D0123793

ALSO BY ANNETTE KOBAK

Isabelle: The Life of Isabelle Eberhardt

JOE'S WAR

JOE'S WAR

MY FATHER DECODED

Annette Kobak

ALFRED A. KNOPF

NEW YORK

2004

THIS IS A BORZOI BOOK
PUBLISHED BY ALFRED A. KNOPF

Library of Congress Cataloging-in-Publication Data
Kobak, Annette.
Joe's war : my father decoded / Annette Kobak — 1st ed.
p.   cm.
ISBN 0-375-41184-4
1. Kobak, Joe, 1920–   .   2. World War, 1939–1945—Prisoners
and prisons, Russian.   3. Soldiers—Poland—Biography.
4. World War, 1939–1945—Campaigns—Western Front.
5. World War, 1939–1945—Psychological aspects.   6. World
War, 1939–1945—Cryptography.   7. Post-traumatic
stress disorder.   I. Title.
D811.5.K5836   2004
940.54'12438'092—dc21   [B]   2003056197

Manufactured in the United States of America
First Edition

For Joe and Pam,

with love

Every story of investigation and of conjecture tells us something we have always been close to knowing.

—UMBERTO ECO

CONTENTS

AUTHOR'S NOTE

This is not a war story in the usual sense. It's an excursion into the Second World War on a very personal mission, to try to make sense of my father's silences. Even the discoveries I've made on that score have been small scale, although one of them opens up a new perspective on Polish involvement in the war, and widens out into a broader panorama of secrecy. My father had no particularly heroic role in the war, though having put the pieces together now, I know he was brave in quietly resourceful ways: he was brave in protecting his family by a lifetime of silence, for a start. And he was brave as a young man in not being felled by successive war blows randomly striking him. It was an uninvited bravery, he'd be the first to say. Indeed, what I love about his story, and what I sensed even before I knew it, was that it was such a foot soldier's story, an unwilling foot soldier's story, one who never intended to have anything to do with war at all but was quietly minding his own business in Lwow in Poland when war decided to change his plans. His silence after the war, which I grew up with, was not so much a question of protecting dramatic secrets, though secrets there were, as trying to manage his fear and confusion. He—and my mother by osmosis, although she knew nothing of his story either—didn't want to pass on this fear and confusion to me, but of course by bottling it up and laying it down in the psychic cellar he outlined its contours to me.

His story was a sliver of war, like the stories of so many others, particularly from middle Europe, stunned as they were by the successive blows of Nazism and Stalinism and the cold war. But there was also some form to it: I sensed it had some meaning, if only I could put it together. When I finally did so, I found it told me most of what I needed to know about the nature of any war, and a lot that I didn't know about the origins of this one. Which is why I want to add it to the bookshelves, as a small counterweight to the deplorable fact that not only did dictators like Hitler and Stalin cause unprecedented trauma in millions of lives, which has knocked on down the generations, but that history now grants these two dictators far more shelf space than it does to people who brought their whole humanity and intelligence to bear on trying to stop such horrors. This book is peopled with such men and women, and with others who were simply caught off balance by the monster from outside, as Milan Kundera called twentieth-century history, and did their best in the circumstances, like my father.

If my father, Joe, had not been a very young soldier, he might not still be alive now—a youthful eighty-three-year-old—and I would never have known what had happened to him before he came to England, and why he was so enigmatic. There is barely a trace of him in official records, and no one left who knew him from that time. So I also offer this in the hope that it may stand in for others who were not so lucky, and that it may throw light on their behalf, too, on some lesser known landscapes and legacies of the war.

Map of Joe's Journey

JOE'S JOURNEY

1939–1941

<←•••• December 1939
←——— January–June 1940
←– – June 1940–December 1941

MILES
0   100   200   300

KILOMETERS
0   100   200   300   400   500

(POLAND)

Berlin ◉   Warsaw ◉

"GREATER GERMANY"

Lwow

Krakow
● Baligrod   Ustianowa

◉ Prague
"PROTECTORATE OF
BOHEMIA/MORAVIA"   SLOVAKIA

Munich ●

Vienna ◉   ◉ Budapest

(AUSTRIA)   HUNGARY   Lake
Balaton

AND

Zagreb
Venice ●   ● Trieste

ITALY   YUGOSLAVIA

◉ Rome

ONE

ANOTHER COUNTRY

The parents unconsciously passed
their unmastered personal history on
to their child at a tender age, often
simply by way of glances.

—ALICE MILLER

| 1 | **THE SILENT SLAV**

It didn't occur to me to ask my father as I grew up why he had nothing from his past before the war—no pictures of himself when young, no family photographs, no mementos of any kind. He was a man without a past, and I failed to notice. Since I grew up alongside the void, it seemed natural to me, as natural as the way his eyes oscillated continuously, or the way he slept with a hammer under his pillow.

Throughout my time at home in southeast London—first in a flat in Crystal Palace and then in a small, semidetached house in a drab suburb called Anerley—my father was often taciturn, irritable and cowled with gloom. His whole manner discouraged questions about himself, even if I'd been disposed to ask them, which, like most children, I wasn't. I was also my parents' only child, and, like most only children, took on the adults' coloring more than usual, being outnumbered. If the grown-ups weren't talking about something, I wasn't talking about it either.

The only facts I knew about my father as I grew up were that he'd been a soldier with the Polish army in the war and had ended up in London, where he'd met my English mother—who was in the women's air force at the time—playing table tennis. At the end of the war he'd taken a job as a watchmaker at Bravington's in Kings Cross, and at the same time studied in the evenings for a physics diploma somewhere in London. I thought he was Polish, because he'd been in the Polish army and had three Polish friends from those days. It wasn't until much later that I learned he was born in Czechoslovakia, so was technically Czechoslovak. By the time I began asking these questions, he was anyway "naturalized" British; and by the time I really started to ask him questions, he had emigrated to Australia.

After a bad war, I've read, the officers stammer and the ranks become mute. My father, who had been a foot soldier, ran true to form, his silence aggravated by being in a foreign country whose language he didn't speak at first. Although I didn't consciously know about his past, I sensed its presence by bumping up against the no-go areas protecting it. I also unwittingly adopted them as my own, and it's partly through butting up against their barbed presence in myself that I've unravelled his story, half a century later. Like the secret establishments omitted on an Ordnance Survey map, my father's past wasn't overtly acknowledged, but was very much there.

My English mother had a past and a visible one, although she was almost an orphan herself. Her mother had died when she was four, and she and her two sisters and brother were packed off to a rackety boarding school in Sussex where their first sight was of a small coffin being hustled out of the building, and where they were seldom visited by their dashing dental surgeon father, who was having problems of his own with four small children to support and a tempestuous love life. He died prematurely, too, when my mother was sixteen, and shortly after that she joined up in the WAAF and the war was on. Even though they must have been short on care— they would often be the only children left at their Dickensian school in the holidays, and it would be closed down in the end, its headmistress committed to prison—my mother and her siblings had photographs of themselves as children, buoyant and bouncy on pebbly beaches, and pictures of their ancestors. All of them grew up energetic and outgoing, sure of each other, and of where they had come from. Although my mother's father had left only debts financially, she had pieces of furniture from her past in our Crystal Palace flat: a tapestry prayer chair, a cabinet, a round mahogany table with brass clawfeet.

My father's few possessions were all to do with the war, and most were khaki, a dull color on the face of it, but as potent as Proust's *madeleine* to me. The first time I was asked to dance by a stranger was with a French soldier in Le Lavandou when I was fifteen, under the aegis of my French penfriend's family. It was exciting enough to be asked to dance the *paso doble* in a beach nightclub, the air thick with pine and the sound of crickets, let alone to feel the rough, clean khaki uniform, familiar from infancy. Later, in the sixties, I used to shop at Laurence Corner, the secondhand military store, just north of the Tottenham Court Road, favoring khaki flak jackets worn over a miniskirt. And a year or two later, against the grain of the times, I even married someone who had been a soldier. So there were the germs of an obsession there, and maybe that's what obsessions are: objects waving their hands in the air, trying to draw attention to something unresolved.

My father's tough, woolen, pocketed khaki uniform hung in my parents' wardrobe in our flat in Crystal Palace, its navy blue cap rolled under one of its epaulettes. At some point the uniform disappeared, but underneath it, stuffed in a back corner alongside a growing pile of *Reader's Digests*—always particularly well thumbed at "Laughter, the best medicine"—was a khaki silk parachute, its swathes of slippery material and eyelets rolled into a ball tied with white silk cords. It provided for our small household for years, a cornucopia amidst the postwar rationing, barely dwindling, it seemed, as my father clattered away on the sewing machine treadle, turning it into pocket linings, pajamas, an eiderdown cover. As a

Joe and the author, 1949

child, I slept in khaki silk pajamas he'd made, underneath a khaki eiderdown. No wonder something of his war rubbed off on my dreams.

I had a recurring nightmare of footsteps coming along the corridor to our flat, of the door opening slowly, and an ogre standing at the door. I know it's an ogre as soon as I hear the footsteps, and I run and hide behind the old mahogany radiogram, with its frayed brown weave behind a sunset fretwork. The ogre thuds over, knowing I'm there, and I wake in terror, my heart beating to the rhythm of his footsteps. Is the ogre my father? Did I, like many war babies tucked into comforting mothers' beds, resent the reappearance of my father when he came back from the war? Did he, slender and traumatized as he was, seem frightening with his uniform and his gruff, heavily-accented voice? I'm sure we babies born flanked by war breathed in extra doses of anxiety that never quite left us.

I was left to my own devices from an early age, a latchkey kid, as my parents were both out at work from when I was four—my mother working as a dental nurse an hour away to the south, my father working at Bravington's. I took myself off on the trolleybus down Anerley hill to school (longing to scroll out the buff-colored ticket from the machine like the bus conductor) and let myself back in with a doorkey on a ribbon around my neck. In the holidays, I used to roam around in the nearby Crystal Palace grounds with other children from the block of flats where we lived. Once or twice we managed to get across to the giant metal dinosaurs which prowl on the islands in the lakes. They were built by the Victorians, awestruck at having discovered that such creatures once existed, and conjuring up what they thought they must have looked like. We climbed up into the dinosaurs' echoing insides through holes in their bellies, and roared out from their mouths at passing lovers. In a photograph my father took of me in the Crystal Palace grounds with the dinosaurs, I'm not the freewheeling urchin I remember, but stand solemnly, with a proper coat and dress, looking sad. It's taken me all this time to turn around and notice those dinosaurs roaring silently behind me, and figure out what they were.

My father's three Polish friends from the army sometimes came to the flat for lunch on a Sunday: Władek, Stanley, and Ted—Władysław, Stanisław and Tadeusz, as they'd been in Polish. My father became animated and boyish when he was with them, quite different from the moody, grumpy person he was for much of the rest of the time.

Ted would bring whiskey from the pub in Herne Hill where he

worked. He was small, cheery and stocky, the type of Polish immigrant who fuelled Hollywood after the war, like Gene Kelly, who—
you only notice later when you're grown up—is very short from
shoulder to waist. My father always seemed to defer to Ted. Stan
was gangly, chain-smoking and intellectual, his dry reddish hair
ruffled and unkempt, kept that way by raking it periodically with
long nicotine-stained fingers. He was a bachelor, with a nervous
edge I found appealing. He never had any money, and would come
from Balham by bus, glad of the home cooking as much as the
camaraderie. I only saw Władek a few times, as he went off to
Argentina when I was small and we never heard from him again,
except for one letter to me in which he said he hadn't been eaten by
crocodiles. I marvelled that he could guess that it was exactly what
I was worried about. Before he left, he gave me a Teddy bear, its
body long like a newborn baby's, its brown face solemn, the hump
on its back and its low growl when you bent it over suggestive of
grown-up cares.

My father seemed the youngest of them all. I could see he was
proud to play host to them, bending down with exaggerated courtesy at their elbows, looking intensely into their faces to ask them
what they'd like to drink, wringing his hands in anticipation. His
light brown backwash of wavy hair, usually brushed away from his
forehead, would spring forward. After lunch, the men would unfold
a card table and settle down to playing cards, setting their amber
drinks reverentially beside them, along with a brass ashtray made
from an old bombshell. My father was the only one who never
smoked. They would speak in Polish, a passport into a more raffish,
virile land. The air grew thick with smoke and the mellifluous,
clashing consonants of a language neither my mother nor I could
speak. I wanted my father to teach me, but he laughed it off, saying
with mock gruffness: "Oh you want to learn Polish, do you, well,
what on earth do you want to learn that for?" Although it wasn't
funny, he would say it as if it was, and more to impress Stan and
Ted and Władek than to answer my question. I would draw them all

in a sketchbook, for want of anything better to do, and for want of other children around. They were completely unself-conscious, and I became an observer. Outside the flat, the air of an English winter afternoon that had never quite roused itself into daylight would congeal particle by particle into twilight. Inside, the air would thicken with smoke, the peeling mica in the grille of the coal-burning stove would crackle with heat, arms would describe more fulsome arcs, or thump down triumphantly on the table as some-body won a game. When my father won, he might brag aban-donedly, beating his breast with pleasure, or he might shrug it off gently as if it wasn't him but some outside force that had done it. Once Władek had gone away, my mother would join in the four-some, playing as volubly as they did. She smoked from a cigarette holder, which seemed to give her more control than she usually had.

In due course my father taught me a few numbers in Polish—*jeden, dwa, trzy, cztery*—as well as poker and canasta. I was the only child any of them had for a long time, and became good at cards, although I never did manage to cut and deal the cards as whistle-fast as they did, or fan out thirteen cards in one hand, or flip a whole pack through the air from hand to hand like an accordion. Card playing seemed to be the natural activity of grown-ups when-ever they got together.

On our own on a Sunday, we would listen to *Forces' Favourites,* which later became *Two-Way Family Favourites.* Jean Metcalfe, Cliff Michelmore and André Kostelanetz's "With a Song in My Heart" were as much part of our furniture as the mahogany radi-ogram in the corner. "Lance-bombardier Frank Medway stationed in München-Gladbach would like us to play Pat Boone's 'I'll Be Home' for his sweetheart Valerie in Luton. It won't be long now, he says." "The forces," along with card playing, seemed to be where the adult action was. The forces were definitely with us. To have been in the forces seemed to give people weight and anchorage. My mother's relatives had all been in the forces in the war, as she had been. I knew my father had been a soldier, too, but that somehow didn't rate as being in the forces, which seemed to be an exclusively English thing. My mother's brother was so much in the forces that he stayed there, commanding his own RAF station, an aura of glamour around him as a result. He was clearly part of what won the war. However, neither he nor any of the other relatives, nor anyone else we knew, ever asked my father about his war, and I sensed that my father's part in it, whatever it was, was best left unsaid. He wasn't an officer, for a start, and then he was foreign, so his part in it was liable to be murky. For of course we knew—we kids who played "Japs and Germans" in the back garden of the block of flats—that it was foreigners we fought in the war, and it was we, the British, who won the war against them. It was Churchill and Douglas Bader and the Dam Busters who won the war: all British. Part of the reason I didn't even think of asking my father about his previous, foreign life is that I didn't know the right questions or even geography, and part was that I felt uneasy about what I might find. His past was literally a foreign country. If I did now and then venture a question, he would comically exaggerate his usual brow-furrowing, then growl and pounce at me, shooing me away from the thing he didn't want to talk about, or running at me in a slightly manic way, the way he ran at a cat if he saw one in the garden.

He was unpredictable, and remote in some way. He was liable to be either very gruff or very jokey in ways I couldn't gauge. He liked jokes, particularly corny ones, and he liked to give people surprises. My mother was never consulted over the rare purchase of some new bargain item for the flat; he would smuggle it in and then uncover it with a flourish, like a conjurer. He also had a trick where he carefully folded and rolled a white cotton handkerchief to turn it into a mouse, and then made it suddenly jump up his arm, to scare you. This was his party trick; men of his generation—my uncles, my friends' fathers—often had party tricks.

I felt protective of that part of my father that others didn't see, and tried to tune myself to the wavelength that brought out a special knowledge in him, so different from the preoccupations of most of

The author with dinosaurs, Crystal Palace, 1952

the grown-up people I encountered at my primary school, or within my mother's family. It was like bright sunshine between clouds, and I tried to catch it when it came. He would tell me the difference between sodium and mercury streetlamps, or of Einstein's theory of relativity, which I would briefly grasp before it slithered away and I was left only with the image of a train being still inside even though it's moving at speed. He would say, scientists tell us that nothing travels faster than light, but in fact thought travels faster than light. He explained the mysteries of minus numbers: picture a ladder going up an apple tree, he would say, and imagine its rungs being the plus numbers. Now picture a hole beside it, with another ladder going down into it: *its* rungs were *minus* numbers. They go up, too, just like the plus numbers, even though they were going down into a hole, see? His blue eyes would flicker excitedly as he held his propelling pencil in the air, waiting for the penny to drop. I took in that what's underground is of equal value to what's above the ground. It would never get me far mathematically, but it would emotionally. He explained to me why people from a far planet would see the ancient Egyptians, or perhaps even dinosaurs, if they were to look at our planet through a telescope. He told me that the future of the world lay in something called computers, mark his words.

When I was about eight, he acquired a Vespa and on Saturday mornings took me up to a cinema near Victoria Station showing nonstop cartoons. I loved riding pillion on the scooter, and quite liked the cartoons, though my father liked them far better. He shook with laughter in the small, near-empty cinema at the quacking shape-shiftings of Tom and Jerry, Goofy and Donald Duck, with their propeller legs. At about the same time *The Goon Show* burst onto the airwaves with the gusto of the Americans liberating Paris, and it liberated my father, too. It exploded with major generals and land mines, it disrupted space and time and little people's stories. It was the war again, this time as farce. Better still, the Goons didn't know they were therapy, and neither did my father, who listened to them chortling with glee. It brought out the boyish side of him, the sunny side, so often submerged in the depths of the armchair where he sat brooding, half awake and half asleep, wearing premature frowns like an overcoat that was too big for him.

What totally absorbed him was anything technical. He seemed to be able to make or mend anything, and often sat hunched under a bright light at his desk repairing some colleague's watch, an eye-glass held in place by an overhanging brow, poring over a universe of tiny starry cogs, rubies and enamel faces which he held in tweezers. He made a leather case for his Kodak camera, hanging up an old blackout curtain in the bathroom to develop and print his photos. He found a cheap photo-tinting set from some market in the East End, and for a while all our curly-edged prints, cratered with drips, were awash with opaque-colored beauty. I didn't have toys— we children from the block of flats had gas masks for our imaginary games, or made mudpies, or threw balls against the wall—but my father did buy me a gyroscope and a secondhand brass microscope. My prized possession was a metal box he made, with flashing lights, knobs, a Morse code button and an earpiece on the end of a wire, which my friends and I used to transform us into Lemmy and Jock from the radio serial *Journey into Space*. My father's prized possession, which he was unaccountably attached to, was a rough brown army blanket with a yellow CM *AEV 1936* printed on it.

I wasn't bookish as a child for the good reason that we had no books, apart from a dog-eared copy of *Swiss Family Robinson* in a version for foreigners, and for some reason a medical textbook with illustrations of conditions so leprous I thought I'd get the diseases just from touching the pages, which provided some kind of perverse excitement for my friends and me. We would take a quick look at the scabby pictures, then snap the book shut, pulling faces and gagging.

All the same somewhere along the line a science fiction story I read etched itself on my memory. It was about a young boy growing up in a village, who began to notice strange things about his life, although on the surface all was agreeable and ordinary. For one thing, he was the only child in the village for a long time, and for another he was the only person who always had to wear green. And then, every time he expressed a wish it would come to pass. He wanted a brother or sister or grandmother, and one would appear. He'd always been told there was a Wall around the village which no one was allowed to go near. Everyone else accepted unquestioningly that going beyond the Wall was forbidden, and didn't approach it. But as he grew up he wanted to discover what this Wall was, and what lay beyond it. One day he decided to go and find out for himself. When he got there, he discovered that the Wall was transparent and went up and up, curving back over the village. Somehow—I forget how—he began climbing the Wall from the outside, until he saw the village spread out beneath him, and real-

ized that the Wall formed a dome enclosing the whole area. Then he
saw a notice on the Wall:

EXHIBIT A:

HOMO SAPIENS

This is the last known example of the otherwise
extinct species of *Homo sapiens*. The genuine
"human being," in its immature form, can be
identified by the green clothes it is wearing.
The rest of the creatures are robots.

The story certainly scared me, but I also identified with the boy's
feeling that all was not right with the world he was in, that what he
was being told didn't quite match up with what he sensed and
observed.

In August 1953, just before I was ten, my father applied for British
naturalization. His application form included an oath of allegiance—"I, Joseph Kobak, swear by Almighty God that I will be
faithful and bear true allegiance to Her Majesty Queen Elizabeth
the Second, Her Heirs and Successors," an oath which moldered in
the corridors of power for five years before the naturalization was
granted. But the process itself, together with the fact that he now
had his physics diploma, enabled him to solidify his position by
applying for a mortgage and a better job. So by the time I was ten,
and had just started at my secondary school, he had become a
research assistant in the furnace department of the British Coal Utilization Research Association (BCURA), at Leatherhead in Surrey,
some thirty miles out of London. It was shortly after this that we
moved down the hill to Anerley, to our own small terraced house in
Warwick Road. Although our position improved formally, we lost
something, too: the spark and possibility for adventure always latent

in the curving hills outside the block of flats, in the surrounding motley, individual houses, in the diverse ages and kinds of people living around, in the Crystal Palace grounds on the doorstep, in the sweeping view we had from our balcony out of London and all the way over to hills in the distance. At Crystal Palace we were poor, but we weren't trapped.

Once installed in Anerley, my father's own iron curtain seemed to come down as firmly as the Soviets' had a few years before. Tied to the treadmill of driving on his scooter through the outer suburbs of London to Leatherhead every day to work, he would come home late and slump in a chair in front of the television. We had beans on toast around the television watching the news ("Nation shall speak peace unto nation"), or spaghetti from a tin on toast with a poached egg on top, or chops with potatoes and vegetables steamed to extinction in the prized new pressure cooker my father had bought, its ferocious head of steam filling the kitchen with condensation and a vicious hissing, as if gasping for air or preparing for nuclear fission. Its inordinately heavy parts, as angular and clunking as those of the Sputnik which the Soviets would launch three years later to the alarm of the West, entailed a laborious process of washing up out of all proportion to the task they were doing, let alone the one they'd replaced: blanching vegetables in a pan of boiling water. It was the same with the egg-poacher. It was a great relief to me to discover years later that you could poach an egg simply by dropping it into boiling water.

My mother got a new job, too, as a secretary to a motoring organization in Croydon. She drove in on a scooter called a Quickly, a game and disingenuous name which suited her well. As for me, instead of walking the mile and a half to school with my schoolfriend Ingrid as I had done from Crystal Palace, along the Crystal Palace parade, past the Crystal Palace tower (where John Logie Baird had been the first to broadcast a television picture in 1937), turning down the leafy hill and in through the gates to Sydenham High School—which to its credit never let on to scholarship girls

like me that there were also fee-paying girls like Ingrid at the
school—instead of that, I would walk down a dreary flat road of
identical terraced houses to a noisy, grimy main road and wait for a
bus. The thirty-minute bus ride was conducive to melancholy, and
then I walked up the hill to school on my own. In the evening, I
would still get back before either of my parents, but now there were
no pals to play around with in a communal garden. No one
approaching my own age surfaced in all the seven remaining years
of my living there. Indeed, from all those hundreds of cheek-by-
jowl houses, the only neighbor who surfaced was Lily next door.
On top of this, we had no telephone—something that was beginning to be unusual by the late fifties even in Anerley.

Lily and Arthur, her toothless husband, had a telephone, in spite
of the fact that he spent his old age lost in the depths of an armchair
in the back room, his head and hands framed by antimacassars, like
a Francis Bacon pope, without the authority or rage. They had a
telephone even though they had no visible friends or family or
indeed income, being retired. If ever a message had to be got
through to us, it came through Lily. The doorbell would ring and
Lily would be there, with her orange-dyed permed hair, her carmine
lipstick stained into the thin delta of her lips, her ample bosom covered in a mauve crochet cardigan, and her slippers on. She would
cackle with ack-ack laughter as a prelude to every utterance, though
the beady, shrewd eyes behind her glasses countermanded any joy
in the laugh. The hair, the laugh, the lipstick, the gaudy mauve crochet were her shot at gingering up the lackluster world of Anerley,
and it was a good shot.

When the doorbell rang, my father's eyes would look up startled and vulnerable from behind the pages of the *Daily Mirror,* out
of all proportion to the event. True, it was a rare thing to happen.
People didn't come unexpectedly—and rarely expectedly, either—
although once two CID officers had turned up unannounced, to
interview my father about his naturalization. Even my father's Pol-

ish friends no longer came. If the doorbell did ring, my mother
would answer it and he would listen, tensed, until he heard it was
Lily, when he would settle back behind the newspaper. He would
never answer the door himself. If Lily were coming in with news of
a telephone call for us, the blue eyes would flicker above the paper
until he knew who it was. It would usually be one of my mother's
relatives. Very rarely, as I grew up, it might be a call for me from
one of my friends, though I didn't encourage it. To brave the pha-
lanx of loudly ticking clocks, the bloom of antimacassars, the layers of dark ornamentation studded with polished horse-brasses, let
alone the silently nodding Arthur, and to lift the heavy black parrot-
beaked receiver, was more than my tongue-tied heart could bear.

My mother, who vaunted my father's intelligence and put down
her own, would pussyfoot around his moods, so entrenching them.
If she ventured some remark which seemed to him foolish, he simply wouldn't reply, burying himself further in his *Daily Mirror.*
Often he wouldn't look at her when she said something that
annoyed him, but looked at me, with a look of collusive exasperation, as if to say, "How do you expect me to exist in this atmosphere?" My mother took this as normal, as punishment even for
not having said the right thing, and I took it as normal, but felt it
shouldn't be. It pained me to see her diminished and crushed, and I
felt anger, never expressed, against my father for treating her this
way, and against her, too, for laying herself open to it and doggedly
coming back for more. There was an increasing tension around, and
no small talk to oil the cogs of communication.

Although I was used to the silence and tension, I began to notice
as my world opened up that it wasn't usual. It wasn't, for example,
like *Life with the Lyons,* which we listened to religiously on the
radio (almost literally, since it was a ritual, and revealed something
of how things could be, in a better world) and which seemed to
embody all the desirable norms: a mother who is a housewife and
carries on perky repartee with a father when he's back from work

("Hi, honey, I'm back from work!"), teenage brother and sister who breeze in and out and get into scrapes, friends of the family who pop in and out all the time, a dog who barks.

My friends rarely came round to our house, and if they did, they found my father scary, hunkered away gruffly in the back room. He felt no obligation to be nice to them or even to greet them. The worst sin, apart from simply arriving in our household at all, was anyone wanting to smoke. It had to be made clear to any visitor that smoking in the house was simply out of the question. If asked why, my father would look thunderous and shake his head in agitation: "No. No smoking, just no." Something had changed since his Polish friends stopped coming. It would be years before I found out why smoking triggered this behavior, but at this stage it was also just part of a general obsession with keeping control of his home patch. Strangers were dangerous. There was no smoke without fire. Ironically, like much of what my father has done, his anti-smoking stance is now fashionable and mainstream even if his manner of delivery still wouldn't be so.

The inertia of Warwick Road meant that, like water finding a course, we all sought life elsewhere. As it happened, my elsewheres would place an increasing wedge between me and my parents.

First was school. Work being immeasurably more interesting than home, I threw myself into it. I was drawn to languages, and French, particularly, became a lodestar for a different and desirable kind of life. My French teacher was one of that first generation of women teachers to be widely university-educated, women who had often bypassed marriage because of the shortage of men after the First World War. Miss Pool had been sighted on the arm of a man at a theatre in London. It was also rumored that she'd had a nervous breakdown, in spite of (or perhaps because of) her dazzling, brisk smile, her high intelligence and sense of fun. All these things gave her cachet and respect amongst us, particularly the nervous breakdown. Miss Pool had a flat in Westminster, and would invite some of us round for omelettes and salad with garlic, then off to see *A Bout de souffle* or *Jules et Jim* at the Curzon Cinema. This was a glimpse of sophistication which eclipsed all other ways of life once I'd seen it, and I cleaved to it. When I was thirteen I went to Paris to stay with a French penfriend, and a whole warm climate opened up of Routiers cafés and *oeufs mayonnaise* and draught red wine in green bottles from the grocer's. When the French family took me down to their small house in a village in the Alps, there were mountains, bike rides alongside rivers, ducks trussed up and gentle-eyed in the cellar before being beheaded and cooked for supper, and postboxes which told you the last time the letters had been collected. Two years later, when we went to the South of France, there was that nightclub and the *paso doble*. No wonder I wanted to read French at university, when the time came.

I learned German, too, and when I was fifteen, thanks to the educational opportunities of the late fifties, went on a term's exchange to a school in a picturesque mountain town near Frankfurt, replete with fairy-tale castle. The film *The Great Caruso* was a hit at the time, and I fancied I was living in Heidelberg amongst carousing students singing, "Drink, drink, drink." With two older brothers in the German family I lived with, two sisters around my age, and a mixed instead of single-sex school, the opportunities for meeting boys expanded exponentially—and quite different kinds of boys from the few I had so far encountered at Ingrid's parties. Indeed, Ingrid's admirable Norwegian mother had taken me aside and warned me firmly that German boys were a very different kettle of fish from English boys, and I found she was right. They were virile young men for a start, with no spots or spectacles, and they were lean in spite of often drinking some seven pints of beer in the afternoons after school was out ("Drink, drink, drink"). Later, this would catch up with them and they would turn overnight, like bolted lettuces, into heavy paterfamiliases.

Another thing that was different about them was that most of them seemed to have weapons in their cupboards, and you didn't have to know them very well to be shown them. There were small revolvers, there were duelling pistols, there were swords. There were uniforms, too, GI uniforms being the most favored, but also the occasional closet Nazi uniform. The father in the German family I was with, it transpired, had been a member of the SS, and, as I saw it then, he certainly looked and acted like it. He was a science master at my *Gymnasium,* and would take his plump, blond younger daughter into his study for a noisy beating, the expression on his face afterward leaving no doubt that he took sadistic pleasure in this ritual. His stout, smiling wife carried on ironing as if nothing were happening. Sometimes he would say, with a challenging gleam in his eye, "You see, Hitler was right, it was the Communists we should have feared."

Our class went on an outing—a *Klassenfahrt,* the occasion of ribald titters to my non-German-speaking schoolfriends back home—to Berlin, where my sketchy ideas about the Second World War were first challenged. It was 1958, thirteen years after the war and three years before the Wall went up, and we got special tickets to travel into East Berlin by underground. Apart from the stark dereliction, what surprised me most were the outsize banners draped over public buildings saying: THANK THE GLORIOUS SOVIET ARMY, WHICH SAVED US FROM FASCISM IN 1945. I wondered why we should be thanking the Soviet army, when it was surely the British who saved Europe from fascism, with a little help from the Americans. And why were the Russians still living in the past like this, vaunting themselves over a war that was long gone?

I didn't think to ask my father anything about this. It didn't occur to me that he might know, although it did occur to me to wonder why he seemed to have no objection to my studying German and living with a German family, when as far as I knew he had fought the Germans in the war. Indeed, two years later, just before I went up to university, our two families met up in the Austrian Alps when my father took us on an enterprising trip through the South of

France, Italy and Austria in our newly acquired Mini. He was clearly at ease with meeting representatives of his former enemy, and I could see that somehow the German family and he, although they had a minimal vocabulary between them, spoke the same language in a way he didn't with the English.

These foreign excursions of mine were a legitimate and mostly state-funded escape from Anerley. My father's escape route was through his work. He set up a workshop in the garage and started to make most of our furniture there: a plywood veneer gramophone with splayed fifties-style legs, a splayed-leg coffee table, all the kitchen cupboards, which he then painted in pink gloss. His research job made him more sober and serious. He began—to my eyes—simultaneously to have an exaggerated respect for his bosses (who seemed to me when I met them unworthy of his deference) and yet to have a philosophical, saintly indifference to any thoughts of ambition. He seemed to me far more intelligent than his "superiors" but doggedly committed to deference and absolute, quiet submissiveness, as if his heavy accent sentenced him to it.

My mother's escape drew us into its wake: we began to spend more time with her family, visiting her sisters or brother in their substantial households in the country. This coincided with my father's Polish friends ceasing to come. Perhaps the suburbs were getting us in their genteel clutches so that pub-owning or louche bachelor Poles were no longer welcome. Sent off to stay with aunts and uncles in the holidays, I began to be an older sister to the cousins, and also aware that on the face of it we were the poor relations. The cousins had toy farms, toy cash registers and tennis lessons, all part of their natural congruence with English values, which I began to sense I didn't quite possess. My father was too volatile and yet withdrawn for English tastes, and when he did put on a sociable front, he could become obsequious. My mother's family patronized him, I saw, and although he took it in his stride, I didn't.

I was developing a prickly, second-generation immigrant pride of my own, which even spilt over into the relative haven of school life. My schoolfriends' families had coherence and color: Ingrid in her large, shabbily grand house, with its basement dedicated to teenage life and black walls painted by her art student sister and decorated with album covers of Jailhouse Rock, Sidney Bechet and Françoise Hardy; or Mary, with her tumbledown, sprawling bunga-low languorously set in an overgrown garden, her many brothers and sisters lounging on unmade beds absorbed in reading one or other of the well-thumbed books littering the house, her unmade-up, bespectacled mother standing at an old kitchen range with an unmistakably sexy yet classy gleam in her eye, book in one hand, and stirring with the other an eternal pot of inimitably tasty stew. From such families I began to sense that we didn't quite have any ground to stand on. That we didn't quite pass muster: the muster of my own vigilant eye.

So I studied more. Torn between art school and university, I took the safe option. I got into Girton College at Cambridge, which had a girls-only austerity that appealed to me. But I incorporated the art too, by helping set up a university artists' group when I arrived. There I met the man I would marry: gregarious, bluff and funny, at ease in English life—and an ex-soldier. Meanwhile, the world around us was changing. In the bitter winter of 1963— in which, we would learn later, Sylvia Path committed suicide in London—slips of paper were passed round the dining tables of Girton one evening alerting us to the fact that Presidents Kennedy and Khrushchev were on the brink of war over the Bay of Pigs. This seems an uncharacteristically alarmist thing for a college like Girton to have done, and I wonder what they thought we should do about it, except perhaps go home for our last hours on earth.

Home for me felt increasingly distant and diminished. It was like a rocket launcher that had served its purpose and could now, I arrogantly believed, conveniently fall away. The discrepancy between my future husband's upper-class background and my own was bridged by jocular references to me as "the paragon of Penge"

The author in 1965

(a signally unprepossessing London suburb). I felt its patronizing edge, but could do little about it since I was the chief culprit in dismissing my provenance. Meanwhile, I had no real idea who I was, except that I didn't feel solidly in the world at all, but for much of the time, when I wasn't learning or painting, fundamentally uneasy.

At that time, most Girton graduates went on to worthwhile and eminent careers in the diplomatic or civil services or as headmistresses. By 1966, however, England was finally breaking out of its postwar sobriety. I wanted to pick up on the artist in me, and also the more frivolous side, so I wrote to the new women's magazine called *Nova*, pointing out that they had no art criticism and volunteering for the job. I got the job, but soon married and left the magazine to follow my new husband, Reg, as he took up an eccentric post researching kinetic art at the Massachusetts Institute of Technology in Cambridge, Massachusetts. I got a job as a subeditor at the university press there, and in the summer of 1967, as the summer of love was unfolding in a haze of dope on greens and open spaces everywhere, we were taken across the States in a Volkswagen bus on a Frank Lloyd Wright trail with a California architect friend, his wife, and their four children under five. We travelled from Cambridge up to Chicago, then across the Rockies and on to New Mexico. Along the way, Bob and Weezy—still barely into their twenties—introduced us to the splendors of camping along the edge of the Grand Canyon, as well as to a total novelty, the "credit card," by which magical means we were all enabled to stay at motels. We only found out later that the card belonged to his father, but these were freewheeling times in America, and perhaps—my much older conscience hopes—he'd agreed to it.

We might have stayed in America, but got homesick and returned in the autumn of 1967. Just before we got back, my father, liberated from the conventional fatherly role which had never quite suited him, and picking up on the fact that Czechoslovakia was about to try to liberate itself, too, drove my mother down to France, turned left and carried on to a village near Kosice in Slovakia, characteristically not telling my mother of his plans until they were nearly there. He turned up at the house where his elder sister had lived almost thirty years before, not having seen any of his family since, and knocked on her door. She rushed around crying with joy, her first thought that she should tidy up the duvets hanging out to air. To my father, in these early Dubček days, Czechoslovakia was once again the smiling country of cherry trees he remembered from his childhood (he would tell me much later), although it wouldn't stay that way for long.

Back in England, Reg and I had a son in the year the first American spaceship was launched; all seemed to look to the future and I couldn't have been further away from thinking about the war, or indeed my father. Then, just as I was expecting a second baby, my father's research plant was closed down and he was made redundant. The prospect of applying for jobs at fifty-one, in a language which he had still not fully mastered, daunted him, so when the giant Australian Broken Hill Steel Company approached him with the offer of a job, he jumped at the chance, even though it meant emigrating to the other side of the world. Indeed—I would discover much later—precisely because it did. He had never relished the thought of growing old in England, having a fastidious dislike of the accoutrements of the elderly, as well he might have done living next to Lily and Arthur. The prospect of a more outdoor life suited him well. I cannot remember any agonized discussions about whether they should go, and I can barely remember the hurried good-bye to them, said for some reason on the windy corner of a central London street. I was glad for them to go, feeling they might well have a more interesting life in Australia than Anerley and the British Coal Utilization Research Association had afforded them. I thought it was a wonderful opportunity for them at their age, and I was also, in truth, glad for my sake, too. The chasm between their expectations and my new life felt unbridgeable, and not to have to negotiate it would be a relief. Yet at the same time I managed to resent them for bunking off and leaving me without even such feeble familial support, I griped to myself, as they'd given me before.

Reg and I moved out into the country, to a village somehow aptly called Wendy, and we had a daughter. I fell in love with my children and tried to be the kind of nonchalant, jam-making, vegetable-growing, pot-stirring English country house owner I'd always wanted as a mother myself, a cross between Mary's and Ingrid's mothers, with a French châtelaine thrown in. There was no room in this role, nor in my marriage, for the complexities and ambiguities of my past, and I could only deal with them by denying them, shoving them away in a cupboard to be sorted some time later. The fact that I didn't look the part was a good indicator that the role fitted me badly, but I kept trying to fit my coltish frame into the image of no-nonsense yet openhearted country pragmatism I admired. The repressed parts would out, of course, and they did so in the long run. My marriage came apart when our children were fourteen and twelve, by which time we had moved back to London.

My first act of self-assertion was to move out to a country village, perhaps in an attempt to retake the country on my own terms. My second was to write a book about a rebel, Isabelle Eberhardt, a maverick of the late nineteenth century, born to Russian parents in Geneva, who had travelled in the Sahara dressed as a Muslim boy and drowned there in a flash flood, at age twenty-seven. Through Isabelle, I began to tap into a kind of questing, spirited melancholy which accorded with my real feelings as opposed to those I would have liked to have had. Through her, I got in touch with a more European sensibility, which suited me better than the subtle scanning of English social radar for lapses from form. After a while, when the children had left home, I also took back my maiden name.

My parents came back to visit us once or twice whilst we were at Wendy, but the visits were often fraught. Our lives were literally a world apart. They were building their own house in the sunshine in Australia, on the outskirts of Newcastle, up the coast from Sydney, and we were bringing up children in the depths of the English countryside. We were at our maximum distance apart, and it wasn't until my marriage broke up that I started to want to pick up the pieces I'd left behind from a much earlier rupture.

TERRA AUSTRALIS INCOGNITA

JANUARY 1989

DISTANCE FROM DEPARTURE 2,527 KM

DISTANCE TO DESTINATION 14,509 KM

The screen scrolled again to show a map of the world with a diagram of our plane sitting like a fly over Moscow. Flight information like this was a new feature since I'd first made the long-haul flight from London to Sydney eight years ago. I looked through the scratched lozenge of the window beside me. The jumbo jet's wing sections glinted in the sunshine, feathering to adjust to the airstream, like a bird, as if taking pleasure in the process. Below us were canyons of cloud, haloed with the brilliant light of what seemed like an accelerated sunset, and below that—10,016 meters below, the screen told me—was the Soviet Union. Gorbachev's *perestroika* was obviously having an effect: here we were in a Qantas airplane being allowed to fly over what had been a forbidden continent. It reminded me how we'd begun to see Russian spokesmen on television for the first time recently, exotic and unheralded, their deep glottal bonhomie cut with sideswipes of irony.

My father seemed to be opening up, too. When I'd first visited my parents in Australia in 1981, ten years after they'd settled there, he'd begun to tell us about his background for the first time, prompted by the curiosity of an Australian friend. From that point, I knew the outlines of Joe's story: he was an eighteen-year-old student in Lwow in Poland when war broke out in September 1939, had run into the countryside to escape the invading Nazis only to be met by the Red Army coming the other way as the Soviets took over the city, kept his head down for a few weeks at his college with martial law all around, until he was rounded up arbitrarily whilst queuing for bread and put into a makeshift prison yard. He'd escaped from there—if he hadn't, we now know, he would have been one of the quota sent off to the Siberian gulags—but then realized it was becoming too dangerous to stay, under what would later be called the Terror, and so managed to make a perilous lone journey back to his home village in the Carpathian Mountains, which, since the Nazi invasion of Poland, was now under German control. A few months later, he had to escape again on skis when the Gestapo put a death warrant out for him for helping take refugees across the border, and after another long and uninvited journey, he ended up fighting on the front in northern France with the Polish army. After France fell, he and his unit made their way down to Bordeaux, where they were rescued by a Scottish coal-carrying tanker, which took them to England. There he spent the rest of the war, and met and married my English mother, Cecilia Ayling, known as Pam. His was a not-untypical individual story of Second World War displacement. There was adventure there, and that interested me; but what drew me in was something I couldn't yet put my finger on.

My biography of Isabelle Eberhardt had been published the year before, and I'd decided I wanted to write my next book around my father's experiences: his journey out of middle Europe, and my journey toward him. My editor suggested other, more commercial subjects—a double biography of Kim Philby and his father, the Arabist St. John Philby, or a biography of Greta Garbo—which I could see were good ideas, but not for me, I said, even if I were up to them. I didn't want to live vicariously for years with spies or film stars who had most likely had a double life, more persona than person. So she agreed gamely if impatiently that I should get this personal book out of my system first. What I didn't yet know was just how long this would last, or that it would take a decade and a half of change—in me, my father, and the outside world—for the story to become clear. I also didn't yet allow myself to see, as I signed the contract, that the justifiably slim advance would barely cover two months' family living expenses, let alone a decade of research.

I had put today's newspaper (perhaps still not yesterday's, since our plane was flying into the future) into the pouch in front of me before I settled down for the "night." An extraordinary, dark and medieval thing had just happened: copies of Salman Rushdie's book *The Satanic Verses* had been burned in the streets of Bradford, in Yorkshire. I was almost his contemporary, but felt suddenly older than him, the way I'd felt with my contemporaries who had become hippies. I'm a typical second-generation immigrant, toeing the line: my father's no-go areas had subliminally schooled me to respect boundaries which other people had a strong investment in keeping. I didn't know whether I thought it courageous to blast a flamboyant way through other people's sensitive territories, as Rushdie had done with the Muslims', or simply callow and unwise, a squandering of precious recklessness. I probably felt that first you had to breach your own taboo areas before you could earn the right to do the same with others. And I sensed that, as with all taboo territories, there were liable to be vengeful gods slumbering on the threshold, ready to be provoked.

Hours and continents later, after a stopover in Bangkok, I watched the striped, flame-red dunes of the Great Sandy Desert in Western Australia roll out below like a landscape from Mars. The odd tiny, sunlit cloud hung in the air, exuberant and flighty, its shadow a flat, map-shaped blot on the desert below.

Three days later, still sleepless from jet lag and the unaccustomed feeling of being back under my parents' roof for only the second time in twenty-four years—an only child back under their rules of engagement—I lay awake at daybreak listening to the cackling kookaburras ushering in the sun like demented court jesters, their cascades of squawks boomeranging back from some infinity peculiar to the ether of Australia. Then came the liquid descant of the magpies, nostalgic even the first time you hear it, like a primeval memory. By midday, all was torpor, and even the crickets had handed over the day to the sun. Outside, the temperature was 37°C. in the shade. Only the mynah birds with their masked bandit eyes shuffled amongst the vine leaves on the veranda, pecking shiftily at the ripening grapes.

The veranda was a new addition since my last visit. My father had made it from bits of wood and steel gleaned from the steelworks, and with fixtures from the store of salvaged screws, nails, hinges and oddments that he had painstakingly brought over from England, and added to ever since. Now they were ranged in cut-off milk bottles on homemade shelves in the cavernous, windowless workroom he had made for himself in the basement of the house. On other shelves lay his watchmaking kit: vials of tiny rubies and starry metal cogs alongside eyeglasses and rusty Old Holborn tins containing springs, loose hands, and enamel watchfaces fissured with hairline cracks. On a top shelf stood an old Bakelite radio, faded Bata shoe boxes, a pile of cracked leather straps and loops of old rope. In a new addition, saws, pliers, hammers and chisels hung on a plywood board over the felt-pen outline of their shape. My father's life was getting sorted.

Soon after arriving and renting a bungalow near the steelworks, my parents had bought this plot of scrubland in Wallsend, on the outskirts of Newcastle, where my father had built their two-story house after work and at weekends. The land was cheap because it banked up far too steeply into the bush, with its peeling eucalypts and forest fires. When I'd first come eight years ago, there were just one or two other net-curtained brick bungalows on the road below, in frigid imitation of English dwellings, with only the odd plumbago or hibiscus bush in the garden paying homage to the sun. Now, Invermore Close was filling out with more ambitious dwellings, which reached out for a more congruous language. Beside my parents' house was a two-story hacienda built by former Yugoslavs, welding together race memories of peasant homes that lodged the animals down below—now Holdens and Nissans—with fantasies of what living in a subtropical climate might be: undulating terra-cotta roof tiles, open brickwork balconies, expansive white arches. In every back garden, the iron web of the clothes hoist dried the clothes almost quicker than you could peg them out on a hot summer day in January.

The day before, we'd driven into Newcastle, which had also metamorphosed over the past eight years. Founded as a penal colony in 1801 after the discovery of coal there, the port initially had a reputation as one of the most brutal outposts of the convict system. Perhaps to compensate for this, when it became a free town in 1824 its buildings took on an exaggerated Victorian sobriety, turning their respectable brick backs on the dazzling sun, the gaudy parakeets and galahs in the air, the bone-colored dunes of Stockton beach stretching sixty uninterrupted kilometers up to Port Stephens, the penguins occasionally washed up there, the intermittent sighting of sharks. When I'd come before, Newcastle was still a city built around coal and steel, trying to ape its namesake in England, grim, worthy and industrial. Now it was on the cusp, beginning to turn outward to the sea, blossoming into postmodern prettiness. Arched cafés, parks and boulevards with stately tropical palm trees and decorative lamp-posts were proliferating along what had been its industrial shore.

We'd driven back in my father's new car, a beige Ford Falcon saloon, which seemed a solid and prosperous car for him—for us—to have. In England, we'd only got a car as I was leaving home—the Mini, which my father had tinkered with and modified. He'd done the same with this new vehicle, equipping it with homemade dials to monitor air-conditioning and what not, and a burglar alarm that stopped the car in its tracks minutes after being stolen—and would

have clamped the burglar's foot to the pedal if it hadn't been illegal.
Thus he refined his dialogue with his machines. His Slav taciturnity
had always been balanced by the attentive rapport he had with
instrumentation. As we zigzagged back up the short, steeply cam-
bered hairpin drive to the house, the dials emitted a hail of nerve-
jangling beeps that set him frowning in agitation, looking in the
rear mirror and jumpily fiddling with switches. Every shot at getting up the drive, I would find, would be accompanied by these
squawks and alarms, making it feel like a national state of emergency. Arriving at the front door brought the relief of having survived Stalingrad, or Dunkirk.

Today, we were going to start recording memories of his early
years in Czechoslovakia. I had little idea of what he was going to
say. I now knew he'd been born in Czechoslovakia, before going to
Poland as a student, but didn't know how he'd got there, or what
either of these countries meant to him or anyone else at the time. We
settled in the dining room after lunch, the green curtains drawn
against the blazing sun, the mynah birds' rustling now a weak
diminuendo, the only sound intermittent clatterings coming from
the kitchen next door as my mother dried the dishes. (Clatterings
whose pitch and message I would hear and decode only when I listened to the tapes months later.) My father put an after-lunch glass
of whiskey on the shelf of the lampstand beside him. This wild piece
of craft was something he'd secretly made the year before for my
mother's birthday from a rubber tree he'd chopped down. Carved
from a whole, S-shaped branch, its rough bark, scarred with natural
hieroglyphs, was lovingly varnished. It had a lampshade at the top
and a platform for a drink halfway. He was proud of the feat of getting the wire to run right up the middle of a curving branch. Alas,
he'd given it to my mother with a flourish, and in a long line of such
occasions, she—longing for a bought present, a necklace, a dress—
had burst into tears. Like birds against a windowpane, they hurled
themselves against the same misunderstandings, never adjusting
from the doomed ritual. That's how I thought, the only child, back in

the forgotten impasses. The only child now divorced, too demanding to "put up and shut up," as their generation had done.

Since coming out to Australia, my father had become known as Joe, rather than the more sober Joseph he'd been in England—or the Józef he'd been christened. I'd begun to call him Joe, too, rather than Dad, since he'd been in Australia, just as I'd started to call my mother Pam. The easygoing "Joe" seemed to loosen him up in my mind, just as Australia had loosened him up in reality, and anyway "Mum" and "Dad" felt too childish for me now that I had my own teenage children. If there was also a camouflaged intent to hurt on my part, signalling: you've forfeited your right to these titles since you've been away so long, on the other side of the world—and there was—then I would grow out of it. But not yet. For the time being, both parents took it on the chin, not challenging my right to name things how I pleased.

Joe crossed his legs, tanned and youthful in their old bleached beige gardening shorts, and although he seemed unfazed by the microphone on the table, his brow set in an anticipatory furrow above his bifocals. There was an elusive reserve between us. I felt the gulf of my ignorance, and sensed that although he was agreeing to cooperate, if I didn't ask the right questions he wouldn't volunteer information. To my pleasure, I found he'd given some thought to where he would start.

"When I first went to school in Czechoslovakia, instead of learning to read from books, you learned to read from enormous pieces of brown paper on wall, with simple words in Slovak on them. Slovak was basic language of that school. But what struck me when I looked at them carefully at one stage was that underneath were originals in Hungarian language, with Slovak words pasted on, and they were pasted only very slightly, so that if necessary you could remove them and go back to original. Previously to that Austro-Hungarian Empire was trying to introduce their own languages—German in west and northwest, and Hungarian in parts of Slovakia and Moravia, Ukraine, and probably little bit of Poland.

At that stage, being in Austro-Hungarian Empire, you could move in enormous area and all you had to do was change your language. Most people were trilingual—you had to have three languages otherwise you couldn't get around. When you are six you also speak to people who are eighteen years old and they remembered what had happened in past, and from what I understood from past, rule of Hungarians was not docile, it was quite brutal. They didn't like German and Hungarian language imposed on them. When they told us what it was like for them before, we didn't like that. As child you only have: you like, you don't like it. It was better for us now, we knew, than for people under old system."

Nearly half a century of speaking English had failed to convince my father of the point of using "the" or "a"—distinctions none of the Slavonic languages, he told me, bother with. ("And it works?" "It works beautifully.") Even with language, he was economical. He would recycle language, if he could.

"Under Habsburg Empire Slovak was still spoken, except there were so many dialects that if you moved as little as fifty kilometers away you probably wouldn't understand people. Then after First World War, when Czechoslovakia came into being, people went around collecting Slovak words to create common language. For instance, there would have been up to six names for potato, and they were so different that in one part of Slovakia it would be called *bandurka* and in another *zemiak!* Now, the difference between *bandurka* and *zemiak* is unbelievable—and they could have been in next village. So they decided which word would be official word, and official word was then *zemiak*. Around seventy percent of language was new. By time I was conscious of language, it was normal, adapted Slovak language—official language—but we also had our dialect still. We were speaking both languages because elderly peasants around did not bother to learn official language, and you had to speak with them."

My father took a sip of whiskey. His memory, I was beginning to realize, was like his workshop. In all those mute years, he had squirrelled away observations for future use, not yet knowing if they would come in handy, or what they would turn into. The Aborigines (and ancient Greeks) would say that our stories are what we are here for. For many of us now our stories are on the bitty side, which may be what makes us fretful.

"Other thing which struck me as unusual at school," my father resumed, "but not until later on, was that at end of school year, you were given your certificate with number of subjects on it—normal subjects started with religion, then language, writing, reading, et cetera—but two subjects were above all others in importance: behavior and keenness. I was very good at behavior, I was very quiet. I liked listening. Also I was very inquisitive, I wanted to know. I was able to read when I was four, long before I went to school. I wanted to know why my sisters opened something and then told me story from it. Later on in school, our teacher knew I was interested in books for older children in Czech language, which has slightly different vocabulary from Slovak, but which you can read with little bit of effort. They were mostly on philosophy, and few were on history. But there was very little history printed about Czechoslovakia at that point. So I read about history of France, which was written about in Czech language. I got fascinated with Napoleon, and learned that he could read book and listen to something else and absorb both subjects. It occurred to me that it was something I had been doing too automatically. All of children from village from ages of seven to fourteen were being taught in same room at school, and I would listen to older children's lectures whilst taking in my own."

On the round mahogany dining table between us—one of the legacies from my mother's family, and here in Australia a solid talisman of continuity and provenance (particularly in Newcastle, and particularly in Wallsend)—a pewter dragon, curled around the lid of an ornamental dish, looked up at me with its one green eye. Joe unfurrowed his brow, and his blue eyes looked at me in childish candor, their irises flickering from side to side. By now I knew why they flickered like this: he had a condition called nystagmus, in which the eyes oscillate continuously from side to side.

"And then there were summer vacations, lasting from middle of June till beginning of September—other vacations were purely religious days, like three days for Christmas. Most people just lived from land where we were, growing vegetables and fruit, and with chickens, one pig and maybe few cows. We boys and girls would spend whole summer vacations helping farmers, or swimming in river. My two elder sisters and older brother were already growing up, but my younger brother and sister and I used to be with group of children. You did not have sort of private family things, and very seldom would you see only two or three children playing together. We were always active, always running everywhere. I think because we were so enjoying it we were helping people without realizing it, because there were so many little jobs farmers wouldn't have time for. There would be fortnight when we would help picking strawberries, then we were all picking raspberries, then blackberries, then mushrooms—we were all busy with whatever was in season. No one thought of reward—we were given baskets of fruit. And most houses had few fruit trees or even orchard behind them, which ran down to river. There was custom there that if you walked along river path and did not pick something from the smallholders' or peasants' trees, they would be offended. They were proud they could produce something good. But if you tried to pick it and put it in your pocket that was different story altogether, because argument was why put it your pocket and carry it about because when you want it you just take it from tree fresh, there's no need to hoard.

"Then harvesting and threshing machines used to come. Straw would be put on one side, and husks put in barns to feed cattle. As boys, our job was to stamp down on these husks. Usually there was shed with loft in half of it, and we used to climb up ladder and jump into these husks. It was such fun—and all in anticipation of getting bit of bread. First sack of wheat that came out of machine was rushed quickly to farmer that had this harvest, quickly ground to flour, then rushed to farmer's wife. She was racing to bake first loaf of harvest—this absolutely white bread. It wasn't loaf of bread, it was art. She made very long roll, cut it into three pieces and plaited it. She put it into hot oven and baked it and then took it out, brushed it with egg yolk and put it back in to glaze it, so it was—glowing with glory. Taste was—oh—indescribable! She brought it outside to us and work stopped for while." He paused, laughed and pulled a long, rubbery face. "Probably if I had it now I wouldn't like it.

"That was first treat of harvest. Second was when farmers went to gather potatoes. When they were digging them out and putting them in sacks to take away, we were picking dried stalks from potatoes, and these were burned on fields, and what we did, we buried potatoes in fire and we had potatoes that tasted like nothing on earth, fantastic taste.

"Another aspect of life in that village was people cultivated flax to make own clothing from it. When flax was first gathered, it was tied in bundles, put in water to soften it or whatever, and then placed on riverbed with stones on top of it to keep it underwater. Unfortunate part was, it also poisoned some fish. When it was collected later, it was spread to dry and then put into small gadgetlike threshing machine. After that it was combed, and so on. What then happened—as tradition rather than necessity, though it probably started as necessity to save light—was they would all congregate in one house to spin it. This spinning would be done silently, with only shushing of spinning wheels. Then tradition was to have storytellers there whilst they were spinning. Usually they were very old men, and they enjoyed doing that. They were often homeless, and they were given food and lodgings. If we were allowed to go, we had to be back by seven. But it was getting dark on walk home, and we were frightened by stories, particularly one of them about how if you hear noise behind you, you mustn't look back, or you will die.

"Basically what it was, there was cooperation amongst people. They helped each other—individually they knew they could not survive."

3 | DREAM STATE

I was glad to hear that my father's childhood had been happy—
the kind of rural childhood I'd have loved—as I knew that he
wouldn't have an easy time later on. And yet a faint alarm bell
rang. I hoped it wasn't too idyllic, too dreamy. I hoped that my
father, now sixty-nine, wouldn't be seeing the past through rose-
colored spectacles and a glass of whiskey. It wasn't until later,
when I caught up with the history of Czechoslovakia at the time,
that I realized that the rosiness wasn't just my father's, it was
Czechoslovakia's.

Czechoslovakia in the twenties, I found, was living out a
dream—a "wild romance" even, the British *Morning Post* had
called it in 1926. It had started on October 28, 1918, two years
before Joe was born, when the new philosopher-president Tomáš
Garrigue Masaryk had ridden on horseback up to the statue of St.
Wenceslas in Prague to declare Czechoslovakia's independence,
and it would last for almost twenty years, until the country was dismembered at Munich on September 19, 1938. For my father, born
in November 1920, it was as if the world had been made anew: a
new country, with a new name, greater boundaries, its own language, its own president, and above all a new pride.

Tomáš Garrigue Masaryk

The new republic was full of hope and promise, and Masaryk was its hero: the sage of Prague, as H. G. Wells called him. As the first Czech-speaking professor at Prague University for five hundred years, Masaryk had conceived the idea of resurrecting old Bohemia and Moravia and putting them together with their neighbor Slovakia to create a new nation—the nation they had once been, nine hundred years before. Memories were long in middle Europe, I was finding. Perhaps they always are in suppressed countries, or individuals. In between, Slovakia had been under the rule of the Hungarians for all of those nine hundred years—hence the deposed Hungarian words still lurking behind the new Slovak ones in Joe's primary school. For their part, Bohemia and Moravia—the Czech lands—had at first experienced a great flowering: Charles IV had made Prague the seat of the Holy Roman Empire and built most of its glories, including the first university in middle Europe in 1348, and Jan Hus had established Protestantism in the land a century before Martin Luther (and been gruesomely martyred at the stake for his pains). But in 1526 all this had been quashed by the arrival of the Habsburg dynasty, which opportunistically took over the throne of Bohemia, made it hereditary in perpetuity, and killed or executed an estimated four fifths of Bohemia's aristocracy. Even more disastrously for the future of the Czech lands, the dynasty imported its own aristocracy and rulers instead, establishing German as the first language, and high Catholicism as the religion.

All this was still the case over three hundred years later, in 1850, when Masaryk was born: Czechs were relegated to being largely a clerical class for the Habsburgs, and the capital, Prague, was the unwilling legislative outpost of an ailing empire. Some Czechs didn't object: Austrians and Czechs had intermingled over centuries now; speaking German gave Czechs a leg up in their professions; and being under the umbrella of the Austro-Hungarian Empire, as the Habsburg Empire became, provided protection from the Germans and Russians, as well as such everyday bonuses as pensions. It was a familiar trade-off: identity for security, however irksome the humiliations.

And yet . . . having to show deference to leaders not their own bred a characteristic Czech attitude: surface compliance masking inner resistance. This could bloom into surreal black humor, as it did later in the writings of Franz Kafka or Jaroslav Hašek (creator of the Good Soldier Schweik), both born in Prague in 1883 into a later phase of the conditions Masaryk experienced: both writers in different ways apeing deadpan obedience to the letter of the law to show up the insanity of its spirit. It may have been no accident, either, that the Austrian Sigmund Freud, the great theorist of repression, was born in Moravia into the same atmosphere, six years after Masaryk. This split psychic life had also bred a mistrust of officials and institutions, and a tendency to trust instead only the unassuming scholar, writer or philosopher, or the man in the street, the "little Czech man." I recognized my father's attitude in all this, which he may have picked up subliminally from an older generation. I realized that what had looked to me like his excessive deference toward authority was in fact an effective parody, giving him some other, inner freedom, though I didn't yet know what that was.

Authenticity, though, will out, and there was another spirit in the air, too, as Masaryk grew up, born of the industrial revolution and the subsequent nationalist movements in Europe after 1848. This was the Czech revival or "awakening," a need to go back to the country's cultural roots, seen as naturally democratic and vernacular, in contrast to the feudalism and hierarchies of the Habsburgs. Masaryk's contemporaries Dvořák, Smetana and Janáček celebrated the new spirit musically, whilst linguists retrieved the Czech language and the historian František Palacký wrote the first history of the Czech lands. (It reminded me that even in the twenties there was a dearth of Czech history in my father's primary school.)

Masaryk himself epitomized the country he re-created: born in Moravia, the son of a Czech cook and a Slovak coachman father, he bridged its geography. He also embodied its yearning for the philosopher/everyman: starting out as an apprentice blacksmith, he'd developed into a philosopher and formidable scholar. Apart from Czech and Slovak, he spoke German, Italian, English, Hungarian and Russian, and read Arabic, Latin, Greek and Sanskrit. In 1878 he'd married an American, Charlotte Garrigue, and travelled to America three times before the First World War to lecture on Bohemian history, particularly in Chicago, with its large community of Czech and Slovak immigrants (by 1914, 20 percent of Slovaks had emigrated, mainly to America).

Although the core of Masaryk's writing and thinking was concerned with Czech history and the problems of small nations, his engagement with the wider world was equally passionate. He wrote two intellectual histories of Germany and Russia of massive learning and scope, and also volumes on the social and political dilemmas unfolding around him at the turn of the twentieth century. Prussian militarism and "Supermanishness," Russian Marxism,

European fin-de-siècle nihilism and anti-Semitism, American mate-
rialism and "decadence" were, he felt, all aspects of a misguided
response to modern challenges. He proposed his own solutions:
instead of revolution—its impulse always aristocratic or philistine,
he thought—he proposed "reformation," progress through cooperative, "small-scale work," allied with an ethical, realistic humanitar-
ianism. The party he formed to put his ideas into practice in 1900
was called the Czech People's (Realist) Party (even its realism put
modestly in parentheses). All ideas and ideals, he felt, including
philosophic ideals, should be judged only on their "sound gains to
life." Like Palacký before him, he discerned two threads running
throughout Czech history: a desire to search for the truth against
any authority and a yearning for freedom. Jan Hus's credo had been
"Defend the truth," and Masaryk's own motto, which he would give
to Czechoslovakia, was "Truth conquers." The forging of the
Czechoslovak Republic would at last make truth and authenticity
concrete.

No leader at the time had a greater grasp of European history
than Masaryk, and none a more considered ethical viewpoint. This
gave him a great advantage over the Western statesmen who were
trying to rebalance the European map toward the end of the First
World War, and who were all at sea in the arcane crosscurrents of
middle Europe's past and present. Extraordinarily, as in a dream,
this advantage levitated Masaryk and his much younger colleague
Dr. Edvard Beneš to a level where they sat at the same table as the
great powers, even though they were technically the nonappointed
leaders of a nonexistent country. During the war, Masaryk was
operating out of exile in London, where he worked as professor of
Slavonic Studies at the University of London, and the industrious
Beneš (only thirty when war broke out) from exile in Paris, where
he was studying and earning a living as a journalist. They were
joined by a roving Slovak astronomer and war hero, Milan Štefánik
(who would die in an air crash in 1919). From their respective

exiles they argued that the proposed new country, "Czechoslovakia," was essential to the future peace of Europe. Beyond that, Masaryk also argued the case for an eventual United States of Europe, to maintain that peace.

In his book *Czechoslovakia's Case for Independence* (1917), Beneš stressed that its naturally peace-loving people had been endlessly thwarted by three foes: the Germans; the Habsburgs, who "made use of the Germans to exterminate the Czechs"; and finally "the Magyars, the traditional allies of the Germans, who tried to extirpate the Slovaks." "There is not a single period in the history of this people," he wrote, "which does not record a conflict with one or another of these three enemies. . . . During these twelve centuries the Czechs were never the aggressors." Beneš even cited a German, Bismarck, to prove his point: "Whoever is master of Bohemia is master of Europe. Europe must therefore never allow any nationality except the Czechs to rule over it, since the Czech nation does not lust for domination. The natural boundaries of Bohemia are the safeguard of European security; and whoever tries to move them, will plunge Europe into misery."

All this was not just in the country's own interests, Masaryk, Beneš and Štefánik argued: the new Czechoslovakia, the geographic heart of Europe, should be the fulcrum of the "balance of power" that would thwart for all time the possibility of another devastating war like the one from which Europe was reeling. The country would be an "active custodian of freedom" against the proven warmongering of Germany and Austria on one side and the potential new threat of post-1917 Bolshevik Russia on the other. It would be a bridge between West and East. So effective was the men's lobbying that Czechoslovakia was born, with, for the first time, viable mountain frontiers to its west in the Sudeten Mountains, and to its east in the Ruthenian Carpathians. So effective were they that the Allies were persuaded to make the breakup of the Austro-Hungarian Empire a war aim, something not even imagined at the start of the war. And so effective was their advocacy that it fuelled the intellectual push for independence of the swath of other middle European countries created at Versailles from 1918 to 1919. As a bonus, Czechoslovakia inherited at birth well over 70 percent of the industry of the former Austro-Hungarian Empire, even though it had composed only just over a quarter of its population. However, this would prove a poisoned chalice, as would the fact that amongst its ethnically mixed population of 13.5 million, it inherited over 3 million Germans—1 million more than its population of Slovaks.

For the moment, though, in the twenties, Czechoslovakia was riding high, the "picture democracy" to emerge out of Versailles, blessed particularly by France. "We were a small nation," Masaryk wrote later, "in an unfavourable geographical position: in effect it imposes upon us the obligation to be more alert, to think more, to achieve more than others." And they did, and had. Masaryk recalled "with what sureness we fulfilled the mandate of the whole nation; how we set out with naked hands, and how at the end we returned bearing them freedom, the Republic, Slovakia, Ruthenia—it still seems like a dream to me. . . . You see how it is: the method must be absolutely practical, reasonable, realistic—but the aim, the whole, the conception is an eternal poem."

"Oh yes," said my father, when I asked him if his happy memories of Czechoslovakia had a lot to do with its being a newborn, optimistic country. "It made you feel that you were just born, because everything was created for nation—from all these dialects, for example, there was new language for new nation. Everybody was looking forward to something new, something that did not exist, and you were part of it. One of reasons that new Czechoslovakia was happy nation was that it was clean and proud. You always stood upright, you walked with your head held high, if you stooped or something you were considered mentally unsound.

"There were two nationwide gymnastic clubs, *Sokols* and *Orols*—Falcons and Eagles they would be in English—which competed with each other. They had started before First World War, on western Czech side, and spread through nation, so as to have people physically fit to fight if necessary. They were not allowed to train as soldiers, but they were allowed to train as athletes. You started gymnastics at age of two. You could hardly walk and you raised your head and arms in unison. When I was about nine this competition began to develop into jamborees, with thousands of schoolchildren coming together, trained at certain gymnastic routines. The best from each school were chosen to go to jamboree, paid for by state, and spent a week or so wherever jamboree was taking place. Imagine some ten thousand children in square, never having met before and performing synchronized routine—without music, since square was too big and there would have been time delay in sound, which would have broken uniformity. Of course, everyone tried to get into it—it was like winning Nobel Prize. We liked gymnastics. They were very important. It was only later on we were told that one of reasons it was formed was to have fit people for fighting."

Later, I would discover how vexed the question of whether to fight or not fight was for Czechoslovakia, and would continue to be. Masaryk's own interest in the matter was of long standing. In 1887, 1889 and 1910, he'd travelled to Russia to discuss it with Tolstoy, who took the pacifist view that if you didn't oppose force with force, the original force would "grow lax and stop killing." Masaryk agreed, up to a point. "I am a convinced pacifist," he wrote, "—but I love the army! I want peace, but that doesn't mean that I am going to meet aggression unarmed, rather the contrary. I want practical not Utopian peace; that means that I exert all the power of my brain and all my love of my nation and humanity to keep the peace; but also, if necessary, to make war. So let's be brave and manly and as strong as we can be." And Masaryk had personal cause to be thankful to the army: a major card in his hands at Versailles had been the paradoxical fact that his nonexistent country had managed to acquire its own army. Some seventy thousand disaffected soldiers, unwillingly conscripted to fight on behalf of their imperial oppressors and against their fellow Slavs the Russians and Serbs, had contrived to desert or be made prisoners of war in Russia and France. They came to be called the "Czech Legions," and through their fighting on behalf of the Western Allies they had helped earn Czechoslovakia its passport to nationhood.

"A train track ran behind sawmill where my father worked, and on First of May there was holiday, and we used to go and wait for train to come. It was decorated for occasion with red flags and ribbons, and with flags in national colors, white, blue and red. We loved colors, and fact that we were given free ride to town and back again. Of course now I realize that First of May is Communist celebration, but then it was just free ride.

"Every year after harvest army had maneuvers, where they had to lug machine guns and rifles across river, only hundred meters away from bridge. This made no sense to us, not to simply use bridge, but otherwise we just enjoyed maneuvers because it was something unusual and special. At end of maneuvers, brass bands would play and army kitchens would be open to us children, so we could finish off what soldiers didn't eat. We weren't particularly hungry, it was just we felt, 'One day I shall be doing this, I'll be eating this when I'm grown-up, let's taste it.' There was enormous pride in army. When I was eleven, one man from our village was called up, and when he came back on leave he had little dot on his epaulet, he'd been promoted—to, well, less than lance corporal, but we were so proud of him, so proud to know someone who'd been promoted. Masaryk was to us man behind it all. We may have been preconditioned to like him, it's hard to tell now, but everybody looked on him as father figure and many songs were about him. On October 28, our national liberation day, commemorating founding of Czechoslovakia in 1918, we would march and sing anthems, and after that we'd sing a song about him: 'Little father, you are old, you have gray hair on your head, but as long as you are with us everything's going to be all right.' As it happened, that is way it worked out."

We had come to the end of the tape, and we adjourned. "Is that all?" Joe asked, with a brisk nod and a matter-of-fact smile, already in another mode, keen to go down to the "usable past" of his workshop and get on with his next project, trying to mend an old Longines watch I'd been given. My local watchmaker (and Longines themselves) had given up on it as out of date, but I thought if anyone could mend it, my father could.

4 | SLUMP

I f Czechoslovakia was a newborn country, born into a fairy tale, it was also a long, narrow newborn, born vulnerable, since the many countries bordering it, with the exception of Romania, were jealous of its birth. Austria, Poland and Hungary all resented having parts of their erstwhile territories lopped off to create the new country; and there were two, more dangerous fairies who had not been invited to the feast at all, and who would take long-term revenge: Germany, which bore the brunt of opprobrium for the war since its co-belligerents the Ottoman and Austro-Hungarian empires had ceased to exist; and Russia, now frozen out of the European club for its Bolshevism. The German hostility was the greater because the 3 million and more Germans who had colonized western Bohemia for generations as overlords were now living there as subjects, with Czech their official first language instead of their own. The tables had been turned. Hitler would call them "Sudeten Germans," refusing to acknowledge them as Czechs, and adopting a term coined in 1902 to describe the Germans living in the westerly Sudeten Mountain range. Typically, he pushed its boundaries, using it also to designate all Germans wherever they lived in Czechoslovakia. He would also energetically fan the residual pique of some of the Bohemian Germans until he could use it as a fire to light war in Europe, and a smokescreen to hide his first plain territorial aggression. Only two weeks after independence, the first Czechoslovak prime minister, Karel Kramář, had made a point of saying, "It is our desire and pride that no one among us who is not a Czech should feel oppressed or unfree. . . . We do not wish to imitate the Austrian system."

The Western Allies, criticized after the Versailles settlements for their inadequate grasp of the tangled history of central Europe, and with problems of their own, began to back away from their previous protégé. Even Czechoslovakia's great ally, France, began to cool.

"Was there a feeling in Czechoslovakia as you were growing up," I asked Joe the next day, "that the Versailles settlement was artificial?"

"No, because as far as Czechoslovakia was concerned, history of Czech lands went very far back, much farther back than Hungary, because Hungarians were nomads, who came with Genghis Khan, and by that time Bohemia had existed for long time. They had history behind them and feeling was in Czechoslovakia that at last barbarians—because this is what Hungarians were known as—were being subdued and Czechoslovakia will develop back into what it used to be in past ages. That feeling changed later on, just before depression came. Feeling came then that France was not doing anything, was very noncommittal and backing off suddenly—because Czechoslovakia had really been born in France during World War I. And there were other things, that communism was beginning to creep in little bit in places and specially during depression." It was then, he told me, he heard his parents beginning to use a new word, "crisis"—an unfamiliar, imported word. He didn't know what it meant, but it was clear it was something bad.

.   .   .

Later, when it was all over, it would be called the slump or the Great Depression. It blew like a tornado through world economies in the years following the Wall Street Crash of October 1929. Banks and companies collapsed, bringing in their wake a cycle of unemployment and protectionism, a decrease in world trade, more unemployment, social problems and disaffected people on the streets.

There were already special problems in Europe that made it fertile soil for extremists. Economically, the newly emancipated states of central Europe had largely exchanged financial dependence on Austro-Hungary for dependence on the West and America. The United States had set up loans after the end of the First World War to help rebuild Europe's war-torn economies and at the same time to boost its own economy with interest on the loans. The chief beneficiary of these loans was Germany, partly because the terms of the $33 billion payment exacted by the Allies from Germany in war reparations were beginning to seem dangerously harsh in a climate in which, by 1923, German inflation was spectacularly out of control, with, notoriously, a wheelbarrowful of marks needed to buy a box of matches and 4,200,000,000,000 marks to purchase one dollar. Politicians were pointing out that Germany, the only surviving belligerent nation, had been unfairly saddled with these debts at Versailles and had taken the flak for them all.

The chief aspiring politician to point this out of course was Adolf Hitler, who, in November 1923, a year into his leadership of the Nazi Party, had just surfaced as the thuggish leader of the "Beer Hall Putsch," an attempted takeover of Bavaria which landed him in prison. It was here—in what he called "my university at the State's expense"—that he wrote *My Four and a Half Years of Struggle Against Lies, Stupidity and Ignorance: A Reckoning with the Destroyers of the Nazi Party Movement*, which he was later persuaded to simplify to the snappier title of *Mein Kampf* (*My Struggle*), just as he simplified his name from Adolf Schicklgrüber. This simplification was no accident: in 1936 he would give an interview to a French journalist, saying, "I will tell you what has carried me to the position I have reached. Our political problems appear complicated. The German people could make nothing of them. I on the other hand simplified the problems and reduced them to the simplest terms. The masses understood this and followed me."

The American loans had stabilized Germany's economy during the late twenties, and Hitler's apocalyptic predictions of disaster began to look overwrought—until the Wall Street Crash, when America was forced to call in its loans and the underpinning for the German recovery collapsed. Fascist and Communist movements alike took advantage of the vacuum to pour scorn on the vaunted virtues of democracy and capitalism as lodestars to the future, and by the mid-thirties, most of the reconstituted countries of central Europe were reverting in panic or mistrust to military dictatorships or monarchies. In 1931, even the government of Great Britain, a relatively stable country, had to form a coalition in order to prevent the growth of extremism.

The exception to all this was Czechoslovakia, which remained a flourishing democracy right up until Munich. It was so democratic that it was the only one of the succession states to continue to allow the Communists to participate in its elections. Masaryk had criticized Marxism on ethical and religious grounds, and had found Bolshevism to be "a communism of misery and disintegration," deploring its "orgy of ignorance, violence and corruption." But he accepted some of Marx's criticisms of the capitalist economy and was in favor of social reforms to benefit the working classes. And although he wrote against tsarism and Bolshevism (the child of tsarism, he felt), he also loved Russia and was in sympathy with the long-standing strain of Russophilia in the Czech lands. For the Czechs, Germany was the historical enemy, and they had been inclined to idealize the Russians as Slav brothers. This had been reinforced at the end of the First World War by the soldiers from the Czech legions in Russia who had brought home tales of a heady new workers' state.

Although Czechoslovakia maintained its democracy, its economy was hit badly, particularly in the German-speaking manufacturing districts. Hitler, rising to power at the same time, encouraged their disaffection with the slogan *"Heim ins Reich*—Home into the Reich," with that cozy abbreviated *"ins"* reinforcing the suggestion of almost climbing back into the protective lap of the Fatherland. His tactical sentimentality masked the usefulness of the Sudeten "problem" to him: not only could it provide a rallying cry and potential casus belli, but also he was all too aware that Czechoslovakia—a mere quarter of the old empire, yet already the "purse of the Habsburgs" with its silver mines and minerals—had inherited that massive 70 percent of its total production after the war. Hitler, eyeing it from just across the border as he grew up in Braunau, Austria, was incensed that what he saw as German riches should go to this new country. Moreover, he had a particular hatred of Beneš, whom he saw as a chief architect of the Treaty of Versailles.

Beneš, previously foreign minister in the new republic, became its president in 1935, when Masaryk retired aged eighty-five and in poor health. Masaryk died two years later, in 1937; he was fortunate not to live to see his country and dream destroyed a year later at Munich. He had been acutely aware of the roots of the Nazi threat which he saw growing on his doorstep from 1933. He saw it developing inexorably from the "Prussianization" of the German people, which he had long warned against, a militarism that "created the basis for a policy of force in theory and practice." He was concerned that "In modern war, adversaries do not face each other eye to eye, hand to hand. They destroy each other from a distance, abstractly, invisibly, killing through and by ideas—translated into the tongue of Krupp. . . . Militarism is an attempt of the superman to escape from diseases which it nevertheless aggravates." Masaryk's memoirs, *The Making of a State,* deal only with the years 1914–18, but they were written in 1936, and in them he is also clearly shadowboxing with Hitler. When he writes that "In truth, the German superman, the Titan, is a nervous creature who seeks

Edvard Beneš as a student in Paris, 1905

relief from chronic excitement in death or in war, that is to say, in an excitement still more acute," it is hard not to see Hitler's personality foreshadowed from birth to bunker. Hitler had already set out his credo along these lines in *Mein Kampf:* "Man grew great in eternal conflict, in eternal peace he perishes." Hitler never challenged Masaryk: he knew that Masaryk knew his history better than he did, and that with him he couldn't get away with lies about a "thousand-year German Reich" and its historic entitlements. He also knew that, unusually amongst the neighboring leaders at the time, with Masaryk he would have been dealing with a moral force.

In spite of the intense afternoon heat and brilliant Australian January sunshine, Joe was back there in his mind's eye, shaking his head

Masaryk and Beneš in the early 1920s

as if to try to slough off the grayness and depression. "People had to draw on their savings to live," my father said, furrowing his brow. In 1930, at the start of the depression, his father's sawmill was shut down, and the family, now with seven children, moved some eighty kilometers away to the town of Medzilaborce, where his father got work as a stoker.

"It was very very dark period in children's lives because wages were very very low and you had to fight for job, for any work there was. My father's job was on night shift and he was also working days at brickworks. He was doing two jobs for quarter of pay. We barely existed, and things got worse and worse. We all had to do work around house, collecting wood from forest, and mushrooms and so on. Whole area was crisscrossed with trenches from severe fighting during First World War, and where trenches had collapsed was ideal place for mushrooms. Once we found opening into trench and saw something bright inside. We crept in and found cannon pointing out at us and saw brightness was buttons on uniforms—and in uniforms were skeletons. We got really frightened and ran back home to tell our father and we went there again with him and couldn't find it. It had disappeared altogether. We knew those trenches intimately.

"Situation was becoming desperate. My father's family originally came from Lwow, and he considered going there, where his brother still had farm, but it could not support two families—and it could not be sold, because there was no one to buy. All my father could find was work in sawmill in village called Baligrod, across border in Poland. There was dwelling attached to job, although it was quite primitive. My father wrote from there telling us to come, and we packed up and got on train from Medzilaborce to Poland. As soon as we crossed border, my mother started to talk in Polish instead of Slovak. We went from station to Baligrod in horse and cart, and arrived in December 1933. We arrived in evening, and I started school in morning, in different language. There was similarity in language, but sometimes words which were very similar could mean opposite—like 'fresh' and 'stale.' All work was unpleasant, laboring—you did anything and everything. There was never any fun any more, you were just trying to exist. It was below poverty."

A slight pall settled on us as I sensed how grim this period had been for my father, and yet couldn't find the words to help him out of it all these years later. He was slipping several countries and decades away, an ebb tide. I think now it was probably the right thing to do, to let him reexperience this gloom attached to its origins, without any attempts at rescue. It had all been locked away in a gray miasma, like the countries behind the iron curtain for us. Now we were beginning to map at least the foothills.

His family had moved to Baligrod just after my father's thirteenth birthday, and from that moment on he was living in Poland, with Czechoslovakia left behind to the south across the Carpathian Mountains, a paradise lost.

Joe had been in Baligrod for over two years when, in June 1936, he got a scholarship to study art in Lwow in Poland. This was fortunate, since he was now fifteen, and to stay on at home with no means of employment in the village would have been burdensome for the large family. However, when he reached Lwow, he found there were no places in the art school after all and the only remaining opening was in a technical college to study electromechanical engineering for four years. "It was take it or leave it, but in fact I began to like subject, particularly instrumentation, automatic control, that type of thing." He was given lodgings in a kind of boarding school, a *Bursa,* with three dormitories, sleeping a total of some sixty pupils. They would set off for their college in a crocodile in the mornings, annoyed at having to walk like children when they were fifteen or more. "I got very high marks in all subjects," my father says matter-of-factly, nodding at the ground. "My parents were delighted, but it was also sacrifice for them, because I could have been contributing to family welfare." Whilst he was studying in Lwow, he only saw his parents in the Christmas vacations. He would work through the Easter and summer vacations, as half their course was theory and half practical.

"Did you know I am qualified blacksmith?" asked Joe suddenly, pulling a long, teasing face, eyes wide and staring at me, daring me not to be impressed. His deep, Slavonic voice growls, "Ye-e-es. You see? You see, there are things about me you couldn't have guessed." His foot jogs up and down. I am impressed. I'm beginning to realize how he could have built this house in Australia on his own, and where all his practical expertise started.

"After first year I was engaged by man who was installing electricity in buildings. He also gave me work during termtime, doing technical drawings for him, of electrical circuits and so on. Then, in second summer, I was put in power station. In third summer I was sent to firm called Romer making electrical equipment, where there were girls stamping out washers from Bakelite on machine. Boring thing, and they hated it. I thought, there must be better way. It suddenly struck me that when you press key on typewriter it moves one space, so I designed machine to do it using this principle—very fast. There was also young man there who was two years older than me, Zbigniew—Zbyszek for short—and he was my co-lodger in digs we were in during summer. He was watchmaker, and taught me bit about watches. He said I should get best timepiece which existed, it was Omega watch, and he had one which one of his clients hadn't picked up for years and so I managed to get it for very little. I was fully self-supporting by now, and could even help my parents."

"This must have been around the time of Munich, Joe," I said. "Were you aware of what England and France were doing to Czechoslovakia, breaking it up and handing it to Hitler on a plate?"

"Oh yes," Joe said, "we knew about Munich. There was censorship in Poland under cohort of aides of former President Piłsudski who were running country at time—he had died a few years before—but there were daily newspapers in Poland. They did not meddle in international news, but there was weekly newspaper and few pages of it were basically international news. We knew about Munich. There was great disappointment about way it was conducted. Britain and France appeared to play chickens. And I knew that Beneš after death of Masaryk was already less than paper shadow. He was not liked by majority of Czech people and also not trusted, due to his softness. But then I had no spare time to find out much else, I was eager to earn money with work, and busy with studies."

"And did news about the fear of imminent war percolate through?"

"Well, there was no-radio rule in *Bursa,* and even if you had radio, you had to buy license, which we couldn't afford. But there was radio station nearby on hill, and after lights-out in our dormitory we would insert piece of wire between planks in floor, connect it to small coil of wire and adjustable capacitator, and listen in through homemade cat's-whisker headphones. Usually, all we heard was Chopin concerts!"

"What about when the threat of war came nearer to your new home, Poland, a year later, in 1939?"

"I just remember one headline in paper: 'Is it war, or is it peace?' That was summer of 1939. Then suddenly bombs came few weeks later, on September 1, war was on and everything collapsed. Everybody was shattered by it and we didn't know what to do.

"I moved out into countryside when fighting started, with Zbyszek. It lasted about eight or ten days, then within fortnight Russians started coming in so we retreated from country. We had run eastward because we were thinking of running away from Germans and hoping that England and France and Belgium would come and rescue us. This did not happen; instead, Russians came from east. We almost ran back to Lwow. It was vacation—we hadn't taken much, just decided to get away because shells were falling. We got to village and asked, 'Could we stay night here, and could you spare little bread?' We stayed in barn for few days. When Russians started pushing in, there was great upheaval because in that area in addition to small farmers and peasants there were largish estates. There were very rich and very poor in that area. Even before Russians came, peasants started dividing estates left empty by owners—who often lived in France, and came back occasionally to hunt, leaving estates for others to manage. The peasants took cattle amongst themselves, anticipating communism. Russians when they came dispersed estates that were left—two for you and ten for us.

"We first heard Russians were coming when we came across Polish motorized regiment on road with few very light tanks and they were going toward Romania and we said, 'Why are you going there?' and they said, 'As far as war is concerned, it's all over because Germany and Russia have signed pact that Poland is going to be divided and already Germans have stopped pushing eastward and Russians are going west.' As soon as Germans had passed Lwow, they stopped and there was vacuum there, taken up by Russians. Germans retreated by some sort of agreement from rest of Lwow, and Russians just filled it in. Polish soldiers on road said they were trying to get either to Hungary or Romania to be interned as prisoners of war—this way, they said, our lives are going to be saved. We said, 'Can we join you?' but they said no, unless you're in uniform you may find yourself in trouble. Anyway, even at that stage there was always hope that England, France and Belgium would intervene and there would be some agreement. I was determined to finish my education and I had only one year to go before I went on to Polytechnic where I could get degree. This is one of reasons why we turned back to Lwow.

"We knew what would happen when Russians came in—we knew way they would behave, from history, from experience. Almost first thing when they entered Lwow, first thing I remember seeing were civilians eight abreast and twenty deep being marched under bayonets in street. I looked at them and they did not look like criminals to me. They were being taken to labor camps. Almost within day or two enormous statues were built, mostly of Stalin's head and Stalin, put in streets wherever there was space—suddenly structure appeared with face of Stalin on four sides. It was beginning of very unpleasant time. I found myself under Russian occupation, whereas my parents, who were living less than 150 kilometers away, were under German occupation, and there was borderline and that was end of it.

"There was emptiness at first, no one knew what to do. For example, in our college they did not know whether to open or not, to accept students or not. Then they were instructed to open, and we enrolled as normal. There was no fear, just—blank emptiness. You were falling down and you did not know when you would hit bottom. You were falling through space and there was nothing on sides to stop you falling. You knew you were destined to disappear somewhere, somehow, but you didn't know how. It wasn't fear, it was fear of not knowing. If there was fear, it was fear of not knowing. But behind all that, there was some hope about West coming in. But this did not happen."

Joe's legs were crossed, and his foot tapped in the air. He looked down in a philosophical, buttoned-up sort of way. "We enlisted at school. Many lecturers were missing, called up for Polish military service. During vacations almost full mobilization was declared in Poland. There was general call-up. Many lecturers were at age group for military service. Many did not return, because either they were killed in action or escaped into Hungary, many as prisoners of war. Later on, Hungary became puppet of Germans and these people suffered enormously.

"I enrolled—there was no other option. Germans started war on September 1 and England declared war on September 3. This gave us hope that Germans would have to withdraw from Poland. But nothing was happening. There was lot of confusion, rumors, false information on radio and newspapers—for example, that two hundred Polish bombers had bombed Berlin—and we did not know whether the declaration of war by England was true or not. We knew things were going badly as first refugees from west started appearing in streets. The continuous air-raid alarms and bombings did not help either. Then when Russians moved in, they took over various posts. The director of our college was replaced by Russian—although all Russian replacements spoke Polish to us. Before, there had been PE in mornings on Tuesdays, Thursdays and Saturdays, but when Russians took over that stopped, and we had to go and chop wood to heat college. Or we would be digging trenches—I don't know what for. That turned into digging trenches all day on Saturday, and then became Sunday as well—except that in morning on Sunday you were also obliged to go and carry banners declaring *Batiushka* Stalin—our 'little father' Stalin—greatest man in world, and you had to march and proclaim your loyalty to him. If you did not go and they found you somewhere else, well, you probably disappeared. There were very few students who dared not go, because it was very easy to determine if anyone was missing. You would march class by class in columns, carrying individual banners, or banners stretching over four people. We did this in center of city, in the Alleya Ulanovska, which is almost one and half kilometers long. We marched up central walkway lined with trees, then down wide street alongside. We joined groups from other colleges—all groups would assemble in side streets and then feed into main street.

"I was marching alongside my friend's sister once, and we were in last line. We had been given banners and there was one with single picture of Stalin, and we were quarrelling because neither of us wanted to carry it. One of military people came over and said, 'What's going on?' and we were saved by student with bright idea of saying, 'Well, commissar, there is only one banner to carry and there are two of them and each wants to carry it.' So the commissar said, 'Right, as punishment, neither of you will carry it.' Absolutely brilliant idea. It saved us!

"Russians were supposed to come as friends—with Germans, you knew they were enemies. But we also knew about oppression of Russians, and that prewar border between Russia and Poland was up to seven kilometers wide of plowed fields so that any footsteps would show up in it. We knew about all these things. But restrictions came much faster than we expected. We thought it would be more gradual. It all happened within less than fortnight, so quickly that people didn't realize that it was happening. It happened—that was it. Russians came in and declared that two Polish *zlotys* were worth one ruble—until then, it had been other way around. They came in with rubles, and bought everything. They bought things by kilo—even shirts. They bought grain, and wheat and shirts, and sent them all back home. Within almost hours shops became empty, and there was nothing to buy. Every morning you would see queues of hundreds of people. Initially shopkeepers were really pleased, but suddenly they realized they were left with lot of paper in hands, and no supplies.

"Within less than week, era of queues started. It was very difficult to get any food at all—*Bursa* was purely place to sleep, not to eat in. You were almost looking through garbage bins for food. Then coal merchant suddenly managed to get loaves of bread from somewhere and people wanted to buy them because they had worthless money and nothing to spend it on. There could be queues of maybe thousand people waiting for bread. If you saw queue of about two hundred it was almost useless joining it. Often you did not know what you were queuing for, you just knew something was there to buy. Many of girl students worked in restaurants in evenings. Amongst students there was feeling of unity—that we have to help each other otherwise we will vanish. Russians would order stuff in restaurants, then leave much of it, just to show they could afford to. Russians became disliked very fast. There was no attempt to make friends, it was authority all time, aggression all time, even with normal soldiers. It was not individual aggression, but probably preconditioning—they had to do something and that was done. It was not just soldiers, but lots of uniformed people in streets.

"If you were not on your own, there was always danger. Maximum of three people could walk together—if you were four, that was considered demonstration! But they would snatch you apart as two or three people walking together and interrogate you, and they were very clever at it and talked in Russian and it was very easy for us to slip up. If your story didn't tally, you were taken off, as assumption was you were talking politics, and that was forbidden. You weren't told rules, you just picked them up. You developed very sensitive antennae. We soon realized you had to get your story to tally from start, before you set off. Every small region had commissar who was sent order that his quota for this week is to supply forty people, for example, and if that didn't work, they would grab anybody they saw in street. We knew that people were being taken to railway station and put in wagon which was going east. We didn't know why, and it wasn't until later we heard of labor camps.

We realized then that walking in crocodile was blessing after all because it protected us."

"Did your parents know what was happening to you?"

"There was no correspondence between east and west of Poland. I wrote to my parents, but later found no letter ever arrived. I suppose there would have been telephones in Lwow, but you probably couldn't phone outside. Once, Marshal Zhukov came and spoke with us. He was only high-ranking Russian who felt for people, not only for us but for his own people. The way I saw it, he didn't like to see what they were doing, what they had to do. He would have preferred that they did not have to do it. He spoke of the advantages of communism, but at end had reservations about means of bringing it: 'even though I don't like doing it, this is way it's going to be done.' So I mentioned, very quietly, 'If you don't like doing it, why do you do it?' He said, 'This is system. You go with it or you perish.' "

The tape was nearing its end, and we called a halt for the day. My father went off to watch golf on television. The weather had clouded over and my mother and I decided to take the opportunity of cooler air to go for a long walk along the sixty-kilometer beach at Stockton. When we went to say good-bye to Joe, he was asleep in his swivel chair in front of the television, head thrown back, exhausted.

TWO

PARALLEL JOURNEYS

Quieter go, further get.

—UKRAINIAN/RUSSIAN PROVERB

5 | BRIEF ENCOUNTERS

I t's March 2001. I've decided to make the journey my father made from Lwow in Poland—now called Lviv, and in the Ukraine—back to his home village of Baligrod in the Carpathians, following in his December 1939 footsteps. As I write up his journey sixty-two years afterward, I shall be walking alongside him, a ghost of the future. This journey, a loop around into my father's past, is also a loop into my own past. Roger, who is travelling with me, is someone I met briefly thirty-five years ago, before I was married. I hadn't seen him since—though I'd read a book of his with admiration—until a chance meeting last year. In between, we've made long journeys with our lives, bringing up families, getting divorced, and being free agents. As Heraclitus said, you never step into the same river twice.

I wouldn't have ventured on my own into the regions we are about to go through, and even Roger, a more seasoned traveller, wouldn't have done so. First, the Ukraine, ten years into independence, has more pressing economic problems than to make itself tourist-friendly, and we don't speak the language. Then, from Lviv we'll be heading for Joe's home village of Baligrod in southeast Poland. Joe had gone by train from Lwow to a small station called

Ustianowa, before jumping off and walking the last stretch through the Bieszczady Mountains for two days. I find it's impossible to make that journey by train now, as the line is disused. There are only one or two border crossings between Ukraine and Poland that foreigners are allowed to use, so we will have to loop up to one, and then go back down to Ustianowa by bus. From there, we shall walk through the Bieszczady Mountains, which, our guidebook tells us, is a relative wilderness of beech and fir forests, except for the unsettling presence of nine wolves to every human. The bonus is that we may see the occasional bear, bison, wildcat or moose. The downside is that they are referred to as "the major European predators."

When I ring the Ukraine Embassy for information about visas, the recorded message tells me in clipped tones and dated English vowels, at a cost of 60p per minute, and very slowly, how to get an entry visa for the country. No visa is required for the Czech Republic, Slovakia or Poland, where we're also heading, but Ukraine requires a visa. It isn't made easy to get, and doesn't bode well for the country's nascent tourist industry. The visas are expensive; you have to be formally sponsored by a business or a private individual in Ukraine; and the application form is more like an interrogation: "Have you ever been charged of any criminal offenses anywhere?" "Have you ever been deported or prohibited from an entry to Ukraine?"

I turn up at the embassy and am admitted by what looks like a bouncer. As I join the visa queue under a framed photograph of a smiling, relaxed President Kuchma alongside a large map of Ukraine combed with waving, golden corn under a blue sky, I begin to take on the air of nervous shiftiness of the other people standing in line. I hand our forms over to the immaculately groomed, doll-like beauty behind the counter, with her smart suit, no jewelry, but deep red lipstick and fingernails. She coolly declines to give me the visas. When pressed, she says I need not only the hotel confirmation, which I have, but a "tourist voucher" from Intel, the Russian travel agent. When I later find that we'll have to pay another £80 (about $120) for this privilege, I refuse to be party to such a racket—especially since I thought Ukraine was an independent country, and no longer tied to the apron strings of Moscow.

When I ring the embassy to say so, I'm told that if the woman on the desk that morning had said I had to get a tourist voucher from Intel Moscow, then I had to do so, and that's that, because she's the vice consul. This takes me aback—she's certainly an exotically camouflaged vice consul, and I wonder why she's vetting the applications personally. I also wonder what she knows about me that made her refuse the visa—and whether I should know it, too. I'm beginning to feel the cold chill of being politically undesirable. It takes another visit to the embassy, and several calls to our Lviv hotel, to persuade them to issue the visas. Ukraine doesn't seem to be heading for an imminent tourist boom, especially since its currency, the *hryvnya,* is as difficult to get hold of from abroad as it is to pronounce. The guidebook tells me, "Today in Ukraine the reward for doing one's job will not support a family, so when a Westerner comes bearing hard currency, some have trouble distinguishing the concept of 'free enterprise' from that of 'highway robbery.' A generation that feels robbed of what was theirs now feels that it's their turn to take their due." This doesn't sound too promising, so I've decided to look up a friend of a friend who is from the Ukraine to get some travel tips for a country which is proving as difficult to get into as my father found it difficult to get out of.

Vera lives in a road of neat brown suburban houses on the outskirts of northwest London almost identical to my parents' old house in Anerley to the southeast. When I speak with her on the telephone, her voice has the same sweetly matter-of-fact, contained tone I encountered in the vice consul and in officials on a visit I made to Russia in 1977—a tone of calm camouflage. I realize that Vera will have been brought up entirely under Soviet communism. On our way into what is definitely the front parlor, with heavy brown furniture and lace mats, we pass by the back room. Vera's toothless mother waddles up from watching Russian television to greet me, grinning but perfunctory, in Ukrainian.

Vera is eager that I should get a good impression of Ukraine, and has laid out a book of photographs of Lviv: beautiful color pictures of churches, the Opera House, mellow Austro-Hungarian facades in gold, terra cotta, sage green and Habsburg yellow, with ebulliently arched entrances and exuberantly carved wooden doors, some topped with a lion's head. All are bathed in golden light, all lack weather—particularly rain—and above all, people.

The population of Ukraine, Vera tells me, used to be 52 million and is now 49 million, thanks to Chernobyl. So 3 million have died—half the number, I can't help registering, since we all live with the number in our heads, of Jews who died in the concentration camps. Vera, an ophthalmologist, is proud of the new Ukraine, which is now the second largest country in Europe. After gaining its independence in 1991, there was 1,000 percent inflation for two years, with the shops empty of goods and the assistants just sitting around reading books. Factories closed, and there was rampant unemployment. From 1994 to 1995, the economy began to recover, and people began to be able to get a wage again.

"Ukraine has been responsible within the Soviet Union for making tires for buses and for television cathode-ray tubes," Vera tells me. "Breaking apart from Russia was like suddenly cutting off a hand and expecting it to do everything that whole body had done on its own. So. It was difficult economically. It was the same with all former Soviet republics."

She brightens as she adds that two years ago there was a summit meeting of eleven heads of European states in Lviv with the theme "The human dimension on the European and regional integration, and its role in the building of new Europe." The human dimension seems a promising thing to be thinking about. Assuring me over and over again that the Ukrainians are "nice people, friendly people," she shrugs off tales of corruption and scandal, and says that we might have to offer the odd bribe here or there—in dollars, preferably—for a seat on a train or so forth, but that'll be the extent of it.

"Enjoy your visit"; she smiles with real sweetness. "Lviv is very beautiful city."

Back home, I catch up with the recent news from Ukraine. It seems a fraught time to be going. Ukraine's president, Leonid Kuchma, a Russophile who has been in power since 1992, has just been accused of having a journalist murdered. The charred and headless corpse has been found buried in a wood, and moreover, the former opposition politician who smuggled the evidence out has just applied for asylum in Britain—which, together with the foot-and-mouth epidemic raging in Britain, probably won't raise our stock with officialdom in Ukraine. There have been riots in the streets, and headlines such as "Crowds Demand Resignation of 'Killer' Kuchma." An article in *The Times,* entitled "Moscow's Friend Who Once Looked West," reports that "Despite its mineral-rich 'black earth' and near monopoly of Soviet-era high technology, Ukraine has sunk to the status of sick man of Europe under a regime widely assessed as one of the most corrupt in the world." This is what we were heading into, on a trip we've decided to take more or less on the spur of the moment—and with no Ukrainian or Polish between us.

In my quick trawl of the best means of travelling to Ukraine, I've struck up a telephonic friendship with a mellow-voiced Hungarian travel agent who told me that if we are going to Lviv, I ought to meet her elderly neighbors, Wanda and Lucjan. They would be my father's generation, and they had a difficult time getting out of Poland, too, though in their case it was because they were Polish-Jewish. All the rest of their families had perished, she said, in the Warsaw ghetto.

"He is quite old now—in his nineties—but she is a young thing of eighty-eight and has some very funny stories about Lwow. They're both doctors. I think they've been back to Lwow recently." She said she'd call me back when she had spoken with them, and did so. As a result, I've been out to see them. They live in a street which is a leafier and more spacious version of my parents' house in Anerley, and Vera's in North London. Greater London has thousands of streets like this, veins and arteries of terraced suburban houses with porched entrances and bay windows, their front gardens now harboring solid, gleaming cars as well as beds of standard rosebushes. They are built for safety and anonymity, not to stand out from the crowd.

Much further down the line, my chance meeting with them will help unlock one of the enigmas of my father—although to my mind, in a quest, especially an emotional quest, nothing is accidental.

6 | LWOW-USTIANOWA, 1939

During that time it just so happened that they were rounding up students in streets for no reason whatsoever, just if you happened to be in street, or somewhere."

It was early November 1939, just before Joe's nineteenth birthday, and two months after Hitler had invaded Poland. He was in Lwow, in the Soviet-occupied part of partitioned Poland, whilst his parents were now in Nazi-occupied Poland, over a border that hadn't existed two months before.

"I was caught in one of these nets on my way back to lodgings in late afternoon; I'd jumped off tram when I saw queue for bread and joined in queue. A person in uniform grabbed me, he was not soldier but he had red bar around his hat and revolver and bayonet. All Russians had bayonets. He and another man in uniform rounded up all of us in queue—about dozen of us. We were taken through streets to somewhere on outskirts and then through into quadrangle of large house with enormous iron gates. We were pushed in, and guard said, '*Oyee!*—Go in!'—well, it means 'come' and 'go.' We crouched around wall of cobbled courtyard, no one was talking. You didn't talk to each other, you were scared to talk even to neighbor, you don't know reaction, or whether person is not planted there. And there was no more frightening thing than when you don't know what is going to happen to you. We were all wondering, why are we there? The guards didn't tell us, didn't do anything to us, we just didn't know. We spent night there sitting on cobblestones, our closeness to our neighbor kept us warm. I do not remember any food.

"The next day, I thought, if I don't get out of here I shall never get out, and—this is one of reasons why I always wanted an Omega watch, because at that time I had that Omega watch I'd bought from Zbyszek—I approached Russian guard who was marching up and down by gates and said very quietly, '*Tovarich, tovarich, pusti mne*—let me go, let me go.' Nothing. He was young, like me. I said, '*Tovarich, tovarich, dam vam tschassi*—I'll give you watch.' He looked at me and still walked by with stern face. I said again, '*Tovarich, tschassi*,' and suddenly he turned toward me with a bayonet pointed at me, like that, and said, '*Oyee!*—Get out!,' march in front of me, and I thought, well, that's it, because they have power of shooting anybody like that, and he marched right through small gate at side of iron gates, closed door and then said, '*Davay tschassi*,' and then I gave him watch. Then he said, '*Udiraj!*—Get lost!'—and I was free. I was never so glad in all my life as I was then. It was just pure bribery that I got out of that."

This was the fourth day of our talking together about my father's past. The horrors of arbitrary arrest without any pretext made me think of how prophetic Kafka had been in *The Trial* and *The Castle* about the new barbarities to come and reminded me that Joe is also a Josef K. "Did you begin to feel guilty when you were arrested?" I asked him.

"Um . . . yes. I just thought at that time that if somebody told me that I have done something, I would have thought about it and said yes, that's probably what I'm guilty of. I could, I would have confessed to almost anything then. But I still had that type of will in me that I must get out somehow or other, and that if I could get out I knew I could outwit them. This was one of things I knew. I knew their mentality, I knew ways they were thinking, and if you know how a person thinks, you can always find a way of breaking that . . . um . . . finding their—"

"Achilles' heel?"

"—Yes, this is what I found in that prison, I found their Achilles' heel. I decided there was no future under Russian occupation for me, there was very little hope for me to complete my degree. I went back to *Bursa,* and became very good boy. I had obeyed rules because I so hoped all this would blow over. But constraint appeared to be so restricting that air one was breathing was rationed. It was second half of November and I started planning how to escape from Russia and—um—easiest way to escape was to be very rich, so they asked for volunteers to join, well, there were various openings. There was opening at University of Kharkov in Ukraine; they paid your fare there and gave you certain amount of money to establish yourself as student, so I enlisted for it, and didn't go. And there were openings to join Russian air force as pilot and of course to do that you had to travel to Moscow for interview, they gave you money, so I enlisted for that, for everything that was available, because by that time I had decided, I shall not stay here. Also they had—still have—monetary system which is two-tier system, one is internal system which is rubles, and other which is international which pays much more, and all these things were paid in international money. Also on December 18, Russians made announcement that Polish money had lost its value, it was no longer valid currency. You could buy twenty *zlotys* for one ruble. I was able to buy enormous amount of Polish money, which was useless under Russian occupation but still had value under German occupation where my parents were. This was moment I decided, right, I'll exchange all this and I'll escape back to Poland."

"Did you go to Moscow?"

"Yes, journey was paid—but we were paid money and given rail warrant as well, money was some type of premium, if anything went wrong you could fall back on it. I went with my rail warrant to

register in Moscow. I felt really safe with my beautiful warrant"—
my father took a sip of whiskey and chuckled ironically—"especially when I came back. When you got there, group of uniformed
people took you to subway. I thought subway magnificent, I'd never
seen underground—it had enormous columns, it was something
unbelievable. Then you were taken to building. I was apprehensive
that this was trap, but seeing people with same documents as me
going to same office, I thought it must be okay. Then I was taken
back to train, then back to Lwow, all in one day. They said they
would send for me when they required me. I tried now to plan my
escape, getting information from others who were also preparing."

"How did you know they were?"

"You have . . . feeling, difficult to describe how you know. Feeling was among all students, all people in same age group—you feel
uneasy. Someone else is getting information on what does that station look like, et cetera. Fortunately for me, I knew area I was going
to reasonably well, I knew what it looked like, where forests and
fields were, where there were no trees. There was no information
about outside world. We didn't know whether there was war in
West—didn't even know what was happening in next street, only
what was happening to us. By this time, digging trenches was
becoming difficult because there were frosts, and I didn't know
why they were doing it, digging trenches. My object was to somehow get legally out of Lwow and to have bit of money to bribe if
necessary. You got money by devious means. You had to change and
adapt, alter mental state.

"Around December 12 I'd already decided, it's time to go. The
way I planned, school holidays were around Christmas and I
needed suitable story for why I have to go west. I couldn't travel
over border, so I had to try to get as near to border as I could. I
would say my parents are peasants, they need me for cutting trees to
create more fields for growing grains—I couldn't say to work in
fields, because they were frozen. You couldn't say trees in area
where there were no trees. I started going to various offices to get

permit to travel. It was not easy, offices were open only when I was at college. I managed to squeeze hour out of classes—first I had to get permit from college to get permit to travel. I went to administrator, and told him my story—he swallowed it. It was so simple, he had to believe it! About December 14 or 15 I went to get travel permit. I got pass for after holidays started, to relieve pressure on trains. Holidays started on Wednesday, I got pass for Thursday.

"I got on train, wearing school uniform with tie, navy blue double-breasted jacket with silver buttons with little target on left arm to indicate college—ours was 160 with little T indicating technical college. Over that was light gray civilian suit. Then pair of lace-up shoes and over that galoshes to save shoes and also because I knew I would have to cross frozen river and in leather soles you couldn't run across ice, rubber gives you more grip. Over that was navy blue ex-Polish police force greatcoat, very long and warm, very good material. Then on head, light balaclava to protect ears against frost, with beret on top of that. I left behind pair of shoes. Trains had open carriages, with wooden benches and passage on side. You could see everything. I was sitting there trembling. Before I went, I was advised by students, arm yourself. Weapons were everywhere, just lying around from 1939 war that had just ended— German-Polish War from September 1 until Russians moved in on September 17. At that point you could get them [weapons] just like that, you could just pick them from dead bodies. There was probably trend from what had happened in past to keep weapons if you found them. In this case, idea was that France and England and Belgium would soon be coming in against Germans, and there would uprising to assist them, and we would have weapons.

"I took one automatic pistol—and it was Josko, my older sister's husband, who was policeman, who mentioned to me that it's possible to conceal pistol on your arm like that, you have holster fitted to your arm, and if you jerk your arm like that then pistol will fire. This is what I had, I had practiced. And I had hand grenade. I thought, if anything happens, I will blow everything up including

myself because I just couldn't face being captured. I was just nineteen at that time and you have different viewpoint then.

"There was vacant seat next to me and then man walks in at
Lwow station, Polish, and says, 'I'm member of delegation from
Moscow,' and started telling me how he'd attended very important
Communist meeting. He started showing me documents about
future of Poland in cooperation with Russia, how communism
works and so on. I told him I know Moscow underground—but it
was one-sided conversation, and I thought I would do anything to
get away. We went four stations, I came to where my permit
expired, but it was still quite distance from border. He was still talking and I thought, I'll risk another station and try to get to
Ustianowa, just before border, when door opened and two NKVD
men came in. I thought, you're in real trouble here, what do you do?
How useless weapons were—all those preparations useless—I had
no time to put hand in pocket, he would have grabbed me. But I had
hand grenade and at that time I was little bit enthusiastic and very
much patriotic and extremely foolish, and I thought if I have to do
something, I'll take as many Russians with me as possible—just
silly young ideas. Meanwhile, my neighbor was talking on loudly
and two men were watching him and me, and I was nodding my
head as he was speaking. Man examining papers couldn't escape
his voice. I was next to window. NKVD man looks at man's documents and asks, '*Vi razom?*—Are you two together?' He said yes."

"Why do you suppose people trusted you like this," I asked him,
"like the guard in the prison did? Was it to do with the way you
looked?"

"No, not way I looked. I was very shy and said very little most
of time, but people trusted my voice—how can I put it?—it was
such that when I talked, they listened. Usually I asked question, it
was inquiring rather than dictating.

"NKVD man didn't look at my pass, then went along examining
other passes. I was hoping we wouldn't stop at station before men
left. People's papers were all in order—nobody risked not being in

Joe as a student, 1939

order or you'd be sent to labor camp. I excused myself from that man and got off train at station. It was Ustianowa Station, third station before Leske-Lukawitze. I alighted from train at opposite side, so that train was between me and station. There were no platforms, and it was one-track rail, but for some reason there was carriage on same side as me, old cattle truck with no wheels. I thought, that's nice place to hide. Track at Ustianowa ran on high area—you looked down from train on undulating country below. I'd intended to lay in dip below track, but hid behind truck. There was no snow up until then, even in Lwow—it was very unusual. It usually starts to fall on December 6, St. Nicholas's Day, but this year there was none. I waited little while to see if there was any activity on station. There was no movement anywhere. It was barrackroom-type station. Rail runs east-west there, San River runs north-west, directly south from me, and one kilometer away was beginning of village spread along banks of little stream."

Joe was tense and took a deep intake of breath.

"There was some kind of depression there—so it must have been stream. I crossed track to look over toward village, keeping behind slight hill to protect me from being seen from village. When I looked at village, it was dead. It was about midday. Law was if you see stranger in village you had to report him, if you didn't you were committing crime which was punishable. Being winter, there was no work in fields; most of people just did not want to know anybody. These were times of uncertainty. People knew risks of arrest, and they knew you could be taken away if you saw someone you didn't know and didn't report them. There were cases where people were tested by disguised NKVD man. Traps were laid. So when I looked at village and it looked dead, I assumed there had been instance of this—news spreads very quickly, especially amongst peasants, there's great loyalty."

Joe sucked in his teeth and worked his jaw.

"I was looking to see if there were any guards on station. After while, I started walking toward valley. It was about five kilometers from me. It took me about two hours walking slowly to reach spot where I could see river. As I walked, because of frozen fields your steps make noise; it was disturbing, but I consoled myself that no one was there to hear. Everything was empty."

Joe got to this point in his narrative and then carried on for about another ten minutes until the end of the tape. What happened next was strange. In taking the tape out, I tested it quickly, and found that it had failed to record. My heart sank. All this remembering was quite taxing for Joe. I'd noticed he'd been holding his breath quite a bit, and now this key bit of his story was lost. I knew from the radio interviews I was doing at the time for a living that a second take of people talking always loses the immediacy of the first. But since I hadn't been committing it to memory, relying on the tape, I realized we were going to have to do it all over again—and if we were going to have to, better right away, I thought, like getting back on a horse as soon as you've fallen off. So we went straight back and did it all again—and what emerged at this point was a different story from the one he'd told me. In fact, he asked me to stop the tape at the point where he got to Ustianowa, as he wanted just to talk through what had really happened. I jotted down notes in a notebook instead.

Crouching behind the carriage at Ustianowa station, he saw there was another man who'd dropped off there, who was obviously trying to escape too. The man said, "Which direction are you going in?" Conversation is very cautious in these circumstances and very very precise, Joe said: you don't answer directly, you say, "Oh, I'm going west, where are you going?" The man said, "Do you mind if I join you for a while?" And Joe said, "Not at all."

So they set off toward the San River together. After a while two Russian guards appeared and accosted them, telling them they were going to be taken to a nearby Russian patrol station. Joe and the other man looked at each other and realized they were trapped, both escaping and with no chance at all against the guards. The other man, older than my father, said, "Oh, I need a nature stop; you go on and we'll catch you up," so he and one guard went behind some bushes and Joe and his guard walked on.

Joe realized what the other man was intending to do and kept glancing back behind him until he saw the man coming out of the bushes alone, and he knew what he had to do. "I had no option but to take care of the other man," is how he put it. How? I asked, a little shocked, with your pistol? He said, oh no, with a small metal rod 15 millimeters in diameter, 30 centimeters long (his time working at a precision instruments factory standing him in good stead), which he had in his greatcoat pocket. It "kept him asleep for while," my father said. Do you mean you killed him? I asked, trying to imagine it and not quite getting there—getting the iron rod out without the guard seeing, my slender nineteen-year-old father bringing a blow down on a uniformed (presumably bayoneted) Russian guard hard enough to kill him. "It was life or death," he replied.

Earlier on, I'd listened to what Joe had said about having a pistol and grenade in the same matter-of-fact way that he'd told it—as if it were perfectly natural to equip yourself with pistol, grenade and metal rod for a train journey of some hundred kilometers. Now I realized that to have forearmed himself like this he must have known how bad the journey could turn out to be. This was Stalin's Terror, being spread to the fringes of the Soviet Union's new empire. This area had been under first Nazi, then Soviet occupation now for four months; quite enough for such a regime to cow people, to have changed the whole moral climate.

I didn't ask him enough about this incident at the time. Partly it was because I was very aware that this was the first time he was talking about it and I didn't want to break the spell and make him retreat. I was also still quite diffident with him, not at ease. My father's mode of talking was very precise and based on facts. He scorned loose talk, and shrugged off most things to do with the emotions, shaking his head and saying, "I don't know about that." It was quite difficult to get a to-and-fro conversation going with him in the ordinary way. If you asked him a question, he would reply to it thoughtfully and as accurately as he could, but he would never ask one back. So I was constrained in my questions, constrained by my historical lacunae and by our mutual inhibitions.

They were not helped by the fact that we had lived for seventeen years at the other side of the world from each other. When my parents first went out to Australia, they sailed on a ship which took six weeks to get there. They went with all their possessions in packing cases, invited and sponsored by the Broken Hill Company. In 1971, telephone calls had to be booked ahead, especially at peak times like Christmas, and you never knew when the call you'd placed would come through. Sometimes (my father told me much later) they would be waiting up until four in the morning for a call to come through. From our point of view, the calls would often come at awkward times: too early in the morning, too late at night. Because of this, the expense, and our general telephonic dysfunctionality, we tended to keep them to a minimum. As for letters, they have their own constraints, especially between parents and children. If a letter takes ten days to arrive, you are wary of mentioning fleeting moods that will have passed by the time the letter arrives. You are wary of mentioning insoluble difficulties like a marriage breaking down. I tended at the time to keep my letters remorselessly upbeat, studded with exclamation marks. When I read Sylvia Plath's letters to her mother, I recognized with a groan a full-throttle version of my own appeasing, good-girl letters. My mother's letters were "newsy"—their generation's version of the same thing, which is to say, gentility. It was very rare for my father to write a letter. It was just accepted, as with many men of his generation, that it was not the kind of thing a man was expected to do. With my father, all this has changed now, and the change started here, when the tape recorder so synergetically broke down.

The two men, my father and the stranger, walked on for a little while together, then the man said to him, "Well, we've done a favor to each other. I'll go my way and you go yours."

In the evening, I asked my father why he hadn't told me that part of the story before. He said that he was very worried about letting something like this be told, as that episode would have been remembered in Ustianowa and the family of that Russian guard was probably still alive. If they found out who had done it, he or I might be visited with reprisals, all these years later. He was wanting to protect us from this. He looked at me with his slightly startled, oscillating eyes blinking with tears, and told me that ever since I'd written to say I was coming over to write about his past, he'd been having a recurring nightmare that he'd killed a man, and when he looked down at him, he found he'd killed his brother. I looked at him with tears, too, and we just stared, half-startled, half-crying. Of course, it was not only his brother, the Russian, he'd killed—and all war is in essence that, killing your brother—but it was something in himself. It was his young blood he shed, if blood there was; it was his loss of innocence in the world. He knew it was his fault, and he knew it was not his fault. Something, I could see, had paralyzed his emotions in that moment, like a locked back which needs a chiropractor's blow to unlock it.

Later still, when I got back to England, I was reading about Claus von Stauffenberg's failed assassination attempt on Hitler in July 1944, and came across a chilling speech Heinrich Himmler made two weeks later in Posen:

> We shall introduce here absolute responsibility of kin. We have already acted on that basis . . . let no one come to us and say: what you are doing is Bolshevistic. No, don't get this wrong, it isn't Bolshevistic at all, but a very old custom practised among our forefathers. You can read about it in the Teutonic sagas. When they placed a family under the ban and declared it outlawed, or when there was a blood feud in a family, they were utterly consistent. When the family was outlawed and banned, they said: "This man has committed treason; the blood is bad; there is traitor's blood in him, that must be wiped out," and the entire clan was wiped out down to the last man.

Whether the Bolsheviks first thought of it, or the "Teutons"—in fact it operated in England in Jacobean times, and no doubt in many other times and cultures—the dogma of collective responsibility is an extremely economical way of spreading terror. It kept the whole of the village near Ustianowa quiet; it kept Czechoslovakia quiet after Munich; it kept Poland (on the whole) quiet after Hitler's *Blitzkrieg* against it; it kept many Germans quiet; it had kept my father quiet for fifty years, I thought. All the Stauffenberg family were executed as a result of Claus's assassination attempt, including a three-year-old child and an eighty-year-old distant relative.

There is, however, another layer to this episode. In August 2000, after an incident I shall come to later, the barriers of reserve between my father and me were broken down. As a coda to a note to me about this, he wrote: "I am now going to free myself from a millstone I have had round my neck ever since the birth of your book." And he told me in brief what had really happened in the hills beyond Ustianowa. I wrote asking him to expand on it, and to be sure to let me know "what happened, what really happened. It's very important for me to know. The book is really about truth and lies, and the great obstacles to telling the truth sometimes, political and internal."

He wrote back the following letter. You will notice that he writes with an almost full complement of definite and indefinite articles; this is partly because he's got better at it since a decade and more ago, partly because he writes them in more than he speaks them. Also, though, it's because my part in the distortion of the truth has been to eliminate all articles from his speech, so that you always know it's my father, a foreigner to the English language, speaking . . . His letter ran:

> . . . To answer your question, I must go back to the time when I was held in the courtyard. The soldier that was on guard was just a bit older than I. All the other men were of mature age. When I asked him to let me go and offered him the watch as a bribe, he opened the small gate and took me outside and said: give me the watch and ordered me to get lost. I know that the watch was a prize beyond his belief, but soon after it set me thinking why he took me outside. He could have taken the watch

and nobody would have raised a finger. That thought played on my mind and made me accept that there are Russians who are kind, or maybe he took pity on me because we were of similar age.

Now the train. After the train departed, I started walking away from the station on a country road along the track. After some time I met a mature man walking in same direction. He asked me where I was going and I said west. He said something like that's where I'm going. He spoke Polish with an accent I did not recognise. There was not much conversation. He kept making remarks how much he hated Russians. After a while we saw two men in Russian uniforms coming towards us, carrying rifles. When we met they reversed their direction and told us to come with them. They were quite young and the blue bands on their caps indicated that they were probably NKVD. They talked between themselves, but one asked some simple questions mostly from me. We walked for some 15–20 minutes when the Polish man asked to be excused for a call of nature. The Russian that spoke to me kept walking and I went with him. After about 20–30 steps the road twisted due to trees and bushes and obscured our view behind. Almost immediately there came terrifying shout from behind and the Russian that was with me turned and started running back. In that moment a thought struck me that this is a chance to gain freedom without violence so I started to run in the direction where I was originally going and after very short distance turned left into pastures covered with scattered bushes, mostly rose hip bushes. I knew I was running in the direction towards river

San, which in this area was a Russian–German demarcation line. When I thought that I am safe from pursuit, I stopped running and started walking. After about one kilometre I noticed a line of trees some two kilometres ahead stretching from left to right and was guessing that it must be the river bank.

I had told him in my reply that this second version of the story sounded much more like him, and he now responded:

You have guessed right. I had a gun and I knew how to use it. Yet in a split second my brain must have analysed several thoughts simultaneously. The NKVD men did not threaten or harm us. The shout came from the Russian because the word was not in Polish language. The man that was with me was already several steps away and the result of violent conflict could go either way. Yet I changed the story because I felt bad about it. Even now I wish that it would have better [sic] if the incident never happened. I am still troubled whether my action should have been different. But at least now I feel clean that you know what really happened.

And now that I do, I'm left with two stories—both plausible, and both possibly refracted in the nightmare. Did he "really" kill the man but have second thoughts about the possible repercussions for himself and me, and so invent a cover story of running away? Or did he "really" run away and invent a cover story for himself that he'd killed the man, to keep his self-respect? As soon as I heard it, the second explanation sounded far more likely to me. The nightmare he'd had, which I was sure was genuine, would have applied to both versions. Yet in a way it doesn't matter. The emotional truth

is there in both stories, and exactly the same: this incident is
steeped in trauma for him, as the cocoon of silence and reworking
attest. More, my father's dilemma is the dilemma of wartime,
although he hadn't yet reached his time of war: if you refuse to
die, you have two alternatives—as Masaryk and Tolstoy had
rehearsed—to kill or give in. Both will blight your life, and both are
unacceptable. You've chosen neither of them, and you are often a
young, untested man (now woman, too). You don't want to be in
this position, with these choices. And afterward you don't want to
tell, because this is too dark a self-knowledge to take back into
everyday life without becoming a pariah. Some people are more
robust than others; some have clearer causes to fight for than others,
which is the luck of the national draw; some have homes and homelands to go back to where they will reclaim and bolster their sense
of self.

I remember the ogre-father of my own nightmares, and wonder
if I wasn't picking up on some banished creature my father had
buried inside him.

7 | LVIV-USTIANOWA, 2001

Flat, scattered flakes of snow are falling as Roger and I arrive in Prague. It's the tourist trough of the year, so we've managed to get a room cheaply in the Art Deco Grand Hotel Europa on Wenceslas Square. From here, we shall be travelling on tomorrow to Lviv by overnight train. I open the old fluted French windows just above the long boulevard and watch the slush and afternoon twilight turning the scene sepia. It all looks like 1950s Paris, with lacy wrought-iron grilles circling the street trees, checkered cobbles, newspaper kiosks, and cars parked at a relaxed angle to the broad boulevard—no parking meters, no attendants, no traffic jams. Leaning out of the window, I can see up to the left the statue of St. Wenceslas on horseback on his plinth. Legend has it that the young duke—who would be butchered by his own brother at the age of twenty-two—found himself faced with a much larger marauding German army, and grieved at the loss of life his countrymen would incur by fighting them. He'd adopted Christianity, against the wishes of his mad, bad mother, and decided to propose instead a duel with the head of the German army, a duel which he won. The other part of the legend (apart from charitably making the snow

warm for his servant) is that he subsequently made terms with the
German army, which would earn him the rueful epithet "first man
of Munich" after 1938.

Yet he has distinguished ghosts around his statue now: Tomáš
Masaryk riding up to it to declare independence in 1918; Alexander
Dubček speaking from a balcony in 1968, ushering in the brief
"Prague Spring"; the crowds surging up to the good king (Václav in
Czech) in November 1989, beginning to break up the one-party
state in the "velvet revolution."

The next morning, we have the day in Prague before taking the
sleeper to Lviv. A tram takes us up the hairpin bends to the castle
high on the hill on the other side of the river and past the Czernin
Palace. Its facade is both rigid and overblown, like a barracks disguised as an iced cake, the bad faith of the man who had bankrupted
the local area by having it built, Count Czernin, ambassador to
Venice, still locked into its stone. Perhaps the architecture even
attracted its subsequent history, as it became a barracks under the
Austrian Empire and then, when the Nazis took over Czechoslovakia, served as headquarters for the notorious "Protector of the
Reich" (two weasel words in one job title) Reinhard Heydrich. It's
here too that Masaryk's son Jan, four days into his appointment as
foreign minister in the postwar Communist government of 1948,
allegedly threw himself out of a top-floor bathroom window to his
death forty-five feet below—the third "defenestration" in Czechoslovakia's history. A few weeks before in London I'd asked an
elderly Romanian journalist I met whether people now knew if Jan
Masaryk's death was suicide or murder. "Oh, everybody knows
what happened," he told me with a twinkle; "he was suicided."

From the Czernin Palace, we walk along and up to Prague Castle, where, apart from the tourists, groups of two or three palace
guards stride easily across the courtyards, their blue three-quarter-
length coats swinging, their youthful faces in animated conversa-

tion. They look benignly theatrical and unmilitary, and they are: President Havel chose to have their uniforms designed by Miloš Forman's costume designer on the film *Amadeus,* echoing those of Masaryk's First Republic and combining the old and new in an almost tongue-in-cheek way. We pause at the feet of the brand-new statue to Tomáš Masaryk—"TGM"—in the castle precincts, now back in place in his country's and capital's history. Airbrushed out under communism for his ties with the West—although his ties with Russia were just as true and engaged—he stands relaxed, looking down onto garlands of flowers with red, white and blue ribbons strewn at his feet. It was only a week ago that this statue was unveiled, in the presence of President Václav Havel, by U.S. Secretary of State Madeleine Albright, herself of Czech extraction. Speaking in Czech, she said:

> For me, like the more experienced among you, the memories are strong. I was only four months old when President Masaryk died, but in every other sense I grew up with him. My father worked for his son. My family talked about him often. I would look at his picture and think to myself, "this is how a President should look." I would study his writings, and think, "this is how a President should inspire." I would research his actions and think, "this is how a President should lead." What an example he set! He was a teacher who never stopped learning; a philosopher who never stopped doing; a lover of peace who never backed away from a fight; and a pragmatist who never stopped believing that the future could be made better than the past.

Alas for Masaryk and his foreign minister, Beneš, the democratic castle—and all the democracy in the world—could not protect their country from the one thing that can scupper democracies and for which they make little provision: a tyrant bent on warfare.

In the gathering dusk, we go back to the Hotel Europa to pick up our backpacks and have tea before setting off from Prague Station for Lviv. The rooms and facilities are just as they were when the hotel was built in the 1920s, the paint and plumbing untouched, the now-rusty radiators embossed with Art Nouveau patterns. The magnificent, broad sweep of the shabby-elegant central staircase drips with waterfalls of glass chandeliers and bevelled glass lanterns with low-voltage bulbs. Like the walls—sometimes painted in the colors of autumn fields, sometimes inlaid with mahogany veneer—they burst with an exuberant twining of geometric and natural motifs. Stylized grains, fig leaves and fruit spill from hard-edged patterns embarked on an improvised and fruitful journey of their own. Everything is embellished, everything exudes a muted, celebratory joy.

It's March 15, the Ides of March, the sixty-second anniversary of the day that Hitler invaded Bohemia and Moravia. We arrive at the elegant, vaulting arches of Hlavni Station to take the overnight train across the Czech lands and Slovakia to arrive in Lviv the following evening. We've booked a first-class sleeper to ourselves, which, for a thirty-six-hour journey with bunks, costs the same as a second-class three-hour train journey out of London. We lay out our banquet of sausage, cheese, bread, fruit and wine on the table (with washstand under the lid) with the thrill of children camping out, then settle down for the night, rocked to sleep by the rhythmic *da-da-da-DA* of the heavy old steam train, which could well date from Masaryk's time, too.

Suddenly, at half past midnight, we're woken by a grinding and juddering, and then by a ferocious banging on our door, and even more ferocious shouts, just in case we haven't got the message. We unlock and untie our door (the British Foreign Office advice on travelling in Ukraine says, "If travelling by overnight train it is safest to be accompanied by a trusted companion. In any case, it is strongly advised that you secure the compartment from the inside by tying the door closed with wire or cord"). We squint out at burly mustachioed Slovak passport control officers demanding our passports. The tradition of middle-of-the-night bullying by over-uniformed people seems to have lingered on in central Europe. After passing the passports around suspiciously in the corridor outside, amidst more gruff talk, they stamp them and hand them back. I try not to feel cravenly grateful.

We lock the door again and just begin to drift back to sleep when three quarters of an hour later the same thing happens, and then again half an hour later, like sleep-deprivation torture—and this time they indicate grimly that we must put on our boots and coats and go outside onto the platform. There is a definite hint of sadism and—am I imagining it?—even revenge in all these rituals. We find ourselves having to step through a tray of disinfectant laid out on the station platform, because we are British and currently plagued with foot-and-mouth disease. No one else on the train has to do this, we have the privilege all to ourselves, and indeed from the few laconic faces blearily peering at us through the train's smeared and sooty windows, we are probably the only tourists on the train. (No wonder, going to Ukraine in the middle of the night in mid-March.)

I feel bad about not speaking a word of the languages of the countries we're travelling through: no Czech, no Slovak, no Ukrainian, no Polish. But even with a moderate facility for languages, I find myself tongue-tied trying to remember simply the different words for hello, please, and thank you in these languages. It surprises me that none of the border control guards appears to speak one word of English or French or German either (the latter brought out rather circumspectly). I'm trying to remember what Irina told me about bribing the guards. We can't do it in *hryvnya* as we've failed to find anyone in England or Prague who would deal in them, so we still haven't got the local currency, but we do have a wad of one-dollar notes suitable for bribing or paying. For bribing, we'd have to know what we wanted to bribe them to do, apart from leave us to sleep, and then convey this in sufficiently effective body language to get results. Meanwhile, I note that the signs in the carriages are written in Czech, French, German, Italian, and Ukrainian, in that order, bespeaking a polylinguism we haven't found. (No Polish, tellingly, although it's Poland that shares a border with both ex-Czechoslovakia and the Ukraine, not France and Italy.)

The next morning, I find that the youngish red-haired guard at the end of our carriage who has custody of our tickets not only speaks some German, but even better is prepared to give us a tray of breakfast. At 8:30 a.m. there's more jarring and shuddering and oily squealing and the train pulls in at the Slovak-Ukrainian border station of Ciesna, marked with the angular Ukrainian crest based on the trident, ancient symbol of authority. More police swarm officiously onto the train, this time with a sniffer dog and in shiny new uniforms with *Policia* on the armbands, leather satchels draped over one shoulder and leather holsters with a gun over the other. We hope we'll pass whatever new leprosy test this is with the flying colors we did in the middle of the night. This time, they give us complicated forms in Ukrainian—which is in Cyrillic script—with lists of questions to which you only have to answer yes or no. We could make a stab at it, but could get it horribly wrong. We try to indicate that unfortunately we can't understand the form and they just talk louder at us in Ukrainian and look skywards: what kind of fools don't speak a single word of Ukrainian except "hello" and "thank you," and even that badly? The kind of fools we are beginning to feel: an asylum-seeker kind of fool.

One of the officials then asks for something that sounds like "medical cards from Stansted" and we root about obligingly in the many pockets of our well-worn jackets but know we won't find them, whatever they are, as we haven't got them. The *Policia* ask for passports again, and we're on safer ground, handing them over earnestly in a bid to look efficient—or even sane. We're rewarded by one of the police taking the passports, then pointing at Roger and gesturing "outside!" I move to go with him, but am told to stay where I am—they want only him. He's disappeared before I've realized we've broken a key rule of travelling, particularly in virtual police states, which I've now no doubt this is: always stick together.

Suddenly, there's a monumental judder and the train pulls away backwards, with me in it and Roger somewhere out of it. I run down the corridor to the guard and say in German which has regressed to pidgin, "*Wo ist mein Mann? Mein Mann—heraus. Ich, hier. Der Zug fahrt.*" A potbellied, track-suited man, also with a mustache, is leaning against the carriage window as he seems to have been all night. He looks on with derisive amusement. Next to the guard a pretty, calm Ukrainian girl smiles at me. They let me gesticulate for several minutes, watching my increasing alarm as the train accelerates away from Roger and my passport, and then the guard puts his coffee down and waves at me to calm down in a gesture of no worries. "*Eine Stunde zurück,*" he says, making gestures of going under the train. An hour back. A light dawns, as I remember the Hungarian travel agent saying that they spend forever changing the bogeys at the border to Ukraine. Sure enough, soon we grind to a halt and begin to engage in an impressive feat of engineering choreography amid a welter of rusting rolling stock and overhead grips and hoists which look like something out of a German Expressionist film. I decide to be stoic, pulling back the nylon half-curtain on the window to watch, but before the hour is up, Roger appears with the passports. He's been made to wait alone for forty minutes in the Kafkaesque hangar of a customshouse, with no explanation, even in body language, and no smiles. They finally gave him back the passports and told him to wait there, but he decided otherwise, and walked the half mile up the track back to where he could see the train, pursued all the way by a family of Gypsies, who are now knocking at the window.

The train's revictualling has taken a couple of hours, done with the aplomb and attention a farmer would give to a herd of cattle being shepherded across a road. We set off again past the grim blocks of Soviet-style border control at Ciesna, past dilapidated homemade sheds and allotments, vestiges of a more do-it-yourself, pre-Soviet culture, and arrive at the new, more airy brutalism of Tchop, the official border. We wait here for another two hours, then get up speed to go through the bleak, undernourished plains of southwest Ukraine—the borderlands from which Ukraine takes its name, and which manage to be both arid and currently waterlogged. If there's a river, it's raging with floods, its water a creamy sage green, its banks decked out with a lacy border of debris—broken glass, plastic bottles, streamers of torn bags, cans—even though it's miles from anywhere. I can suddenly imagine all too well the headless body of the murdered journalist Georgy Gongadze, dumped in the woods three months ago, which had created such a stir in the country since President Kuchma's bodyguard had released tapes of the president allegedly discussing how to get rid of him. Growing street protests came to a head just last week in Kiev, when more than eighteen thousand demonstrators hurled stones and bottles at riot police, shouting: "Get rid of Kuchma's criminal regime!" It's difficult to tell from outside just how "criminal" the regime is, and I hope we're not heading into trouble. Despite all the information at our disposal, and with all our relative safeguards, it's not that much easier to gauge the danger of volatile regimes than it was for my father.

Once the train gets into the foothills to the east of the Carpathians, the countryside becomes less raw, as if it's only when the land begins to undulate that civilization can take root. There are wooden houses and kempt plots of land with woodpiles stacked high and tight under the eaves. The soil here still looks parched and poor, but pine and beech forests begin to crest the hills. The only things that speak of money are the immaculately painted Orthodox churches, their onion domes gleaming silver and gold, all presumably restored or built in the last decade, since the fall of communism.

Now we begin to climb up into the Carpathians proper, and the mood changes. There is a natural, bucolic orderliness about the houses strung out along the rivers or on the hillsides, with their neat stacks of logs, their individual haystacks built around a pole, like the onion domes of the churches. The haystack culture proliferates as we climb. Things get more prosperous, fed by the lifeblood of rivers and wood. Things have been done to please the eye now as well as for practicality: houses have decorated balustrades on their balconies, they are brightly colored, with contrasting lozenges on their sides painted with cameos of a deer or tree, like a Swiss chalet. Leftover winter snow pocks the slopes. The long, high train winds through the hills, its head visible to us when it curls. It goes through tunnels, over high bridges and aqueducts that are often manned. There is no shortage of manpower, and the manpower is generally standing around doing nothing in particular. At every tiny signal box or station we pass there is a railwayman or -woman dressed in an orange jerkin, standing to attention and holding up an orange baton to signal the train through. They look serious and proud, as if they are saluting the train, and their radiated pride is infectious. When we come down a steep hill, the train stops for about twenty minutes whilst a man in a fur hat comes along solemnly tapping the wheels to make sure there was no damage to the brakes from our descent. British Railtrack take note, says Roger.

Now that we're back on the plains again, the track is bordered by dogwood and hazel, and increasingly by bigger, scruffier villages as we come toward Lviv. The railway lines themselves seem to be the arteries here. There are few visible made-up roads, and an endless frieze of people walks along the broad edging to the railway— children coming home from school, old men cycling along with a solid center of gravity like figures from the film *Il Postino,* women in scarves carrying large bags of produce, wiry foraging mongrels. I've only seen three sheep on the whole journey, and no cattle. But at every siding there are herds and herds of rolling stock, some old, some new and gleaming, some covered with tarpaulins.

It's dark when we draw screeching into the cavernous old railway station of Lviv. We get a taxi to take us to the George Hotel,

painfully aware that we can only say, "dollars okay?" like some
redneck—and also aware that we could literally be taken for a ride.
What would pass in England as charm—smiles, self-deprecating
grins and shrugs—doesn't play very well in Lviv, I note.

The George Hotel, where Balzac once stayed with his fiancée in
its Austro-Hungarian heyday, is in the center of town, at the end of
the long Prospekt Svobody—the former Alleya Ulanovska down
which my father marched with his unwanted Stalin banner. It costs
about the price of a youth hostel in England. The hotel's long, wide
corridors and tall Georgian doors are from another era, but the dim
wattage is from this one, and the concierge-cum-cleaners sitting
eternally in a room on each floor observing any guest who comes
by are from the previous one, the Soviet. An unmistakable stamp of
the ex-Intourist establishment clings to the hotel. The uniformed
guard in the almost-imposing foyer could be from an era of bell-
boys and grand dinners, or a leftover habit of Soviet surveillance of
visitors. He feels like the latter. In reception, there are brass clocks
set to the times of Lviv, Moscow, Kiev, Warsaw, London, and New
York, in that order. The hotel's own currency exchange booth is
closed, so our first task is to go out and scan the plethora of
exchange kiosks, all still open, for the best rate of dollar-*hryvnya*
exchange. A hand passes us money from behind the grille of the
tiny kiosk as if from behind a burka. The streets are dark and low-
wattage, apart from a brightly lit McDonald's, and we've yet to find
our bearings, or a café. We eventually find one—small and local,
with a menu in Cyrillic. The young waitress and waiter are helpful,
with a patient grace, and in spite of quickly finding the limits of
sign language, we have a delicious, cheap meal with wine.

The next day is a Saturday—our only full day in Lviv—and we
first try to get advance rail tickets for the following day, to Przemysl
across the border in Poland. In the main, romantic cobbled market
square, we find a small tourist office where they speak English.
They don't sell rail tickets, but the director of the agency, a smiling,

sophisticated woman called Natalia, tells her young colleague to take us to where we can get them, and we find ourselves for an hour in the interesting company of Vyacheslav. He not only takes us on a mile-long walk up to the Hotel Dniester, where he says we can get rail tickets, but also shows us the best places to eat that evening. We don't want to take up so much of his time, but he insists with straightforward charm. We go up through the Ivan Franko Park (honoring Ukraine's "second-greatest writer" after Taras Shevchenko), where Lviv University is housed in former Austro-Hungarian government buildings. Vyacheslav is doing a tourism degree in Lviv—he was part of the first intake for a degree which started four years ago. His tourist agency is privately owned, by Natalia. He agrees that the visa requirements are a disincentive to any tourist, and he and other tourist agencies are always petitioning the government about them.

When we reach the Dniester, we find the exchange manned by a tough, middle-aged woman with peroxided hair, breasts like tanks and familiar Soviet Bolshie obstructionism. The tickets would cost 50 *hryvnya* each, she eventually tells us through Vyacheslav, after much prevarication. This is more than double the price we were told at the rail information office (which didn't, however, sell tickets); it's evidently still the old two-tier currency operating. Even Vyacheslav seems surprised at the premium they put on. His intelligence and animation beam out from his face when he talks with us, but when he speaks with Comrade Battleax his eyes slide away dismissively in the same way as hers do, and he takes on an impenetrable manner. He has a two-tier face: he can do spontaneity, and he can do former Soviet deadpan, the keynote expression of this being something like "It's obvious, you blithering idiot."

We decide against the inflated tickets; we'll take our chances at the station the next day. On our way back, we ask Vyacheslav why there are quite so many exchange kiosks, and he says they're not for tourists, as (he says with a smile) there are no tourists, but they're for Ukrainians to save and make money, as they can change it favorably now and then according to the exchange rate. We want to pay Vyacheslav for his time, or at least offer him a coffee or lunch, but he demurs gracefully. Whatever two-tier or black market systems operate, there is one universal currency as testable as gold between the teeth, and that is the smile. When they have it, Lvivians seem to have a noticeably sweet, unguarded version of this currency, and they seem to have it in abundance. When they don't, they have a blank, fierce, defended look, which we will get to know all too well in the following days.

It's market day, and on our way to the outskirts of Lviv to try to find Joe's *Bursa* we linger in two bustling markets, buying fruit for the next day's journey, breathing in the market air. The street trees in Lviv, straggly anyway at this time of year, are noticeably polluted and stunted, but the produce here is plentiful and bursting with health. The first market is just a line of rustic people sitting on folding stools with baroquely gnarled parsnips and carrots, dense, fat, earthy little leeks, horseradishes, turnips, beetroot, russet and other apples of all sizes and shapes spread out on old hemp bags in front of them: a producers' market, what would be the height of sophisticated organic food in London. The quality of the food may account for the general well-being of the people, in spite of the low level of prosperity. The graceful Austro-Hungarian buildings seen through such a rose-tinted filter in Vera's book are here indeed, and make Lviv a fundamentally ravishing city, even more so for the fact that most of their red or yellow ocher, sage green, dusty pink, or light blue paint is peeling and shabby. There is hardly any building work going on. Many of the streets are cobbled, with generous cobbles slewing diagonally across the road and then shuffling back into right angles on the pavement. There are no parking meters and few street markings apart from pedestrian crossings—you can still park for the most part right outside where you want to go. Heavy ornate wooden doors like those in Prague, framed with wide stone arches with stone lions' heads above them, give directly onto the pavement and open up into balconied courtyards much like the one my father was imprisoned in.

Joe has given us a map of how he remembers Lwow, and where his college was, although it's still not easy to find the way because even Vyacheslav's agency has maps only in Cyrillic, and no one seems to know the location of the college. The Cyrillic map Vyacheslav gives us has Omega watches advertised on it, I note with pleasure. In spite of the fact that Vyacheslav has told us that the first foreign language being taught in Lviv schools is now English rather than Russian (with German as a second choice), few people speak any English at all—although I haven't earned the right to surprise. We set off in the general direction of where the *Bursa Grunwaldska* had been. We pass through the other big undercover street market, its produce stacked high on trestle tables and women skirting its entrances with bunches of violets and primroses. A huge pig's head looks abashed and mournful on a butcher's slab.

No one has heard of "Jack's Hill" (*Góra Jacka,* as my father knew it), but when we turn off Zielona Street we can tell from the topography we're getting close. There's a mellow old nineteenth-century building with fading salmon-colored paint and pine trees flanking the entrance, young people going in and out briskly, carrying musical instrument cases. As we peer in through the iron gates at the back wondering if this is the *Bursa*'s courtyard, a vivacious man in a beard and black leather jacket asks if he can help. I explain my mission (in German) and he tells us he is a teacher here, and this is now a specialist music school for talented musicians from the age of seven to eighteen. Its name is no longer *Bursa Grunwaldska*—which, after all, commemorates a major Polish victory against the Teutons in 1410, and this is no longer Poland. He doesn't know of "Jack's Hill," but we realize the hill is right behind us—the hill that had the radio station on it which Joe's cat's-whisker radio tapped. We walk up to find there's now a gray Soviet-era block on it, still part of the technical college. As we walk round the back, we discover the old college, very dilapidated, a two-story building around a courtyard with mangy, undernourished trees and a line of washing hanging from one to another. I sit on an old bench and cry for no apparent reason.

The next day is likely to be the most taxing of all. We're taking the train out of Ukraine just over the border into Przemysl—the oldest town in southern Poland after Krakow, although we won't have time to see it. From there we need to press on to Ustryki Dolne by bus, and will arrive there late and with nowhere booked to stay. This is the only way we can now get to Ustianowa, the station my father had arrived at from Lwow: by looping up to Przemysl, then taking a bus to Ustryki Dolne, and another bus back down to Ustianowa. Joe had gone by train directly from Lwow to Ustianowa, but Polish-Ukrainian relations haven't yet thawed to the extent of reinstating the direct rail line link.

Lviv Station by daylight looks no better than at night—a daunting complex of grim, neglected halls with an anxious, military feel. We go three stories up to another cavernous hall, where window no. 25 is open and labelled promisingly "For Foreigners," but the woman at the desk turns out to speak no foreign language at all, and has no interest in communicating. But we get our tickets, for 22 *hryvnya*, and find our train, with its snowplow in front and eyes like Thomas the Tank Engine. We clamber up the iron ladder and settle down in a carriage imbued with the same harsh, poverty-line nervousness as the station. There are three tiers of benches up each wall, none upholstered, all made of wood covered with torn plastic, the two top ones folded up now. I imagine them all full up, legs from the upper benches hanging over those sitting beneath, or perhaps piled with chickens in boxes. But we have the boxed-in bottom benches by the window to ourselves, and can draw back the lace half-curtain and look out. Most people getting onto the train are wheeling trolleys of boxes, or red-and-blue-checked plastic storage cases stuffed full of—what?—blankets and suchlike, it seems, to be sold over the border. For some reason, four separate people hold Hugo Boss carrier bags.

Outside, the gray, depleted, ground is awash with meandering floodwaters. There are no hedges, just patches of tilled land unaccountably stitched into a field in the middle of nowhere. Then it becomes more cultivated, with mustard-colored wooden houses studded with satellite dishes, and apple trees in the garden with trunks whitewashed neatly a few feet up to prevent disease. Everywhere, there are dogs. At three in the crepuscular afternoon, we arrive at the concrete block of a border customshouse, surrounded by an inordinately wide platform, which would make it difficult for anyone to make a run without being seen from the lookout tower. The customs officials come through the train and get us all to fill in a declaration in Polish that we have no narcotics, ammunition, and so on, and detail how much money we have and in what currency. We tell them we have *zlotys* and $150 and they gesture: show us, and we pull them out and prepare to count them when they wave them away, which is just as well as it was a wild guess. They go off with our forms and passports, and when we look concerned the man in the opposite seat says, "Normal," to us with a grin, although he is guarded about getting into further conversation whilst officials are on the train.

There's an hour's wait, then the train sets off again, with our passports not returned. As we pull away slowly from the border, we see that the roads below the rail track have double rows of strong, high steel wire fences, and the whole area is surrounded by open fields. Our passports are given back, and our *"Deklaration"* stamped, but we're quizzed in Ukrainian about where we're going to, and the peaked-capped guards get us to stand up whilst they look under our seats. Then there's another long wait, with the lavatories all still locked, as they have been throughout the border crossing.

The border crossings are orchestrated in stages. This is no doubt for bureaucratic reasons, though it's hard not to feel that there's an intent to unnerve, to say: Don't think you're through with this yet. I sense a rising paranoia, even though I'm travelling with a companion, legally, in peacetime, and protected in the background by my government and hopefully by international human rights legislation. Joe had none of these things, and must have known he had a very slim chance of coming through the border ahead, crossing from Soviet terror to Nazi terror, without extreme danger. In addition, he was only nineteen. The double fence reminds me that the German word for "border," *Grenze,* is an onomatopoeic word, ferocious and barbed, embodying the angst around its meaning for a country which has constantly sought to expand or defend its borders. In English, "border" is almost benign, redolent at most of Bonnie Prince Charlie.

The train creaks and grinds at two miles an hour for some ten miles as it skirts the border. At Przemysl Station we pile off the train, along with about two hundred men and women with trolleys and plastic sacks of goods to trade over the border, all crushing and herding together to get up a ramp into the customs hall. Faces are grim and harsh, and a couple of scuffles nearly break into fights. Then two women take hold of us and gruffly gesture to us to jump the queue and work our way through to limbo under the plastic barrier, which we do, passed through by helping hands and unsmiling faces. When we look back, we find that two others trying to do the same are getting manhandled violently back. There's a lot of raw, volatile energy, a bagatelle of darting, guarded glances.

It's dusk in Pzremysl and we find a bus to take us through the Bieszczady Mountain foothills to Ustryki Dolne, arriving at eight-thirty in the evening to a deserted bus station and a dark and closed town. At least we are now in *Rough Guide* territory, and it has warned us that in Ustryki Dolne accommodation can be "very hard to find in the summer hiking season and completely deserted or closed at any other time," so we take a taxi to the one hotel they recommend ("all pretty basic, but this has the most chance of rooms"). The bafflingly sour taxi driver takes us by a circuitous route up to a hill on the outskirts, to a bleak, pitch-dark barracks of a hotel behind even more pitch-dark pines. As soon as we pay him he disappears in a flash, before we discover that the hotel turns out to be closed for the season, as he must have known, and we then have a two-mile trek in the dark to find our way back down into town. Eventually we find a small hotel, with a room in the eaves. No restaurant or café is open, and we eat our apples and chocolate in our room to the accompaniment of the television showing a World War II drama. A Nazi soldier comes into a room with a cowering family in it, humiliates the family and rapes one of the women. It's raw and lifelike, and you feel that to the people who made it it's not drama.

Next morning at the tourist office we book ahead into a hotel at our next stop, Polanczyk, which we'll reach after a day's walking across the hills from Ustianowa, following the route my father took after he got off the train and encountered the NKVD officers. We get some money changed and then stand for an hour at a bus stop with others, whilst three men lay paving stones in front of us. If there's a way to lay paving stones viciously they are doing it, throwing up dust and hurling down the slabs, scowling. A couple of teenagers are in animated, conspiratorial conversation, but apart from that there's a marked absence of the gentle, interested looks and sweet smiles we'd encountered in Ukraine. It's exactly the opposite of what we'd been led to expect: Ukraine was meant to be the rougher, poorer, and more surly of the two countries. We see and feel the change, without yet knowing where it's coming from.

When the bus finally arrives, there's another long wait because the driver's ticket machine has broken down, reinforcing a bad mood that is clearly endemic, etched as it is into his features. We get on and ask for two tickets to Ustianowa and are met with a stream of what we know (without any Polish) is furiously cross-patch abuse. He shouts, he gesticulates in exasperation, he refuses to give us tickets. Why? Like the taxi driver, this is his job, to take passengers: what could possibly have provoked this outburst? Perhaps bad Polish is a hanging offense in these regions? The bus falls quiet, uneasy with this drama, trying to pretend it isn't happening, until a solid, matronly woman halfway down the bus gives him a long, firm piece of her mind possibly along the lines of "for God's sake just give them two tickets, you old bugger," and he grudgingly hands over the tickets. After a few stops, we get off at Ustianowa, resisting the urge to wave him a tongue-in-cheek good-bye as by now we're a little wary of the rules of give and take in what are beginning to feel like badlands.

Taking our bearings, we see a valley down to the left, with hills rolling up away from it into the distant Bieszczady Mountains, and a road winding up the nearest hill which will be our route. First, though, we clamber up a bank to the railway station of Ustianowa on our right. It's a deserted and godforsaken place, with one disused track and no platform, although there's a small station building where the shed had been in my father's time, and which he'd hidden behind. The skies are overcast, and the trees and bushes at their most barren although the distant hills are fringed with firs. We take in the huge sweep of the panorama we're setting off into.

8 | BALIGROD, 1939 AND 2001

My father had some sixteen miles to walk across the hills from Ustianowa to his parents' home village of Baligrod, which was now under Nazi occupation. Once he had run away from the Russian guards and come within sight of the San, he said, "I started walking more cautiously along a gully leading toward the river, as I expected border guards along river. Edges of gully were covered with bushes which shielded me from being seen. I knew that river would be frozen. As I walked, because of frozen fields your steps make crunching noise, and this was disturbing, but I consoled myself that no one could hear. Everything was empty.

"I was looking for suitable spot to cross river, and noticed two guards patrolling along river on sort of track this side of river. They were three hundred to four hundred meters apart, then they walked toward each other and met. Also, that stretch of river was straight, so I thought I would walk left, toward village, to find better area. When I got there, there was bend in river, but further on there was also guard with dog—big dog, four-legged dog."

Joe pulled a face boyishly.

"Whole river and border were patrolled continuously. Soldiers not only had rifles but also machine guns. Russians carried only Russian weapons, very primitive and old. They had revolvers in leather holsters—I was surprised, because leather was very valuable in Russia. My pistol was Belgian, 7.3FN, little flat thing. I've seen it fired, but I've never fired one, although I think I would know how to use it. It was like talisman. I saw that man with dog never met up with guard—there was gap of about two hundred meters between them. There was no coordination of time, they walked in same direction sometimes so sequence got out of phase. I moved bit nearer. Dusk was falling—it was about four to five o'clock. I noticed layout—there was steep bank, and I was up on higher bank, and couldn't see edge of frozen river on this side. On other side, I could see about twenty- to twenty-five-meter-wide ridge of pebbles. After this ridge, there was depression, after that willow rushes and bushes. I slipped over road and bank and fortunately there was quite bit of cover on bend and they couldn't see me on bank, amongst bushes. I was sitting waiting to cross, contemplating what to do—whether to just run, or throw grenade to explode it so I could run under cover of confusion. I was getting cold, which was good sign because once you start getting warm, it means you are freezing to death. Death by freezing is hallucination—you start feeling warm, you start dreaming you're in front of fire, then just slip into nothingness. This has been said by people who were freezing and who were revived. I was moving my fingers, every part to try not to freeze.

"It was getting darker, and moon came up, which started spoiling things. One cloud slightly obscured it. I must have been there altogether for about one hour, and I knew that if I didn't move I'd freeze to death, so I started running when cloud came over and at that very moment there was another man on right, on straight bit after bend, who also started running. He started first. I noticed shadow, and figure running. I ran sliding like a sleigh across river, I must have broken Olympic record, then hit ridge on other side. I fell over, and heard shot as I was falling. As I was moving so fast, I rolled over and over, completely out of breath and absolutely scared. Fear started overtaking me. First I did not realize why I couldn't see. After while it came to me that my eyes were closed"— he laughed—"I opened my eyes, it was relief in one sense but not hearing anything I thought I was still wounded somewhere. Even when it is still, you can hear any slight movement, and then I heard myself moving, so I started to check whether I was wounded somewhere. I moved my hand, then arm, then other one. I moved my left leg, that was all right, but when I tried to move right one, I couldn't.

"Fear gripped me that I might have been shot. I started to move toes in right leg and found I could, so I couldn't be injured very much. There was sufficient light from moon to see that reason I couldn't move it was because my left leg was pinning it down! When that happened, I thought I was all right. But I was frightened, absolutely frightened. How to get away from there? You did not know whether they were going to follow you, or what to expect on other side, with German patrols or anything. I rolled over a bit away from river and started thinking. First thing I did was throw away grenade across river, and then crawled into bushes. Further on, there were few trees, and screen becomes thicker for you. I realized they were not following me, and then saw that other man crawling along like me and I spoke with him in Polish. We thanked each other for saving each other's lives—he said, 'You saved my life,' I said, 'No, you saved mine.' "

Now, as I write over a decade later, I wonder whether Joe had transplanted a bit from this episode into his original telling of the "killing" of the NKVD man. I hope he has, for an odd reason. When he'd told me before of the conversation after this incident, about each man going on his way and saying he'd done the other a favor, it rang true to me at the time—but now, once he's told me that he'd actually run away and left him, it's unsettlingly realistic. To cover up a traumatic episode is understandable, but to embroider it with a conversation which couldn't have taken place is for some reason more worrying. It would subtly spill into the realms of lying for the sake of it, and I find I can far more readily cope with the idea that my father killed someone with his bare hands than that he had *gratuitously* lied.

"I walked toward lights of village, came to house with lights on, and I knocked on door. Door opened, and I spoke in Ukrainian, because in peasant villages Ukrainian would be spoken in that area. You start with religious greeting—'May God bless you. Would you have space so I could sleep here tonight?' They say, 'Where are you going, where did you come from?' and I say, 'I've come from across the river, I'm going to Baligrod.' They had bench in hall, between bedroom and kitchen, and let me sleep there."

"Would they have had sympathy for you," I asked, "coming out of the Russian occupation?"

"Peasants under German occupation were much freer, they could move freely from village to village. Border was guarded on one side only. Nobody from German side tried to escape into Russia. Others who'd escaped from Russian side before had brought news of what was happening there. As long as you identified yourself as being of that area, you were accepted."

"Who were the Russian border patrols after?"

"Well, they said they were protecting people from Germany occupying whole nation."

"In spite of the Nazi-Soviet Pact?"

"Politicians were saying one thing, and others were saying something else. Commissars had duty to inform people that they were coming in as friends, to protect them. Then there was another group, Russian soldiers and German soldiers who knew they were going into war. There were three levels of information and you had to distinguish which one is which, and realize that all were lies, except the one the soldiers knew, which was that war was imminent. There was continuous hatred against Germans—Russian hatred of Germans was greater than their hatred of Japanese, and they were at war with Japan all the time, with continuous skirmishes along border."

"Why then did Stalin make the pact with them?"

"I don't know that, but if he made it calculatingly, it was clever move. Other possibility was that Germans needed breathing space for attack on Belgium and France. Or that there was some agreement on parcelling out Europe—Germans had already shown willing to parcel Poland. Another possibility was that Russians at that time may not have been ready for war. Or they made a pact to wait and see Germans being completely weakened by West so they could step in and conquer whole lot. These are politics that first of all I did not concern myself with then and they are too complex for me today."

Joe shook his head dismissively and took a sip of whiskey.

On our walking map for this part of the Bieszczady Mountains, we've highlighted the tracks we need to follow across the hills, and our path takes us down into the valley and up the road we've seen from the station. Roger's only concern is possible encounters with wild dogs, having seen the whites of their eyes in the Romanian mountains a while ago, so he looks out for fallen hazel branches and whittles them into dog-fencing staves with a penknife bought in Lviv. My concern is about finding a bed for the night: I don't relish the idea of leaving in the morning not knowing where I'm sleeping that evening, especially after a long day with a backpack in a country whose language I don't speak, but I'm trying to wean myself off this settler frame of mind and segue into a more vagabond spirit. I wouldn't mind trusting to fortune so much if the nights weren't too cold and damp to bed down under the stars at a pinch, or if the Bieszczady didn't have bears and wolves lurking in them somewhere. Tonight, however, we're booked into a small hotel, so what with that and the staves, we're both setting off on the right foot.

At the top of the road, just before we strike off across country, there's a lane lined with freshly cut logs, and a couple of loggers come down past us. They don't greet us with their eyes, let alone a

friendly nod, as you would expect in a country area with no one else
around. Perhaps memories are long around here and they think we
look like Germans. Perhaps old brainwashing about reporting
strangers on pain of death dies hard even after sixty years. If the
Moi tribe of Vietnam can still describe the mammoth in vivid detail
even though it died over ten thousand years ago, perhaps to the
Boyks and the Lemks—the indigenous people of this southeastern
area of Poland—the memory of fairish-haired strangers walking
into their territory is as traumatic as if it had happened yesterday.
Perhaps something in our manner or dress rubs them the wrong
way? I have a flashback to being a seventeen-year-old *assistante* at
a Catholic school in central France and coming down to breakfast
in a black shirt and realizing from the frisson running through the
table of nuns that something was amiss, but not working out what.
Then again, my school history didn't get as far as the Second World
War, and my general knowledge didn't get as far as Fascist black
shirts.

It may even be that we look offensively happy—for we are
happy. Until now, our journey has been a wintry one, and the dog-
eared tail end of winter at that. Today, it's been sleeting until we
reached Ustianowa, but once we head off on an old droving track,
its high banks lined with butterbur and wild violets, across hills
undulating into the distance, a buzz and warmth seeps into the air
and our spirits lift: it's the cusp of the season, beating with the
unmistakable soft pulse of the first day of spring. I've sent my
father a copy of the map of the territory we plan to walk through,
asking him to mark his route on it from memory. It's made him fretful in the way older people get when something in reality doesn't
gel with their knowledge of it, and they fear they may be losing
their memory. What worried him was that the map showed a huge
lake between Ustianowa and Baligrod, and although he knew that
countryside very well, he couldn't remember a lake at all. I then
found out it was an artificial lake, created some thirty years ago for
hydroelectric power and water sports. My father breathed a sigh of

relief at escaping his brush with senility—but we realized that the lake would now cover the place where he skidded across the river.

Dogs bark us through the first village we come to, Lobozew Dolny, passing us on to the next one like relay batons. They are mostly behind fences of quite prosperous-looking detached houses, although a couple of strays run up to us, little suspecting we'll turn into two blood-curdling Cyranos with our staves. There's a shop in the village, and we get some cheese and bread and 7-Up and sit on a bank feasting on it as the sun breaks through. We can glimpse the lake in the distance, with a dam crossing it, and aim to cross the San there, hoping there's a footpath over the dam. After some two and a half hours' walking, we reach the vast fjordlike lake, and take another ten minutes to walk over the broad concrete span of the dam.

All is unsettlingly out of proportion: on our left, the lake itself is artificial and too huge, the wind brushing uniform wavelets over its massive, dead surface; and on our right is a vertiginous drop to the hydroelectric system down below, with helicopter pads, pylons, office blocks, and hangars like some hideaway for M in a downmarket version of a James Bond movie. Somewhere down there, underneath the new mass of water, is the spot where my father skidded across the frozen river, obliterated now by the blank water in the same way that blank faces seem to have obliterated people's expressions. Memory, I sense, is an unwelcome commodity in these parts. I kiss one of the small pinecones I've picked up along the way and throw it down into the dam, thanking the old river underneath for preserving my father.

Before I set off from England, I found out about the new lake from the Internet, which yielded a felicitous translation of an Italian text:

An other attraction of the Bieszczady is the Jesioro Solinskie, the artificial lago of Solina. The dam was constructed in 1968 and the lago that was come to create, called "sea of the Bieszczady," has one surface of 21 kmq. It can be visited in boat; along the numerous rivers tourist villages are fates modernly to equip you.

Solina, at the other end of the dam, is evidently aspiring to be such a tourist village, but the fates have failed so far to modernly equip it with anything but two closed tourist bars. We've done some ten kilometers by now, with another ten to go to get to our room in Polanczyk. We're spurred on by walking on springy turf through pretty beechwoods running steeply down to small bays in the lake, which suddenly looks pea green and Mediterranean and eminently visitable by boat as it laps at the shore. It reconciles me a little to the flooding over of the past: perhaps leisure and pleasure and hydroelectric energy do well to blot out memories in such vexed borderland areas.

A man in his late thirties draws alongside us, with cap, wool jacket and sturdy brown boots. We ask, inasmuch as we can, if this is the way to Polanczyk, and he says he's going there and will accompany us. For the next hour or so we're in his voluble and energetic company, talking continuously, with not a word of a common language between us. It is tantalizing, and exhausting. There is so much we would like to ask him, and so much evidently that he would like to tell us, and he does, smiling all the while and with a slight stutter. All I gather is that—possibly—Baligrod is full of Gypsies, but that is only if he said *Zigeuner,* and if *Zigeuner* means the same in Polish as in German;* and that they have recently laid a telephone line to Polanczyk, which is why there is such soft, turned, sandy soil under our feet. Or maybe not. These are slim pickings for an hour and half, and guesswork at that.

*My father tells me later, "You are right, it means gypsy. *Cygan,* in Czech, Slovak and Polish (and maybe in Russian) also means a cheat, a fibber. Also a person who is unable to tell the truth. I am certain that in some manner your guide was referring to the second category."

At the crossroads to Myczkow and Polanczyk, the man asks a woman at a kiosk the way to our hotel. She doesn't know, but two girls with a two-year-old called Patrisk in a pushchair do know, and indicate that we should follow them. It's dusk now, and we walk on down toward the southerly part of the lake and Polanczyk along a newly built road. We are joined by an old woman in a headscarf who grasps my arm and hand and propels me along with toothless cackles, patting my arm and asking vivacious questions, which I answer with a haphazard repertoire of shrugs and laughs and smiles and squeezes. Then she takes both of our hands together, nods vigorously as if blessing us, and departs, waving merrily. One of the things it's surprisingly difficult to figure out if you don't understand a word of someone's language is whether a person is unhinged or not. I daresay she went back and said the same thing about us.

"Well, next morning, I got up and found snow had fallen—eight, ten inches. I asked directions to Baligrod. It was heavy going, and my long overcoat dragged in snow. As I was approaching next village, I saw two German soldiers walking toward me—we were some seven to eight kilometers from border. They had long overcoats like mine, and helmets, balaclavas and thick scarves, and you could only see small amount of their weathered faces. They were old, in forties—well, that's what I thought then. As they came, I was just walking, I had nothing. Soldiers' rifles were strung across shoulders, there was no reason for me to raise my hands. They asked me where I was going, where coming from. 'Across the river.' *Haben Sie Waffen?* I still had the pistol, but regretted it. I said no, no weapon. They told me to go to the *Kommandatur* as soon as I arrived in Baligrod to get permission to stay.

"I got to Baligrod early in afternoon and went to my parents' house, small detached house almost at end of village. They were not there, they'd moved few houses up. There were normal emotional scenes. It was year since I'd seen them. My mother was there

and younger sister. Others came later. Before they came, I asked
where *Kommandatur* was; they had requisitioned previous administrative building opposite school, which was part post office, part
hotel. It was frightening moment going to report. I entered building,
I didn't know what to expect. There were guards everywhere. I told
man I came to report. He took me to office where there was young
captain in his early twenties sitting behind desk. I addressed him
first in German: 'I've come to report myself, I studied in Lwow but
my parents live here and I want to help parents.' He spoke Polish to
me, and was very obliging, saying, please sit down. Even before he
asked my name he said, 'So you come from Lwow and are student?
Tell me of secret underground organizations students are developing there.' He said, 'Well, you'd better tell me because under table
there is grenade and if you don't tell me, it's going to go off in one
and half minutes.' This threw me, from such kindness. I knew bit
about grenades, though, and you cannot set grenade, you cannot
time it. Secondly, if it's under table, we both go up if it goes off. I
told him that and told him I knew nothing about politics, my interest was in study only. From then onward his manner changed, he
just took details. I told him I knew nothing about student organizations in Lwow, I didn't even know if they existed.

"Later on, through whispering rumors, I heard his name was
Zielinski, though he was always addressed as 'Herr Commandant.'
Same rumor said he was professional soldier, a corporal, in Polish
army, and became *Oberleutnant* for Germans. Perhaps he was from
western Polish border with Germany, where loyalties are sometimes divided. Whether he was pure Gestapo or military Gestapo, I
don't know. Uniform wasn't pure army uniform but not pure
Gestapo, either. I don't think I've seen pure Gestapo in our place,
but I'd recognize it. They had bands with Gestapo on arms—
he didn't have that. He was in charge of a bit more than just village
of Baligrod—villages were close together, and in some, no soldiers
were billeted. Many villages were too small to accommodate more
than half a dozen soldiers and most were in training, throwing

dummy grenades and so on. I felt sorry for many of them. There were some elderly soldiers there, many from Austria, in their forties—to me it was old, anything over thirty was old. Some three or four weeks later, I saw them on exercises, going uphill and falling over in snow, throwing those grenades. I thought this shouldn't happen to elderly people.

"Soldiers were billeted in people's houses—a room was allocated to them, and they made two children sleep with you in same room. You had no option but to tolerate it. There was soldier in my sister's house, an Austrian soldier, forty-fiveish, who had duties as cleaner at *Kommandatur.* He was not very agile. During evening, he would come in, he didn't have meal with them. Most of Germans were young—it was old Austrians who were drafted, none would have volunteered.

"As I sat there, I wasn't really frightened. Fear left me from moment I crossed river and fell over. That was frightening moment. It did not matter from then onward. You come to stage where you think fear that was there was so enormous that nothing else can equal it—you come to think that even death probably would not frighten you, probably arrest might because you don't know what to expect. As long as you know what to expect, you don't really feel fear. He was very polite, there was just that one moment when he tried to frighten me. He explained what situation is, we may be called to do some work—Polish people, that is—and he did not specify what, but said that for instance if road gets blocked you may be called in to clear it. You also had duties about reporting to *Kommandatur.* You had to report once or twice in week, according to what you were told. He asked me what I would be doing in Baligrod. I said, 'I don't know at moment. I'll try to find job to help parents.'

"Zielinski had slim, slim face. I didn't take to him. One was preconditioned—we knew they were our enemies. It was: Make life as difficult for them as possible without endangering anyone else's life or freedom, because by spring there is going to be offensive from

France and Belgium and all this is going to blow over and everything will be back to normal. It wasn't fraternization, it was: Keep
your distance because they are not our friends. In Russian occupation, it was: Keep your distance even though they are supposed to
be our friends, because you knew consequences. Here at beginning
I did not really know what was happening, there was no time to get
information even from mother, so I had to stay calm and do what
was necessary. It was fortunate probably that this was just before
Christmas—Christmas was Sunday, and this was Friday. Zielinski
was looking forward to his leave, planning celebrations, in festive
mood.

"Later, when I got home, father and brother came in, there was
very restrained talk on my part. We did not really know what to talk
about. I could not talk about what happened in Russia. I just said it
was very unpleasant. Remember, I hadn't seen them for over year,
it's always difficult to pick up threads. If things happened, you're
afraid to open up, to tell about troubles you went through because
they may be nothing in comparison with what they went through.
You may think you've been through hell, but it may not be anything
in comparison. No one knew what had happened to people in
Lwow. There were rumors of people being taken away, et cetera,
but no real communication. It was also Christmas, and nothing was
happening."

Eventually we arrive at our newly built chalet-type hotel, which
overlooks the lake on one side and on the other the Sanatorium
Plon, looking like something out of Thomas Mann's *Magic Mountain*. I feel exhilarated from a day's hard walking in clean air, with
that buzz that walking right through the point of exhaustion and out
the other side can give you. The hotel is small, cool and modern,
with generous pine staircases and hessian carpets, and no kitsch. A
delightful young woman who speaks English offers us a choice of
rooms, and we take what is virtually a suite: bedroom, sitting room,

bathroom with vast triangular double bath of a kind I'd hitherto unaccountably thought naff. Now I'd like to stay here for weeks. This hotel seems to go back to the word's roots in "host" and "hospitality," a wayfarer's rest. We bathe and wash our hair and change—back into the same clothes we will wear every day for the whole twelve-day trip give or take this or that (quite testing to my vanity, as this is still a new relationship). The only honor we can do to the wonders of the establishment is to take off our walking boots and wear shoes. In the restaurant down below, the owner takes us through the menu in fluent English, which he learned in Lytham St. Anne's in Lancashire, staying with his English brother-in-law after the fall of communism. After that he worked on a cruise ship operating from Miami, which is where he learned his trade. We have a meal that would do credit to the Ivy in London or Balthazar in Manhattan: borscht with tortellini, fresh local carp in cream, and a magnificent ice cream sundae, all with fine local wine. Then the waiter brings split cooked bananas with ice cream saying it comes with the compliments of the owner.

A dense twittering of birdsong wakes us early, but by the time we come down to breakfast soft flakes of snow are falling and the season has slipped a gear again. A magnificent breakfast of egg salad with slices of local cheeses, ham, and salami, and a large pot of tea sets us up for our longest day's walking. The total bill at the hotel for accommodation and meals comes to 260 *zlotys* each— around £24 ($36).

"How to explain mood?" Joe continued. "It was elation in one way. I was very pleased to be back home, they were pleased to have me, but already there was underlying apprehension, what does future hold? In such a place as Baligrod, there was no hope of proper job. Fear was that because of my age, one month over nineteen, there may be pressure put on to join German army. It was already happening with young men, especially Ukrainians, who were more easily swayed because of tense feeling between Polish and Ukrainian people—they thought Poland grabbed Ukraine, and that it should have been free country. There was feeling that if you have sufficient persuasion, you can persuade Ukrainians to join army. They felt occupied by Poland. As far as Jews were concerned, they were reluctant to go into national service and found all possible ways of getting out of it—there were three million there and hardly any were willing to serve, and this led to resentment. They claimed to be pacifists because of their religion. But this was not true of Ukrainians: they were just as willing—or unwilling!—to go as everyone else. There were hints that in other places Germans had started recruiting youngsters, through threats to their family or bribery. But for moment, things were very very quiet, there was no pressure yet to recruit people from other nationalities. In background, thought existed though.

"So we had Christmas. There was very little to celebrate with, and although we were all together again, there was underlying anxiety. I only remember working one day as casual worker, so it was very uneasy existence there. My father did have work, in sawmill, and my younger brother was employed on part-time basis. Meals were whatever we could lay our hands on—potatoes, cabbage, sauerkraut, occasionally rice, very little meat. They were very simple meals.

"I was slightly nonreligious by that time—no, I must not say that, I'm a nonchurch person, by church, I mean temples and buddhas and anything that congregates people in one place where they chant, I'd had my share. But it was custom to go to church on Sunday morning, and so I did. Vicar was plumpish, jolly person, and he tried to get me into his flock. Soon, a week after I arrived, he asked me to drop by for chat. I was already beginning to feel uneasy, with no job and no prospects of job, or even of moving away to get job, and I could not continue my education. I was lost. We talked about life in village, about how young people were unsettled there because they do not know what future holds. Then he said, 'By the way, do you play bridge?' I said I do, little bit. 'How about dropping by from time to time, I'll get two others and we can have game?' This was very exciting for me; at least there was something to do in evening and somebody to talk to, because talk at home was mostly about everyday life. Here was talk on different level, where food was not of primary importance. Vicar was in his thirties, but looked older than he was—or perhaps he was older than he looked. Fortnight after I arrived, he suggested I come and to my great surprise one of players was Zielinski. Other I think was teacher. We spent evening playing bridge, then said goodnight. Meanwhile, reporting to *Kommandant* had to go on once a week. We spent about two evenings a week playing bridge, there was nothing else to do there, no cinema. Books were very limited, libraries did not exist. People could borrow before from school library, but that seemed to have lapsed."

Poring over our map, we decide that we can avoid walking along a road for a mile to start with by cutting through the hills to the west of Polanczyk, although there is no marked track here. This brilliant shortcut turns into a very long cut as we begin to hit the far more challenging terrain of steep hills covered with pine and beech forests and deep valleys with streams at the bottom, and eventually come out onto the road we would have been on before, only two crucial hours later. Still, we reach the village of Bereznice-Wyzna in reasonable time, by around two in the afternoon, having covered almost half of our journey to Baligrod. The most mountainous part is ahead, and we begin a long, steep climb (I now see what the tourist office means about "even if easy, demand to times one sure resistance because of their length") up a rocky droving track cut deeply into the hills.

We are expecting to count the tracks turning off to the left, so confidently indicated by our current map and, after about two miles, to take the third one, which will cut through to a track lead-ing to Baligrod. However, it's difficult to make out whether a "track," when we hit it, is a real route or just a dead end into bram-bles, and meanwhile our compass tells us that our route is heading too far north and west. The fact is, there are no viable routes down to the left: we've turned back and tried a couple, and ended up in valleys with unbreachable streams, then had to climb back up again. By now the snow has stopped, but the air is damp and utterly still and when we find a clearing we realize we are in the middle of mountainous, forested hills reaching away darkly as far as the eye can see, with not a living soul or habitation in sight, right up to the distant horizon. It's so inhospitable that we haven't even seen or heard any animals here—no deer, or rabbits, and scarcely any birds, apart for the odd buzzard. On the other hand, there don't seem to be any bears either, though I'm wondering if bears are nocturnal. Then I remember the nine wolves to every five humans there are meant to be here, and hope we don't qualify for 1.8 wolves each.

It's getting late—a quarter of four—and we recognize with a sinking feeling that we are lost. I wish I'd brought the detailed 1939 maps of the area that Roger had copied in the University Library in Cambridge, and which I've been using only for research, not think-ing they might be useful practically. When I get home, I will find that they would have shown us clearly that the third and fourth paths ended up—after a long descent—as dead ends. The people who made those maps obviously knew the terrain intimately, and our current Polish *mapa turystyczna* cannot compete. With maps, as with people, there are layers of knowledge, and with both, it seems to take some hard footslogging in difficult circumstances to under-stand what you're really dealing with.

"On one occasion vicar asked me how long I'd been living there, if I'd been to college, I told how we used to go mushrooming when in season, and picking raspberries—"

"Raspberries?" I interrupted, at the risk of breaking Joe's train of thought. "Do you mean blackberries?"

"Oh, no. Where they used to fell trees for sawmills, they would take logs for firewood, and leave only leftover thinnings and branches for charcoal burners. Area would be devastated. But on these areas, some three years later, raspberries would start to grow."

I'd interrupted, but what was becoming a pleasure to me was to find that whenever I queried my father about something, I would uncover some further layer of information—small, like the raspberries, or large, like the incident with the guards after Ustianowa, but all refining the truth in an illuminating way. This is not true of everyone, and I was beginning to appreciate having a father who shared what seems to me the particular mystery of the world—that you can go on looking and looking into it, and never cease to find new things. In fanciful moments, I sometimes think the world may have been organized for us by some divine parent exactly for this purpose: so that we will never get bored, never get to the end of our explorations of matter.

"Sorry, Joe—you were saying about the vicar—"

"Uh, yes. Vicar said, 'In that case you must know mountains quite well.' 'Yes,' I said, 'right up to Czechoslovak border,' because there were berries there size of pea, dark bilberries, excellent in pie. It was quite some distance to get to furthest berries, about sixteen to eighteen kilometers, but because we liked them we sometimes used to go and get them there. He asked, 'How difficult would it be to go across mountains in winter?' 'Not that difficult,' I said, 'provided you were on skis'—you couldn't walk, because terrain wasn't gentle. Mountains were covered mostly with pine trees and they have branches that slope downward, starting at almost ground level. When snow falls, snow stays on and area underneath tree is snow-free. But when weight increases, snow sheds and on side there's heap of snow and some underneath. This meant that there were undulating places if trees weren't dense. In one place snow may not be more than one foot deep, further on ten foot deep, and unless you know terrain, you don't know. Only way you can go is on skis because you don't sink much in powdery snow. And conversation ended at that. I was almost into my fourth week, and was getting annoyed at myself that I came to help parents and they were keeping me.

"Then vicar started conversation about snow and said, 'You said it wouldn't be difficult to get across mountains on skis. How difficult would it be if six people were on skis?' I said, 'If they knew how to ski it would not be too difficult, but you would have to select route which is not patrolled.' As far as I remember, he said, 'You know mountains very well. Could you find route that's not patrolled?' I said, 'There are so many; they haven't got enough people to patrol, and it's unhospitable terrain.' Few days later, he suggested it would be nice gesture if I could smuggle some people across border. He said, 'There are some people in hiding at moment and only way they can gain freedom is to escape across Slovakia to France. If you met a group of people like that, would you be willing to take them up to border and point them where to go?'

"Few days later, occasion came. Round town he knew where there were no patrols, but you still leave ski prints in snow. You wouldn't use same route twice, or until after snowfall. He mentioned these people would be at certain place, six kilometers away. Someone else must have taken them there—these things are very delicate, you can't talk about them directly. Even your answers, you never gave direct answer, not yes, you said, somebody might be able to do it. It had to be like that because you had to be on your guard against everyone. I got on very well with that vicar, and thought, this is a man you can trust, but word your answers in such a manner that you cannot be pinned down. I went there; there were about five men, already shivering, obviously undernourished for some time. I had two pairs of skis, one pair constructed mostly by me, speed skis, very narrow but very fast. I was on normal ones that night. It was too cumbersome to maneuver in confined spaces, and also going was uphill. I used to do ski-jumping in Medzilaborce in Slovakia, where there were quite good ski slopes, and we used to build our own ski jumps from logs, compacted with snow on top. Also there was proper ski jump at Lwow."

We now have to use our wits and compass to try to get ourselves to the nearest habitation shown on the map—a village called Zernica Wysna, which lies a bit north of our route, but shows a clear track going across the hills from it to Baligrod. We could also perhaps get some information there, and if things get really bad, a bed for the night. The only consolation is that, apart from the overnight comfort of Polanczyk, the journey is becoming more and more like Joe's: harsh and scary. We have an apple and some chocolate each, and water. We decide to get ourselves to the highest possible point so that we can get the best overview of the landscape, and after walking from east to west up and down the steep undulations of more beech forests, with their golden leaves and many tangly brambles underfoot, we come out onto a huge clearing on a hill. I say to Roger, "We're out of the woods!" knowing I'll never use the expression again without a feeling of joy. From our vantage point, we can see a river way down below, and from our map and compass readings we know that it must end up at Zernica Wysna. But snaking up over the hill the other side of the river, in the direction of Baligrod—which is at least some five miles away—is a promising-looking path and we wonder whether to take that instead, even though it isn't marked on the map. It would be quicker, if it worked. If. We decide to take the safer bet of the Zernica Wysna path, and it's just as well: when I get home, I find from the old maps that that path would have led us back to the southeast, miles away from Baligrod.

After we've walked along the wide logging path by the river for a mile—with its welcome evidence of human activity sometime in the past at least—and with dusk just beginning to coagulate the air, and fear doing the same to our hearts, Roger sees some apple trees, and says, "This must have been a village, these were orchards." And then we see a bend in the track ahead and I hallucinate the outline of a cottage roof with smoke coming out of a chimney, just breasting the trees ahead. As we turn the corner, we suddenly see it's no cottage, but a ruined and spooky church sitting on top of a hummock of land by the river, looking desecrated. Not only that, but the village of Zernica Wysna is up on the other side of the river, or rather, what remains of it: some kind of gaunt, hollow-eyed garrison, its windows smashed in, empty and hostile and closed like some of the faces we've encountered. Nothing else is there.

Who has been holing up in that garrison, and when? Is it from the war, or from the 1946–47 civil war I'd read about between the Ukrainian Patriots and Poles, or from later Soviet occupation? Whatever it was, for the moment, this is not a place to hit at dusk, when you are lost. This is not a wayfarer's rest, a friendly watering hole, it's a place to get out of as fast as you can while you're still alive. It has the horrible air of a place where in the past people haven't done so. We go gingerly into the church and as our eyes get used to the gloom we can see the traces of a painting of St. Christopher on the wall (promising for us) and a Virgin Mary, and in a small crude alcove there is a roughly hewn wooden cross. The floor is rubble, and the walls are crumbling, but it has a roof, and Roger says if we can't find the path to Baligrod, we'll have to stay here. I say I'd rather take my chances with the wolves and the bears and the hypothermia, and he says, "There really will be no choice, you know."

With even greater urgency, we set off to find the footpath that should lead to Baligrod. It's difficult to be sure with these paths, but by a careful reading of the topography Roger finds what he thinks must be the path. The bad news is that to get to it, we have to ford the fast-running river across a fallen log with no handrails or footholds. So we bump our way along the log on our backsides, our backpacks lurching. It's now late in the afternoon.

"I met them in latish afternoon. I told my parents I was going to spend night with my sister, who lived not far from vicarage. I would sometimes spend evening there. Her husband was by then in army, and had been interned in Hungary. He wasn't prisoner of war, just disarmed and kept in camp. I preferred to go at night—even with no moon, there is sufficient illumination to see from stars, and there was less possibility of being caught. I brought them to border, then there was question of going downhill to village not far from there, two kilometers from border. I gathered that arrangement existed from then onward they'll be put on train, and then they'll be able to move to France.

"I left them there, pointing toward village, and arrangements were obviously that someone is going to take them over there. It was long journey home, and by time I got back, it was coming toward noon. There was no problem in entering village without being seen, there were so many trees around, and houses were surrounded by trees. Usually there were no questions whatsoever about where are you going, where have you been, and this was blessing in certain way because I did not want to tell anybody any lies. I did not want to lie in family, definitely not in family.

"It was about two weeks later there was another consignment, and again it was suggested that oh, if something like that happens, would you be prepared to take them? This time I said, 'Well, it's all very well, but I'm doing a job, I'm doing something, I'm doing it for nothing, and consequences could be very drastic if I am caught doing this and I think I should get some monetary reward for this.' And then it was pointed out to me that if I go to that village in Slovakia, all I have to do is to take few packets of tea with me, and exchange them in shop for pepper, and when I come back my prof-

its would be 2,000 percent! You could do this because tea was really
scarce in Hungary and Slovakia, but they had plenty of pepper,
which was very expensive in Poland.

"So on that next trip I went right up to village and got pepper
for tea. It was only just getting light, but village shops are different
to anything you see in town, they don't have hours of opening, the
shop opens when there is customer. You knock on the shop's door
and that means there is customer and you have to serve customer
otherwise he may go—well, he wouldn't go anywhere else because
there is nowhere else to go but it's nice to have customer. I
exchanged tea for pepper and brought it back and it wasn't difficult
to dispose of it in our place, as there were quite a few shops and
they just dispersed it amongst themselves.

"That was time when I started thinking about getting away.
Once these two groups got away, I thought, well, they are going
across, they are going to France and I knew at that time there were
connections in Budapest, and I knew language through Slovakia, so
there was no problem about that. So I started thinking about going
because spring was not all that far away and it would have been
quite all right to join Polish army in France and come as liberator—
this is youth, this is thinking of youngster, it's moderated to certain
extent as you grow old. But at this time, too, everybody believed in
it; my parents for instance had a chest of drawers filled with clothing, and at bottom of lowest drawer was Polish flag because they
knew they were going to put that flag up when spring came, when
liberation came.

"This would have been about March 14, there was small group I
took over. This time I didn't take any tea or anything like that
because you cannot do things too much or you flood the market!
There was another way of gaining money, it was to buy and sell dollars, but I didn't do that, I just took people, because by that time I
had made up my mind that it would be my last group. After that I
would go because snow would soon start to melt, and once that
starts it would be very difficult to cross mountains, so it would have

been my last trip. I was coming back and for some reason I wasn't really late—it was afternoon—and when I wasn't far from Baligrod in mountains I saw four figures moving slowly and I could see that they were trying to hide so they wouldn't be seen. I was wondering what was going on because I had several routes to come back and only my younger brother knew route I might be taking. He did not know what I was doing, but in unspoken way, with hints, he knew when I was not at home with my parents or sister then I'm somewhere else—he didn't want to know what I was doing but on second expedition when I brought pepper in and I was able to get some money for it and gave it to my parents of course it became known. When they asked, 'Where did you get money?' I said, 'Well, I smuggled tea,' so although there was no indication that I was dealing with people, he knew I crossed border."

The track is long and uphill and it's getting dark. We've been walking for seven hours altogether, with backpacks. There are still no lights or signs of life anywhere to be seen in the hills all around. Once we reach the top of this hill, we shall know if Baligrod lies the other side or not. If it doesn't, we shall have to go back to the hateful church, and I may abscond. In spite of the endorphins stimulated by the sheer walking, it's been hard going today and Roger manfully (used with full feminist awareness, and still used) insists on carrying my backpack as well as his own for this part of the journey. I'm not sure I could have done this last leg without that. As we breast the top of the hill in darkness, we look down and see a brilliant sight: the twinkling lights of Baligrod some two miles away down below.

"On that occasion when these four figures appeared I didn't know what was happening and suddenly three of them stayed back, hiding behind oh, quite small three- or four-meter-tall pines, and one

figure started walking on skis, not in hurry, and my brother had pos-
ture that I could recognize at once and although I couldn't see him,
I knew it was him. He knew I would choose one or two routes to
come into village and he was guessing which one I might take, so
he made himself reasonably visible so that if I'm in that area I
would have been able to see him. And I saw him and seeing that he
was on his own, I came to him, and he said, 'Well, there are three
people here, take them and don't come back again because there is
warrant at office. First of all it's for your arrest and from then
onward there are inquiries about you.' And he said what had happened is that Austrian soldier who was billeted with my sister he
came home and said that *Kommandant* was looking for me because
he wanted to play cards, and when he got home my mother said,
'Oh, he's probably with my daughter,' so he went there and I wasn't
there, so he wanted to know where I was and he said there's going
to be inquiry and arrest. He just said that to my sister, he didn't say
what to do or what not to do, so my sister contacted my brother and
said, 'There is no point in him coming here because he's going to be
arrested,' and arrest normally meant"—Joe sighed—"well, it could
mean that you were shot, it could have gone as far as that. And my
brother says, there are two women and a boy there—"

"Where did they come from?" I asked.

"Oh, I don't know, they were in village somehow, and it's possible that vicar contacted my brother. Circumstances were such that
you don't ask questions, you don't have time for this, the imminent
arrest hanged so heavily that everything else—well, you don't care,
you don't even ask who people are—you're told, take them across,
and that's where long journey started. Because boy he was only
about thirteen or fourteen years old, he was on skis and there was
woman of maybe twenty-six or -seven, she was not boy's mother,
there was no relation between these people. And then there was
other woman, she would have been probably approaching fifty and
to me it looked as if she weighed one hundred kilos and she was
not on skis, but had snowshoes. I knew she couldn't make it on

snowshoes—it's very very heavy going on them even if you are fit, and this was mid-March and the snows were starting to melt, which meant they melt on top and during night they freeze, so there is ice crust formed on snow and in some places crust holds and in others it doesn't and you fall through. Now with skis there's no problem because most of time snow holds, but with snowshoes, once you get in it you cannot get out.

"By that time I knew she was doctor, escaping to Hungary, and it was just mentioned that if there is any problem, any medical problem, I am doctor and can deal with it. She was trying to be helpful; you just accept it and don't ask questions. I saw these snowshoes were no good whatsoever, so I decided to tamp snow for her as we went so she could walk on it. The boy tried to help with tamping, other woman was not skilled enough on skis, and neither had strength or weight to help, so instead of having two people in trouble I preferred her to stay on skis. I had about fifteen or sixteen kilometers to go to border itself and it was tamping snow with skis to make it firm enough for her not to sink, it was really hard work. It took us ages to get there. I think it was practically dawn when we arrived, and we'd set off in afternoon."

"So you'd been walking for two days and two nights solidly, with no sleep?"

"Yes, it would be. And just because you crossed border it did not mean that you were safe, because Slovakia was given some type of autonomy by Germans and you did not know whether there weren't one or two people who would act unfavorably toward you. I was still tamping across border. We went to that little village, and there I met first surprise."

Seeing the lights of Baligrod is a great moment—until, that is, we reach the village, which is strung out along the river with no hinterland but the hills, and find that the welcoming lights were merely tall streetlights, and that otherwise the whole place looks closed down for the evening, its shutters literally and metaphorically pulled down. The gas station is closed, the couple of places that look like shops are closed, and the prospect of walking up the paths to knock on any of the mainly wooden bungalows and houses is daunting. I cannot imagine anyone opening the door to a stranger in a place like this at night. So we walk along the long road that is Baligrod, looking for anything that resembles a hotel or café and knowing we won't find one. I suddenly recall my father saying when I told him we were going to Baligrod: "It's a dump, you know." Finally, at around nine o'clock, we find the blessed (and somehow counterintuitive) sign NOCLEGI, meaning "Rooms," up on a utilitarian block of flats. Even better, as we walk round to the door, there are lights on and a neon sign saying: THE RITZ. Well, actually it says, BAR, but the impact on us is the same.

We knock, and a startled barman takes us through a heavy door into a saloon, with a blaring television up on the wall and two locals sitting up at the bar. They turn slowly, staring at us as if we're apparitions, and we no doubt look it. We feel like the couple of Americans walking into the Slaughtered Lamb pub on the north Yorkshire moors in *An American Werewolf in London,* greeted with a sudden wall of menacing silence where there had been merry chatter. *"Dzien dobry,"* we say, knowing we should be managing "Good evening," not "Good day," but unable to remember the words.

"As we entered village, older woman said, 'I can take charge from now onward,' and I said, 'What do you mean?' and she said, 'It's all right, there's dentist here, I know him, and he'll arrange rail tickets for us and we'll go to Budapest.' That was really pleasant surprise, but you think now all my troubles are over, then there is the thought in background, is it right, is she telling truth? There is always that little nagging question, is this true, or is there something else in it? But we went to dentist and sat in his small waiting room—I don't know how he managed to make living in that village, but he gave us coffee and bread and it was most welcome. As I was sitting there, I tried to get up and that was moment I discovered my legs wouldn't hold me, they just collapsed underneath me. She came straightaway and felt underneath my knees and said, 'You'll require probably operation, you've damaged your knees,' and we hobbled somehow or other to station and got on one-wagon train—diesel train—to next main station.

"When changing train, I had problems even getting to it, even climbing up steps; fortunately, my arms were strong enough to pull myself up. We got into train and it was crowded with soldiers—oh, it was crowded. I was hoping I would get seat somewhere, but I was sitting on floor with my knees in pain, I could not find position where I could sit without pain. It was long journey, very long, because I think it has taken us practically all night to get to Budapest, whether we were waiting at stations for long time I don't know, but it went on and on and on. Of course, during that train journey I was drifting from sleep into consciousness; as soon as I woke up and tried to move, pain came. But when we got to Budapest, she lived up to what she said: she ordered taxi for all four of us, and went straight to hospital and left me there, then went with others and arranged lodgings for them and said she would come back. She was taking really good care of us. The doctor at hospital treated me for my knees—there was water on knee or something, it needed slight incision to remove pressure. And woman doctor said, damage is not too bad, now just a little rest is needed; well, little rest was last thing I wanted, I just wanted to disappear, to go to France. I didn't want to stay in Hungary—they were extremely pro-German.

"I stayed in Budapest eight days in all, four of them in hospital. I was able to move around quite well by then. Doctor took all four of us out one evening for meal at YMCA, she was really taking care of us, and from what I discovered later she had quite a bit of funds salted away in Hungary, which was one of reasons she tried to get there. She introduced me to nightlife, drove me to a show and clubs, and we ate really good food—I'd never experienced that type of thing before.

"I wrote to my parents from Hungary and said: I'm safe. I don't know if they ever got it."

I can just about remember the Polish for "red wine" and ask for some, and they duly present me with a martini. They haven't any food except crisps, and we eat three packets each. Never have they tasted so delicious. We down another martini and beer and the barman then comes over and offers us one more on the house. By this time we're speaking at least the language of smiles, although not getting much further as regards information. I'd like to ask about the garrison up in Zernica Wysna, but even with Polish I suppose I'd be wary of broaching a subject that could prove sensitive and quickly get me out of my depth, especially with three martinis inside me. Anyway, for the moment, we're just grateful to have a roof over our heads, and arrive in the haven of Baligrod with feelings of relief approaching those Joe must have had. The barman takes us to our room at the end of a dilapidated institutional-type corridor which also houses a pram and a rudimentary shower and basin, as well as rooms off to the side evidently used by his extended family. There are three put-you-up beds covered in stained brown bobbly material with brown plastic ends, with the odd empty bottle, paper wrapping and condom under them. We sleep like kings, and are charged only £10 (about $15) for the privilege.

The next morning, Wednesday, March 20, we set off south through the length of the village trying to find Joe's old house, which was opposite a sawmill. Joe has told me that no Kobaks exist in Baligrod anymore; after the war, his older sister moved down to Kosice in Slovakia and his parents and other siblings, along with much of the population of southeastern Poland, were "relocated" to the west of Poland—in their case to a region somewhere near Wroclaw. On the way we pick up some cheese, salami and sweet bread rolls from the grocer's, and stop off in the main square to eat them. The square is laid out like a small park, with thin trees dotted around and a couple of squat firs. In the middle is a paved area with a Second World War tank up on a plinth in the middle of it with a chain-link fence around. The tank's gun is pointing—perhaps accidentally, although in areas with long and bloody memories such things are not usually accidental—toward Ukraine. This whole area, I find later when I get home, has been crisscrossed with layers of vicious civil war, which have only recently begun to come to light. In the only book in English on the subject, Neal Ascherson calls it "an episode so dreadful—and so firmly suppressed by the Communist authorities of Poland and the Soviet Union—that it has taken fifty years for a candid account to appear in English. This is the genocidal war fought between Ukrainian and Polish partisans in the borderlands either side of the River Bug, a merciless war of mutual extermination which cost tens of thousands of lives— almost all civilians—and which was routinely accompanied by massacre, rape and torture on a Rwandan or Bosnian scale."

It all started at the time my father was in Baligrod, as the Nazis moved in. Hitler, exploiting local grievances, courted Ukraine as a weapon against Poland, offering it autonomy as an eastern territory of the Third Reich if it would join in the fight against the Poles. Ukraine felt bitter toward Poland, as it had lost its short-lived two-year independence to the Russians in the 1920 war, whilst the Poles had not only clinched theirs, but also on the way taken over western Ukraine, including Lwow, for themselves. So an army of partisans, the Ukrainian Patriots' Army (UPA), had grown up to fight for independence in these borderlands. It was a vengeful guerrilla army, which Hitler immediately exploited to do his dirty work for him. He fielded them to fight the Polish resistance against the Nazis, and to provide guards for the Nazi concentration and extermination camps that he began to establish in Poland soon after the outbreak of war. (It is noticeable, for example, how many of the guards at

Plaszow and Auschwitz, outside Krakow, mentioned in Thomas Keneally's *Schindler's List* are Ukrainian.) Two years later, in 1941, a special, and notoriously cruel, Nazi SS division was formed from these Ukrainian partisans, the XIV Division *Galizien*. They took to the hills—some of them the hills we've been walking through. The Carpathians, with their dense, impenetrable forests and camouflaged mountain hideouts, gave them perfect cover.

Then, in June 1944, as the Nazis were beginning to lose the war, they were thrown out of the Bieszczady area by the incoming Soviet troops. The Galician division was defeated by the Soviet army in a major battle in the Volynhia district, north of Lwow, but one third of the company—some five thousand men—still managed to escape southwestward and most of them went and holed up in the Bieszczady. These men were still collaborating with Nazi *Einsatz* groups, the "special" units dedicated to the extermination of prominent professional people and others whom they considered war criminals. Since the Soviets now occupying the area were even less welcome to some than the Nazis had been, and since many of the Ukrainian "Patriots" or "Fascists" were related to people locally— the borders having shifted like a sinuous belly dancer for centuries—loyalties were divided and above all drenched with fear. To try to distinguish who supported whom in these circumstances was an impossible task and bred entrenched suspicion in the population. Worse, the fighting, which continued up until 1947, well after the war had finished for the rest of those involved, descended into vicious barbarity.

The Polish partisan who gave the first English account of the fighting—as late as 1999—Waldemar Lotnik, says there was "escalating bloody revenge." The Polish-Ukrainian carnage was spliced with Nazi carnage. The Nazis took "routine reprisals" on Polish villages in these borderlands as they retreated from the Russians in the spring of 1944. They would come into people's houses, murder their sons in front of the family and rape the women. I think of that television program in Ustryki Dolne of the cowering family and wonder if it's playing on an eternal loop, at least in people's minds. Lotnik says that in one village, all the women were raped, no matter how old or young, and then the village was razed to the ground. Then the other side would do the same to a bigger village, and so on.

> We reacted to their attacks, which reached unspeakable levels of barbarity, with a ruthlessness of our own. . . . While I never saw one of our men pick up a baby or small child with the point of a bayonet and toss it onto the fire, I saw the charred corpses of Polish babies who had been killed that way. If none of our number did that, then it was the only atrocity that we did not commit. . . . This was how the fighting escalated. Each time more people were killed, more houses burnt, more women raped. Men become desensitized very quickly and kill as if they knew nothing else. Even those who would otherwise hesitate before killing a fly can quickly forget they are taking human lives. In fact, in order to kill it is necessary to forget that the victims are human; as soon as eye contact is established, it becomes difficult to pull the trigger. On both sides teenagers were the worst perpetrators of atrocities.

Lotnik was fighting in an area northeast of Baligrod, near Lublin, where the worst of the atrocities took place, but they spread in a rash down all the Ukrainian border, under cover of the Carpathians. The incoming Soviet army, using terror tactics itself, was also both victim and perpetrator in these atrocities. In these Carpathian regions, whole areas became the provinces of virtual bandit kings. Once the war had ended and the Soviets were in charge of Poland, this gave the Soviets a convenient excuse to tighten their security grip on the area: at the end of the war, the Polish Communist authorities, knowing that the area was a potential cauldron of trouble, had decanted the entire population of the Bieszczady region, either into the western areas of Poland bordering on Germany or into the Soviet Union. This wholesale evacuation of some two hundred thousand people, code-named "Operation Vistula," was one of the biggest transfers of population in European history. The inhabitants were given two hours to pack up and leave with whatever they could carry. Although my father's family ended up in the Wroclaw region in the west of Poland, he thinks they were "resettled" there before this diaspora, although information was impossible to come by once the iron curtain had descended. About a quarter of the original eighty thousand or so people "resettled" within western Poland have now returned to their parents' or grandparents' homes—a few trickling back in the late fifties, but most coming back since Poland regained independence. Perhaps this accounts for the closed faces we'd found in these areas. Perhaps whole geographical areas can be traumatized, just as much as people.

As we sit eating our breakfast in the gathering sunshine, a crocodile of young schoolchildren falls higgledy-piggledy out of the school opposite—my father's school—all in different-colored clothes, and looking round at us with easy curiosity when I take their picture. We take up our backpacks and cross the road to look at the peeling, hollow-eyed facade of the defunct Greek Orthodox church, with its squat onion dome more like a pumpkin. And there we see evidence of those atrocities having reached Baligrod—the tip of the iceberg, no doubt, in that this is the acknowledged evidence. There is a plaque to the memory of forty-two men from Baligrod, who were massacred at mass in the church by a group of Ukrainian "Patriots" in August 1944—shortly after the Soviets had moved into the area. Ukrainian Patriots, no doubt, who had been taking refuge in the hills we'd walked through. No wonder that deserted barracks at

Zernica Wysna had spooked us so. No wonder that tank gun is pointing toward Ukraine: it is, I realize, definitely no accident.

No wonder, too, that Polish-Ukrainian relations are so slow in thawing that the railway line between Lvov and Ustianowa is not yet up and running again. A stone plaque outside the church lists the names and birth dates of all who were killed. There is a Kopacz, Antony, a Kowalczyk, Jan, and a Kosdas, Adam, but no Kobaks. Later, I will send my father a photograph of the plaque, and he translates the inscription:

NAMES OF POLES MURDERED BY
ORGANIZED GANGS OF UKRAINIANS ON
6 AUGUST 1944 IN BALIGROD

At the bottom a legend reads:

EVERLASTING PEACE TO THE MURDERED,
SHAME ON THE MURDERERS

My father tells me: "the word 'to murder' in Polish has two degrees: *zamordawac,* to murder generally, and what's used above, *pomordowac,* which means calculated, premeditated, planned, cruel multiple murder."

We will not find out the extent of these atrocities until we get home, so for the moment we walk along the road with spring in our step. Straw-colored hills etched with dark green copses of fir slope off and up on either side, birds sing, and everywhere things unwittingly delight the eye. Wooden houses line the street in a natural disposition, each with a scattering of fruit trees around, most with sheds and neat stacks of wood at the side, some with satellite dishes, some with an array of small wooden beehives painted in different colors—the colors we saw on the houses in Ukraine: mustard, light cobalt, red ochre, black, turquoise, the colors of an early Renaissance painting. Thanks to Roger, steeped in wood and its

culture, I see that the real art in Poland lies in its wooden houses
and beehives. In Baligrod each house is a variation on the theme of
a central porch flanked by rooms with wooden windows either side,
the grander houses having steps up to a multiwindowed porch.
Most are painted different colors; some have characteristic whitewashed walls at the side with crossbeams sticking out attractively
from them. There is much decorative woodwork, over the porches,
around verandas. Happily, the Poles and Ukrainians seem to prize
their skills in this area. In Lviv, before we left, we managed to fit in
a quick trip up on a tram to see a *skansen,* a sprawling but well-
maintained outdoor museum of wooden architecture which is evidently as well-funded as the Orthodox churches we'd seen. After
we leave Baligrod we will visit another *skansen* in Sanok, where
long, low wooden houses, often painted with stripes along the horizontal planks, are topped by thatched roofs of impressive crafts-
manship, each a virtuoso poem distilled within its function.

As we reach the end of the village, we see a huge ski slope in the
distance, the one my father used. To the right, the old sawmill is
still there. We find a couple of houses opposite the sawmill which
could have been my father's house, but it's not clear. I should call in
and ask if anyone knew of the family, but I funk it: we have a bus
leaving at midday from the other end of the village, and no Polish,
and in a sense I'm replete with whatever it is I wanted to know.

As we walk back through the village, we note again that people
passing us tend to avert their eyes, all but the children. This is a big
village, but we are strangers, and there are, we sense, too many
things buried here, buried in muddied and inglorious circumstances,
for it to be possible to look a stranger in the eye. There is one new
house in the village, with no roots in the architecture or functions of
the past, a whitewashed Disneyland of a house with garish orange
slashes of roof and open orange fences, and nothing in the garden
but two regimented rows of knee-high triangular pines, badly
placed. This is a house which has set its face against the past,
brashly whitewashed over it, just as Lake Solina with its hydro-

electrics and its windsurfers has washed over its river past. At the post office, I send a card of Baligrod to my parents in Australia—cameos of its new village church, its old Orthodox church screened by trees so that it doesn't look dilapidated, its tank in the square. It's sixty-one years to the month after my father left in such dread.

On our way out of the village we pass another Orthodox church, newly built, sinister and hideous to my eye, its thin pointing spires menacing and out of proportion in the way Mormon churches can be. And then, opposite the bus stop, is the bleakest sight of all: a huge Jewish cemetery, with a long rectangle of paving stones surrounded by dense, high, dark pines, and in the middle a huge stone monument of a shield with two black swords cut into it. Behind the thick trees stretching back almost as far as the eye can see are row upon row of identical white marble graves, each with the Star of David on it in black: mass graves. There look to be more dead people here in Baligrod, dead in horrible circumstances, than there are living. Perhaps my father, always so accurate with his vocabulary, was literally correct in calling it a "dump." Later, when I get home, I look up the Jewish cemetery in Baligrod on the Internet and find the International Jewish Cemetery Project, which lists all the Jewish cemeteries all over the world. It is a mammoth project of homage and memory, rescuing millions of people from oblivion by simple listing; listing of cemeteries, listing of circumstances, listing sometimes of names. Everything is done matter-of-factly, with a sad, wise, possibly angry reticence, a reticence similar to my father's. There is also a site for the World Monuments Fund Survey for the U.S. Commission for the Preservation of America's Heritage, which mentions that

> Bereft of their rightful Jewish guardians in the community, deserted cemeteries suffered from considerable neglect and vandalism after the end of world war two and through the 1970s. . . . There are also, throughout Poland, scores of sites of

deportations, executions, massacres and mass burials of Jews, only a few of which are marked and/or
designated historic sites. The vast majority of Jewish cemeteries that were sites of executions and
mass burials of Jews during world war two have
not been given monument status by the Polish
government.

Although my father was not Jewish, I can see that he was fortunate to escape when he did in March 1940. What was to come in
this area was even worse than what he was about to encounter, and
that would be bad enough. Although he has kept his own silence,
the mass silence here is more unforgiving, more stony-faced. It has
begun to be broken, with Waldemar Lotnik's harrowing tale, with (I
will find out later) other long-buried horror stories from this area
beginning to emerge. For his part, the first president of newly independent Ukraine, Leonid Kravchuk, made a public apology in May
1992 for the atrocities of the Ukrainian-Polish fighting:

We do not conceal and do not keep silent. During
the Second World War Ukrainian chauvinists
killed about half a million Polish people in the
eastern regions of pre-September Poland. Like-
wise, for a number of years after the war Polish
villages burned and people perished. Ukrainian
chauvinism is an abscess on the healthy body of
the Ukrainian nation, a pang of our conscience in
respect to the Polish nation.

As for us, we are leaving against our best instincts. We've been
happy in Baligrod, which may have laid to rest some ghosts.

THREE

HINTERLANDS

The time was past when man had
only the monster of his own soul to
grapple with, the peaceful time
of Joyce and Proust. In the novels of
Kafka, Hašek, Musil, Broch,
the monster comes from outside
and is called History.

—MILAN KUNDERA

9 | A "FARAWAY COUNTRY"

The Munich Pact was not directly part of my father's story; he wasn't in Czechoslovakia when the calamity happened. Yet unknown to him, Munich was behind everything which would shape the rest of his life from the outbreak of war until the breakup of the Soviet Union. If he had been able to tune his cat's-whisker receiver in to what was happening behind the scenes in the weeks leading up to Munich, it wouldn't have helped him avoid his fate as a powerless individual; all the same, there's some late-coming satisfaction in finding out what really precipitated the loss of both his countries, Czechoslovakia and Poland. Conversely, perhaps if the powers-that-were had been aware of how many individual fates they would be decimating in the decades to come in their decisions, and how far more devastating the consequences would be for some, it might have given them more pause for thought. Or maybe not.

When I looked into the history of Munich, I was taken with a book called *I Saw the Crucifixion,* long out of print. It was written just after the Munich debacle in 1938 by a newspaper correspondent from England, Sydney Morrell, who had been following events from the ground in Prague. I'd had to remind myself in reading about the Second World War that it wasn't being reported daily on television and radio as events are today, and that accurate information was extremely difficult for the public to come by, especially from faraway countries—which, as far as England was concerned, was notoriously anything south of Calais that wasn't in the British Empire. And I'd come to rely on eyewitness reporting—like my father's, in his layman's fashion—to get a better picture of what was really going on than what the newspapers or even historians said.

I was particularly struck with Sydney Morrell's independent surefooted judgment, and with his diligent sleuthing, all of which took him to the right place at the right time, and to the right conclusions. I imagined him as a Hoagy Carmichael figure, wearing relaxed, 1930s double-breasted suits, strolling down Wenceslas Square with his Jack Russell terrier, Pop, and his pregnant wife, Mary—until things suddenly turned dire. Since my father wasn't in Prague when "Munich" happened, Morrell became my eyewitness instead for this short period, and I supplemented his observations with trawls through the contemporary archives whenever there was something he wasn't able to know at the time.

As it happened, Morrell had arrived in Prague sixty-three years to the day before Roger and I had, on March 15, 1938, the Ides of March. He had arrived from Austria, two days after its annexation, or *Anschluss*, by Hitler into the German "*Reich*," where he'd been reporting on the increasing violence and thuggery of the Nazis there. He came over the border into Czechoslovakia because everyone knew this was where the next push of Hitler's *Drang nach Osten* for *Lebensraum* would come—slogans Hitler had adopted for his tactics, as if giving words to the concepts of appropriating land to the east and expanding your living space justified them. As with "simplification," Hitler knew what he was doing: he told his friend Ernst Hanfstängl: "There is only so much room in a brain, so much wall space, as it were, and if you furnish it with your slogans, the opposition has no place to put up any pictures later on, because the apartment of the brain is already crowded with your furniture." It's curious that people didn't challenge him on his vocabulary, and still don't retrospectively. Calling himself "the *Führer*" was a verbal self-aggrandizement people accepted as if it were a valid title, and historians still do. The Eskimos, apparently, have a word for "leader" that they only ever use ironically, which seems a subtle and economical way of nipping grandiosity in the bud.

Now that Austria was taken over by the Nazis, western Czechoslovakia—Bohemia—was surrounded on three sides by the expanded "*Reich*," clearly vulnerable to a pincer movement cutting the country off at its waist to incorporate Bohemia, too, into Germany.

"When foreign correspondents start flocking into a capital, it means that something is getting ready to happen," Morrell wrote. "But the Czechs didn't see that." Coming over the border at the Czech customs point of Mikulov, on the southern border with Austria, he had watched two Czech officials going through his baggage. He asked them what they were going to do when Germany attacked them. The customs officials smiled at each other and one said, "If Germany attacks us we shall fight. We aren't Austrians. Hitler can't take us the way he has taken Austria. We know the Germans. We've had to live beside them for a thousand years. They ruled over us for three hundred years, and tried to Germanize us, and they failed." He leaned over earnestly. "The men and women up there in the town, they know what it's like to be ruled over by Germans. They belong to all kinds of parties now. Some Communists, some Socialists, some what you call Conservatives, and some are Fascists, but we'll all fight together if Germany attacks us."

"And supposing your allies, France and Russia, don't help you?" Morrell asked.

"Then we'll fight alone," he answered instantly.

Morrell had arrived at Mikulov at twilight and could see a ribbon of lights running all the way down the frontier toward Bratislava, lighting up the work of thousands of Czechs who for months had been digging a line of forts deep into the mountains, fortified with steel and cement and new guns—Czechoslovak-made guns. Morrell knew that even the British army was now buying its Bren guns from the Czechs as they were superior to those made by Krupp in Germany—as Hitler also knew. The Czechs had seen Hitler's aggressive intentions toward their new country, plainly set out already in *Mein Kampf* and recently rehashed in Nazi speeches. Accordingly, Masaryk put into practice his philosophy of ensuring a defensive army against tyrants. Unfortunately, the black irony was that the more effectively Czechoslovakia built up an arsenal against Hitler, the more desirable it became for him to seize. It was part of his tactic to take over the weapons of his enemy to beat them with, which he did both literally and metaphorically. He'd already done it with the notion of "self-determination," dear to President Woodrow Wilson and the negotiators at Versailles, turning it around and waving it in their faces: if it's self-determination you're after, let's have it for the 3.5 million Germans, locked, according to Hitler, within the "tyrannical" country of Czechoslovakia. The Sudeten Germans wanted self-determination, too. And if Czechoslovakians were so keen on gym societies and vast communal gymnastic displays to build up the morale and physique of their young people, why he'd do that, too, and outdo them at it.

Czechoslovakia in March 1938 was in good shape, as Morrell knew and could see. Its economy and armed forces were strong, with thirty-five armed divisions against Hitler's twenty-one, and the most effective air force in Europe. And, under Beneš now, who had inherited Masaryk's mantle the year before, its morale was still high. Morrell had left an Austria full of swastika flags, noisiness, and Nazi brutality, and found Czechoslovakia "an island of peace." In the towns, people sat quietly in cafés; there were no processions, demonstrations, or troops as there had been in Austria, but "if the need arose every man was a soldier."

A few weeks later, Morrell decamped from Austria for good and brought Mary and their terrier with him to Prague. On one of those maverick, unseasonably warm days that herald the next season, he strolled down Wenceslas Square with Pop, noting with approval that the terrier didn't have to be muzzled in Czechoslovakia, as he had been in Austria. As they wove their way through the crowds promenading along the broad avenue, Morrell reflected that there was no more agreeable city in Europe to be at that moment. You could buy real tomato juice from America, cereals and cigarettes from England, home-produced silk stockings and tailored suits better than those you could buy in the rest of Europe. He passed stalls of versatile traders selling ties, belts, a look at the stars through a huge telescope, and lottery tickets for a new car perched on the pavement. Slovak girls sold sheep's-milk cheeses shaped like swans' eggs, brown from the smoke of cottage fires where they were hung and smoked. There were more newspapers in Prague than in any other European city: nine in the morning and ten in the evening. And there were even more newspapers in German than in Czech; not the sign of an oppressed minority, he noted.

In the evening, Morrell took an English visitor to a film in which Claudette Colbertova explained to Gary Coopera that the cure for insomnia is to spell Czechoslovakia backward. Afterward, they went to a Slovak wine cellar where people roared out Slovak folk songs to the tunes of a man who was dancing around his cello "with the gravity of an elephant around a daisy." A waiter, hearing Morrell and his friend speak English, quietly put a small Union Jack on their table, and people crowded around them lifting their glasses: "*Na zdar!* Long live England! Long live France! Long live democracy!"

But Morrell was already worried that England wouldn't prove the firm ally the Czechs hoped. He had seen how Hitler had manipu-

lated Britain in the 1935 Anglo-German Naval Agreement. The
implicit bargain was that he would be given a free hand in central
Europe, where Britain feared most of all not a Nazi but a Bolshevik
takeover, in return for allowing the Royal Navy to dominate the
seas. The Naval Agreement, Morrell felt, paved the way for
Britain's reluctance to act against Hitler:

> When, next year, he marched into the Rhineland,
> we held back when France wished to deal a blow
> that would have smashed him. I was in Cologne
> that dramatic March weekend and saw the Reichs-
> wehr generals were quaking in their top-boots.
> But Hitler knew more than they did; he knew his
> England.
>
> Early in 1938 Lord Halifax, the British Foreign
> Minister, went to see Hitler at Berchtesgaden and
> came back, as the Germans say, with his face red
> and his ears tingling. Soon afterwards Austria fell,
> and England, who had guaranteed the indepen-
> dence of that state at Stresa, made no move.

Morrell's instincts were running true: evidence he could not
have seen shows how much that visit was a prelude to the sellout of
Czechoslovakia. Lord Halifax, an "appeaser" newly appointed in
February 1938 to take over after Anthony Eden had resigned over
his government's attitude to Italy's and Germany's dictators, told
Hitler that "Although there was much in the Nazi system that
offended British opinion (treatment of the Church; to a perhaps
lesser extent, the treatment of the Jews; treatment of Trade Unions),
I was not blind to what he had done for Germany and to the achieve-
ment from his point of view of keeping Communism out of his
country and, as he would feel, of blocking its passage West." And
the extraordinary thing was that the other dictator who now knew

from this "secret" conversation that England was in some measure privately backing Germany, in the interests of keeping the Communists out, was Joseph Stalin: this conversation was passed through directly to the Soviet leader by two of the "Cambridge Five" NKVD agents at the heart of British security services, Donald Maclean and John Cairncross. From the Russians' point of view, this secret knowledge of what the British were saying in private, as opposed to their public pronouncements, would be the clinching factor in the Nazi-Soviet Pact the following year, which Stalin would see as appropriate revenge for British and French perfidy.

On another beautiful day in that spring of 1938, this time in mid-May, Morrell walked up to the Czernin Palace, passing young Czechs lying on the riverbank in bathing suits and splashing in the shallow weirs. Since independence, the palace had been transformed from barracks to the seat of the Czech Foreign Office, and Morrell wanted to drop in on friends in the press department. At the Czernin all was quiet except for the sound of little bells coming from the Capuchin monastery opposite. He walked along a corridor with offices on both sides, all of them empty as he knocked. He found all six of the press corps in the chief's room, grouped around his desk and frowning at sheets of paper he was holding. Here, what do you make of this? they said. American newspapers were all saying the same thing. The *New York Herald Tribune*'s report was typical:

> Czechoslovakia cannot survive in its present form, the British are convinced. Even if its allies and friends waged a victorious war on behalf of the Czechs, they would insist that the Czechs disgorge their alien minority to forestall any more wars on that score in the future. Therefore the Czechs should be practical and make the best terms with Hitler without any wars at all.

Morrell was appalled. He knew there were diplomats at the British Legation in Prague who disliked the Czechs as "middle-class" people and never tried to understand them. The Czechs were too busy building their state to put on airs, he felt, and the diplomats found the Bohemian castles and shooting lodges of the former German aristocrats far more to their liking. But what about the British government? What had happened in London, Morrell wondered, to change the way the wind was blowing?

He set about sleuthing, and discovered that a few days earlier, on May 10—the day Hitler was in Italy getting Mussolini on his side for what was to come—the first woman member of Parliament, Lady Astor, had given a lunch party at her house in St. James's Square in London so that Prime Minister Neville Chamberlain could privately brief some fourteen American journalists. Chamberlain needed to appease increasingly restless U.S. questioning on his foreign policy, whilst, Morrell thought, needing to keep his own electorate in the dark about what he was doing. However, a few days later some vigilant Labour MPs began to table questions in the House of Commons. Many had begun to put two and two together about the timing of the lunch party and the U.S. reports—and about the presence in London at the same time at Chatham House (on another side of St. James's Square) of the head of the Sudeten German Party (SDP), Konrad Henlein.

What even Morrell didn't know was just how Machiavellian a liar Henlein was. A quiet, apparently mild-mannered man who had come in under the cloak of being head of the Sudeten German gymnastic society—modelled on the Czechs' own—he was in fact clandestinely carrying out the first stage in Hitler's program to take over Czechoslovakia. He was the Trojan horse of the whole Munich crisis (and therefore of the war), smuggling the Nazi Party into Czechoslovakia under the guise of gymnastics. Meanwhile, he and Hitler consistently denied having any links to each other.

Henlein had already visited London in December 1935, July 1936 and October 1937, and privately briefed diplomats and politicians at Chatham House, London's center for international affairs. On these visits he had systematically sought to misinform the British government over Czechoslovakia, painting it as a state "tainted" with Bolshevism. From May 1936, he had a secret personal agreement with Hitler to work clandestinely on his behalf, and had held covert meetings with him at the Berlin Olympics that summer. All the same, it didn't take much to deduce Henlein's allegiances: in May 1937 he introduced the Hitler salute, calling it "the German salute almost universally used and in no sense a provocation to the Czech people," and then openly attended the Nuremberg Rally in September 1937. Yet when, a month later, a *Daily Telegraph* reporter asked Henlein whether "Germany was not, with some justification, considered to be at the back of the Sudeten German Party, Herr Henlein maintained that at no time had Germany sought to influence or dictate his party's policy—or vice versa." But at the height of Nazi power in May 1941, when Henlein could speak freely, he came out into the open, stating that he took the decision as far back as 1933 to "camouflage our movement with a show of legality": "We knew that we could only win if we succeeded in making three and a half million Sudeten Germans into National Socialists, but if we were to avoid Czech interference, we had to pretend to deny our allegiance to National Socialism."

If Chamberlain and his close colleagues were self-servingly blinkered over Henlein's puppet status, and over the moral and political consequences if Czechoslovakia were sold down the river, many others—Morrell included—were not. Parliament itself was operating in an exemplary fashion, asking awkward questions of a government that was already stonewalling by May 4, 1938, when Conservative MP Samuel Vyvyan Adams asked Prime Minister Chamberlain in the House of Commons: "Is the Prime Minister aware that if the Henlein demands were granted, the independence of Czechoslovakia would be effectively destroyed?"

Chamberlain blocked: "That may or may not be the case, but it does not affect my answer."

MPs and others across the spectrum of party politics were deeply concerned about the ethics of a situation where the government seemed to be preparing not only to violate the sovereignty of another country without consulting it but also to risk another "European war." And they, as ordinary MPs, managed to be well informed about what was going on in what Chamberlain would later choose to call a "faraway country."

From the moment he came into power Hitler had threatened "Czecho-Slovakia," as he always referred to it, the hyphen with him a dagger signifying his intent to see it in two parts. Indeed, even before he came into power, in 1932, he had secretly set out his plans, saying, "The Czechs must be expelled from central Europe." To him, Czechoslovakia was the prime symbol of the Versailles Treaty and had to be destroyed. It was also inhabited by Slavs, whom he chose to see as an inferior race, and whom he had eyed jealously as they flourished in their new country just over the border from Braunau. By summer 1937, his intent to destroy Czechoslovakia had become a firm plan, code-named "Operation Green." "The war in the east must begin with a surprise German military operation in Czechoslovakia," Hitler's defense minister noted. "The necessary conditions to justify such an action politically and in the eyes of international law must be created in advance." A few weeks later, on September 14, 1937, the death of philosopher-president Masaryk, aged eighty-seven, played into their hands, removing Masaryk's strong moral authority from the scene—an authority which Hitler never personally confronted.

Seven weeks later, on November 5, Hitler informed his military staff in a key secret meeting that he had decided to annex Austria and "Czechia" by force. (He had already stated publicly in 1936, "Only force rules. Force is the first law.") His rationale was based on exaggerated, hypothetical scenarios: that by 1943–45 the raw materials of Germany (coal, "edible fats," etc.) would no longer sustain its population. Unlike what he called the "satiated nations" such as Britain and France, he sought the remedy not in colonies but near to home. And nearest to home were Austria and Czechoslovakia, nations where he saw an alarming "decline in Germanism" and "instead of increase, sterility . . . setting in. . . . The only remedy," he claimed, "and one which might appear to us as visionary, [lies] in the acquisition of greater living-space."

With this in mind, he presented a timetabled plan for Germany's expansion for a ten-year period from 1938 until 1948. On a separate sheet, he attached a sketch map of Europe with the targeted countries shown in different colors, and dates beside them to show when each country would pass under German control, except for a fringe around the Mediterranean reserved for Mussolini. Even at this early stage, in 1937, he had put a line across France, dividing it in two to show the limits of German influence—what would three years later become "Vichy" France and occupied France. The countdown ran:

Spring 1938	Austria
Autumn 1938	Czechoslovakia
Spring 1939	Hungary
Autumn 1939	Poland
Spring 1940	Yugoslavia
Autumn 1940	Romania and Bulgaria
Spring 1941	Netherlands, Denmark, northern France
Autumn 1941	Russia

At this stage, England was not on his hit list, but Russia already was, showing in what bad faith Hitler would be negotiating the Nazi-Soviet Pact two years later. Three weeks after Hitler had secretly drawn up this list, Britain's prime minister Neville Chamberlain was writing blithely on a postcard to his sister: "Both Hitler and Goering said separately and emphatically that they had no desire or intention of making war and I think we may take this as correct."

Beneš, on the other hand, did believe Hitler intended war. As Masaryk's foreign minister, and then as president of Czechoslovakia after Masaryk's death, he had tried to counter tyranny and dictatorship with the principles of democracy his nation was built on. Above all, he had tried to cocoon Czechoslovakia with treaties. The December 1, 1925, Locarno Treaty, designed to defuse altercations between Germany and its immediate neighbors, provided for mutual assistance between France and Czechoslovakia in the event of an attack by Germany. Czechoslovakia also allied itself with Yugoslavia and Romania in the "Little Entente" (so named, ran the joke, because there was so little entente). However, by 1935 this support was clearly not enough against a rapidly rearming Germany.

Russia was the only potential ally strong enough to take on the Nazis, and Beneš—more of an egalitarian and less of a liberal than Masaryk—had a natural sympathy toward the Soviets. But he knew that to make a treaty with the Soviets would alienate the West and play into Hitler's hands. His solution was to make an alliance with Soviet Russia contingent on prior French support. Even so, there was the practical problem that Russia and Czechoslovakia had no common border and that Romania, in between, was loath to let Soviet troops onto its soil. Still, in the spirit of Masaryk's ideal of a cooperative, democratic Europe, with Czechoslovakia as the bridge between West and East, Beneš had done his level best to get and give support. With hindsight, what he had failed to do was to take two initiatives closer to home: he had not actively courted his closest neighbors, Poland and Hungary (though he had reason not to trust them), instead falling back on the old tradition of seeking allies at a distance; and he had not actively courted his Sudeten Germans, instead relying on fair treatment within the law. After the war he would be criticized for too naive a reliance on "collective security."

Collective security would anyway be rendered pointless, as Hitler had the dictator's contempt for treaties, which he would use and abuse according to his needs. In addition he had a formidable memory, especially for geopolitical tensions, and a grasp of European history which he used like a rapier. His stated view was that "A man who has no sense of history is like a man who has no hearing and no sight"—so for him to be pitted over Czechoslovakia against Chamberlain, a businessman with scant knowledge of European history, was no contest from the start. When British foreign secretary Anthony Eden had visited Hitler in Berlin in 1935 to negotiate the Anglo-German Naval Agreement, he told Hitler pointedly that the English liked to see international treaties kept. Hitler countered, "Surely that has not always been the case. In 1813 there were treaties which did not allow a German army. Yet I don't remember Wellington saying to Blücher, 'Your army is illegal, please leave the battlefield!' " It was an economical way of saying: You too play by the rules only when it suits you.

Calling the bluff on English hypocrisy in this way was a relatively inoffensive use of Hitler's supreme skill, which was to play on people's, and nations', weaknesses. It was a conscious and calculated talent: "I have not come into the world to make men better," he said, "but to make use of their weaknesses." The national weaknesses Hitler perceived around him were that the Austrians didn't know if they were masters in their own house any more, that the Czechs were naive and idealistic ("green," as Masaryk had put it), the Poles programmed for partition, the Russians wanted to be included in the club, the English were snobs and hypocrites, and the French hobbled by overrefined thought processes—and by recent memories of bloody trench warfare on their soil. (France's prime minister Edouard Daladier had been in the trenches, and would do anything to avoid such conflict in the future.) Above all, Hitler played ruthlessly on Germany's own weaknesses: its yearning for unity and yet—primed by its central myth of the gods themselves being defeated by the forces of darkness, the *Götterdämmerung*—its underlying psychic desire for catastrophic apocalypse. "We shall not capitulate," Hitler said early on in the war, "no, never. We may be destroyed, but if we are, we shall drag a world with us—a world in flames."

Hitler had such a developed eye for the weaknesses of others partly because he was so driven by his own. By the time he was turning his attention to Czechoslovakia, and lining up troops on its borders in May 1938, his hypochondria, medicinal drug-taking and insomnia had coalesced into a pathological fear that, as he approached fifty, time was running out for him. This was exacerbated by the state of high tension he was beginning to live in. In May 1938—five months before Munich—he wrote his will. A year earlier he had said, "No one knows how long I shall live. Therefore let us have war now."

10 | MOBILIZATION

Afortnight or so after he had written out his will, on May 19, 1938, Hitler began troop movements on the border with Czechoslovakia—although he denied them, branding reports of them "Czech lies." The next day, on another warm May evening, Sydney Morrell and his wife were dining with friends from one of the legations in Prague when the telephone rang and their host was called back to his office. When he hadn't returned by the end of the evening, Mary left for home on her own and Morrell jumped into a taxi to Masaryk Station, which served the west of Czechoslovakia out toward Vienna. "And there I saw it. *Mobilization.*" He saw a line of horses under guard, and a crowd of soldiers inside the station sitting on haversacks and smoking, waiting for trains. He wasn't allowed in. By now it was midnight, and he went over to Wilson Station, whose trains went up to the German border. More troops there, and no one was allowed on the platforms there either. He walked home quickly to file a report back to London, but couldn't get a line out—either to London or to colleagues in Berlin, Budapest, Vienna or Bucharest. This, he found later, was because the Czechs had their mobilization plans worked out to the last detail, and wanted to make sure that no news leaked out until they were ready. "I was wondering how I could get my story to London," he wrote, "when, at 2 a.m., there came further news. Two Sudeten Germans who had tried to break through a Czech frontier patrol into German territory had been shot dead and the May 21st crisis, as people called it, was in full swing."

By the next day, he had pieced together that most of the legations in Prague had received independent eyewitness reports of German troop movements, so it wasn't only the Czechs who were reporting them.

> The Czechs, when they were satisfied that the German troop movements were really serious, replied by sending their own troops to guard the frontier. And at such unthought of resistance to Hitler, Central Europe trembled. It looked as if war was coming. I sent Mary off on the Dutch aeroplane which flies non-stop across Germany to London.

In Prague, crowds were standing in silence round the railway station, unable to get news of what was going on. In fact, some 176,000 men were under arms that day. Morrell got a taxi to take him up to the Sudetenland—past the White Mountain Hill overlooking Prague, where the Czechs had lost their independence to the Habsburgs over three hundred years before. Although most of the roads near the border were blocked by freshly felled trees, he managed to get up to the border, where a Czech guard made him some coffee and told him he hadn't seen Czech or German troops on either side.

Back in Prague, he found that Goebbels had swung into action, and the German press was trumpeting that this was a Czech Hussite plot to attack the Third Reich, that Czech airplanes were violating the frontier hourly and Czech troops were trying to blow up German bridges. Three days later, Chamberlain was telling a packed

House of Commons that the crisis was over. In his report on that speech, Morrell writes:

> he mentioned casually that there had been rumours of German troop movements from the nineteenth of May onwards but that the German Government had said these rumours were unfounded . . . he ended by saying that the Czechs were now prepared to negotiate speedily with Herr Henlein. When you compared it with what had happened, it didn't mean a thing, but it did the trick. The Czechs, bewildered, found themselves in some indefinable way the villains of the piece as a result of this speech.

The Czech foreign minister called a conference of foreign correspondents at the Czernin Palace, asking them first which language they would like to speak: French, German or English. French was agreed on, and he explained to them what had really happened on May 21, ending, "Gentlemen, Czechoslovakia called up her reserves to resist German aggression and to reinforce the authority of the State in the German regions." "So there it was," Morrell wrote. "The Czechs had contradicted Chamberlain as openly as was polite." But they were hamstrung, unable to argue against Chamberlain for fear of jeopardizing the possibility of England, and particularly its ally France, coming to their aid, and yet with the alternative of accepting impossible conditions from a totalitarian Nazi regime. To concede what Henlein and Hitler wanted would amount to permitting a totalitarian state within a democratic state.

The fact was, however, that Hitler didn't want war quite yet, and was alarmed at the efficiency of the Czech mobilization, which spoiled his plans. What he had wanted was to build up propaganda against the Czechs in order to influence the municipal elections due at the end of May, so preparing the way for the kind of warless

Anschluss he'd had with the Austrians. For what he knew and the Czechs didn't—thanks to Henlein's conversations in London, all of which were reported back to him—was that England wasn't prepared to stand up for Czechoslovakia if it came to the crunch. Henlein's pro-Nazi deputy Karl Frank—the only one of the SDP hierarchy to know of Henlein's direct connection with Hitler—said the reports on British views sent to Hitler "presented one of the most valuable political services rendered to the German Reich. They provided Hitler with invaluable information, indispensable for the carrying out of his international policy."

Although Hitler didn't want war quite at this stage, he didn't want a negotiated settlement with the Czechs over the Sudetenland, either. Even less did he want it after what he felt was the humiliation of May 21. He clearly expressed what he did want to his military leaders on May 30: "It is my unalterable decision to smash Czechoslovakia by military action in the near future"—and he put a date to it—by October 1, 1938 (still within his 1937 timetable of taking over Czechoslovakia by autumn 1938). The "negotiations" with the Czechs were always in unmitigated bad faith. Joachim von Ribbentrop, Germany's foreign minister since February 1938—and an anglophobe as a result of his previous two-year stint as ambassador to the United Kingdom—said on August 18 that year: "the general instruction [was] given to Henlein, namely, always to negotiate and not to let the link be broken, on the other hand always to demand more than could be granted by the other side." This was a pincer movement of the mind. An American historian of Czech provenance, Radomír Luža, writes:

> With Henlein and Hitler working in close relationship, it was virtually impossible for Prague to achieve any kind of settlement. Faced with these dilemmas, Prague followed the delaying tactic of retreat, offering to the Germans, under heavy Western pressure, more and more far-reaching

concessions in the hope that the West would finally realize that the real issue had little to do with the Czechoslovak Germans. It was a unique spectacle. *The democratic Powers were utilizing all available means to press their democratic ally to capitulate before the totalitarian Nazi dictatorship.* (Luža's italics)

The Czech government was being asked to contort itself impossibly to reconcile its democratic system with the Nazi doctrine and demands for the Sudetens—which included that the "official German view of the National Socialist world outlook today should be taught in the schools" and that "the personality of Herr Hitler should be permitted to be brought home to Sudeten Germans by pictures and other means and the Nazi flag be allowed to be flown." Then it was dealt a blow by the results of its own democratic elections in May–June, which delivered the fruit of Hitler and Henlein's maneuverings over the Sudetenland, as the German Czechs polled a resounding 88 percent for the SDP. To the outside world, and particularly Britain, this looked like conclusive proof of what Hitler had been saying: that the Sudeten Germans wanted to secede from Czechoslovakia. Meanwhile, Czechoslovakia was showing and bolstering its morale in the way it knew best: through the *Sokols* or gym societies.

On July 6, Morrell went up to the huge stadium on the outskirts of Prague, where, with a backdrop of hills behind, some quarter of a million people—including Beneš—were sitting in closely packed tiers looking down on an empty arena half a mile long and a quarter wide. Through wide gates in the center came 32,000 men, dressed in white singlets and flannels, many of them aged over forty, from many Slav lands: Czechs, Slovaks, Bulgarians, Serbs, Macedonians, Bosnians, Czechs from France, Austria, South America and the big Czech and Slovak communities in Chicago and New York. Beneš had been one of the founders of the League of Nations, and, like Masaryk before him, had wanted to help build a United States of Central Europe until thwarted not only by Germany's belligerence but by internal squabbles with Poland and Hungary. Now he was doing the next best thing: getting together a Pan-Slav show of solidarity for an enjoyable purpose, with a subtext of showing collective muscle in the face of Hitler's threats.

Most of the participants hadn't met before but had practiced the movements in their own homes whilst tuned in to Radio Prague. The audience waved white handkerchiefs whilst the men and women—in simple white smocks, embroidered at the hem in red—swung their arms, bent, stretched, lay flat, twisted around, sprung up in unison, the patterns and colors changing as pink faces or arms all suddenly showed, the whole picture looking like wind rustling over a cornfield. Then the soldiers of the Little Entente came in, some ten thousand of them in the khaki uniforms of the Czechoslovak infantry, doing bayonet drill; then Yugoslav sailors, barefoot and bare from the waist up; Romanian soldiers building a bridge; Romanian cavalry galloping through bonfires to the cheers of the crowds—all this without anyone shouting orders. Significantly, no Russian or Polish soldiers took part. The display cannot fail to have provoked "an over-sensitive dictator" like Hitler (as the British ambassador in Berlin, Sir Nevile Henderson, called him), particularly since it was a Pan-Slav show of strength—Hitler's political nightmare. No doubt he logged again that the powerful Russia had not been invited, and filed it for later use.

From now on, Chamberlain took it upon himself to take over the direction of Czech foreign policy from afar. Chamberlain's experience of politics, let alone the international scene, was surprisingly limited. The British author Compton Mackenzie speaks of him at this stage as "a Birmingham Unitarian on the edge of the allotted span, with solid business interests and little knowledge of the larger world beyond the experience he had gained as a young man growing sisal in the Bahamas, with little knowledge either of human nature or of literature, who for the lubrication of the party machine had found himself Prime Minister of Great Britain in spite of the fact that he had not entered politics until he was fifty." Undaunted by his lack of international experience, however, the prime minister told the House of Commons on July 26 that he was sending a "mission" to Czechoslovakia to "investigate" and then "mediate" the grievances between the Sudeten Germans and Czechs along the border. The mission would be led by Chamberlain's friend, the recently ennobled Viscount Walter Runciman, whose alleged qualifications for being an independent expert were that he'd been a governor in India, president of the Board of Trade and had inherited a large shipping business—not a massively useful qualification in a country without a coastline (even though Shakespeare had given Bohemia one in *The Winter's Tale*). He and his entourage were already sympathetic to the German cause and toward Henlein—so much so that whenever they encountered it, they would respond immediately to the Nazi salute "out of politeness." Beneš protested that sending such a mission seriously affected the sovereignty of his state, but his cabinet members were forced to accept what was virtually an ultimatum. Chamberlain had declared in his July 26 statement that the mission was sent at the request of Czechoslovakia—a straightforward lie to the House. As Morrell wrote: "This was news to me in Prague. I found no one in the Czech government who was enthusiastic over the idea."

On August 3, Runciman and his entourage settled into a vast suite of rooms in the luxurious Alcron Hotel in Prague. They had private telephones installed—which, Morrell was sure, were tapped, the lines going from Prague to London via Germany. Morrell, walking the territory as ever, noticed that there were some "odd-looking people in the Alcron Hotel suddenly." The Sudetens courted the envoys assiduously. They'd heard that Runciman liked serious music—so they sent in classical music sheets for the string trio which played in the hotel every evening. They knew all upper-class Englishmen liked hunting—so they invited them to sumptuous hunting weekends at the country estates of wealthy Sudeten

Germans. Merrie England. Otherwise, for the fortnight and more that the mission was in Prague, it retired into its shell, rarely emerging from the hotel, apart from two notable sorties which Morrell tracked like a terrier.

On one of them, Runciman's assistant, Frank Ashton-Gwatkin, went to Marienbad, where Henlein was holding an SDP meeting, hotfoot from visiting Hitler at Berchtesgaden. This was the second time Ashton-Gwatkin had met Henlein. Morrell was there in the crowd as three thousand Sudeten Germans "materialized from nowhere" to hear Henlein and Ashton-Gwatkin speak from the veranda of their hotel, above a small placard saying that King Edward VII of England had taken a cure there in 1906.

The second mission sortie was also for a rendezvous with Henlein. Morrell had been tipped off by a colleague in Berlin that Runciman was about to leave for the Schloss Rothenhaus, near the Saxon border, the decrepit castle of a fervent Nazi, Prince Max von Hohenlohe-Langenberg-Liechtenstein, where he would be meeting up with Henlein. By telephoning Czech gendarmerie posts along the Saxon border, and at the previous locations of Runciman and Henlein, Morrell tracked each man's progress with pins on a map until the pins indeed ended up at the same time and the same place: the Schloss Rothenhaus. It transpired that Ashton-Gwatkin had just returned from London with a plan which fulfilled almost all the demands that Henlein had made, and Runciman was letting Henlein (but not the Czechs) know this in advance. So Henlein now turned down the fulfillment of all his previous demands and gave Ashton-Gwatkin a new one to present to the Czechs: abandonment of the Soviet pact. When this demand was duly delivered to Prague, the Czech government refused. It was manifestly clear that the Nazis didn't want a negotiated solution at all, and the Czechs were not about to abandon a bona fide treaty with a country that was looking like their only serious ally against an imminent Nazi invasion. This, however, merely fed into Henlein's previous characterization of the Czechs as pro-Soviet.

In the meantime, the Czechs were actively preparing to defend themselves: in the crowd near the border Morrell saw bespectacled soldiers—previously deemed ineligible to fight—and middle-aged legionaries from the First World War in three uniforms, French, Italian and Siberian. He saw the Czechs still building forts along the border, one every hundred yards. Runciman himself wrote to Halifax on August 10 that Prague displayed no signs of fear or nervousness: "the fabric here is of sterner stuff than was set up in Austria," and the British military attaché in Prague noted on August 22 that "the Czechoslovak General Staff had prepared the Army and the country for war in an almost masterly fashion. . . . Every civilian man and woman was ready to fight somehow." He praised the morale of the army and nation: "They would fight for their very existence and for the maintenance of independence." For their part, the Czechoslovak Officers' Association declared on August 12, "We can die but we can give way no more. Not one step, not one foot."

In these circumstances, it's perhaps not surprising that back at the Alcron, Runciman—whom Morrell always saw "in an old-fashioned dinner jacket and with unusually high colour"—was beginning, like Hitler, to suffer from insomnia. Unknown to most of the players at the time, Runciman was becoming aware of his ambiguous and ineffectual position. He wrote a letter to British foreign secretary Lord Halifax, from Prague on August 10:

> Where are we going? The answer can be given as
> well by you as by me. Success depends on whether
> or not the Führer wants to go to war. If he does the
> excuse will be found easily. In any case I can only
> continue my labours and hope for the best in good
> faith. It is a pathetic side of the present crisis that
> the common people here, and, I am told, elsewhere
> are looking to me and my mission as the only hope
> for an established peace. Alas, they do not realize

how weak are our sanctions, and I dread the
moment when they find that nothing can save
them. It will be a terrible disillusionment for them.

On August 18, he wrote to Halifax: "Insomnia is spoiling my
nights."

Runciman, and all around him, felt an oppressive sense of
countdown, although there was no reason in the world why matters
between the German minority in Czechoslovakia and the Czechs
should not have taken however long it took to sort out step by step
through negotiation. But Hitler was dictating, amongst other things,
the timetable of panic. Throughout Europe, and indeed the world,
all were aware that the date of September 6 was looming, the start
of the huge annual weeklong Nazi Rally at Nuremberg, and a date
which Morrell underscored ominously in black in his diary. Hitler
was deliberately cranking up the atmosphere to fever pitch to suit
his own war aims, driven by his own pathological sense of time running out for him.

Hitler had practical reasons for wanting to go to war now:
because "our economic situation is such that we cannot hold out for
more than a few years" and because, as he saw it, "there is no outstanding personality in England or France" to oppose him. He had
been watching developments on this front in the West ever since he
came to power in 1933; and later he looked back at that early period
and said, "I was a little consoled when I made the acquaintance of
the utter blockheads whom the United States were pleased to send
as their representatives, and later by the apparition of Sir [Horace]
Rumbold, the Ambassador of Great Britain, wrapped permanently
in a haze of intoxication. . . . I recently had the occasion to point
out more than once the degree to which diplomats are estranged
from reality and their abysmal ignorance of political affairs."

Runciman's letter of August 18 was an admission from the
horse's mouth of just how true this was. The future of the country
that was Czechoslovakia, built up with hard work, thoughtfulness

and good faith (with its ordinary quota of failings), was now being passed around like a hot coal in the hands of inept diplomats tied to a makeshift policy conceived in bad faith and adapting day by day to whichever way the German wind was blowing. There were many brave people who saw this and tried to turn the tide of events. They included Social Democrat "Sudeten German" politicians like Wenzel Jasch and Ludwig Czech, as well as German generals who, appalled at Hitler's plans to attack Czechoslovakia, were plotting a coup against him. One of them was Ewald von Kleist-Schmenzin, a forty-eight-year-old Prussian landowner (and descendant of the poet Kleist), who risked his life to come over to England and alert the British government to the fact that Hitler was planning an annihilating war, starting with Czechoslovakia. He managed to get to London, and on August 19, a day after Runciman was writing of his insomnia, he visited Winston Churchill, then working at the Admiralty.

Von Kleist told Churchill that an attack on Czechoslovakia was imminent and would most likely occur between the Nuremberg Conference and the end of September. He said there was nobody in Germany who wanted war except Hitler, who regarded the events of May 21 as a personal rebuff whose memory he must obliterate. Even Hermann Göring, though he would not say a word against war, was not keen on it. The generals were for peace and von Kleist believed that if they could receive a little encouragement they might refuse to march. Churchill said that though many people in England were not prepared to say in cold blood that they would march for Czechoslovakia, there would be few who would wish to stand idly by once the fighting started. He pointed out that the successive Nazi coups had hardened public opinion in Britain.

Von Kleist suggested that some gesture was needed to crystallize the widespread antiwar sentiment in Germany, and particularly to encourage the generals, who alone had the power to stop war. He wondered whether members of Parliament could appeal to the peaceful elements in Germany to assert themselves without delay.

He was convinced that in the event of the generals deciding to insist on peace, there would be a new system of government within forty-eight hours.

Von Kleist also took his message to Robert Vansittart at the Foreign Office, telling him that

> if Hitler carries the day and plunges his country into war he [Kleist] will anyhow be one of the first to be killed, and that he has anyhow come out of the country with a rope round his neck to stake his last chance of life on preventing the adventure. . . . He added that there was no prospect whatever of any reasonable policy being followed by Germany so long as Hitler was at the head of affairs but that he believed that if war was avoided on this occasion as it had been in May, it would be the prelude to the end of the régime and a renascence of a Germany with whom the world could deal.

Vansittart reported his conversation with Von Kleist back to Chamberlain, who passed it on to his new foreign secretary, Lord Halifax, adding: "I take it that Von Kleist is violently anti-Hitler and is extremely anxious to stir up his friends in Germany to make an attempt at its overthrow. . . . Nevertheless I confess to some feeling of uneasiness and I don't feel sure that we ought not to do something." He asked Halifax to get the British ambassador in Berlin, Sir Nevile Henderson, "to comment on it and tell him that we are sufficiently impressed to be inclined to make some warning gesture." The warning gesture would turn out to be an impulsive flight to see Hitler at Berchtesgaden three weeks later.

Once the war he had tried so hard to avert had broken out, von Kleist remained in touch with the continuing plots by German officers to assassinate Hitler, and his son, Lieutenant Heinrich von Kleist, offered himself as a human suicide bomb in early 1944 to kill Hitler. After Claus von Stauffenberg's attempt on Hitler's life on July 20, 1944, Ewald von Kleist was arrested, tried, and beheaded by the Nazis in April 1945, a month before the end of the war.

The British government had kept the decision over what to do about the German officer's desperate plea within the inner triangle of Chamberlain, Halifax and Sir Nevile Henderson—all "appeasers." Henderson's perverse response to von Kleist's appeal was to urge the press to stress the peaceful, benign nature of Hitler:

> I do wish it might be possible to get at any rate *The Times,* Camrose, Beaverbrook Press etc. to write up Hitler as the apostle of peace.... I do feel that it will be a mistake to flatter Benes too much. But give Hitler as much credit as possible. The last word is his. We make a great mistake when our Press persists in abusing him. Let it abuse his evil advisers but give him a chance of being a good boy.

That evening, Henderson went off to the Nuremberg Rally, which was about to give everyone the opportunity to see the "good boy" in his true colors. Henderson in particular, though, remained willfully color-blind.

The eyes of the world were on the Nuremberg Rally, as Hitler intended them to be. It took place in Berlin from September 6 to 13. On the first day Henlein finally came out into the open, flatly refusing Beneš's offer of full autonomy for the Sudeten Germans and severing relations with the Czechoslovak government. As one British member of the negotiating team at Munich, William Strang, would later ruefully admit: "Henlein threw off his mask in the first half of September 1938" and the whole business of demands for autonomy for the Sudetens was shown to be "a cynical farce and a highly successful one." The Czech government now issued Henlein with a warrant for treason, and on September 7 he fled with his family *heim ins Reich*—finally laying his cards on the table. He still kept directing events from across the border. Henleinists smuggled arms into Czechoslovakia, planted agitators and SS troops along the border, and from now until October 1 began to launch terroristic raids on Czechoslovakia with his newly formed paramilitary organization. In Czechoslovakia, the SDP rallies continued, now attended by Italian Fascist journalists as well, as Sydney Morrell saw on the ground. He also noted that the German journalists had begun to go undercover—a bad sign, he thought, as he'd seen them do the same before the Austrian *Anschluss*. The newspapers began to be censored, and people were glued to their radios to try to glean news.

Beneš broadcast to the nation on Saturday, September 10, in an attempt to reassure the population. Loudspeakers were hung from trees in Wenceslas Square, trams stopped and passengers jumped out to listen to what he was saying. "All Prague stood still," Morrell writes. Beneš spoke first—very gently, Morrell says, in Czech, and then in bad German, speaking directly to "his" Germans as *teuere Mitbürger,* dear co-citizens. If the problems over nationalities are settled, he said, the state "will be one of the most beautiful, best administered, richest and most equitable in the world." Once again, though, Hitler took his cue from the Czechs and turned it against them: on September 12, he broadcast to the Sudeten Germans from a radio station in Breslau in Silesia which he'd had adapted to reach them. The speech was also broadcast to millions throughout Europe. Hitler was announced portentously: *"Der Führer hat das Wort*—The Führer has the platform." Hitler brought in his heavy verbal artillery, slamming his old bugbears, democracy and the Jewish people. He sneered at democracies, saying that only two nations in the world were supported by 99 percent of their people— Germany and Italy. He poured contempt on England for hypocrisy in condemning the bombing of Abyssinia whilst bombing the Arabs of Palestine. Now, he said, the great German people were exposed to threats and ill treatment: "I am speaking of Czechoslovakia."

Seven million Czechs were torturing 3.5 million Germans, wanting to annihilate them and handing them over to a slow process of extermination, pursuing them like wild beasts for wearing white stockings or using the salute which was agreeable to them. "I am not," he said, "willing to allow a second Palestine to be created here in the heart of Germany by the actions of other statesmen."

The American journalist William L. Shirer heard this speech from Sydney and Mary Morrell's apartment overlooking Wilson Station, and wrote in his diary: "I have never heard the Adolf quite so full of hate, his audience quite so on the borders of bedlam. What poison in his voice when at the beginning of his long recital of alleged wrongs done to the Sudeteners he paused: '*Ich sprech von der Czechoslovakei!*' His words, his tone, dripping with venom."

Now, winding himself up to a frenzy (he claimed to lose between four and seven pounds in weight when he gave a speech), Hitler threw down the gauntlet to Beneš: "Here I stand and over there stands he. Things must be decided between us." This speech served as the signal for a carefully planned revolt. The crowd began to sing the Horst Wessel song, banned in Czechoslovakia, to parade swastikas—also banned—to smash the windows of Jewish and Czech shops, attack customs and gendarmerie posts, assault German democrats and shoot policemen. The following day, the Czechs imposed martial law in many districts.

Nevile Henderson meanwhile had been to "supper in the SS camp with Himmler":

> Unfortunately I did not get an opportunity to talk politics. He [Himmler] was however very friendly as were all the Germans at Nuremberg with me. Were they thinking to pull wool over my eyes, to detach Great Britain from interference in Czechoslovakia?
>
> Anyway I spent a great deal of my time even with the humblest replying to the constant resent-

ful enquiries as to why we were butting in and
what interests England had there? Very few really
could understand that it was exactly because we
had no interests there and could therefore best keep
the peace that we were playing the ungrateful role
of honest broker.

"Honest broker" was a good, catchall phrase. Henderson's reluctance, even though he was the ambassador in Berlin at such a time,
"to talk politics" with the German leader made it easy for Hitler to
get away with not revealing anything about his plans. He withheld
his speech about Czechoslovakia until the end of the week, milking
the dramatic tension and getting his acolytes to do the preparatory
dirty work for him. Joseph Goebbels—with a particular eye, as
Morrell had said, to England—warned that "the trend of developments in Czechoslovakia is particularly menacing. . . . Prague rep-
resents the organizing centre of Bolshevik plots against Europe."
And Göring, in a mad speech that targeted British snobbery and
anti-Semitism, ranted that

> We know how intolerable it is that that little frag-
> ment of a nation down there—goodness knows
> where it hails from—should persistently oppress
> and interfere with a highly civilized people. But
> we know that it is not these absurd pygmies who
> are responsible: Moscow and the eternal Jewish-
> Bolshevik rabble are behind it.

A measure of the way the eyes of the world were on Hitler at
Nuremberg is the fact that throughout September 1938 nearly all
the editorials in *The Times* of London—an influential organ at the
time—dealt with the issue between him and the Czechs. There was
no doubt in anyone's mind how critical an issue it had become for
European peace, and Nazi propaganda had led people to expect and

dread some pronouncement by Hitler on the issue at the Nuremberg Rally. On the fourth day of the rally, September 10, the *Times* editorial says of Germany's allegations over Sudeten border incidents that it is "not understood in this country why such incidents should have been given so much prominence and exaggeration in the German Press" and that "an attempt to effect a settlement by force would be universally condemned." The following day the paper is more forthright, speaking of Hitler's "hazardous talent for dramatizing politics" and "an atmosphere of indescribable tension" at Nuremberg:

> At moments, fanned by the oratory of fanatics, it has clearly reached the point almost of delirium. The Führer has the reputation of responding instinctively to emotions which he himself has been mainly responsible for creating. . . . He can hardly fail to have in his mind that larger audience which, in Germany no less than other countries, sees no occasion whatever for hostilities over the difference between Sudeten and Czech, and profoundly believes that war cannot settle the problem and must inevitably bring ruin, in lesser or greater degree, to all who become involved in it. So far from providing a settlement it could only bring an intensification of all the disasters of Armageddon, from which we are now partially and slowly recovering. . . .
>
> President Benesh's [sic] broadcast on Saturday was a model of what a public utterance should be at such a time of critical suspense. . . . In contrast Göring delivered on the same day at Nuremberg the very pattern of the wrong approach to an international dispute; and it is discouraging for the victory of common sense that it apparently roused his

audience to a frenzy of enthusiasm. Its tone was an echo of the Prussianism which, between the beginning of the century and 1918, ended by uniting almost the whole world against Germany—and the world is much more ready today to recognise and resist an act of lawlessness than it was in 1914. [Ironic, especially since *The Times* itself would play a role in failing to resist an act of lawlessness.] The speech was boastful and it was ill-tempered. It sneered at Great Britain, it reviled democracy, it referred with vulgar contumely to the courteous antagonist of Germany in the present racial dispute. It was in fact the speech of a bully. . . .

Two days after that, an editorial reports how Herr Hitler

spoke of "seven million Czechs torturing three and a half million Germans," an absurd perversion of the truth which can hardly have deceived his own docile, devoted audience. He even exclaimed that there was a desire to annihilate them. It is lamentable indeed that the head of a great country should talk such nonsense.

Here was some plain speaking. But then, on the fifteenth, under the headline:

DRAMATIC BRITISH MOVE FOR PEACE

comes

MR CHAMBERLAIN TO CONFER WITH HERR HITLER
FLYING TO GERMANY TODAY

—and suddenly the tack begins to change. The *Times*'s editor Geoffrey Dawson looks to have been nobbled—and hobbled. "A Cordial Welcome from the Fuhrer" and "A Bold Initiative," the headlines run, over articles reporting the warm reception the prime minister received not only from Hitler but also from masses of cheering Germans—reflecting von Kleist's and the generals' contention that the mass of German people did not want war. By the twentieth there is a more marked change of tone: *The Times* advocates that Czechoslovakia cede those parts which are predominantly German in order "to make it stronger, more homogeneous"; and by the twenty-second, Geoffrey Dawson is writing his infamous leader saying, "There is nothing sacrosanct about the present frontiers of Czechoslovakia. They were drawn twenty years ago; and they were drawn wrongly in the opinion of many well qualified to judge."

From so authoritative a voice, this was the death knell for Czechoslovakia. Thirty years later, in 1968, *The Times*'s current editor honorably recanted, acknowledging that

> Britain should not have taken up the General's [Mason MacFarlane's] idea [of killing Hitler] but should have done something much more substantial in 1938. It should, against the advice of this newspaper at the time, have stood firm at Munich. That would really have affected history.

"SMALL FRY"

As it was, Chamberlain had seized the ball out of everyone else's hands—even those of the otherwise judicious *Times*—and run with it, and because of the boldness of the move and the severity of the crisis, everyone assumed that he was aiming in the right direction and could deliver. Chamberlain's decision to fly over and see Hitler personally had been taken unilaterally, in a smokescreen of secrecy, not consulting his ally France, not consulting his electorate, and only telling his cabinet one day before the meeting. Above all, he did not consult Czechoslovakia, the most affected party. In his defense, at least Chamberlain was trying to confront Hitler face-to-face with what he was up to in Czechoslovakia, something his ambassador and Hitler's own Foreign Office had signally failed to do. Also in his defense, the sixty-nine-year-old Chamberlain had a mortal fear of flying and had never been in an airplane before, so flying to see Hitler was an act of bravery on his part. However, he went with so little strategy or historical understanding, in such a defeatist spirit and with so many accumulated articles of bad faith, that it was inevitable he would be wrongfooted by a manipulative dictator with a predetermined plan.

He was outmaneuvered from the beginning, when Hitler—who

thought Chamberlain was coming to declare war—made the prime minister come to Berchtesgaden, the farthest point in Germany from England, to meet him. Then, whilst Chamberlain was still in the air, Henlein (now openly Hitler's mouthpiece) announced on the radio that the Sudetens wanted nothing less than annexation, *Anschluss,* with the Reich. Chamberlain hadn't even taken the precaution of providing his own interpreter, or anyone to take notes—and was then indignant when Hitler subsequently refused to send a record of the meeting. The record therefore relies on Chamberlain's memory of the conversation, and the notes of Hitler's interpreter.

When they met in Berchtesgaden on September 15, 1938, Hitler told Chamberlain that "it was impossible that Czechoslovakia should remain like a spearhead in the side of Germany." Chamberlain recounts:

> So I said "Hold on a minute; there is one point on which I want to be clear . . . you say that the three million Germans must be included in the Reich; would you be satisfied with that and is there nothing more that you want? I ask because there are many people who think that is not all; that you wish to dismember Czechoslovakia." He then launched into a long speech: he was out for a racial unity and he did not want a lot of Czechs, all he wanted was Sudeten Germans.

Soon, though, as Hitler got the measure of his opponent and what he wanted, he began to get impatient and put his cards more clearly on the table:

> . . . but all this seems to be academic; I want to get down to the realities. Three hundred Sudetens have been killed [an untrue statement which Chamberlain hadn't verified] and things of that kind cannot

go on: the thing has got to be settled at once: I am
determined to settle it. I do not care whether there
is a world war or not: I am determined to settle it
soon and I am prepared to risk a world war than
[sic] allow this to drag on.

   To that I replied "If the Führer is determined to
settle this matter by force without waiting even for
a discussion between ourselves to take place what
did he let me come here for?"

By the end of the discussion Chamberlain had already made the
one concession Hitler needed, and which would lead to Munich. He
told Hitler that "on principle I had nothing against the separation of
the Sudeten Germans from the rest of Czechoslovakia provided that
the practical difficulties could be overcome." In practice, of course,
as opposed to "principle," Britain was not prepared militarily for
war at this point, as General Hastings Ismay, Britain's chief of
Imperial Defence, pointed out to Chamberlain, suggesting that
Britain had to play for time. However, Czechoslovakia *was* prepared for war, with its thirty-five divisions against the Germans'
twenty-one, its high morale and its determination not to lose its territorial integrity. And Britain and France were honor-bound by
Chamberlain's earlier statement to the House of Commons in
March and by France's treaty to come to Czechoslovakia's aid.

   The cabinet, consulted at the last minute before Chamberlain's
flight, had on the whole approved the line the prime minister said he
would be taking with Hitler, although there were notable excep-
tions. The secretary of state for war, Leslie Hore-Belisha (who
introduced the "Belisha" beacon and was the only Jewish member
of the cabinet), told Chamberlain and the cabinet that all this was
"part of a relentless plan on the lines of *Mein Kampf*." The First
Lord of the Admiralty, Alfred Duff Cooper, said that "the choice
was not between war and plebiscite, but between war now and war
later." Once Chamberlain had returned from Berchtesgaden, it

became clear that the prime minister was capitulating to Hitler in spirit. He told his cabinet that "it was impossible not be impressed with the power of the man . . . the Prime Minister had formed the opinion that Herr Hitler's objectives were strictly limited . . . and that the impression left on him was that Herr Hitler was telling the truth . . . the Prime Minister said that Herr Hitler would prove to be better than his word."

Duff Cooper renewed his objections even more forcibly, along with Lord Winterton, who said that arguments in favor of accepting Hitler's demands to annex whole swaths of a sovereign country against its will could "equally be used to justify acquiescence in the invasion of Kent or the surrender of the Isle of Wight." This was a strong point of law and natural justice, but one ignored by people governing a country that had not been invaded in recent memory and whose sympathies couldn't stretch to imagining how such a thing might feel. As a retrospective spur to that kind of empathy, look at the two comparative maps on page 182. If you stand Czechoslovakia on its head, it happens to bear a passing resemblance to the outline of England, Scotland and Wales. The maps illustrate what would happen if a third of these countries were mauled in the way Chamberlain was preparing to allow Hitler to do. And the analogy would be that an ally like France or the United States had dictated this dismemberment, over the heads of the elected British government, and that there were no seas or viable frontiers protecting Britain from the hostile power which had taken over a third of its land.

Three days after Chamberlain had flown to Berchtesgaden, on September 18, the British and French governments came up with Anglo-French "proposals," allegedly based on Runciman's report. The French government, headed by Prime Minister Edouard Daladier, acceded reluctantly to these proposals after a stormy meeting with Chamberlain in Downing Street in which the French pointed out that it wasn't just the Sudetenland that Hitler was after, but that he was "aiming at something far greater." They were bulldozed,

Cannibalized Czechoslovakia compared
with similarly cannibalized England,
Scotland and Wales

however, by the fact that both the proposals and the report were hastily rigged to conform to the de facto concession Chamberlain had already made to Hitler without consulting his nominal ally. Henderson in Berlin wrote to Halifax on the nineteenth with a complacency even more shocking than before:

> In the circumstances fear and dislike of war have almost disappeared. Indeed in some circles the prospect of a punitive expedition against the Czechs seems to be looked forward to with pleasurable anticipation.

And on the twentieth:

> It's a sorry business but I would rather have local trouble between Czechs and Germans than a world war and that was the issue. It may be humiliating but it's better to keep the peace for a principle than to fight a war in opposition to one. . . . One is now waiting to hear when the Prime Minister will come to Godesberg and the nature of Benes's reply. Prevarication at least, I fear, if it is not open defiance. Much depends on how straight the French or we talk to him, for it is clear or was so in the last forty-eight hours, that he still clings to the hope of dragging us all down in his own ruin. Folly or resentment, perhaps both.

The British minister in Prague, Basil Newton, far closer to the reality of the situation, wrote to Halifax and told him exactly what Beneš's response was:

> President Benes was greatly moved and agitated. His first comment was that as his government had

not been consulted when questions of such deep concern to it had been discussed he did not propose to reply. He was moreover a constitutional President and must refer the matter to his Government and also, he said, to Parliament. . . . Speaking with self control but with bitterness he showed that he felt that, after all the efforts which he and his Government had made, they were being abandoned. . . . President Benes seemed to be wrestling with himself as to the attitude which should be adopted so I thought I might tell him that I realized that he was placed before a cruel decision. I knew the Czechs were a brave people and I did not think the sufferings and sacrifice which would be involved by war would greatly weigh with them but after the first immediate reaction, what should, and I hoped would, weigh with them was the future of their country. . . . Dr. Benes listened with attention but showed that he felt the guarantees which he already possessed had proved valueless. He said he did not believe the proposed solution would prove final or be anything more than a stage towards eventual domination by Germany and develop further German ambitions.

The next day, Newton transmitted to Halifax the text of Beneš's response and his government's formal reply:

1. Czech Government [the familiar lack of definite article!] are convinced Franco-British proposal cannot realize the object of peace.
2. Czech Government have not been consulted.
3. They cannot decide on a question of frontiers without consulting Parliament.

4. State would be mutilated in every respect.

5. Question of peace would not be resolved, because a) minority problem would again arise, and b) balance of power would be destroyed.

6. Czech Government appreciate offer of a guarantee which would open way to agreement if nationality problems were equitably settled.

7. These problems could still be settled on basis of Czech proposals.

8. Czech Government demand application of Treaty of Arbitration with Germany of 1926 and are ready to accept an arbitral award.

9. Czech Government address a final appeal to British and French Governments and beg them to reconsider their points of view.

The following day, Newton cabled Halifax with the reactions of Dr. Kamil Krofta, the Czech foreign minister: "Dr Krofta who was in considerable distress repeated nevertheless that Czech Government simply could not accept proposal and dismemberment of their country all at 48 hours notice." There was deep dejection over the Anglo-French proposals in Prague, where even the pessimists had not expected such a development. On the twenty-second, Chamberlain was due to leave to meet Hitler again, this time at Bad Godesberg on the Rhine in the west of Germany, and the British and French now put the utmost pressure on Beneš to accede to the demands, forcing his hand by saying that the prime minister would have to cancel his visit if Beneš did not agree. Showing how much they'd been infected by Hitler's manic pressurizing, and also by his insomniac dictator's trick of presenting categorical demands in the early hours, the British minister Newton and French minister M. de Lacroix drove from their legations to the Hradschin Palace at 3:00 a.m. on September 21 and demanded that the guard take them to Beneš at once. Morrell writes:

A secretary hurried in his dressing-gown to
Benes's bedroom and roused the sleeping president. Benes was tired, prematurely aged at fifty-
four, and suffering from severe nervous strain. He
went out to . . . face what he must have known was
at last inevitable.

Beneš himself said:

> The French Minister handed me the message of his
> government with tears in his eyes: he had every rea-
> son to weep over the end of a twenty-year-old pol-
> icy to which we had remained faithful unto death.
> What the British Minister felt at that moment I did
> not know. He was cool: while his French colleague
> spoke, he kept looking at the floor. I had the
> impression that both of them were ashamed to the
> bottom of their hearts of the mission they had to
> discharge in the name of their governments.

Both men insisted that Beneš's earlier reply was not enough; he
had to give either complete acceptance or complete refusal, for
Chamberlain needed to take a clear answer to Hitler at Bad Godesberg the next day. In the face of this dire, dictatorial ultimatum,
Beneš asked for time to consider the situation. He pointed out that
this was three o'clock in the morning on Wednesday. Chamberlain
wasn't due to fly to Godesberg until Thursday morning. Surely
there was time for him to sleep and call his cabinet later that morning, and send a reply to London before nightfall? But the two ministers were pitiless.

Realizing he had no option but to give in, Beneš summoned Premier Milan Hodža from his villa on the outskirts of Prague and five
members of the inner cabinet. This dismal meeting started at half
past three in the morning. For four hours, Morrell writes,

Beneš and his ministers went through Gethsemane.
France had abandoned them. France was following
England, and Chamberlain was determined to have
peace at the cost of every sacrifice which he could
force the Czechs to make. There was Russia, but
[one of the ministers] insisted it would take three
months for the Russian troops to find their way in
any numbers to the side of the Czechs. There was
the chance of fighting a war, to fight a withdrawing
action until they reached Moravia and there to dig
themselves in behind the High and the Low Tatras
mountain ranges, until Russian aid reached them.
But then came the news which shattered all hopes
of defence: Hungary and Poland, who had been
waiting all this time to see which way the wind was
blowing, took courage from the attitude of England and came out boldly on the side of Hitler. The
Poles were preparing to march into Teschen on the
east: the Hungarians into Slovakia and Ruthenia. In
their 1,400-mile frontiers, only about 80 miles bordered a state that was not hostile—Rumania.

In the background, the military leaders in Poland and Hungary's
Fascist government had been secretly approached by the Nazis and
offered tracts of Czechoslovakia to which Hitler knew they felt historically entitled in return for letting him break up the country.

The anguished meeting went on until dawn, when Hodža drove
from the palace to convene a meeting of representatives of the
coalition parties making up the government and put the ultimatum
before them. All the while Newton and Lacroix were pressing for
an answer. At 1:00 p.m. Beneš sat down with the full cabinet,
together with heads of the General Staff, communication experts,
and senior civil servants. At 3:30 p.m. Newton and Lacroix called
the Foreign Office insisting on a reply, and the Foreign Office min-

ister, Dr. Krofta, weary and dejected, gave it to them: complete unconditional acceptance. Morrell saw Premier Hodža—who would resign the next day—drive out from the Hradschin Palace drawn, slumped, not saluting the legionaries as they saluted him, followed by the other cabinet members. Crowds gathered, seeing the story from their faces. Soon Morrell saw that all kinds of processions were taking place, including the red flag, people shouting down with Hodža, away with Beneš, long live the army. A soldier cycling down a side street was lifted off his bike by the crowd and above their heads. Crowds gathered around the huge statue of Jan Hus in Old Town Square. A crowd massed up toward the Hradschin, making not for the office of the president but for the giant entrance to St. Vitus's cathedral, where the body of their patron saint and king, Václav, lay. But troops in the alleyway turned them back. It was past midnight and by now there were nearly half a million people on the streets. There were cries of long live the army as the procession moved along the riverbank and toward the Ministry of War. They swayed in front of it, cheering. They had struggled and saved to pay for the enormous military budget which the proximity of Hitler had forced on them year after year. Every day they had watched the growing strength of Germany, and had taken comfort in the thought of their fortifications along the frontier. The cheering rose, then suddenly from loudspeakers came the voice of Hugo Vavrecka, the newly appointed minister of propaganda, almost weeping as he spoke, yet trying to calm the crowds. Speaking from Prague Radio Station two miles away, he said:

> Our nation has experienced many a catastrophe in the course of history. It often appeared that our people would be wiped out, but they have always recovered, and times of humiliation were followed by times of evolution. Such a catastrophe is threatening the state and the nation today. You have heard that our allies and friends have dictated to us

sacrifices without parallel in history. But we are not defeated. If our government, with the President of the Republic at its head, had to decide to accept such cruel conditions, it was because they wished to spare the whole population useless bloodshed. [The ghost of Wenceslas appears . . .] It is not lack of courage that has prompted our leaders to make this decision which has stabbed us all straight to the heart. Often more courage is needed to live than to commit suicide. [The ghost of Masaryk, dead for only one year, appears . . .] In the whole world there cannot be any decent men who could say that we behaved as cowards when we authorized our Foreign Minister to tell France and Great Britain that we have decided to make this sacrifice for the sake of world peace. We shall not reproach those who have left us in the lurch. History will judge them. We face the future with our heads high.

In England, Winston Churchill—a simple member of Parliament without any cabinet responsibility—immediately published a declaration deploring his government's action, saying, "The partition of Czechoslovakia under pressure from England and France amounts to the complete surrender of the Western democracies to the Nazi threat of force. Such a collapse will bring peace or security neither to England nor to France. On the contrary, it will place those two nations in an ever weaker and even more dangerous situation."

Even Hitler himself was nonplussed by this easy victory. He later said, "I did not think it possible that Czechoslovakia would be virtually served up to me on a plate by her friends." They had simply handed over to him all the zones which were more than 50 percent ethnically German without plebiscite, together with all fortifications and war matériel there, so dismantling the whole western mountain border with Germany, and making it impossible for

Czechoslovakia to protect itself. But now this was no longer what Hitler wanted: his demands, as ever, had been to stir up unrest preparatory to war. So, when Chamberlain flew over to see him again on September 22 at Bad Godesberg—with German divisions already massing on the border with Czechoslovakia—Hitler raised the stakes again, to Chamberlain's astonishment. Hitler said, "Do I understand that the British, French and Czech governments have agreed to the transfer of the Sudetenland from Czechoslovakia to Germany?" "Yes," said a smiling Chamberlain, thinking he'd done just what was required. "I'm awfully sorry but that won't do anymore," said Hitler, "this solution is no longer of any use."

Chamberlain was stunned as Hitler put his new demands: German army occupation of the Sudetenland by October 1 and the expulsion of all non-Germans within the territories. Hitler now lectured him, saying that "Czechoslovakia was an artificial construction, which was called into being and was established solely on the grounds of political consideration." It was "a state which possessed neither a history nor tradition, nor, indeed, conditions of existence." It is at this point, above all, that Chamberlain and Great Britain betrayed Czechoslovakia, for in the face of this volte-face by Hitler, Chamberlain failed to challenge him—he didn't have the history to challenge him—as the record shows: "The Prime Minister said that he did not wish to dissent."

The unpleasant phrase "conditions of existence" might have rung warning bells for Chamberlain, as might Hitler's next reference to "the necessary surgical operation on Czechoslovakia." Hitler now said that he "fully realized that the Prime Minister and the British Government had done their best to perform the necessary surgical operation on Czechoslovakia in the most peaceful manner." Chamberlain, however, was merely "disappointed and puzzled" by Hitler's attitude; in doing what he'd done, Chamberlain said, he'd been "obliged to take his political life in his hands. . . . He had actually been booed on his departure today. Herr Hitler interjected that he had only been booed by the Left." Now

Hitler turned the screw on Chamberlain, softening him up and then staging a melodrama:

> Herr Hitler [said] that he personally would much prefer a good understanding with England to a good military strategic frontier with Czechoslovakia. The Prime Minister said that he would not get a good friendship with England if he resorted to force, but that he would if he agreed to achieve his aims by peaceful means. Herr Hitler said that the decisive element was speed, because whilst they were sitting there they were at the mercy of events, and an irreparable incident could occur at any minute. . . .
>
> If the Prime Minister knew the territory and the people as well as he did, he would agree that the idea of a conflict between Great Britain and Germany on account of such people was simply absurd.

At this point Hitler was interrupted by a messenger bringing a doom-laden announcement that "twelve Germans had been shot by the Czechs in Eger," which orchestrated incident gave Hitler the cue to repeat that "the essential element was speed. If Prague fell under Bolshevik influence, or if hostages continued to be shot, he would intervene militarily at once. It was an intolerable strain on his nerves to hold his hand in view of constant Czech provocation."

Hitler's nerves were an issue, though Chamberlain didn't spot it. William Shirer did, though, reporting from Bad Godesberg. He saw Hitler as he walked into the meeting: "Every few steps Hitler cocked his right shoulder nervously, his left leg snapping up as he did so. I watched him closely as he came back past us. The same nervous tic. He had ugly black patches under his eyes. I thought to myself: 'This is a man on the edge of a nervous breakdown.' "

The next day, the twenty-third, Chamberlain and Hitler had another conversation in which Hitler once more attempted to soften Chamberlain up through snobbery, then harass him with theatricals: "He, Mr Chamberlain, was an Englishman, and he, Herr Hitler, came from Nieder Sachsen, so that possibly they could in the distant past claim common ancestry." (Hitler was later reported to have said to colleagues: "The gift of command comes naturally to everyone in Lower Saxony. Wasn't it from there Great Britain got its ruling class?") Then von Ribbentrop came in and announced "in a portentous tone that M. Benes had ordered general mobilization." To his credit, Chamberlain now riposted that

> Hitler had placed one and a half million men under arms and had moved his tanks, his aeroplanes and his troops to their appropriate stations. In the circumstances it was not surprising that the Czechs felt themselves threatened. Herr Hitler might declare that he had no confidence in the Czechs, but the latter, in view of what had been done, could not be expected to have much confidence in Herr Hitler's intentions.

When he returned home later that day, Chamberlain noted that "the whole thing was in terms of dictation, not in terms of negotiation." Yet still "The Prime Minister believed that Herr Hitler was speaking the truth. He thought he had now established an influence over Herr Hitler and that the latter trusted him and was willing to work with him." However, Chamberlain told the House of Commons three days later what terms Hitler had demanded: immediate separation from Czechoslovakia of all the areas shaded on his map. "These were to be completely evacuated by Czech soldiers and officials and occupied by German troops by 1st October." By this time Masaryk's son, Jan, was serving as the Czech minister in London, and these proposals were put to him. He stated that the reply of the Czech government was "that they considered Herr Hitler's demands in their present form to be absolutely and unconditionally unacceptable." When the French ministers Daladier and G.-E. Bonnet were told this, they told Chamberlain they would fulfill their treaty obligations if Czechoslovakia were attacked, and the British government said, "we should feel obliged to support them."

As Hitler now announced that he was going to invade Czechoslovakia on September 28, France mobilized one hundred army divisions, and England put the entire Royal Navy (under Duff Cooper) on alert and declared a state of emergency in London. In Czechoslovakia, morale rose: for the second time (after May 21), the popular response to the call for mobilization was enthusiastic, with 1 million soldiers deployed by September 28. All the main roads were mined and blocked, and a total blackout covered the country. "Some of the foreign correspondents," Morrell says, "took rooms on the outskirts of Prague to be able to sleep without tension and without the awful feeling of being completely alone that the blackouts give you." For seven days, from the Bad Godesberg meeting on September 22–23 to the end of the Munich Conference on the thirtieth, Czechoslovakia was geared up to defend itself, supported by Britain and France—seven days which could have preempted the Nazi push east.

For the first time, it looked as if Beneš's policy of giving Hitler the rope to hang himself—allowing him to go so far in his demands that he would show the Allies his true colors—was paying off. Even more so since Hitler now had a sudden, unexpected reverse. Seeking to rouse popular support for war with a march-past of one of his army divisions in Berlin, he stood on the balcony of the Reich Chancellery reviewing the troops and saw to his dismay how few people had turned out to watch, and how many were turning away from the parade or ducking into nearby shops and subway entrances to avoid it. The German people, he could see, didn't want another war. Meanwhile, unknown to him, plans were being put in place by his generals to have Hitler arrested for treason in Berlin the moment he gave the order to invade Czechoslovakia. Hitler's chief of staff of the army, General Ludwig Beck, the most dedicated of the senior staff against Hitler, had resigned at the end of August, and was on hand to help the German officers secretly in their high-risk plot. Even diplomats of the German Foreign Office under the secretary of state, Baron Ernst von Weizsäcker, were involved. "Every possible opportunity was taken," writes the historian Patricia Meehan, "to inform and warn their opposite numbers in Britain" of Hitler's warmongering plans and of high-ranking German opposition to them.

Suddenly there was strong opposition to Hitler from several sides. Hungary, it was true, stood ready to invade Czechoslovakia in its own interests, but on the other side of Hungary was Yugoslavia, pledged and ready to come to the aid of the Czechs; Poland was ready to try to reoccupy Teschen in northern Moravia, but on the other side of Poland was Russia, pledged and ready to come to Czechoslovakia's aid once France had stood by its pact. All of a sudden, with the Allies, Czechoslovakia, Yugoslavia, Russia, his own generals, Foreign Office officials, and a large part of his own people standing against him, Hitler was potentially outmaneuvered. Some of this he didn't know about: it was above all the lack of war readiness of his Berliners which now persuaded him to step back from the brink. And so on the twenty-seventh he wrote to Chamberlain assuring the Western Allies that if they yielded the Sudetenland, it would not result in the destruction of Czechoslovakia, and "he would even be glad to join with England and France in guaranteeing the rest of Czechoslovakia from further aggression."

All this was—with hindsight—shockingly scuppered by Chamberlain making the wrong move at the wrong time. Chamberlain replied to Hitler—in what he called "one more last letter—the last last"—and read it out to the House of Commons just before setting off for Munich on September 28:

After reading your letter I feel certain that you can
get all essentials without war and without delay. I
am ready to come to Berlin myself at once to discuss arrangements for transfer with you and representatives of the Czech government, together with
representatives of France and Italy, if you desire. I
feel convinced that we could reach agreement
within a week.... I cannot believe that you will
take the responsibility of starting a world war
which may end civilisation, for the sake of a few
days' delay in settling this long-standing problem.

At the end of his speech, Chamberlain makes an important
omission. He says, "I have now been informed by Herr Hitler that
he invited me to meet him at Munich tomorrow morning. He has
also invited Signor Mussolini and M. Daladier." In the flurry of
congratulation in the House, no one seemed to notice that the Czech
government had suddenly been dropped. In fact, although Chamberlain presented himself as the moving force behind these "negotiations" with Hitler, it was the Italian ambassador, Count Grandi,
who had taken a key role in persuading Hitler to the negotiating
table. Halifax reported that the Italian ambassador in London
"would not conceal from me that, although the Italian nation would
do whatever Signor Mussolini told them, the idea of war, and particularly, perhaps, war by the side of Germany, was unpopular. We
had, however, constantly to have regard to the mentality of dictators. It was very difficult for us here to understand it. It was nearly
all the time a problem of psychology."

In Prague that same day, Morrell turned on the radio to hear
Chamberlain broadcast to the nation, and picked up on his ambivalence:

Somehow it clashed with all the other news
about preparations for war. It was not a war

speech ... when a Prime Minister is going to lead
his country into war he does not say how horrible it
is to be dragged into a war "because of a quarrel in
a faraway country between people of whom we
know nothing." You bang the drum and blow the
trumpet in a million subtle ways. You talk about
saving democracy and a war to end tyranny. But
Chamberlain did not do so. He went on: "However
much we may sympathize with a small nation confronted by a big powerful neighbour, we cannot in
all circumstances undertake to involve the whole
British Empire in a war simply on her account. If
we have to fight it must be on larger issues than
that ... I am myself a man of peace to the depths of
my soul. Armed conflict between nations is a nightmare to me, but if I were convinced that any nation
had made up its mind to dominate the world by fear
of its force, I should feel it must be resisted."

And so it was that Chamberlain flew out to Munich on September 29. The day before, the British representative in Prague, Basil
Newton, had written to Halifax:

The President [Beneš] telephoned me at 7.30 p.m.
and said that he had heard there was to be a conference of four powers at Munich tomorrow. He
accordingly asked me to convey the following personal message from himself to Mr Chamberlain:
    "I beg Mr Chamberlain to do nothing at
    Munich which could put Czechoslovakia in
    a worse situation than under Anglo-French
    proposals. . . . Poland is now beginning to
    deliver threats and has given a kind of
    ultimatum to take effect by next Friday.

The people will be driven to desperation by such treatment. I ask Mr Chamberlain very earnestly for help because it is our real desire to contribute to peace. I beg therefore that nothing may be done at Munich without Czechoslovakia being heard. It is a most terrible thing for her if negotiations take place without her being given an opportunity to state her case."

Chamberlain, wrote Compton Mackenzie shortly after the war, "replied to the appeal of the President like a complacent schoolmaster. . . . Mr Chamberlain was completely unaware of putting the slightest strain on Czechoslovak goodwill. He was like an irritable surgeon who tells a patient not to fidget when he is probing with his knife. He was as little distressed by the spectacle of a small State gasping out its life as he would have been by the sight of a salmon safely gaffed."

Czechoslovakia never was given the opportunity to state its case. The head of the Central European Department at the Foreign Office, William Strang, who was with the British delegation, and (belatedly) critical of Chamberlain's conduct of foreign affairs as inadequate and naive, wrote: "The Munich Conference was a hugger-mugger affair." Once again there were no formal arrangements for note-taking. It was left to Sir Horace Wilson, accompanying Chamberlain as his chief adviser, to write a brief account of the meeting from memory. He admitted that the lack of notes was "only one unit in the chaos that ruled for the last five hours." Present were Chamberlain, Wilson, from France Daladier and his deputy Alexis Léger, from Italy Benito Mussolini and his foreign minister (and son-in-law) Count Ciano, and Hitler, von Ribbentrop and the diplomat von Weiszäcker from the Ministry of Foreign Affairs (who would prove to have been a moderating force on Hitler; and whose son would be Germany's president from 1984 to 1994). There was a

German interpreter, Herr Schmidt. A small Czech delegation led by the Czech foreign minister to Berlin, Dr. Vojtěch Mastný, arrived in Munich to a reception at the aerodrome which was "roughly that accorded to police suspects," as one of them wrote.

They were driven by police car to the Hotel Regina, where the British delegation was also staying, only to find that the conference had been under way for some four hours and they were not invited or able to contribute or communicate. The foreign delegations were swept into the "Führer House" and the meeting began at 12:30 p.m. on September 29.

Chamberlain raised the question of Hitler's demand that the Czech evacuation should be completed by October 10 "without existing installations having been destroyed," saying he had had no opportunity to consult with the Czechs on this point.

> This led to a tirade from Herr Hitler (who was oth-
> erwise calm throughout most of the Conference),
> his line being that if—having asked him to stay his
> hand—we were not prepared to take the responsi-
> bility of ensuring the concurrence of Czechoslova-
> kia we had better let him resume his way! He
> was, in due course, soothed. . . . In the course of [a
> subsequent] discussion the Prime Minister raised
> the question of the representation at the Confer-
> ence of the Czech Government. The conclusion
> was reached that the heads of the four Powers
> must accept responsibility for deciding—in the
> circumstances—how the situation should be dealt
> with.

So much for a nation's sovereignty, for international law, for treaties of support. After an interval for lunch—during which the French delegation failed to turn up to consult with the British as arranged—the conference was hurried through the conditions Hitler stipulated. The Allies tried to insert a clause for debate about financial issues resulting from the transfer of territory, but were told later that "it had been lost." There were "many tedious waits," and "after very long delays due to inefficient organisation and lack of control, the Agreement . . . was signed a little before 2 a.m. on the 30th September and the proceedings concluded by brief expressions of satisfaction." On one point, though, everyone was evasive: how to tell the Czechs. No one wanted to confront Beneš. Chamberlain and Daladier agreed to speak with Mastný, the Czech foreign minister still sitting in the hotel room, and "he was given a pretty broad hint that—having regard to the seriousness of the alternative—the best course was for his Government to accept what was clearly a considerable improvement upon the German Memorandum." The considerable improvement was that the occupation of Czech territory would take place "in stages," from October 1 to October 10, and that Hitler made the "concession" of occupying 11,500 square miles of territory instead of 12,000. Chamberlain's adviser William Strang, exculpating himself later, wrote:

> To the professional diplomatist accustomed to the decencies of international life, the Munich Conference was a distressing event. . . . What was disturbing was that, at an international conference, four Powers should have discussed and taken decisions upon the cession to one of them of vital territory belonging to a fifth State, without giving a hearing to the government of that State. The decision, after it had been reached, was merely communicated at the dead of night to representatives of the government concerned by two of the participants in the conference, for immediate acceptance under brutal duress from the beneficiary.

The following day, Chamberlain had a conversation with Hitler in his flat in Munich, which the German interpreter Herr Schmidt recorded:

> *Prime Minister:* He was very pleased at the result of yesterday's proceedings, and he hoped that Herr Hitler was equally happy.
>
> *Herr Hitler:* He was particularly happy, especially that the hopes of many millions of Germans had now been fulfilled. . . . Their sufferings had indeed been terrible. . . .
>
> *Prime Minister:* . . . he was obliged to consider the possibility that the Czech Government might be mad enough to refuse the terms and attempt resistance. In such an eventuality he wanted to ask Herr Hitler to make sure that nothing should be done which would diminish the high opinion of him which would be held throughout the world in consequence of yesterday's proceedings. In particular, he trusted that there would be no bombardment of Prague or killing of women and children by attacks from the air.
>
> *Herr Hitler:* Before answering the specific question, he would like to say something on a point of principle. Years ago he made proposals for the restriction of the use of the air arm. He himself fought in the Great War and has a personal knowledge of what air bombardment means . . . even if the Czechs were mad enough to reject the terms and he had consequently to take forcible action, he would always try to spare the civilian population and to confine himself to military objectives. He hated the thought of little babies being killed by gas bombs.

Again Hitler runs rings around Chamberlain—"small fry," he would later call these men of Munich—ending up with this po-faced piece of false sentimentality worthy of a pantomime villain. Chamberlain took it all at face value, and now turned to other issues: a possible truce in Spain, armament restriction, international trade, and Anglo-German relations. With this last in mind, he had drafted an agreement on the desirability of better Anglo-German relations, leading to "greater European stability." Would Herr Hitler sign it? As Chamberlain spoke, Hitler "ejaculated at intervals '*Ja! Ja!*' " and immediately agreed to sign the document, the core of which ran:

> We, the German Führer and Chancellor and the British Prime Minister . . . regard the agreement signed last night and the Anglo-German Naval Agreement as symbolic of the desire of our two peoples never to go to war with one another again.

This, which Chamberlain would vaunt as a major concession from Hitler, was of course laughably easy for Hitler to agree to, especially as England was not as yet on his hit list. The Munich Conference had lasted eight hours. Morrell wrote:

> and in those eight hours four statesmen, sitting in armchairs in the Führergebau at Munich's Königsplatz, transferred to Germany three million Sudeten Germans and nearly eight hundred thousand Czechs, with their homes, killed the best democracy in Europe, and poisoned all respect for England among the small nations of the world. These are not pleasant things for an Englishman to write but I think that other Englishmen who don't realise these things should understand that England lost far more than the Czechs at Munich.

12 "A NICE QUIET SLEEP"

I t fell to General Jan Sirový, head of the Czechoslovak armed forces, to give the news out on the radio "in his harsh soldier's voice." Morrell writes:

> Crowd scenes in Prague after the Berchtesgaden Plan were nothing in their complete despair compared to the scenes in Prague that night. I have never before seen people walking blindly along the pavements with tears streaming along their faces; I have never seen crowds, furious with a helpless fury, arguing with policemen to join them instead of obstructing them . . . now this same soldier-premier had accepted even worse conditions—and there was no-one else to whom they could turn. They were a lost people.

Then Minister of Propaganda Hugo Vavrecka took the microphone, saying in a "grief-stricken voice":

We had to consider that it would have taken the Russian army weeks to come to our aid—perhaps too late, for by that time millions of our men, women and children would have been slaughtered. It was even more important to consider that our war by the side of Soviet Russia would have been not only a fight against Germany, but interpreted as a fight on the side of Bolshevism. And then perhaps all of Europe would have been drawn into the war against us and Russia.

On September 30, the Czech party leaders and cabinet met, and received the ministers of France, Great Britain and Italy. Without letting them speak, Foreign Minister Kamil Krofta told them: "The President and the Government submit to the conditions of the Munich Agreement which has come into being without Czechoslovakia and against her." The French minister Lacroix attempted to express condolence, but was cut short by Krofta: "We have been forced into this situation; now everything is at an end; today it is our turn, tomorrow it will be the turn of others."

Prime Minister Beneš then broadcast the news to the nation at 5:00 p.m.:

We have had to choose between making a desperate and hopeless defence, which would have meant the sacrifice of an entire generation of our adult men [again the ghost of St. Wenceslas], as well as of our women and children, and accepting, without a struggle and under pressure, terms which are without parallel in history for their ruthlessness. . . .

We were deserted. We stood alone. . . . It is our sacred duty to preserve the lives of our people, in order that it may not emerge weakened from this age of terror, and in order that we may not be obliged to abandon our belief that our nation will rise again, as it has done so often in the past.

The German Social Democrats, who had fought against Henlein and by the side of their co-citizens the Czechs in the Sudetenland, and who would be the first to bear the practical brunt of Munich, sent out a message:

> with admiration we do homage in this hour to the small Czech nation which has to bear the same blows of fate as we do. May it, when this ordeal is over, go forward to happier days. The task of collaboration between the nationalities will remain vital in central Europe. From the depths of our hearts we wish that it may yet be crowned by a successful conclusion.

As for Chamberlain, he returned to his hotel after Munich, sat down to lunch, and "complacently patted his breast-pocket and said: 'I've got it!,' " as William Strang, who was there, records. Strang continues:

> It was clear from Daladier's demeanour at the London talks in September and at Munich that he felt deep shame at the course of action which he found himself constrained to follow; and he was much surprised, on his return to Paris from Munich, to be greeted by popular acclaim instead of by hostile demonstrations. It is doubtful whether Mr Chamberlain shared these qualms.

Chamberlain didn't appear to share these qualms and famously—infamously—stepped off the plane triumphantly waving his piece of paper signed by himself and Hitler. Yet the slightly curdled expression on his face as he read the joint statement on the steps of Downing Street showed a bridled unease. He concluded:

> My good friends, for the second time in our history, a British Prime Minister has returned from Germany bringing peace with honour. I believe it is peace for our time . . .
>
> Go home and get a nice quiet sleep.

By the time Chamberlain came to report to Parliament on the Munich Agreement on October 3, Hitler's armies had begun marching into Czechoslovakia, and Chamberlain's tone was more defensive:

> Before giving a verdict upon this arrangement, we should do well to avoid describing it as a personal or a national triumph for anyone. The real triumph is that it has shown that representatives of four great Powers can find it possible to agree on a way of carrying out a difficult and delicate operation by discussion instead of by force of arms, and thereby they have averted a catastrophe which would have ended civilisation as we have known it. The relief at our escape from this great peril of war has, I think, everywhere been mingled in this country with a profound feeling of sympathy.

At this point some MPs shouted "Shame!" and Chamberlain countered:

I have nothing to be ashamed of. Let those who
have, hang their heads. We must feel profound
sympathy for a small and gallant nation in the hour
of their national grief and loss.

Mr Bellenger (MP): It is an insult to say it.

The Prime Minister: I say in the name of this House
and of the people of this country that Czechoslovakia has earned our admiration and respect for her
restraint, for her dignity, for her magnificent discipline in face of such a trial as few nations have ever
been called upon to meet.

The army, whose courage no man has ever
questioned, has obeyed the order of their president,
as they would equally have obeyed him if he had
told them to march into the trenches. It is my hope
and my belief, that under the new system of guarantees, the new Czechoslovakia will find a greater
security than she has ever enjoyed in the past. . . .

Two days later, the first fruit of this greater security was that
Beneš, the philosopher, the inheritor of the mantle of Masaryk, the
democrat, was forced to resign by the Nazis. Beneš's share of the
responsibility is held to be that he failed to take more initiatives
whilst he had the moral, political and strategic advantage, and
failed to make any energetic propaganda effort to counteract false
Nazi propaganda. But, as Radomír Luža writes: "President Beneš,
despite all his weaknesses, remained a towering figure beside the
Chamberlains, Horthys [Hungary's dictator], Bonnets [French foreign minister], Becks [Polish foreign minister] . . . with their political cynicism and ignorance."

Beneš was visited on the day of Munich by representatives of all
parties and of the army, trying to persuade him to allow Czechoslovakia to fight unilaterally. To one of them, Beneš replied:

It was not Hitler who defeated us but our friends. . . . In spite of everything . . . I believe in the ideals of democracy and humanity. True, in many ways, I have been disappointed. I have been wrong. I have now come to realize that the big powers and great nations, even in the present times, do not consider small states and small nations. They treat them as they find it convenient at the moment. . . . It is a hard decision, to accept the conditions and save the country, or to go to war and be massacred . . . we can retreat without losing honour and prestige, preserve the state, and hold, as it were a mortgage against the western states . . . waiting . . . for a future accounting. This will certainly come, for the big powers have not solved anything for themselves by sacrificing Czechoslovakia, and events will go on.

The immediate fruit of "greater security" for Czechoslovakia was, however, bitter, and its sour aftertaste would last right up until the present. The newspaper *Lidové Noviny* wrote: "If the world is not to be ruled by justice but by force, then our place is on the side of those who possess the greater force and the greater energy of decision. There is nothing else left for us. Let us seek unity with Germany." As Sheila Grant Duff wrote at the height of the terrible ensuing world war: "the Nazis had achieved the political demoralisation of Europe long before they achieved its physical domination." And the longer-term consequences were equally dire. Historian J. W. Brügel writes: "the memory of the bitter humiliation the Czechs suffered at Munich is ineradicable: it may well be that the non-involvement of the Soviet Union in the whole business enhanced the chances for communism amongst western-minded people." The wild but familiar irony is that the fear which drove

Munich conjured up exactly what it was trying to prevent—and even worse. For in the long run the whole of central Europe was subsumed under the great bugbear of communism, and cut off by the iron curtain from any dialogue at all with the West.

As for the United States, American reaction to Munich was mixed. The United States's ambassador in Prague, Wilbur Carr, had given very accurate reports of developments all along. However, the ambassadors in London and Paris, Joseph P. Kennedy and William C. Bullitt, were strong appeasers. President Roosevelt had appealed to Hitler and Beneš on the September 26 in a way which "practically put the causes of Nazi Germany and Czechoslovakia on the same level." For Beneš the appeals presented "the last heavy blow." Roosevelt appeared pleased with the Munich Agreement, his Department of State commenting that "the peace results . . . afford a universal sense of relief." Another American, the journalist and writer Martha Gellhorn (on the spot again as she had been in the Spanish Civil War) had an opposite and forthright view. Looking back on the moment of Munich she writes: "The moral of that moment in history has lasted for me permanently: never believe governments, not any of them, not a word they say; keep an untrusting eye on what they do. Cheering crowds greeted Daladier in Paris and Chamberlain in London, when properly both men should have been stoned."

For the most part, European public opinion did cheer the agreement enthusiastically. Russia, however, had seen what was coming, which included the fact that Munich would put the Nazis that much nearer to their borders, with Poland the only, deeply vulnerable, buffer in between. On October 4, 1938, Soviet Deputy Commissar for Foreign Affairs Grigory Potemkin said to the French ambassador Robert Coulondre: "My poor friend, what have you done? For us I see now no other way out except a Fourth Partition of Poland." It was left to Winston Churchill to sound the most accurate and prophetic note in the House of Commons on October 5: "We have sustained a total and unmitigated defeat . . . We are in the presence of a disaster of the first magnitude which has befallen Great Britain and France."

And not only Britain and France: in Germany, the generals now gave up in complete dismay. All their plans were shelved, and they resigned themselves to follow Hitler into the abyss ahead. After the Munich Agreement General Halder, one of the key generals plotting against Hitler, whom he saw as a "madman," was "in a state of complete collapse, weeping, and asserting that all was lost." (Shortly after the outbreak of war, his co-conspirator Admiral Canaris said: "Halder has suffered a complete mental collapse.") It was a year later, after engineering the Nazi-Soviet Pact, that Hitler said, "Our enemies are small fry. I saw them at Munich."

In France, an era passed away: the end of the French system of alliances, the end of French influence in central Europe. The French newspapers were more candid in their evaluation of what had taken place than the British. *L'Epoque* was typical:

> The peace of Munich has left us less strong than we were yesterday, since we have lost an ally, and more than thirty German divisions will be available to be turned against us. If we were incapable of resisting the formidable German menace in the past when we were stronger, how will we resist the next time when we will be less strong?

In England, a few voices spoke up with the kind of clarity that vaults ages and continents. As soon as Chamberlain returned from Munich and reported to his cabinet, First Lord of the Admiralty Alfred Duff Cooper resigned. Three days later, on October 3, he gave a speech to the Commons explaining his resignation, a speech which preceded the prime minister's own accounting for his actions at Munich. Knowing that he is going quite against the grain of public opinion—"I was caught up in the large crowd that were demonstrating their enthusiasm and were cheering, laughing, and singing;

and there is no greater feeling of loneliness than to be in a crowd of happy, cheerful people and to feel that there is no occasion for oneself for gaiety or cheering"—Duff Cooper says:

> I have always believed that one of the most important principles in . . . the conduct of foreign policy should be to make your policy plain to other countries, to let them know where you stand and what in certain circumstances you are prepared to do. . . . During the last four weeks we have been drifting, day by day, nearer into war with Germany, and we have never said, until the last moment, and then in most uncertain terms, that we were prepared to fight. We knew that information to the opposite effect was being poured into the ears of the head of the German State.

It was not for Czechoslovakia that we should have been prepared to fight, he went on, just as it was not for Serbia, or even Belgium, that we fought in 1914:

> We were fighting then, as we should have been fighting last week, in order that one great Power should not be allowed, in disregard of treaty obligations, of the laws of nations and the decrees of morality to dominate by brutal force the Continent of Europe. . . .
>
> I had hoped that it might be possible to make a statement to Herr Hitler before he made his speech at Nuremberg. On all sides we were being urged to do so . . . even by Germans who were supporters of the regime and did not wish to see it plunged into a war which might destroy it. But we were always told that on no account must we irritate

Herr Hitler; it was particularly dangerous to irritate him before he made a public speech, because if he were so irritated he might say some terrible things from which afterwards there would be no retreat. It seems to me that Herr Hitler never makes a speech save under the influence of considerable irritation, and the addition of one more irritant would not, I should have thought, have made a great difference, whereas the communication of a solemn fact would have produced a sobering effect.

Duff Cooper had hoped that at least Chamberlain would make the position clear at Godesberg, but again he'd failed to do so: "Sweet reasonableness had won nothing except terms which a cruel and revengeful enemy would have dictated to a beaten foe after a long war. . . . The moment I saw them I said to myself 'If these are accepted it will be the end of all decency in the conduct of public affairs in the world.' " And then came Munich:

> I had thought that after accepting the humiliation of partition [Czechoslovakia] should have been spared the ignominy and the horror of invasion. . . . The German Government, having got their man down, were not to be deprived of the pleasure of kicking him. . . . We are left, and we must acknowledge it, with a loss of esteem on the part of countries that trusted us.

At every step, Duff Cooper himself had clearly stated his recommendations at the time. He now itemizes the ways in which Hitler has betrayed his every word, and predicts how ill-founded the prime minister's "confidence in the good will and in the word of Herr Hitler" will be, concluding:

I have given up an office that I loved, work in which I was deeply interested and a staff of which any man might be proud. . . . I have ruined, perhaps, my political career. But that is a little matter; I have retained something which is to me of great value—I can still walk about the world with my head erect.

Many people within the government and Foreign Office would not be able to say the same. Most of these were what we now call appeasers; but there had been another, more ruthless and pragmatic strain of thinking within Whitehall which also colluded obliquely with Hitler. There were those who resisted attempts by high-ranking Germans to get rid of Hitler because—perhaps understandably—they feared a return to a strong, Prussian Germany and wanted Germany's unconditional surrender or nothing. This strain would only grow as the war progressed, so that by the time Count Claus von Stauffenberg's assassination plot on Hitler of July 1944 had failed, John Wheeler-Bennett, official historian at the Foreign Office political intelligence department, could sum up the advantages of that failure and even, shockingly, of the subsequent vicious Nazi purge:

By the failure of the plot we have been spared the embarrassments, both at home and in the US, which might have resulted from such a move, and, moreover, the present purge is presumably removing from the scene numerous individuals which [sic] might have caused us difficulty, not only had the plot succeeded, but also after the defeat of Nazi Germany. . . . The Gestapo and the SS have done us an appreciable service in removing a selection of those who would undoubtedly have posed as "good" Germans after the war. . . . It is to our advantage therefore that the purge should continue, since the killing of Germans by Germans will save us from future embarrassments of many kinds.

After the war, the Foreign Office was aware of the incriminating nature of some of its documentation, particularly about the events of September 1938, and preemptively published *Documents of British Foreign Policy* in a doctored version to exonerate itself. Lord Cranbourne, undersecretary of state at the time of Munich, having declared publicly that "our case is overwhelming and should be given to the world," added to the pool of hypocrisy and bad faith by then writing the opposite privately in a letter to Eden. It concerned the record of the meeting between Hitler, Sir Nevile Henderson and Sir Horace Wilson which had taken place on September 26, three days before Munich:

> That is a really dreadful document. Our readiness to bully and batter the Czechs, and to do anything, however contemptible, to avoid a war makes one blush, and is bound to create a deplorable impression, both in the US and in the occupied countries themselves. Would it be very disingenuous to leave it out?

Would it be very dishonest? would have been a more honest question.

After Munich, the Czechs were left to pick up the pieces of their shattered and compromised country. Meanwhile, Hitler had been given the unexpected bonus of validation by the West: Beneš, talking of Munich to Compton Mackenzie after the war, said, "Munich was Hitler's first real victory because it meant his recognition in the eyes of the whole world as a responsible statesman."

Writing from the perspective of 1964, Radomír Luža mourns that

> A world of freedom and tolerance had passed away.
>
> Very few happenings are so decisive that they split the history of a nation into two definite parts. Such events, if they occur, leave their mark forever on the soul of a nation; they nurture a new state of mind, for nothing can be the same after such explosions. Munich was such a cleavage for the Czech nation, and it still remains buried beneath the surface of the national consciousness.

Sydney Morrell, who stayed on in Prague for a few weeks longer, wrote that now the Czechs felt the whole world was against them. As a Czech friend told him: "We wanted to sing with the angels, but now we must howl with the wolves."

13 | LEARNING TO KEEP QUIET FAST

And so, a year before war was declared, Czechoslovakia went under, divided and ruled by the Nazis. Thanks to Nazi censorship—and to that of the quasi-dictatorship in neighboring Poland—my father in Lwow was unaware of the extent of the degradation of his native country. He was, however, aware of the growing threat of the Nazis, who, in one bound—like the game of Grandmother's Footsteps, with the West apparently turning the other way—were now sitting on the border of Slovakia with Poland, less than a hundred miles away. As yet, though, it seemed to pose no personal threat to Joe, who was thankful to have a place studying electromechanical engineering and to work in his free time drawing up plans for electrical circuits. Czechoslovakia's fate in that year, from September 1938 until September 1939, got swept under the carpet, and once the war had broken out in earnest, Europe had other things on its mind than recapitulating that country's trauma. With hindsight, we can fill that gap.

"The Wenceslas Square was poorly lighted, as if all the street lamps were slowly burning down. The row of shops across the way, with their names painted in the strange, untidy Czech lettering, did not shine as they used to, and only Bata's neon sign glowed at this end of the street." Martha Gellhorn is describing the Prague she came to in October 1938, its population demoralized overnight, its lights dimmed. She came from reporting on the Spanish Civil War, where, as in Prague, she "had no qualification except eyes and ears." The description of post-Munich Prague comes from her novel *A Stricken Field* (1940), in which the protagonist Mary Douglas, an American war reporter—her alter ego—comes back as she had done to this metamorphosed Prague:

> The crowds moved slowly, as if they too were strangers, uncertain of directions and having nowhere to go. She could not find one face to remember. They all looked alike and no one seemed to have slept, or eaten, or gone shopping, or made love, or transacted business successfully or unsuccessfully, or done any of the things that leave a mark on the eyes or mouths of passers-by. They're all waiting, she thought . . . even despair would be better than this, despair would have shape, and bring the faces to life. But these people looked gray and empty and she thought, so that's the way it goes; they learn to keep quiet fast.

As Mary Douglas sits discussing what has happened with some fellow journalists, noting that the Czechs are now once more forbidden to speak Czech but must speak German, a novelist called Novak tells her:

> "The Germans take what they see, and from one day to the next, no one knows what more they will grab. Now at Pilsen they have taken the most important electric power stations, the way they

have here." (Ah, Mary thought, so that's why everything's dim.)

One of the journalists, Tompkins, says the Czechs are running so scared of "Adolf" that their censors are doing his work for him, but another journalist says they are not simply scared but cynical and disabused:

> "After all, the Czechs got a pretty good idea of how world opinion stood nobly by and defended the weak and virtuous. I think they're right to please Adolf and let the rest go. Adolf's who counts in Europe."
>
> "Anyhow," Tompkins said, ". . . Adolf wants it to look like everyone was welcoming him with flowers and heils and the English and French would rather not know what a stink it all is."
>
> "The story's dead," said Thane. "The Nazis have won again, and that's all there is to it."

And the story on Czechoslovakia did go dead, like the eyes of the people in the street. For a long while, the Nazis had won again, and that was all there was to it. In countries as in individuals, the stages of demoralization and corruption follow on as quickly as a martial arts sequence once the initial breaking blow has been struck. For Czechoslovakia, the process began at Munich on September 30, 1938, and was completed by the outbreak of world war less than a year later, on September 1, 1939. For Czechoslovakia, as George Orwell said of Western Europe in 1940, "The 'democratic vistas' have ended in barbed wire."

On October 1, 1938, Beneš was told to resign by Göring, who conveyed that unless he did so, the Munich Agreement would be applied to the whole country "with ruthlessness." Almost overnight the army's fighting spirit gave way to indifference. A leading Czech collaborator with the Germans said, "Our soldiers having been brought up in too much modesty and obedience, limited themselves to curses and tears." Beneš submitted his resignation on October 5. In a broadcast to the nation, he stated: "In order not to jeopardize the life of our State in the new circumstances, I think that as President I should no longer stand in the way." Privately, to Compton Mackenzie, he said, "Physically, I was utterly exhausted, a broken man with indescribable feelings in my heart and with grave thoughts in my head." In danger from the Nazi regime, he was persuaded to leave for voluntary exile in London on the twenty-third. "Bohemia's best sons," he had written twenty-one years before, little suspecting he would share their fate, "abandoned by their allies, were obliged to take refuge for ever in exile." In early 1939, he would take up a post lecturing at the University of Chicago. To cap it all for him—and relatives of his would die in concentration camps—he would be reproached for this exile.

From now on, the Nazis referred to Prague as an old German imperial city, and on October 7, in a divide-and-rule policy, they made the republic a federal state within which Slovakia was given internal autonomy. On the twenty-first, Hitler said, "It must be possible to smash at any time the remainder of the Czech state should it pursue an anti-German policy." At the end of November, the aged and infirm Dr. Emil Hácha was sworn in as president of Bohemia and Moravia in place of Beneš. His room for maneuver was minimal, especially since the Western democracies gave him no support. Hitler travelled through the Sudetenland in early December, astonished not to find the hospitals full of Sudeten Germans who'd been attacked by Czechs; he had begun to believe his own propaganda.

In the new year, the Nazis stirred up trouble to crisis pitch in Slovakia, forcing it to secede from the Czech lands or be partitioned by its neighbors—chiefly Hungary—ready and waiting on its borders. The treacherous Catholic priest Jozef Tiso was installed as premier of Slovakia, and Slovakia became the first satellite of Nazi Germany. The Nazis now continued to build up a crisis in what was left of Bohemia and Moravia, filling the press with trumped-up tales of atrocities against the persecuted Germans. On March 10, when the German troops were already massing for an invasion of Czechoslovakia, Chamberlain made a statement that "the international outlook was quite serene and that there was no cause for anxiety." That same day, Home Secretary Sir Samuel Hoare said that "there was now an opportunity to discover the road to peace, the greatest that had ever been offered to the leaders of the world" and that he "now envisage[d] a cooperation between five men in Europe—the three dictators and the Prime Ministers of England and France—which might create a Utopia in Europe in an incredibly short space of time." Trying to understand the crises arising in his country, Hácha travelled to Berlin in mid-March to speak directly with Hitler, at the suggestion of his pro-German foreign minister, Dr. František Chvalkovsky.

A special train took the seventy-six-year-old Hácha and Dr. Chvalkovsky to Berlin, leaving Prague at 4:00 p.m. on March 14 and arriving in Berlin at 10:40 that evening. Meanwhile, at 5:30 p.m., whilst Hácha was still on the train, German troops crossed the Czechoslovak border, and at 6:40 they occupied the industrial center of Moravska Ostrava. There was no Czech resistance as no Czech army units were there, but as soon as the Germans encountered the first Czech troops, they were fiercely resisted.

Hácha was received by Hitler in the presence of Göring, Ribbentrop, Wilhelm Keitel and others at 1:15 a.m. on March 15, Hitler once again wrongfooting his opponent from the start by panic timing. Hitler had never met Hácha before and a month later Göring told Mussolini that "the Reich Chancellor was completely surprised" by the president's submissiveness. Quickly taking advantage of Hácha's frailty, Hitler told him that in view of the Czech "provocations" and the confusion following Slovakia's "independence," "he had given the order for invasion by German troops and for the incorporation of Czechoslovakia into the German Reich." The troops would invade Czechoslovakia from three sides at six o'clock that morning. Any resistance would be ruthlessly crushed.

The French ambassador in Berlin gave an account of how the devastating interview turned into tragic farce. For several hours, Hácha and Chvalkovsky protested against the violent scenario offered to them. They refused to sign the document, asserting that their people would curse them forever if they agreed to it. With all the energy at his command, Hácha opposed the status of a protectorate which Hitler intended to impose on Bohemia, adding that no people of the white race had ever been placed in such a situation. The German ministers, however, moved in for the kill. They literally chased Hácha and Chvalkovsky around the table on which the documents were laid out, continually pushing the papers in front of them and thrusting pens in their hands. If they refused to sign, they kept on repeating, half of Prague would be destroyed within two hours by German airplanes. And this would be only the beginning. Hundred of bombers were awaiting orders to start, orders which would be given at six o'clock in the morning if the documents remained unsigned. President Hácha, an old man in a state of physical depression, broke down and lost consciousness. He was only resuscitated by injections given by Göring's personal doctor; his feelings on being brought round into this dire context can only be imagined.

Hácha insisted on telephoning the cabinet in Prague in the early hours of the morning. The Czechs recognized there was no possibility of resistance since without fortifications, without proper western borders and without allies the republic was defenseless. At 4:00 a.m., Hácha, "overcome, maintained only by injections, and with death in his soul—gave his consent," as a French observer wrote. He and Chvalkovsky signed a declaration prepared and cosigned by Hitler and von Ribbentrop, expressing the Führer's "determination to take the Czech people under the protection of the

German Reich and to guarantee to it an autonomous development of its national life in accordance with its particular characteristics."

Anyone who knew Hitler's mind, his contempt for Czechs and weasel way with words, would have recognized what he meant by "in accordance with its particular characteristics." The Czech-born historian Vojtěch Mastný—son of the Czech ambassador to Berlin Vojtěch Mastný, and now a leading cold war scholar—writes that "Having himself emphasized in his first words to Hitler the close dependence of his country upon Germany, Hácha was hardly in a position to question the substance of this statement. But except for insignificant details, he also left unquestioned its devious wording, which was a masterpiece of deceptive understatement." The term "protectorate" is a euphemism, saying one thing—protection—and doing another—quashing the independence of a country in a back-hand way without conquest. Emotionally, it is something like rape within a forced marriage of unequal partners.

The first word of the German occupation came from Radio Prague at 4:30 a.m. on March 15, the Ides of March, a suitably treacherous date. The broadcasts repeatedly warned the population not to offer resistance to the German army, which would start advancing at six that morning. At 5:00 a.m., Goebbels read over Radio Berlin a proclamation by Hitler stating that the excesses committed by the Czechs against their ethnic minorities and the secession of Slovakia had led to a breakdown of the republic. It was now coming back into the Reich—*heim ins Reich*—where Bohemia and Moravia "had in fact belonged for over one thousand years." The ghosts of Masaryk and of the patient historians of the nineteenth century must have been weeping, if not gnashing their teeth with rage.

Troops entered Prague at 9:00 a.m. and by the afternoon were in possession of the whole country. People woke up that morning to an unusually severe blizzard, with iced roads and drifting snow, and to the sight of hundreds and hundreds of vehicles rumbling by plastered with snow, as Nazi troops suddenly occupied their city. There had been no hint of this in the heavily censored press, no rumors of further demands, no preparation. The impotence they felt led to bitterness and silence, especially since they had well-founded fears about the intentions of their new rulers. The Prague government itself was caught unprepared by the catastrophe, which had blown up as suddenly as the snowstorm. The occupation came so swiftly that there was no time even to destroy military stock. The snowstorm meant that no aircraft could take off, although one plane did succeed in reaching London with the secret files of the intelligence section of the General Staff. Hitler himself said later that he had given the Czechs an ultimatum, "otherwise German aircraft would be over Prague. I would have irremediably lost face if I'd had to put this threat into execution for at six o'clock fog was so thick over our airfields that none of our aircraft could have made its sortie."

Somewhat astounded by the ease of his opportunistic invasion of Bohemia and Moravia, Hitler now made another spur-of-the-moment decision: to visit Prague himself, that same day. But once he and his party set out on the Berlin-to-Prague railway, he suddenly changed his mind and had the whole train diverted to a junction in the Sudetenland, just before the Bohemian border, where he brooded for two hours, unsure whether to carry on or go back. In the end, he decided to go on to Prague by car. His motorcade drove along icy roads congested by his own advancing troops, all caked with snow from the blizzard. Night had fallen by the time they reached the outskirts of Prague, and the German army had already taken possession of part of Prague Castle, which they now hurriedly prepared for Hitler's surprise arrival.

After driving through streets emptied by the curfew and by fear, Hitler and his party slipped into the castle so inconspicuously that the Czech cabinet, in a crisis meeting in another part of the building, had no idea they were there. Hitler, a teetotaler and vegetarian, celebrated with Pilsner beer and Prague ham. For him, *l'appétit venait en mangeant,* and he had now swallowed Czechoslovakia whole. Hácha reached Prague Castle after Hitler had already arrived. In a terrible symbol of the extent of Hitler's triumph and Hácha's humiliation, Hácha was received by Hitler at the castle with a pumping handclasp, along with the mayor of Prague and the minister of defense, the former General Sirový.

The following day Hitler gave a speech from the Hradschin proclaiming that "For one thousand years the provinces of Bohemia and Moravia formed part of the *Lebensraum* of the German people." Czechoslovakia, he said, had "showed its inherent inability to survive." It was an uneasy triumph, though, since Hitler could not fail to notice that, unlike in Austria, there were no cheering crowds, and he never returned to the Czech lands.

On March 18, Hitler appointed the servile Konstantin von Neurath "Protector" of Bohemia-Moravia. On the twenty-fifth, von Neurath told the Czechs, in sentences writhing with tortuous half-nelsons, that "according to the Führer's will, the Czechs should be treated in a conciliatory manner, though with the greatest strictness and relentless consistency. . . . The treatment according to strict principles should obviously be fair." The only consolation for the Czechs at this stage was that since they were the first incarnation of a "protectorate" by Nazi Germany, it was in the Nazis' interests to make it a reasonably appealing prospect. Therefore the German occupation for the moment was less oppressive in everyday life than many had feared. Many Czechs slipped back into the psyche of the underdog, hamstrung by a measure of guilt at the memory of what now seemed their imperfect democracy, and, like the French later under Pétain in 1940, and like any cowed people, prepared to accept paternalism as a trade-off for their sheer existence.

Hácha led the way in making the best of a very bad job in a speech broadcast to the Czech people on March 16, after his return from Berlin:

> When twenty years ago all Czech hearts were filled
> with joy, I stood apart from those historic events.
> My joy about our unbelievable success was over-

shadowed by anxiety about external and internal
guarantees which would assure permanence of our
success. Now, after twenty years, I can see with
grief that my anxieties were not without foundation. What we held for a solution to last for ages
proved to be merely a short episode in our national
history. . . . By our union with [Germany] the former unity of the Reich has been restored.

On the same day, Chamberlain and Halifax reported to the
British Parliament on events in Czechoslovakia, blandly untroubled
by guilt. They commented on Germany's action "in a tone rather of
sorrow than of anger. They were, they said, unable to regard it as
other than inconsistent with the spirit of the Munich Agreement. It
was also in conflict with Herr Hitler's repeated statement that he
desired to incorporate in the Reich only people of German race."
However, it seemed that "Czechoslovakia had disintegrated of its
own accord, that the President had asked Germany to intervene, and
that Herr Hitler had been graciously pleased to take the country
under his protection and would respect its autonomy." Since that
was so, the British government conveniently regarded itself as
"being definitely released from the guarantee which had been given
to Czechoslovakia at Munich and which had never yet been properly defined" (said airily, again as if it were the Czechs' own fault!).
However, the mood of his own country was against him: Compton
Mackenzie wrote that "The indignation of the country clarified even
Mr Chamberlain's turbid mind," and the next day the prime minister made a speech in Birmingham apologizing for his previous
speech, excusing it on the (shameful) grounds that the government
had not had time to digest the information or form an opinion on it.
Mackenzie wrote: "A tortoise coming round the corner would have
been too quick for Mr Chamberlain to be sure whether it was a tortoise or a tiger. He went on in his speech to ask in the accents of an

old lady who has had her purse snatched by a footpad: 'Is this a step in the direction of an attempt to dominate the world by force?' "

After March 15, 1939, all Czech nationals had to decide for Reich or Protectorate citizenship, and national sovereignty disappeared. Hitler ordered the Czech army to be demobilized and military service abolished. A new secret police was proposed, the "Czestapo." The German army seized 1,582 airplanes, 501 antiaircraft guns, 2,175 guns, 469 tanks and armored cars, 43,876 machine guns, 1,090,000 rifles and 114,000 pistols, all of which incalculably bolstered their ability to fight the terrible war they would unleash on the rest of Europe (and eventually, Russia). They also took 200,000 technical designs and patents and the whole of the gold reserves of the Czechoslovak National Bank, amounting to some £18 million pounds (about $27 million).

Early in 1939, Beneš had left London to take up his post at the University of Chicago, where he was to give a series of lectures on democracy. Chicago was the second most populous Czechoslovak city in the world after Prague, and it was here that Masaryk had also come as professor whilst in exile during World War I. In March 1939, Beneš broadcast to the American people about the plight of Czechoslovakia, saying that there would be no order until the crimes that had been committed in Europe had been wiped out, until there was once more respect for people's word and respect for honesty—honesty of the individual and the state. Real courage must take command again and require that "brute force must stop." "I must end," he said, "with an appeal to the American people. I would beg that they do not permit such conceptions and ideas as are now trying to dominate Europe to be tolerated in this free country."

That same day, President Roosevelt recalled the American ambassador from Germany and the American minister from Prague. U.S. opinion was behind him, and the isolationism which had helped create the background climate for Munich was temporarily stemmed. The next day, Beneš warned the world: "Do not believe that it was a question of self-determination for a minority. . . . With the subjugation of Czechoslovakia, freedom is being guillotined."

In April 1939, the British government introduced conscription. In June, Beneš was voted "the most outstanding man of the year at Chicago University." Several universities offered him honorary degrees. He and Jan Masaryk, Beneš's former foreign minister, addressed meetings all over the United States. In July that year, Beneš and his wife left America to live in Putney, southwest London, where he began to form a government-in-exile and to coordinate a resistance movement and "one of the best intelligence networks in Europe," built on the intelligence officers who had fled Prague earlier. Beneš was greatly helped by the fact that General Alois Elias—secretly one of the most prominent members of the Czech resistance—was made premier of the new "protectorate" in April 1939. From the beginning, he was in regular contact with Beneš whilst adopting a line of surface compliance with the Nazis.

The capitulation of Slovakia enabled Nazi troops to begin to concentrate on the Slovakian border with Poland. On April 28— eight days after his fifty-first birthday—Hitler annulled the German-Polish nonaggression pact. On May 23, he had a secret discussion with his commanders at which the final decision was made to invade Poland. He said, "The question of sparing Poland can therefore no longer be considered and we are left with the decision to attack Poland at the first suitable opportunity. This time there will be fighting. The war with England and France will be a life and death struggle." Now England was targeted by Hitler, too. Three months later, on August 22, von Ribbentrop went to Moscow and the next day stunned the world by announcing the Ribbentrop-Molotov pact.

For the Czechs, the Nazi-Soviet Pact meant that they lost their one remote possibility of salvation—an East-West alliance between Britain, France and Russia. Also, the regime at home became harsher: listening to a foreign radio became a criminal offense, the Nazis took full control of censorship, people found guilty of subversion were threatened with severe sentences, including death, and the Gestapo rounded up prominent Czech politicians, intellectuals, priests, Social Democrats and Communists, and sent them to concentration camps—the first of which, Dachau, had been set up already in 1933. These punitive measures were being brought into the German part of the Reich, too.

On September 1, at 4:45 in the morning, the German army swept into Poland and launched its *Blitzkrieg*. For the Czechs, there was some bitter consolation in that they had been predicting a wider war all along, and also in seeing that in spite of the West's declaration of war on Germany, it still let their Polish ally succumb.

For my father, with one homeland already lost behind him, the war was just beginning.

FOUR

BOMBSHELLS

You may not be interested in war,
but war is interested in you.

—LEON TROTSKY

14 | SITZKRIEG

I t's January 1940, and my father is in Budapest, with just the clothes he had on and a pair of skis. He cannot go back to his family in Nazi-occupied Poland, or to Slovakia, now hand-in-glove with the Nazis, and he cannot stay in Hungary. Although technically still neutral, Hungary is Germany's old ally, and hovering on the brink of a new German-Hungarian alliance. (It will soon trade its sovereignty to the Nazis in exchange for getting back territories it lost to Slovakia at Versailles.) Above all, my father now wants somehow to get to France. His idea is that he will wait out the war there—which is still the "phoney war" (*Sitzkrieg*, or "sitting war" in German)—and then come back into Poland again once the West has dispatched the Germans, as he's sure they will.

"I became little bit more mobile, and woman doctor managed to acquire—whether she bought or scrounged or whatever—she acquired car, and contracted driver—he was taxi driver in Krakow and he readily agreed to drive. He was waiting to go to France as well and I think she must have met him where they were processing passports et cetera. Many people were going by train, escaping anyhow, and we got him as driver. It was just question of waiting for suitable time to go. In addition to driver there was young cadet officer who was studying medicine, and who was coming too. We were introduced when we went to office supplying passports, and for some people clothing. Well, they looked at you first of all and decided what sort of modification to make to your face, how to rearrange your age, they added or subtracted years from you, so that you would not fall within military age. If it was difficult to disguise age, they told them to pretend that they were lame or something. Taxi driver was very first one we came in contact with, he was older, probably around thirty, though he looked about forty-five. He didn't talk much about himself. He'd crossed over border with Polish army. When Germans invaded Poland, people who were already in army were fighting, but not everywhere and his regiment must have retreated to Hungary, as several did, and they were interned there. Then they escaped from these camps and their prime goal was to go to Budapest because in Budapest it was possible to arrange with Polish office to escape to France. From internment camp, there was no possibility of doing this. So he managed to get to Budapest, and there he was being processed to be suitable to go to France. Hungarian authorities were pro-German but lethargic. The railwaymen at stations and so on were not vigilant. But to leave country was little bit more difficult. You had to have documents, which only Budapest could supply.

"Hungarians had affection almost for Germans, which was overhang from Austro-Hungarian Empire—they had empathy toward Austrians and therefore toward Germans. Czechoslovakia, part of Ukraine, and Poland were peoples who were enslaved— if First World War had not occurred, these Slavonic languages would have disappeared because at school, depending on whether you were under Hungarian or Austrian domination, you were taught either Hungarian or Austrian and your native language you only spoke at home. Within two generations, native languages would have disappeared, and Hungary probably felt they had been deprived of their destiny, they could have conquered so much and probably rearranged world or something like that. They felt superior, but apart from that there was no animosity—they felt superior, but probably not younger generation. They did not know really where to go, they were just following leader, and their leader at that moment was Horthy and he was admiral and he had boat on River Danube—probably he was admiral of fleet, he may have had two boats. This is song we used to know as children at school, '*Horthy Miklosz kattanay vayog*'—it was derision about him being an admiral and having to ride horse. But Hungarian people when I saw them in Budapest they were just like people everywhere else— there was war somewhere, between nations, and they were sympathizing with one party but they had no active role to play in it, they were just outsiders. Obviously they were worried what may happen, but at that time feeling was, they were hoping Germany would win, although feeling was also Germans most probably would lose.

"My own passport was made out to be sixteen years old, although I was just nineteen now. I passed for that. First of all, I was very very skinny, I was average height, good height for that era in history—five foot eight was good height—but I was slim, and after about three months in Russia and two months in Germany where food was rather scarce I was even slimmer. I don't remember what cadet officer went as, he couldn't have passed for less than military age.

"Budapest was city of statues—everywhere you went at every corner, on every street statues, statues, people just standing up, people on horses, people with swords in air trying to swipe at something. Bridges, too, so many bridges over Danube—it appeared to me it was almost covered with bridges—and of course bridges were connecting two towns—on left bank of Danube was old town of Buda, I think it means 'home' or 'house'—and on right bank which was hilly there was town called Pest, that was new town. When they started building bridges these two towns became joined, as Budapest.

"Eventually we got our day of departure from Budapest and as we were ready to go we discovered that a fourth passenger was introduced into our group, he was captain in Polish army, professional captain, but now he had civilian clothing and he assumed command. The three of us did not like it but there was no way we could object to it. So we started in very tense atmosphere because we were under impression that only three of us were going to go, but within few days we had become very friendly. Very little was said about our past or our future, just about what was happening at that very moment. That woman doctor also gave me letter of introduction to consulate in Paris so I could apply to Sorbonne and continue studies there, and also quite bit of money to go on with. The other three they were supplied by Polish authorities with small sums of money which would pay for food and hotel until they got to France.

"We started in car from Budapest, atmosphere was beginning to ease little bit and suddenly there was horrible noise in car and we didn't know what had happened. We went on for little while, but since there was no point in going if something was wrong with car, as we wouldn't be able to repair it along route, then decision was taken to go back to Budapest and check what was wrong and have it repaired. As we returned toward Budapest at one stage noise suddenly disappeared, so we travelled another kilometer or so and decided to turn back after all. As we turned back, that noise came again and we said there is something wrong and we turned back again, and as we did so we noticed surface of road changed and that was what was causing noise. It was great relief to us, and we turned back again toward Yugoslavia, but we had lost over hour of travelling.

"Car was blackish, with running boards, and driver and usually captain sat in front and two of us behind. Dashboard seemed very sparse, but there was speedometer and at one stage on stretch of road toward Genoa we reached speed of 100 kilometers an hour— that was quite something—I had never travelled at that speed in vehicle before, it was like breaking sound barrier. When we got to Yugoslavia, we were welcomed—they just looked briefly at our passports and checked exit visa. We felt relief that all our papers were in order. They were very friendly in Yugoslavia—Yugoslavs felt as brothers to Czechs. One reason was knowing any of Czech languages—and especially two languages from Czechoslovakia and in addition Polish—you could converse with them, you had about sixty percent of vocabulary. But Yugoslavia itself was not as closely knitted as Czechoslovakia, for instance—not only country but people. They had two alphabets, Cyrillic and Roman, this already divided them into two groups; and then they had more languages on top of that, with more difference between them than we had, so they had sometimes more friendly feeling toward Czechoslovakia than toward their own people in their own country."

"What nationality do you *feel*, Joe? I've never really known."

"I feel that I belong to Czechoslovakia. My loyalty is to my family; my father and mother were Polish but they lived in Czechoslovakia and my loyalty is toward family, as son would feel toward parents—but as citizen I feel loyalty toward Czechoslovakia. It gave me much more basic grounding about life than Poland did. I learned very much more about how to appreciate life in my childhood in Czechoslovakia than I did in Poland—reason may be that I was much more free there, free of worries. Czechoslovakia still appears to me as country of sunshine and Poland appears that there are always clouds there; it isn't true, because we had some beautiful summers in Poland and in winter night skies were so clear and full of stars, but to me feeling was always that beyond these Carpathian Mountains, toward north, there is country where there's nothing but clouds."

"Do you think you're more of a Czech type than Polish?"

"I wasn't Polish type—but I don't think I would have been even if I had been born in Poland. I think there is something in myself that would not have agreed with some actions that were taken in Poland. Not by authorities, because I couldn't help that, couldn't do anything about it, but small things, some national characteristics I did not quite like. There were some characteristics in Czechoslovakia that I did not like either, so I am neither here nor there, but basically I'm more of Czech origin than anything else. What I didn't like about Czechs was organizing of people, regimenting. It started at school—"

"—but you seemed to like that?"

"—I liked it because what it meant to me as boy was gymnastics, which got you through to jamboree, that was something to be enjoyed. But today's expression is cloning—that did not appeal to me—everyone was supposed to be like everyone else. I admired for example in that regimentation physical activities, that you should walk proudly, your head up. At school during lessons we had to sit upright with our arms folded behind us all the time. This was to straighten your back and keep you awake—this was discipline I did not dislike because it improved your physical well-being—you felt better this way. But to make everybody equal, I did not like that. There was for instance feeling that if somebody was invalid or something it was their own fault and they were ridiculed. For instance, left-handed people were considered as invalids, that there was something wrong with them. So normally when babies were born and put in cot, both their arms were bound to their body and then after while their right hand was released so they would become right-handed."

"What were the Polish characteristics you didn't like?"

"What I didn't like about them as group was their unnecessary generosity, which led to drunkenness and often to fights. When they gathered somewhere, let's say wedding or pub, it was inborn generosity that nobody wanted to be left out without buying drink for somebody else; it was cumulative so after while everybody got drunk and those that were still capable of standing got into fight. In Ukraine, they were more placid people—that could have been because they were normally peasants, poor relations of people working in industry or offices. But that was probably their own fault, because although they were attending Polish or Czechoslovak schools they were trying to preserve their own language in Cyrillic alphabet and there was that feeling that they were really separate nation, they did not want to assimilate with Poland or Czechoslovakia."

"But the Yugoslavs felt like brothers as you were travelling through—"

"Yes, although we weren't there long. There was lot of rain at that time, snows were melting in upper countries—in Austria and Germany—and Danube was swelling quite lot. There had also been floods around Lake Balaton in Hungary. We were supposed to shoot through Yugoslavia in one day, but three of us decided we would spend at least two days because we wanted to detour little bit and see places like Zagreb and Lyublyana. Captain objected to it, and objection was overruled. He kept quiet about it. We had very provisional routes, no official map, just piece of paper with names of towns that we would go through. We were navigating by names of towns. We set off from Budapest in morning, but we lost time with that noise on road. We stopped for food along route, and also spent unscheduled night in hotel in Zagreb, because we'd wanted to see it and anyway had to take detour round flooded area. Following day we started toward Italy and Trieste. It was mountainous country before Trieste, with twisty downhill roads mostly, and I was struck with one thing I have not seen before in my life—there was white line painted in middle of road. We had never seen any painting on road, right through Poland, Hungary, Yugoslavia, and now there is road divided into two halves. It was real eye-opener, sort of: oh, it must be wonderful to know exactly where you are, where to drive.

"We went down to Trieste and from there we went to Venice because it was slightly on way. Again, in this case captain did not say anything because he also wanted to see Venice. We went into Venice by bus, and saw St. Mark's and gondolas and pigeons, and when we came back, he started trying to take command again, saying we had two days to cross Italy. And of course being in Italy and not seeing Rome did not appeal to us. And his argument was, not only that we have time schedule, but we haven't enough petrol coupons for that. That was very valid argument, so as soon as we got out of Venice we went to garage and asked how much petrol would cost if we didn't have coupons, and we found that coupons and *lire* were equivalent, so there was no argument from him anymore about petrol, but he still strongly objected to it. But we did go on to Rome with him, though he was more or less quiet from then onward, contemplating what to do, but in Rome he just enjoyed it like everyone else. In one place we spent night in hotel, before we reached Genoa. I shared room with cadet officer, and we put out light and there was noise suddenly, *sshhh* noise, and it felt like something was scraping the wallpaper of room and suddenly I felt something drop from ceiling onto bed, then something else drop. We put on light and room was full of bedbugs, dropping onto us from ceiling out of crevices where paper was peeling off. They're nasty things, like ladybirds, only brown and smaller and flatter, and do they bite! There was feeling of dirtiness that was so distressing, suddenly to be confronted by that.

"In Italy, we saw that people were not concerned with what was happening elsewhere—they were content with their lot. It was 'phoney war' at this time, but also Italians were neutral in sense that they neither welcomed us nor did anything against us. For instance, when we asked about petrol, they treated us just like any other Italians—as if they were surprised we didn't know rules. Cadet officer knew French and Latin, so he got by, adding an 'a' to end of words. Except Romans weren't very good on words for petrol and so on!

"Genoa was big surprise, first time I'd seen town on sea. I hadn't seen real sea before, especially as it was from height. We plodded on because from there it wasn't all that far to Menton, on French border. It was now April 8, and when we arrived at Menton, it was six in evening and already bit dark. And that was moment of fright because that captain said, 'Now I've got you, all of you, you've been violating my rules, I was in command, now I'm taking you to Polish authorities and you'—he said especially to cadet—'will be facing court-martial for that.' So driver stepped out of car, got captain to get out too, then stepped back in again and off he drove. Instead of going to committee in Menton, we drove right on toward Marseilles, stopping night somewhere along route.

"There were information centers along coast to guide us to places where Polish camps were. In this case we were very well off because cadet was speaking French—probably fluently, I don't know. We learned that there is Polish camp not far from Marseilles, camp de Carpiane. We did not make it that day, we spent night in Marseilles hotel. Cadet officer invited us to go into town and we went to restaurant and he ordered some wine and—well, I'd had sip of wine at age of nine at my sister's wedding and ever since then I knew it existed but I didn't know that people were using something like that with their food. I didn't take to it much, I was hungry rather than anything else. We drove to camp next day, still in car. Administration tried to take it over, but driver was experienced man, he managed to drive back to Marseilles and sold car. Major part of payment I took because car was given to me—they didn't want to take any, but I gave them some. We were picked up and said we wanted to go to camp de Carpiane, and people didn't know we had already been there. There we were issued with semi-military clothing. It was beginning of April by now, nights were very cold still."

BLITZKRIEG

rom another world, down below us in Invermore Close, an ice-cream van chimed in vain in the sultry heat. Our imaginations, though, were inhabiting the cold April nights. "By this time I'd already decided that I'm not interested either in going to Paris to continue my studies or in consulting consulate—I'd been told they would arrange it for me either to study in Paris or be transferred to England," Joe went on. "Of course at that stage there was lull, there was no indication that Germans would march on France, after all it had Maginot Line, nobody could penetrate that deep, everybody believed it would protect France."

"I've heard it was called the Imaginot Line afterward," I tell him.

My father laughs. We're on to tape nine now, and he's visibly relaxing, sloughing off years like army kit.

"But I already decided that it would be better just to be with army and return with army and continue my studies in Poland, because it was only way to get back, with Polish army we knew was gathering under French command. I didn't want to start something and then not finish it again. And then, we arrived in Marseilles day after Germany invaded Denmark and Norway, so we knew war had broken out in earnest, so there was more reason for me to join up."

Hitler had not planned to invade Norway and Denmark: they had not been on his list. His plans for the spring of 1940, outlined to his generals the previous October, were to invade first Holland, Belgium, Luxembourg and northern France, and then to use those countries to serve as a base for the successful prosecution of the war against England. After that he planned to turn his attentions east toward the Soviet Union. Neville Chamberlain, however, still heading the British government in April, persisted in believing that Britain could negotiate a peace with Germany—in spite of the fact that Hitler had already bombed the Royal Navy at Scapa Flow in the North Sea on three occasions, killing almost a thousand British sailors. Chamberlain's response during the phoney war was still cautious and preemptive. He wanted to cut off Germany's supplies of war matériel, principally iron ore, which it was getting from Sweden, and he planned to do so from March 20, 1940, by mining the seas around the north coast of Norway to prevent German access to Scandinavia. Delays in this plan—including the replacement of French prime minister Edouard Daladier by anti-appeasement Paul Reynaud on March 20—prevented it from being carried out, and allowed German cryptographers to intercept it. Hitler did a quick about-turn with part of his army and navy to make a surprise invasion of Norway and Denmark on April 9.

Joe has found amongst his papers a small diary he bought in Hungary in 1940 in which he wrote the dates of his itinerary, the written facts some anchorage in uncertainty. He wrote his notes in shorthand, learned at the *Bursa*—"it kept busybodies ignorant of them"—and the notes tell that indeed he arrived in Marseilles at 18:00 on April 10, the day after the fall of Norway and Denmark, and was transferred the next day at 19:30 to the camp de Carpiane.

"We spent one week at camp de Carpiane. It was transit camp— you registered your name that you volunteered to serve in army and that was that. We were still in civilian clothing but they issued us with long underpants made of starched calico so that they made noise when you walked and you couldn't bend your knees, so we walked around like Frankenstein. The camp also had French regiments there who were more or less in charge, and they also had soldiers from French Africa, from Senegal and Gambia, with extremely dark skin and three-inch-long white teeth, and when they smiled you knew you were going to be eaten. They couldn't speak French, we couldn't speak French, so we were in same boat. But they were underprivileged—they were allowed in one part of canteen only and they were not allowed to have any alcoholic drinks at all. Being friends with them, we gave them glasses of wine and then they started opening their hearts to us, all in sign language—how cruel their corporal was, how they didn't like French military police. And they said, give us another glass of wine and we will bring you our corporal's ears, and of course we were not very keen on ears, so we said, all right, we'll give you another glass if you don't bring them—and they said, yes, even better, even better!

"Then we were transferred to place called Bressuire. Many people were ex-servicemen, and so they gave their rank et cetera. All those who had served were told to step to one side and all those who hadn't to other side—and I was on my own. All eyes were then on me from recruiting point of view because I wasn't yet in any category. Three people with notebooks came toward me and asked about my background. I told them I was studying electromechanical engineering. Ah, electricity! Then it's signals—and there I was. This was their type of logic—electricity, therefore signals. People I was with, they had experience of army life. They knew what to expect, they knew what to do, they knew how to react. To me, every step was new. I did not know anything. I was such beginner, such naive person, I did not know how to react to anything. So when they said signals, that was it, I was in signals. I really wanted to go to tanks because I thought it was safe inside tank, but signals it was.

"I gave my proper age—they didn't check with passport, didn't even know I had passport. It was taken from me little bit later, when it was turn to take various documents that were not true, let's put it this way. I gave it to them because there was always thought behind that we would march from France to Germany and all documents would be preserved and there would be document that I was issued with, passport, and then I could declare honestly that I haven't got it. It paid to tell truth because then I don't have to remember lies. Sometimes truth doesn't quite correspond—no, it's always there but seen in different way. Or you may remember something additional that happened there, that had not been disclosed, or you disclose something and later on you forget about it. Only truth you can have is what is written, because then it remains as absolute record. In memory, only certain things remain as absolute record from beginning to end. Others are tinted in various ways because some things become less important in that incident than others.

"Then we went through Rennes, and stopped at military barracks, which from outside looked like fortress or horrible prison and from inside looked like horrible prison, and it was. It was there we were issued with uniforms. And you felt different, because you were exactly same as everyone else. You thought, well, at least I'm one of them now; being in civilian clothing I didn't belong to them, even though they were also in civilian clothing: they knew how to behave, I didn't. Now, when we all had uniforms, even though I still didn't know how to behave, they couldn't differentiate between me and them. We stayed one night there, and from there we went on to camp de Coëtquidan near Rennes—this was purely Polish camp, training camp for Polish Armored Cavalry Brigade. As soon as we got to Coëtquidan, cadet was put with officers, he had rank and profession.

"In barracks there was room full of Morse keys, where people were training. It was noisy, like aviary on unknown planet where birds were chirping all same tune. The corporal said to us, 'You'll be deaf by the time you're thirty from this noise, but don't worry, because you're not going to reach thirty.' I thought I shall never get used to it, especially as I was only novice. You have to learn Morse code, then you have to learn military discipline. I stayed for about one month—it seemed like six months, it could have been three days."

The diary tells us it was from April 27 until May 25.

"We knew nothing of what was going on around. There was no feeling of threat to France—people trusted Maginot Line. British Expeditionary Force was not far from there. We were receiving soldiers' pay—fifteen francs a month, fifty centimes a day, this was just private's pay. We learned that British soldiers' pay was twenty-five francs a day, so there was some jealousy over injustice—French forces had same pay as us. So there is home force being paid much less; it was like later on in Britain when Americans came in.

"We were sent to prepare airfield strip for English and French airplanes—there was tough gorse and very dry and we were supposed to hack it away. Only air force that existed that we knew of by then was German, there was nothing else around, so we were not keen on doing it. When airplanes are around they usually fly around, don't they? So we came to conclusion that they either have no petrol or no airplanes, and as petrol existed for cars, obviously there were no airplanes. It was heavy work, so in my innocence I suggested to corporal in charge, why don't we set fire to it, that will do job for us? And he said, what wonderful idea, so we struck match, threw it in, and it was going beautifully at first except it got out of control and fire brigade had to come from Rennes because it was threatening surrounding countryside. Nobody ever said whose idea it was, report just said, 'Fire flared up.'

"In military training, we were taught rifle drills—how to put it on, take it off, put it next to your foot. That wasn't too bad. Then they decided that they'd put a bayonet on rifle and show us how to pierce an enemy if he ever comes near you. So: rifle is in horizontal position and he says, 'Push! Back! Push! Back!' That wasn't so bad. Then suddenly he says, 'Push! Hold it!' and in extended position like that I fell flat on my face. I was taken before commanding officer of signals and it was really embarrassing, it's criminal offense to drop weapon. I simply explained to him that I hadn't got enough strength to hold rifle with my arms extended. When I stated that, they checked if I had enough strength and that cadet officer saved me because by then he had become a medic, and he signed form saying this young fellow hasn't got enough strength to hold rifle when his arms are extended. This was day or two before we went on to Versailles."

On May 10, a fortnight after Joe had started his basic training at the camp de Coëtquidan, the Germans invaded Belgium and Holland, both neutral countries not prepared to wage war, especially in view of the air- and land power ranged against them—which included an extraordinary sixteen thousand German troops parachuted into Holland like sycamore leaves. On May 14, in another surprise move, and in spite of the 450 kilometers of defensive Maginot Line built from Belgium to the Swiss frontier at a cost of 9 million francs in gold for every kilometer, the Germans invaded France. They did it by simply coming in from newly conquered Belgium through the only gaps in the Maginot Line: the tortuous routes through the Ardennes massif which were thought to be obstacle enough in themselves, and which brought them into the parts of northern France already so devastated during the First World War. As with the Czechs, all those fortifications for nothing against brute force and cunning. Ten days after this *Blitzkrieg* had started—Hitler's own invention, a "lightning strike" designed to create as much havoc and confusion as possible—Joe was sent up to the training barracks for Radio Signals at Versailles, outside Paris.

"We were supposed to train there to go to front line. We were attached to different units from then, though we were all still signals—it was only Polish training center for signals. We were not far from palace at Versailles, at barracks that were misery as far as accommodation was concerned—1914 barracks. There were three or four bunks going upwards, and you had to walk sideways to squeeze between them. Mattresses were filled with 1914–18 straw and lice were prominent—it was just absolute misery there. Lunch

consisted of sort of block of meat which was dripping with blood
and practically nothing else except *bidon* of wine. Some drank it all
at lunch. I never drank it at all, to me it was undrinkable. Another
thing they did there, they put bromide in your food. Reason for that
is that apparently it was subduing men's sexual desires—all that it
did was make people more sleepy. Fortunately I didn't like food
that was given to me because I didn't learn what was in it until
much later. Like most French cities, they had brothels, and venereal
disease was widely spread—this is probably one of reasons why
they put bromide in, because there was no room in hospitals for
people infected like that and obviously they didn't like it, because
not only did they have to use bed, but later on there was punishment
and they had to use military barracks as prisons and there weren't
enough of them. It was cumulative effect that had to be eliminated
and they decided that best elimination was bromide. That was their
way of thinking about it."

If my father and his fellow soldiers had known what surrounded
them, and what was about to confront them, they might have taken
the bromide gladly for oblivion. German victories were proceeding
at a breathtaking pace around them. With Norway, Denmark, Belgium and Holland fallen within a month, the German troops had
managed by May 21 to invade France and reach the mouth of the
River Somme, on the Channel coast. This meant that four days
before my father reached Versailles, the Germans were not only
cutting off all avenues of escape to the south for the British Expeditionary Forces in France, but also staring England in the face from
across the Channel. Three days later, Rommel was writing to his
wife: "My estimate is that the war will be won in a fortnight," and
the same day Hitler told his staff: "The next objective of our operations is to annihilate the French, British and Belgian forces which
are surrounded."

But there had been a setback for Hitler. In Britain, Neville
Chamberlain, who had thought from the outbreak of war in September that "there was no hurry as time was on our side," was run-

ning out of time himself. During a two-day debate in the House of Commons on May 7 and 8, the seventy-one-year-old Chamberlain saw no reason why he should go. However, the next day, the Germans invaded Belgium and Holland and it was made clear to him that an all-party national government was now urgently needed, and that the Labour Party leaders would refuse to serve under him. So from May 10, 1940, Hitler found himself no longer facing the "small fry" of Munich, but someone who would match him in fighting spirit and resolution: the backbencher and constant critic of appeasement, Winston Churchill. Eight days after becoming prime minister, Churchill made his first broadcast to the nation, saying, "This is one of the most awe-striking periods in the long history of France and Britain. It is also beyond doubt the most sublime." The British and French people, he said, "have advanced to rescue not only Europe but mankind from the foulest and most soul-destroying tyranny which has ever darkened and stained the pages of history."

Behind Britain and France, Churchill went on, were "a group of shattered States and bludgeoned races: the Czechs, the Poles, the Norwegians, the Danes, the Dutch, the Belgians—upon all of whom the long night of barbarism will descend, unbroken even by a star of hope, unless we conquer, as conquer we must, as conquer we shall." Yet Churchill's first major engagement of the war as prime minister was going to be a retreat, the evacuation from Dunkirk—reaping the legacy of Chamberlain's inactivity. When Churchill took over as prime minister, there were only forty-five military aircraft at his disposal. (No wonder my father and his fellow soldiers had seen no British airplanes over France.) After his first month in office, there were over a thousand. They were immediately brought into service to cover the mass evacuation of hundreds of thousands of men during the nine-day retreat from Dunkirk. Unfortunately, over the period of Dunkirk from May 27 to June 4, 1940, although 190 airplanes were produced, 194 were shot down. The great evacuation began two days after my father arrived at Versailles. Altogether, 225,000 British, 110,000 French

and 2,000 Belgian troops would be evacuated from French to
British shores. Churchill feared that it would be his "hard lot to
announce the greatest military disaster in our long history," and was
careful not to present this evacuation as a victory, calling it instead
a "miracle of deliverance."

Meanwhile, in spring 1940, an unambiguously catastrophic event
was unfolding in the dark pine forests of Russia, as my father travelled up through France with the Polish army: the massacring of the
fifteen thousand Polish officers at Katyn. It would be three years
before the news of this slaughter saw the light of day, so naturally
my father knew nothing of it—just as he did not know how narrow
an escape he had had by having to leave Baligrod so precipitously.
In early 1940, the Nazis began to deport over 1 million Poles to
Germany for forced labor in factories and fields, many of whom
would die in ghastly conditions, whilst others would return to
Poland after the war broken and bitter. Commandant Zielinski's
mention to my father of getting Poles like him to do work such as
unblocking roads was no doubt the thin end of the Nazi labor camp
wedge—just as the prison yard in Lwow had been the thin end of
the Soviet labor camp wedge.

"It was at Versailles that I met Ted. By that time he was sergeant
and I was designated to his platoon and as platoon we were designated to tanks, so at last, I thought, I was in tanks. By that time war
was going badly. Germans had broken through Belgium, and they
have overrun Maginot Line. It was just matter of time. We knew
about it. Shock came when they dropped paratroopers in Holland
and completely destroyed local defenses from there onward. The
same happened in Belgium, they just shot through Belgium and
bypassed Maginot Line and that was shock, that they managed to
simply go around it. No one had thought of that. We were supposed
to train for quite while—I wasn't even half efficient, or quarter efficient in what I was supposed to do, but I was in platoon and that

was that. Later on"—he looks at his diary—"on June 9 it was, we were attached to armored brigade of General Maczek.

"If things were normal, I would have been there for about six weeks or so until I became proficient. His brigade was already formed. It barely had tanks—probably two or three tanks—but most of soldiers in brigade were from Polish forces in Poland and they knew tactics and everything, and what to do with tanks. Tank is tank, it's like motorcar, once you can drive one, you can drive all. That brigade was formed very quickly, and few more tanks were delivered—this was under French command. Our army was independent, but under French command, and French command decided that we should go to front line"—he hesitates—"huh, basically to save France because everything was falling back and I think we didn't know at that time what was going to happen, we were just allocated to that brigade, and that general, General Maczek, had nickname: Butcher. He achieved his objectives no matter what cost, and he was known for that."

His men may have known him as the butcher, but Stanisłas Maczek had studied philosophy and what he termed "the psychology of sentiments" at Lwow University before becoming a highly decorated career soldier. By spring 1940, he and the similarly exiled General Władysław Sikorski had managed to put together an impressive army of some eighty thousand Polish troops on French soil, drawn from Poles already living in France and from the thousands of Polish soldiers who managed to escape from internment in Hungary and Romania—and the odd independent escapee like my father. Maczek had only recently begun to muster and regroup his Tenth Armored Division at the army camp at Coëtquidan when my father joined it.

"When this was being formed we were still in Versailles and orders to depart were very quick, but before we departed on our last day in Versailles, German planes bombed Versailles, so we knew they wouldn't be far away. Day or so later we were transferred to armored brigade so they could get used to communication with

General Maczek (left) at Coëtquidan, 1940

radio. I don't think there were radios in every tank, it was just too primitive, but as group of tanks there would have been commander who'd be in radio contact with probably another tank unit or anti-tank unit. So this was to give us and them opportunity to cooperate, but there was no time for any maneuvers like that at all. Because as soon as we got round to them we discovered that following morning we were going to be loaded onto train and transferred to front line—it was as quick as that.

"We arrived there probably in afternoon and we saw cars, beautiful limousines sprayed with khaki paint to make them military vehicles. Everything was requisitioned for war, just sprayed khaki with blotches on it. When we joined them, we were allocated to our radio stations. Now this was another disappointment. In my joining signals, I thought we would have a radio station which is nicely covered with metal plates and reasonably safe, and when we got there we discovered that we had truck—front tires were solid tires, that was fair enough. Instead of rear wheels it had caterpillars like tractor, made of half metal, half rubber, and instead of having nice little protection by armor where we were sitting, we were covered with canvas canopy and that was our armory. We were issued with rifles and everybody got three rounds of ammunition to fight war, and there was a very good explanation for it: they said if signals have to fight with rifles, then three rounds of ammunition are more than enough. You were not supposed to fight with rifles. But there was another thing we learned earlier, that a unit in French infantry was issued with machine guns, and then they discovered that firing pins were not there, because some general decided that machine guns are going to be stored in one place which was not far from Paris and that firing pins are going to be stored way down somewhere toward Toulon so that when Germans capture machine guns, they won't be able to use them. So there they were, armed with machine guns, and the firing pins were far away and never arrived. I'm certain there are hundreds of other incidents that are even more tragic than that."

With hindsight, the inadequate British and French preparation for war, which catapulted so many young men like my father into impossible situations, might have been mitigated if the military had listened to the newly established top-secret code-breaking intelligence center at Bletchley Park in Buckinghamshire, which had broken the Enigma code by January 1940—based on the initial work of Polish mathematician Marian Rejewski. Just before the invasion of Norway, Bletchley Park reported an unusual buildup of German naval activity in the Baltic, but the military and government ignored it. As a result, the British and French were caught completely unawares by the German occupation of Norway. Even after this, for a long time no one gave any thought to getting through Bletchley Park's intelligence findings to the troops on the ground, where it could have been of some use.

"We were in station—[inside the] truck, that is, they were called station—more or less hidden by trees, and we were woken early one morning, it was still bit dark, and we were told to get ready, we are going to be loaded onto train and transported toward front line. But there was one incident that night. There was man in signals, but not in our station, this man was trembling with fear all the time, he was trembling he was so scared, and when he woke up following morning his hair was gray—and he had had black hair, and it was absolutely frightening to see him, he was so scared he should have been taken into hospital or put somewhere where he felt safe, he should never have come with us. And there was another one on sister station, another young fellow, he'd been in army before and he had red hair, and he was also scared."

"Were you scared?"

"I must not say I did not feel fear. I did not want to die, let's put it this way. I was always youngest in army, always at least two years younger than anybody else. I said to myself, I'm just nineteen years old, I don't want to die yet. Well, following day we got up very early to load tanks onto wagons. Authorities that be, all-knowledgeable who knew everything about how to carry on war, and how to load tanks onto wagons, had put wagons in yard half kilometer away from us, and so that enemy wouldn't see them, they put smokescreen over yard, beautiful black smokescreen. Previous morning you could see station, and wagons, and that morning you could not see anything, there was just one big black cloud there four hundred meters by four hundred meters sitting there. Preparations were under way to load everything, some engines were ticking over and suddenly there was hum of airplanes, they saw smokescreen, and bombed smokescreen. Fortunately, they didn't bother to bomb us.

"Then we were ordered to move toward Troyes—I was innocent one, I knew nothing, I just followed, this was just about all I could do. But I think we had sixteen tanks in our unit, and later on thirteen motorcycles and antiaircraft guns, and antitank guns—and radio

communication, this last was most important. And that was our
brigade, or it might have been part of brigade. Motorcycles were
fighting vehicles, many with machine guns on them. They were
supposed to be very fast, so they could creep up on somebody and
shoot them very fast. But they were also for transporting officers
from various units, and sometimes for communication too, transfer-
ring messages because you couldn't rely entirely on radio to transmit everything—sometimes if somebody is only half of kilometer
away it is much quicker to send motorcycle than it is to transmit.
But at that time I didn't really know, all I knew that there were tanks
there, and our armor was piece of canvas, that was disappointing.

"When we arrived in Troyes, we were going through suburbs
when bombers came and they dropped few bombs, and then fighters
came along and started spraying place with machine guns. Obviously they could see column and they started spraying with
machine guns. Well, there's no point in sitting underneath canvas
when you are target, so we jumped out and into garden, where there
were cabbages and carrots. I just jumped in and tried to dig myself
as deep into soil as possible, there was firing and bombs were dropping, you name it and it was going on. And Ted also dived into this
garden there, and as he dived there was little shed, or perhaps it was
chicken coop which he was diving toward, so I called to him, 'Ted,
over here!,' and as he was moving toward us, two French soldiers
dived toward that little coop, and as he dived toward me there came
stream of bullets from airplane and they went right through garden
and they grazed Ted's temple and forehead and he grasped at it and
looked at his hand, and it was full of blood. He looked at me as if to
say, 'Look at me, look what you have done to me!,' and within
almost split second of that that coop exploded. Direct hit."

Joe looked at me, startled, his eyes brimming, flickering faster
than usual, the lower part of his face crumpling and astonished, as if
caught in a flashlight—terror-struck that in a split-second impulse
he had caused a friend to be hit, and then seeing those two French
soldiers explode. Then he broke down in tears. It was the first time

he'd done so. My eyes were brimming, too, and I hugged him and said we must call it a day, and he said no, and shook himself and blew his nose.

"We got out of course, this finished, these things don't last forever, it just finished. We got back and discovered that there was no damage either to our station or to our sister station, and—er—we moved." Joe broke down again, and we broke off for the day.

16 | CHAMPAGNE

And yet we came straight back to it the following afternoon, the catharsis driving us both on, Joe barely missing a beat. "When that bombing ended, we started going through streets, there were still houses burning on street. Strangely enough, saying was if bombers come and you are somewhere near, and there is bridge, go onto bridge because they will bomb everything and miss bridge, because they are aiming at bridge and if they are aiming at something they will obviously miss it. So you sit on bridge—and anyway even if they hit it there will be just one small hole because it would shoot through and drop in water and if you got hit on head you wouldn't know about it.

"Our convoy at that stage was only our three stations [i.e., trucks]. There were others, but they were further ahead and there were some behind but we got through without anything. Civilians were badly hit by that, and those two French soldiers. Otherwise there was no time to find out whether there were any casualties. Ted's graze was superficial. We had no bandages or anything like that—we had first-aid people trained in medical things, but they were not with us. So we started moving, and you remember I told you about man whose hair turned gray, and I mentioned another young man, older than I, who was ginger-haired? He was also scared, very jumpy, and as we were going toward Troyes we were stopping in places and he was trembling and Ted gave him drink of wine to settle him down, then he said, I'll have another drink, and when we were in Troyes, clinging to earth, he was in middle of road, shaking his fist at the airplanes, saying, 'You Deutsche Schweinhunds, come down here and you'll see who's going to win, you can't hit me, you couldn't hit a battleship if you saw one!'—he was walking up and down street like that. But unfortunately from then onward he was no good anymore as soldier because he always took his wine and that diminished his responsibility. He was just one of people with us.

"From Troyes, we moved on for about twenty kilometers and met up with tanks, don't ask me how they got there. We were stationed in wood amongst trees and on one side of trees was road and beyond that wheatfields, wheat was still green, this was around early to middle of June, around twelfth. When we met with tanks we stopped and obviously there was some discussion about what to do, where to go, and again bombers came and started dropping bombs. It was very hot and we were in this heavy uniform and as soon as we saw them coming, we knew they would be bombing where tanks were. Rest of us who were not in tanks we ran toward wheatfields, because if bomb drops on your head you've had it, but if you are in open field like that and it drops even about two meters from you, it just makes hole and covers you with earth, but you are safe. Well, safer than being with tanks because if anything hit them there was shrapnel et cetera flying all over place and it wasn't quite so safe. Well, they dropped bombs, and then went off.

"We returned to tanks. Our stations were always parked little bit away from tanks, because tanks were targets, and we started going back to station when fighter bombers came in and they were spraying everything with machine-gun fire. Now that's different thing altogether, you just hid behind tank and you were absolutely safe. They were coming in one direction and when you are behind tank, they can't hit you, because tanks have strong armor. There were not many of these fighters, although it appeared there might have been two hundred because they were ranked about two or three times. As soon as they disappeared, few bombers came back again and we ran to that field and by time we were in that field—I can only speak for myself but others said same, they were so tired—I had had enough. I said now if fighter comes again I'm not moving from here, I'm staying here, I've had enough. And of course they returned, but they must have been out of ammunition, they were just scaring us from then on, so I didn't have to run."

Joe laughs, but he's very tense.

"Would you have run?"

"Yes, you would, no matter what, you were so exhausted, you said that if it happens I can't run, and then you see them coming and few people start running, and you run. It was probably when we realized that no fire was coming from them that we stopped, otherwise I'm certain we would all have been running."

"How were you feeling about this first day of bombing?"

"I was frightened. One is frightened because you are so helpless, you can't do anything about it; we were not organized yet, it was just going there trying to get to where action was, and we were already being attacked before we even met any Germans. So it was situation where we felt: well, where is our air force to protect us, we haven't seen one friendly airplane in sky. In a way it was blessing, because you didn't have to recognize whether it was yours or not, whatever was in sky was German. Antiaircraft guns were not yet with us. All I knew was that we were with our group of tanks, we would probably go together. At my level of military echelon I knew nothing!

"We moved little further off and spent night in that place. You slept very little, wherever there was bit of space. Inside station, there was just about enough room for three people to sit and two or three standing. You slept out in open, found vehicle with high chassis and slept underneath. Nights were quite warm by this stage, so there was no problem with that. You cannot say you woke up at certain hour because you were awake all night really, you were just dozing off from time to time. It was still dark when we got up. At that time we still had kitchen with us and we were given some bread and coffee and we started moving toward lines where we were going to meet enemy. Spot we got to was big, flattish hill with woods and with farmhouse some distance away, and as we were getting there, there was enormous cloud of airplanes coming and we said, well, this is end, this is end of us, but they just flew past, and general opinion was that they were coming from bombing station and had no more bombs left.

"We got to that hill, called I think Montbard. Strange thing happened there. First of all we were told to be very close to tanks, but Ted was saying, 'This is not place for our station, we'll have planes on us in no time.' I wasn't very experienced at Morse code and I think from time when I called Ted away from that chicken coop, he took care of me, and he said to me, 'Don't do any duty on station, you just do various things around station like delivering messages to our commandant, it will be easier for you and it will help us.' So they sent me to major in charge of tanks asking permission to move over to that farmhouse where we could be hidden and not taken as military target. We had antitank guns with us at that point, on our left. We did not know about it, but that was day that Italy stepped into war [June 10] and to demonstrate their willingness to fight they sent Stuka dive-bombers on that unit—it wasn't difficult to find, no matter how you camouflaged yourself. They started dive-bombing tanks and we didn't have antiaircraft guns with us, they were somewhere else, so our antitank guns opened fire—at airplanes! But it was hopeless. If you hit one, you destroyed it, but you had little chance of hitting them and of course these Stuka dive-bombers, that was something we didn't experience before; they screech and scream as they are diving down toward you, it was unbearable, this alone unnerved people. One of our ammunition carriers next to tanks was hit with direct hit and ammunition started exploding in all directions, we were quite distance away and it was just confusion from horrible noise."

General Maczek's own account of the battle around Montbard and thereafter echoes my father's experiences:

> Any man who suffers from such an air raid has the feeling of being personally targeted. He feels absolutely sure it's him the German pilot is trying to get. The passivity involved in waiting around for such attacks increases this painful sensation even more. . . . From the beginning it was perfectly clear to me that the operational mission was quite beyond our capabilities: moreover, we had no idea of the extent of the German tank incursion into France.

Maczek was not at all ready in his own terms when he was called into battle by the French command. His "Light Motorized Division" was to reach combat readiness by June 1941, but the German invasion had led the French to insist that at least part of the so-called division be sent to the front a full year early. It was also against Maczek's wishes that his units be fielded individually, as they were, and not together, but he had to cede to the undoubted *force majeure* of the surprise German invasion. He had an impossible task trying to coordinate forces that were not yet fully operational, especially in the absence of coherent strategies from above or French reinforcements. "Effectively," writes the historian Andrzej Suchcitz, "General Maczek found himself in a sack with the noose tightening." On the ground, my father and the rest of his unit were experiencing the effects of this, as well as the lack of knowledge even in high command of what was going on.

"In charge of our three stations we had youngish man about twenty-four, bit higher than cadet officer, he was aspirant, but he was in charge. He had beautiful uniform, with high leather boots

tight around his calves, really splendid uniform to go to ball. He
was there hiding, as we all were, trying to scratch earth to get
underneath it. I think it was mostly noise that was worse than
bombs dropping. They were mostly missing with their bombs, but
one dropped little bit nearer and when next screech came along he
was looking where to go and he just jumped into big ditch just like
that. When screech ended, bomb dropped elsewhere, and everything quieted and we found that aspirant had dropped into ditch
which was farmer's lavatory. He came out and nobody dared to get
near to him—it was comical to start with and later we took pity on
him. We went to pump and started pumping water and throwing it
over him, from distance at first, and later on from little bit nearer.

"We managed to clean him sufficiently to get near to him and
while all this was going on we noticed there were two army supply
trucks nearby we hadn't seen. We wondered what was in them, and
in one we found French uniforms and particularly underwear, and
that was blessing because we could drop everything we had and put
clean uniform and underwear on. Other truck originally probably
carried only food but all that was left on it was meatpaste in tins,
cheese, cube sugar and bottles and bottles of champagne. It had
been abandoned—obviously French had abandoned it. First we
changed clothes, but when officer came to take his boots off we
couldn't get them off because they were too wet, so we had to cut
them off with knife and from then on he was just like one of us, but
he said if you ever mention it to anybody you'll be court-martialed.
But we kept quiet because we felt sorry for him really.

"We started loading—well, I started loading meatpaste, et
cetera; others were busy with communications. Then we saw German tanks were coming toward us from right, and there was little
bit of skirmish between tanks, so that our tanks moved to right and
that blocked path between enemy and our antitank guns. Our
French antitank artillery was good, German tanks couldn't face it,
they were too weak and it would penetrate their armor, so what they
did they put sacks of sand around tanks in addition to protect them.

They maneuvered toward our tanks and at that moment antiaircraft artillery opened fire instead at tanks. When that happens, of course it couldn't do any damage to tanks, but when antiaircraft shell explodes, it's like firework—there are sparks, lot of smoke and sand from sacks was flying in all directions. One of our people was listening to German communications and heard them broadcasting to all stations: '*Zurück, zurück! Neue Waffe!*' We were saved by that, because they turned round and disappeared, thinking we'd got some new weapon.

"No one was living in farmhouse, it was deserted, there were not even animals there. We were about one kilometer away from front line and people might have deserted because they expected Germans. Our motorcycles scoured countryside ahead as lookouts, so they knew if tanks were coming—it was very unusual for tank column to meet another tank column without knowing. Radio communications could intercept each other, and we had people who spoke fluent German, but they would have to have people who spoke Polish. When battle starts, there's no point intercepting messages anymore, everything happens so fast that what you hear has already happened. When it starts, everyone's on their own, there doesn't seem to be any coordinated action.

"After all this, we moved away, there were few casualties. Our problem was supply—not only food but fuel. Tanks were already very low on fuel. What they intended to do was to move from place to place because by this time locations of German positions were discovered and it wasn't question of attacking only German tanks but also German field artillery and normal soldiers—it was destruction of people rather than anything else. If tanks get at something like field artillery of course they win, because they are faster and very difficult to hit. They made one or two excursions like that, a few kilometers here and there, creating little bit of confusion. We heard Germans saying on radio, we are sending reinforcements, but by time German tanks arrived there, our tanks had gone. This is probably one of reasons why they were running out of fuel.

"We were almost surrounded by Germans by that time, there was one road that was still clear, going to south. Order came that motorcycles should go through, and antitank and antiaircraft guns should break through. Two or three tanks had to be destroyed because of lack of fuel—they were destroyed so that Germans don't get them. All of those could break through cordon, but order said, as far as you signals are concerned, good luck. We were not fast enough to go through with motorcycles, and we couldn't go with tanks, so good luck to you! So we selected route that was as close to motorcycles as possible for some distance. Our maximum speed was about forty kilometers an hour, very slow, although truck could go across field very nicely. We were threading through these various roads like that, trying to go south by compass. By that time we were still fighting, but general headquarters for army was already in England.

"Order to break out toward south or western France came through on June 14, and by that time France had already practically collapsed. We didn't really know about it. Unless you were high up you didn't know what was happening; probably even major who was commander of our tanks didn't know what was happening. Orders came now, though, make your way south and try to make it to England, so we knew France was collapsing. Fortunately, being signals, we started listening to various stations, even to London, so could get some idea of what was happening."

What was happening on that day, June 14, was that the Germans had occupied Paris. It was less than one hundred kilometers away from where my father and his unit were still technically fighting. Once Paris had fallen to the Nazis, the rest of the country could not be far behind, and within three days, Marshal Philippe Pétain, the new—military—prime minister of France, had asked for an armistice with Germany. As it happens, my father's unit was about equidistant from Paris to its left and from the small village of Colombey-les-deux-Eglises to its right, the home (and eventual grave) of General Charles de Gaulle. Now minister of war, de

Gaulle wanted France to fight on (as did the previous prime minister, Paul Reynaud), but was overruled by a divided French government. On June 18, the day France under its new prime minister signed the armistice with Hitler, de Gaulle left France to lead another government-in-exile in London, like President Beneš and General Sikorski before him.

Hitler had orchestrated the signing of the armistice to extract maximum symbolic revenge for the humiliation of Versailles which had so fuelled him. He brought the railway carriage where the Versailles armistice had been signed out of its museum and into the clearing in the forest of Compiègne where on November 11, 1918, Germany, in his view, had been forced to sign away its pride, and now he inflicted the same on France: in twenty-four humiliating articles—including that France should bear all the costs for the army of occupation—France had to sign away its sovereignty, half of its territory, all of its armaments and military forces, its freedom of action and its pride.

Joe went on: "We were trying to get as far away as possible from Germans to get outside circle that was closing on us. Some of roads we were on were not even on maps. We stopped at one spot to rest drivers for while and road was on side of hill, and we didn't know what was beyond hill. There were only two stations by this time—I don't know what happened to third one. I was always running around, it was my duty to investigate, and I climbed up that hill and looked over and there were German soldiers there cooking their meal. I went back to Ted and said, 'They've got kitchen going there, we could have some food.' He said, 'Let's get out of here,' and we did.

"I've seen two of our soldiers attended by medics; there was lot of blood. Medics had ambulance with them, because originally it was thought front would be more or less stationary, and ambulance would go back and forth taking people. That was destroyed at Troyes when we were hit with planes and we knew no matter where we were we would be attacked by airplanes. That meant that front line cannot be stationary, because supply lines and lines of communication would be attacked. We continued there, that was last bit of Germans we saw around there, from then on we didn't have any problems with them. Our food was still problem, though—it consisted of piece of cheese with meatpaste on it washed down by champagne, or cube of sugar with cheese on it, or a cube of sugar with meatpaste on it—and it wasn't very good diet, and we would have given anything for drink of water.

"We did not go through any town at that time, though once we came across farm and we thought maybe we shall be able to buy some bread. One of us had been waiter in France and he went and asked to buy bread and milk. Man said, 'No, I can't sell you that,' so our man said, 'We'll dig in round your farm and defend you from Germans then,' and he said, 'Oh no, anything but that!' And that was so welcome, that bread and milk. We paid him for it, but it was just he was so afraid of antagonizing Germans if they came and discovered he was giving help to Allied soldiers."

Maczek's view of the French "retreat" was tinged with bitter irony, as is my father's. He writes of how "impatient we all were to see some sign somewhere of French resistance asserting itself and some attempt to let loose a counterattack in grand style. . . . As for reconnaissance, only the odd piece of information came through to us, gleaned from here and there, often exaggerated, near panic. . . . Another eloquent sign was seeing empty roads when the Germans were nearby. There was a silence; that before the storm." Maczek retails sardonically how one "Captain Borotra, ace French tennis player, is very happy to share a chicken we offer him, washed down with wine, as we sit in a ditch, but refuses to join us for the operation at Montbard, on the pretext of orders received from above."

"From there we moved on," my father says, "and we had collected other soldiers and it was very cramped inside. So I put belt round framework in roof and hung my arm through it and that was my bed for night. As we were going along we met Polish soldiers in open truck, and they'd mounted one antitank gun on it and two machine guns, so we were armed by then. We also had small weapons—we discarded rifles that were issued to us with three rounds of ammunition because you could find weapons almost any-where, so we got ourselves very short rifles instead of these long ones, which were useless and heavy. We got pistols from that sup-ply at Montbard. I probably wouldn't know what to do with it, but there it was. There was debris all over place, abandoned tanks and artillery guns, and as we were moving south we were meeting more soldiers, mostly French soldiers, just marching along roads. And we were also meeting refugees by that time and that hampered movement along road; there were long queues of cars, but we were fortunate in that we could move off roads and go through fields.

"By that time war was over as far as French soldiers were con-cerned. They just dropped everything, their rifles, everything, although most of them still carried their *bidons,* that was one of sights that was depressing. So when we saw French soldier who was almost limping—he was dark, he was probably Arab—but he still had his rifle, we took pity on him even though we didn't have much space. We rested him on mudguard of our vehicle and he proved real blessing to us because his hearing was so good that with engine running he could hear airplanes. We couldn't speak—he would wave and point in some direction and we would say, all right, we move away.

"By then we had put mattress on our vehicle so that it looked like civilian refugee vehicle. I don't think we were ever attacked by airplanes in that instance. I don't think by that time Germans cared any more; they'd won, they were looking for pockets of soldiers, they were not interested in long column which might have con-tained soldiers. There was, however, incident when we stopped by side of road and there were eleven haystacks there and German plane came and fired toward us so we ran toward haystacks, and I think he had game with us. A bullet cannot penetrate haystack, so he came along beside haystacks and fired at us, and then from other side he did same. I think he was just playing games, though he would have killed us if he could. On third pass he ignited one of haystacks and we thought, oh, he'll run out of ammunition by time he gets to us, but by that time there were only about six haystacks left because others were burning and we were really worrying—we were just running from one to other. But then he just went off. That was last action we have seen.

"We moved south and stopped at hospital at Dijon, and we had treat because we were given platefuls of scrambled eggs, no bread, but that was quite something. We always had problem with petrol supply to our station, it was very thirsty and using one hundred liters per one hundred kilometers, so we had to chuck out our seats and put in two two-hundred-liter drums—this is something that reduced space inside. But when we got to Dijon, one was empty and other one was half empty, and we went to garage and man wouldn't sell us petrol, he locked up garage. There were also civilians there, and later I learned from them that what he'd said was he's keeping it for Boches when they arrive, and that incensed one of men there to such extent that took short rifle he was carrying, stubby little thing, and with butt hit that man on side of his face, and he collapsed. Then other man broke padlock on gate to get to petrol and we filled up, and then he shouted to others, 'Petrol is free, all take it!' I did not see what happened to man who was hit. These things happen so quickly, you see one thing and you don't see another, by the time you look again scene has changed.

"By that time we received orders to move toward Bordeaux because there was ship waiting to transport us to England, but we couldn't go there directly because Germans were already there. We had to go east toward Switzerland, and then across, because rest of France was already filled with Germans. We thought if we could not make Bordeaux, we would cross border to Switzerland and become internees in Switzerland. We were going toward Lyons and it appeared that there was some kind of settlement between French government, and Pétain had taken over by then. There was general surrender: no fighting, and suspension of hostilities. Soon after

Lyons we got some petrol again, we tried to keep our drums as full as possible with petrol. We were still eating our cheese and cubes of sugar. Petrol tanks were full, we weren't. Even if we went through some town, it was very rare that we tried to stop and buy something; we just tried to get through it as quickly as possible in case Germans were already there, or nearby, as we'd have been prisoners of war then.

"We arrived at Clermont-Ferrand—it was night and raining, and there was long downhill drive into town. At that time, we had no markings on our vehicle and so they could not recognize it. We had French uniforms, and our little group didn't have Polish markings on our collars anymore. It was dark, raining, and we were miserable, and we were met by delegation from town hall and they all welcomed us in German language, thinking we were Germans, and they welcomed us as German liberators. And since they assumed we were Germans, we gave them lesson in what Germans do—we shot off their chimney pots and moved on."

"Was there some leftover resentment in this, do you think, from France failing to support Poland when it was invaded?" I asked him.

"Yes, there was that, too, probably. But main resentment started soon after we left front line when we saw these enormous guns, whole column of guns pointing in one direction but there is nobody there, they were just abandoned like that. There was incident earlier on, for example, when we came to bridge which was 'defended' by French soldiers. As soon as they discovered that Germans are fifty kilometers away, they moved away to 'defend' next bridge. I don't know whether it was to save bridge, or to save themselves, or confusion. They were just falling back, back, back. As soon as they found that Germans were coming, they just abandoned everything. I mean, these guns when we saw them all there in some field—that was what we didn't like, and also we didn't like individual soldiers all going along and not one of them carried rifle, but they didn't discard *bidon*. Before that, there was that feeling that Marshal Pétain,

he's victor of last war, he will lead France and everything was
defended, and suddenly you learn that he's the one who's negotiating, and everything is in disarray."

I asked Joe what the mood of the French refugees was like.

"Absolutely depressed. They were moving like zombies, probably because they couldn't go any faster, car after car in one direction, and car after car in opposite direction, it was that kind of
confusion—people were moving from one place and others were
going where those others were escaping from. It was utter confusion, and this added to mood of not caring—just, well, car in front
of me's going there, I might as well follow it.

"After Lyons, about halfway to Bordeaux, around Clermont-
Ferrand, we came to fork in road and there was French colonel
waving pistol and civilians could take either fork, but as we looked
ahead we saw anyone in uniform was ordered to go north and not
southwest. When we got there, that aspirant who had fallen into
ditch before went up to him and asked why, and he said all military
are going to some camp where soldiers are grouped, and he says
why, and colonel says these are orders. So aspirant says, all right,
I'll go and give them order to move. When he came back to our station, he just said, 'Obviously we're going to be taken as prisoners of
war.' Our station was also armed, we had mounted one machine gun
on each side, covered by mattress. Aspirant said, 'We'll give him
his own medicine. Just uncover machine guns and point them at
him and tell him what we're going to do.' He returned and as we
came up to colonel, aspirant said, 'Right, you told us to go that way.
Just look at these machine guns, where do we go?' And colonel
said, 'You go where you like.' And we went toward Bordeaux.

"We spent night and part of day travelling to Bordeaux. There
were quite few regiments of Polish forces waiting there at Bordeaux for this ship to go. We were signals, we kept together as signals, you felt you were among your own people. We waited there
and ship was in dock and it was being loaded already with soldiers.
It was English coal tanker, called *Royal* something, powered by

diesel, and I spent all my time on deck although it was wet and cold because it stank so horribly of diesel."

This was now June 22, 1940, the day that France surrendered entirely to the Nazis. The men's ship left at six-thirty that evening.

"We were directed to port of Le Verdon, near Bordeaux. Order was any big armaments were to be pushed into sea and only small arms were to be taken, so all we really had were machine guns. We loaded little bit of radio equipment, too, and somehow there was large box of chocolates and two boxes same size of small bottles of champagne and this went on board, too, roped together as radio equipment. Then we took our rifles, machine guns and pistols off and our radio station was pointed toward cliff, engine was started, driver jumped out, and station went into sea. This was fate of practically every vehicle that was there. We were probably last column that arrived there and almost very last to get on. I think most of others managed to get through, but some must have been left behind. We were fortunate we had communication; we could listen to what orders were and act accordingly. On other hand, as far as I know that brigade of General Maczek was only brigade that was fighting at that time. Whole brigade was given medal by French after war.

"We set off, and instead of taking shortcut to southeast England, captain decided to go into Bay of Biscay, and we listened to German radio and there was mention about ship that is sailing in vicinity of Bordeaux and there was indication that you will not get very far because submarines are waiting for you. That wasn't very pleasant news, and it was disturbing, very disturbing after all this, specially when we'd had option of internment in Switzerland, and would have been safe. I don't think anybody wants to die. I cannot accept it that people do things because they want to die. Definitely, I did not want to die.

"So we were sailing and as night fell, weather got worse, and by time night fell, it was really rough and became rougher and rougher and we were sailing overnight. Following day, it was still very rough and we heard that captain remarked that he has been sailing that ship for twenty years and has never known Biscay to be as angry as that. But that was saving of us, because weather was so rough that submarines couldn't operate—they couldn't see anything probably. But there were still these messages from Radio Berlin: we are keeping track of that ship, this is public broadcast, there is ship going to England, they don't know that submarines are waiting for them, that type of thing; and then it was toward end of day that radio announced that this ship had been torpedoed. That was relief to us, but we knew that another ship had been torpedoed and they had mistaken it for us.

"From then onwards we were free, but weather was very very foul, and we circled around England and we landed at Liverpool—I think it would have been morning." (I learn later that the ship arrived at 3:15 a.m. two and a half days later, on June 25.) "We were marched in column to railway station and as we walked along platform we noticed this writing etched on windows of train: SMOKING and NO SMOKING. And of course since "smoking" in Polish means dinner jacket, we were surprised that one has to wear dinner jacket to get into train, so we all looked for windows where there was no smoking—and promptly lit up our cigarettes. Entering train itself, second surprise was seeing upholstered seats, which I personally hadn't experienced before. There must have been about three hundred and fifty to four hundred soldiers on that ship. We took up quite bit of room because each of us was carrying quite bit of equipment. I was carrying very short rifle, I'd never had to use it. Also I was carrying pistol concealed in my jacket. My only personal belongings consisted of horse blanket in my rucksack.

"We travelled up to Glasgow and were put into one of football stadiums. I still had some francs left and Scottish banks were still willing to change it. There wasn't much left because most of time I was not eating with army kitchen. Whenever I could, I did not eat there. I just felt that I'd better make best of bad situation. At that time I was smoking. The reason started in occupied Poland, where you could get cigarettes but you couldn't get food, so cigarettes were substitute for food there. Of course, quite bit of money went on cigarettes. Ted was quite heavy smoker, too, and I felt obliged that instead of him having to smoke these horrible French troop cigarettes that they were issued, I usually got Gauloises or something like that which were very much milder and much more pleasant.

"When I got to stadium, well, we disembarked and walked there and just dropped on benches, and I fell asleep and I slept through that night and through next day and slept through night again. I must say Ted was very concerned, he was very protective to me, I think it was in memory of that garden in Troyes. He got really worried so he contacted our doctor, who said, has he eaten anything? Ted said, no, he hasn't eaten anything, he just sleeps. So apparently I was fed with milk or something but I was still asleep. Eventually, I woke up very dizzy and very weak, and I think we spent another night or two in that stadium, and by that time I could eat normally; in fact, I began to be very hungry. After I'd eaten for few days, I weighed one twenty-four pounds in my army uniform and boots—and I'm sure my boots alone must have weighed fifty pounds.

"Soon afterward we were taken on train through Third Lanark—no, Lanark; Third Lanark was football team. We ended up at Douglas, and there we found tents we had to erect ourselves, no mattresses of course, but kitchen was there which was fantastic blessing to me because I was hungry, hungry. I tried to be first in queue for breakfast so I could join queue at end and have another one. I was so hungry I was worried about it, and went to our doctor and he said, 'I can't see anything wrong, I'll prescribe you double rations,' and if you can imagine it, we were given half loaf of bread for breakfast, that's quite lot and after one loaf I still felt hungry. I wasn't gaining any weight at all, just eating, eating.

"When we arrived at Douglas and we opened tents, I felt relief

Joe in Britain, 1940

for first time, I felt that there is somebody that is organizing something for us. Up until then it was hodgepodge, whatever there was grabbed. You felt that you just had to care for yourself—nobody else cares about it, what you do or what happens to you. And even when train was at Liverpool and we entered that train, now somebody had provided something; but you did not know what was going to happen next, and when we were marched to this football stadium and put on benches, it shut down again—sort of, they provide us train to get here and there is nothing here, you are left on your own again. But once we were in that camp, and once I saw kitchen there and they were cooking things, I thought, well, at least somebody is thinking about us. We stayed there about three weeks, sleeping six to a tent, feet toward center, sleeping on blanket. I had my blanket with me—that famous blanket! This was best blanket that existed. In French army they issued blankets for privates, blankets for noncommissioned officers, blankets for commissioned officers, blankets for high-ranking officers and then blankets for horses—going up in degree of quality and I had blanket for horses! It's got its date on it: 1936."

In 2002, through the good offices of the historian and archivist of the Polish Institute and Sikorski Archives in London, Andrzej Suchcitz, I learn a little more. I discover that the ship my father was evacuated on was called the *Royal Scotsman,* and was one of three ships sent to evacuate men from France on June 22–23, all of which were headed for Liverpool. Mr. Suchcitz unearths the load list for the *Royal Scotsman:*

> 147 officers
> 51 cadet officers
> 2,147 NCOs and privates
>
> 1,342 rifles
> 280 pistols
> 66 light machine guns
> 34 heavy machine guns
> 68 mortars
> 25 motorbikes

They were ordered, as my father had said, to jettison all their equipment, but the Polish colonel in charge refused point-blank and insisted—to some units at least—that the soldiers brought equipment on board. In England, it would be particularly welcome after the disastrous armament losses at Dunkirk.

Mr. Suchcitz also tells me about the subsequent fate of Maczek: he wasn't on any of the boats from Bordeaux, but reached Marseilles and then Morocco, eventually sailing to England in September 1940. He arrived in Scotland in October, where he began to re-form the remnants of the brigade for the second time. As part of the Polish First Corps, the First Rifle Brigade then took up defensive positions along the Scottish east coast to deal with any potential German attack on Scotland from occupied Norway—once again, one cannot fail to observe, helping to defend another country whilst never having the compliment returned. Meanwhile, Maczek was preparing to join the Allied invasion of France in 1944. In late July 1944, the division would transfer to the continent as part of the First Canadian Army, where it fought key battles in the liberation of northwest France, Belgium, and Holland, for which Maczek himself would earn the CB and DSO, amongst many other honors. Andrzej Suchcitz shows me a copy of a letter from General Eisenhower to Maczek just before he left for France:

> Dear General Maczek
> I want to express to you once more my appreciation of the opportunity I had last Thursday of visiting your fine division. I was greatly impressed by all I saw and have no fears as to the results when your organization gets into battle. Good luck to you and all ranks under you.
>
> Sincerely,
> Dwight D. Eisenhower

And he shows me a letter to Maczek in slightly fractured English from the town council of the Dutch city of Breda, conferring the medal of honor and citizenship of the city on the First Polish Armored Division for their liberation of the city. I smile at one particular word, thinking that if corroboration were needed for the existence of the Freudian slip (a black slip, this one), this would be it:

> The Town-Council of BREDA considering, that the city of Breda on Sunday 29 October 1944 by the Allied Expeditionary Forces has been liberated

from the heavy joke of the German occupation,
that lasted nearly four and a half years—

—a heavy joke indeed.

After the war, Suchcitz tells me, Maczek made a living in Edinburgh doing various menial jobs. He died there in 1994, at the great age of one hundred and two, having seen his home country liberated at last from a war which for Poland lasted for fifty years.

Andrzej Suchcitz is bilingual in English and Polish, but with the diffident manner of an English gentleman scholar. Yet there is controlled anger within what he writes, meticulously factual as it is:

> Unlike the Polish Government in September 1939, the French government decided that France should lay down her arms and capitulate to Germany. . . . Polish military intelligence built up an extensive network throughout occupied France, providing invaluable information for the Allies regarding troop, aircraft and naval movements, giving warnings of the imminent German invasion of the USSR. This was in addition to supplying the Allies with the secrets of Enigma, even prior to the outbreak of the war, an act of generosity not reciprocated by either the British or the French as far as asdic or radar was concerned.

Wondering, since he's my generation, what his personal story is, I ask him as I'm leaving whether his father fought in the war too.

"Yes, yes," he says briskly. "Actually, he was serving in the Tenth Mounted Rifles Regiment—the nonoperational part of Maczek's brigade in France."

"Goodness. How did he come out?"

"On the *Royal Scotsman*," he said. And he hadn't told me! "Actually, they must have been on the same boat. Small world."

Four months after becoming prime minister, on September 3, 1940, Winston Churchill wrote a letter to all Polish soldiers on his headed paper at 10 Downing Street, saying:

> On behalf of the Government and people of Great Britain, I am very glad to write this line of welcome to every Polish soldier, sailor or airman who has found his way over to help us fight and win the war.
>
> I have heard of the difficulties which have beset your journeys to this country: I realize the hardships which your relatives and friends are undergoing in Poland: but I know that these will only inspire you to further deeds of endurance and valour for which your nation is so justly renowned.
>
> Until the hour comes when through our united efforts you return to your own country, we in Great Britain hope that you will find amongst us a happy, if temporary, home. Together with our joint Allies, we look forward to the day when victory will crown our efforts and we shall help to build a new and better Europe. I know that the Polish forces on land and sea and in the air will play a worthy part in achieving this goal.

I think of his later speech on Sikorski's death in 1943, when he described how Sikorski had managed to muster an army of eighty thousand Poles to fight in France after the fall of Poland. "This army," Churchill said, "fought with the utmost resolution in the disastrous battles of 1940. Part fought its way out in good order to Switzerland, and is today interned there. Part marched resolutely to the sea, and reached this island." Now I know how my father fitted in to this resolute march to the sea, and how he reached this island.

17

"SUNLIT UPLANDS"

Over the past fortnight, Joe had discharged an almost life-long burden, which was sitting now in the neutral care of a score of electromagnetic tapes. I was retrospectively relieved for him that he was on safe ground now, in Britain, and we both felt we could relax. We were coming into the home stretch, it seemed, with the recording, as he must have thought he was when he got to Scotland.

In July 1940, Joe and his company—by now with the title of Signals Company of General Maczek's First Armored Corps—were stationed at Crawford, some thirty miles south of Glasgow in Scotland. There were many more officers than soldiers in the Polish army there, because the officers had escaped from France well ahead of their units—the lucky ones, those who had escaped west and not east like General Anders and those at Katyn. Many of them were high-ranking officers in their fifties, and these "grandads of the woods" were encamped on a stretch between the river and the woods. They had no hope of commanding any units because of the lack of rank-and-file Polish soldiers, which made my father suddenly a rarity. Now that France had fallen, they, like my father, were absorbed into the British army. Joe swore allegiance to the king, signed the British Official Secrets Act, and was equipped with a British army uniform with POLAND in white letters on a red background on the top of both sleeves.

They were not expecting any action that autumn, but the plan was to train over the winter to keep fitness and morale high for the invasion of the continent and the eventual liberation of their homeland. Within the first two months of being at Crawford, the squadron had two battle-ready alerts on suspicion of German air activity, and they were inspected twice by General Sikorski and once by General Sir John Dill, Britain's vice chief of the Imperial Staff. From Crawford the squadron was moved to Meigle, near Glamis Castle, and later to Alyth, north of Perth, where most were quartered in a church, with mattresses and a roof over their heads for the first time in months. In spite of that, their Sunday Catholic mass was scrupulously said outside in the open air, since it was a Presbyterian church.

By now there were only fifteen of them, and it was here that Joe learned Morse properly, and here that he met Władek Kordys, my future godfather. Like many foreigners, Joe found the Scottish accent easier to understand than the English. The villagers were friendly and would organize shows for them in their village hall. "It was very pleasing to come into contact with normal people," my father said, "because we were soldiers and not normal." The local girls enjoyed their company, too, and it's probably in contexts like these that the Poles were found "too charming"—although it seemed to be the Englishmen rather than the Scots who found them so. There were historical reasons why the Scots and Poles found each other congenial. A long tradition of Scottish-Polish relations is still embodied today in a flourishing Scottish-Polish Society. In the seventeenth and eighteenth centuries, thousands of Scots emigrated to Poland as traders, artisans, soldiers of fortune or scholars—there were thirty thousand Scottish families living in Poland at the begin-

Joe in 1941

ning of the seventeenth century, and there was a reciprocal flow at the beginning of the eighteenth century when Polish students came to study Protestant theology. In the next century, many Polish freedom fighters took refuge in Scotland—particularly in Edinburgh— after Poland's national uprising against the Russians in 1830–31. By the time my father arrived in July 1940, the Scots were already setting up many charitable and educational homes for the new wave of incoming Poles. Temporarily, all the Polish troops evacuated from France found a home in Scotland, the initial ten thousand or so Polish troops growing in time to tens of thousands as the soldiers of Władysław Anders's army also arrived in Britain.

Many—like Maczek—stayed on in Scotland. Joe told me that one of the soldiers in his platoon, who had been a crane driver on the docks in Poland, would go around telling everyone he didn't want to be in the army and wasn't made for it. He began ostentatiously searching everywhere for bits of paper, and then compulsively crumpling them up and throwing them away. After some

Joe and Władek, 1941

months, people realized he was going mad, so he was called before the doctor, who discharged him as being of unsound mind. When he was given his discharge paper, he looked at it and said, "This is the piece of paper I've been looking for," and went off and got a job as a crane driver in Glasgow. Joe said it sounds apocryphal but was true.

It was the local people who first told my father and his unit about the Battle of Britain taking place in the skies over southern England. They got news on the radio, via the BBC, but "our bulletins were shaded lightly," my father said, "to give us little bit more heart, but when we were talking to local people we knew truth." On June 18, whilst my father had been in his truck travelling from Clermont-Ferrand to Bordeaux, Churchill had made the following famous speech to the House of Commons:

What General Weygand has called the Battle of France is over. The Battle of Britain is about to begin. Upon this battle depends the survival of Christian civilization. Upon it depends our own British life, and the long continuity of our institutions and our Empire. The whole fury and might of the enemy must very soon be turned on us. Hitler knows that he will have to break us in this Island or lose the war. If we can stand up to him, all Europe may be free and the life of the world may move forward into broad, sunlit uplands. But if we fail, then the whole world, including the United States, including all that we have known and cared for, will sink into the abyss of a new Dark Age made more sinister, and perhaps more protracted, by the lights of perverted science. Let us therefore brace ourselves to our duties, and so bear ourselves that, if the British Empire and its Commonwealth last for a thousand years, men will still say, "This was their finest hour."

And the British Empire, crumbling and outdated as it was, together with its Commonwealth—altruistic in its courage just as it had been in the previous world war—did brace themselves to their duties. The ensuing air battle over England, when Germany bombed the country from July 10 until October 31, 1940, probably was the empire's—if not necessarily the Commonwealth's—finest hour. Britain and the Commonwealth stood alone against a tyrant and murderer who had carried all before him, and Britain endured the bombings and bombed the Germans back, and saw off Hitler's planned invasion—although this was far from the end of bombs being dropped on English cities. Australian, Canadian, New Zealand, South African, Polish, Czechoslovak, French and American pilots (the last volunteers) took part in the Battle of Britain.

There were two wholly Czechoslovak squadrons, 310 and 312, and
two Polish squadrons, 302 and 303, out of nearly eighty squadrons
altogether. All four were barely formed in August 1940, operating
in a language not their own and flying Hurricanes and Spitfires with
which they were not familiar. All had exceptionally high enemy
"hits": more than 10 percent of all the enemy planes brought down
in the Battle of Britain were brought down by the two Polish
squadrons. All the more surprising that as late as 1993, on a monument to the Battle of Britain erected above Dover commemorating
every fighter squadron that took part, neither of the Polish
squadrons is mentioned, although 303 Squadron was the highest
"scorer" of all. The reasons for this I would find out later.

One day in late 1941, my father—now posted to Forfar—was
suddenly summoned and told that he was being sent to London. He
was to report to Stanmore, a suburb in the northwest of London
where the Polish Signals company was stationed. "I was lost, completely lost. There was just me, nobody else, you're not given reasons or anything like that. You get your railway warrant, you're told
where to go, who to report to and that's it."

Plagued with thoughts about what was in store and what he'd
done to deserve it, he found to his relief that Ted was in Stanmore,
too, and they would be working together—not only that, but they
were in a very agreeable building, and even better, they had a Czech
woman cook who had been chef at a Czech restaurant in London.
They were in a group of eight communicating in Morse with partisan cells or people who were being dropped overseas into France,
Germany, Poland and Hungary, and Joe had been selected because
he had both parachuting and radio communications experience—
and no doubt on the recommendation of Ted. (He'd also been noted
for lateral thinking on friendly maneuvers with the Black Watch,
jamming their airwaves with Scottish music.)

One of the eight was the gangly cigarette-smoking Stan I would
later meet as a child. They were reporting both to General Sikorski
and his staff—now based at the Rubens Hotel in Victoria, in the

heart of London—and to the British Admiralty, and most of their work was done at night, when long-distance radio communication could be received. The work was taxing and arduous, trying to pick up and decipher signals from people whom they knew were in hazardous circumstances, and whose lives might depend on the communications they were making. They smoked and drank black coffee all night long, living a twilight existence, doubly cut off from the outside world since they were not only nocturnal but also forbidden to talk to anyone about what they were doing. Then, when Germany turned on its "ally" Russia and invaded it in June 1941—making the same catastrophic miscalculation that had led to Napoleon's downfall—Joe's unit was given the top-secret duty of listening to and decoding Russian signals.

It was at this point that my father met my mother, who had been working as a nurse at Great Ormond Street Children's Hospital, but who was now in the WAAF with the dashing rank of "Leading Airwoman." She first saw him in the YMCA canteen (where Mrs. Attlee, wife of the Labour leader and future prime minister Clement Attlee used to serve) and went out on a double date with him and a friend, and "since Sheila was one of those people who like to end up with the other person's date," she says, "I ended up with Joe." The Poles, she said, looked very smart and they had a novel accessory, which they introduced to British men: attaché cases. For the first three months they went out together, my father didn't tell her his surname, and until 1989, when we began to tape his story, had told her virtually nothing about his past. She accepted it without question. He was very suspicious of everyone, she said. To add to this, there was the Blitz—the German bombing of London, renewed shortly after my parents met, continued in 1942 and then launched again in January and February 1944, a few months after I was born—a "little blitz" in retaliation for the Allied bombing of Berlin.

The next month, the Germans brought in their new weapon—a real *neue Waffe*—the pilotless V1s, or *Vergeltungswaffen,* so called

Pam in 1941

because they were "weapons of revenge" for the bombing of German cities. They were also known as buzz bombs or doodlebugs, their zippy names helping to cock a snook at their terror. Londoners, it was reported, were "more jittery" and "more helpless" than at any time in the war, suffering from "apathy" and "war-weariness." When these attacks petered out, the V2s were launched from Holland and the French coast, and by November 1944, the beginning of a winter of intense cold, Jane Waller and Michael Vaughan-Rees note: "It was a time of something approaching despair, with the feeling of impending victory overshadowed by the daily tragedies." During all this period, up until 1946 when he was demobbed, my father was based at Stanmore and later Boxmoor on the northern outskirts of London, visiting my mother whenever he could in whatever rented rooms they could get in southeast London, which suffered the worst of the Blitz throughout the war.

My mother tells me how she hadn't wanted to leave London when the Blitz came, as she wanted to be with my father whenever he was off-duty. (Londoners had a 1 in 160 chance of being killed by attack from the air by 1944, compared with 1 in 800 for the rest of the United Kingdom.) My mother hadn't wanted me to be evacuated to the country, as many small children were, nor had she

Joe, Pam and the author, 1944

Flyleaf from Joe's "Soldier's Service Book" (Army Book 64 [Part I])

ALL RANKS.

"REMEMBER—Never discuss military, naval or air matters in public or with any stranger, no matter to' what nationality he or she may belong.

The enemy wants information about you, your unit, your destination. He will do his utmost to discover it.

Keep him in the dark. Gossip on military subjects is highly dangerous to the country, whereas secrecy leads to success.

BE ON YOUR GUARD and report any suspicious individual."

wanted to take shelter in the underground shelters because she "hated the thought of being buried alive more than the thought of your number coming up if a bomb hit you." (Once it nearly did, shattering the window by my cot.) In spite of having served in the Royal Air Force until she was pregnant, she became classified as an "alien" when they married, as wives had to automatically take on their husband's nationality. Like all the other Poles in the Resettlement Corps after the war, pressure had been put on them to "return" to Poland. In amongst all this, she said, Joe had never told her anything of his background or experiences, and she had never asked him.

Years later, my editor finds this hard to believe. "Joe would have talked to her—one assumes—" she writes me, "more than to anyone, including his three friends, once he was in London. They're in love, this for him is the moment when he allows himself to make a connection, allows (or resigns?) himself to believe that England is going to be his home and this woman his life's companion; everyone in love tells the other person their story—or as much of it as can be risked, or borne." You would think so, but it wasn't the case. It may be that I've understated the extent to which my father had pulled the drawbridge down on conversation, and how my mother and I simply adapted to it and accepted it as normal: which is why the science fiction story so resonated with me. My mother herself was still only eighteen when she met Joe, and an orphan, and it was wartime. She says now, "I have to tell you that for many years Joe never communicated with me in any way and was very difficult to live with. Then he was very prone to moods, which I reacted to in all the wrong ways. My childhood in itself was a crazy mixed-up business and left a lot to be desired, and quite frankly, I knew very little of the outside world—I was in fact very naive."

As for my father, apart from finding himself pitched into the Soviet and Nazi terrors, and then the chaos of war, he had no English at all when he arrived on these shores. By the time he met my mother, he had a year's worth of trying to pick up the language in the intervals between working nights (with Poles only) and sleeping much of the day. I ask my father now in an e-mail how he feels about his silence and shutdown in his early years in England, and he replies:

I was the youngest soldier posted to the London unit. All the others were professional soldiers aged from late twenties upwards. They had the secrecy discipline instilled in them even from prewar days. I had to fall into it. This was the time when fear was again introduced into my life. Thus during the war I never talked about what my duties were. And almost from the time of joining the unit I realised that there was no future for me in continental Europe. So after we got married this situation of silence continued. And although your Mum and I had practically no contact with her side of the family during the war, there was unmistakable feeling that I had married into a social class above me. Due to my limited knowledge of English, I had a feeling that I did not belong here. This feeling remained with me. After the war I obtained a job as a watchmaker and almost immediately started attending evening classes to move to a better job. The classes were four evenings a week and I went directly from work. I seldom got home before ten at night. During the spare evenings there was homework and again silence. By the time I got a job at BCURA [the British Coal Utilization Research Association], the non-conversation was embedded.

On many occasions I wish the past times were different.

Although my father's was an extreme version of silence, I'm not sure it was that unusual—and it was quite common amongst soldiers returning from both wars. In love my parents might have been, which they were, in spite of the obstacles, but this was before the age of disclosure, and for the average person there wasn't the vocabulary, or habit, of self-revelation. It all reminds me of a documentary I saw about men who'd been in the Burma campaign, where one veteran and his wife told how he had come home from the war and walked in through the door looking like a ghost. Before even saying hello to his wife, he said, "Is there a carving knife in the house?" His wife said calmly, yes, and he said, "Get it out of here." And the wonderful thing was that his wife, without batting an eyelid, without ever asking him what horrors had induced him to ask such a question or what he meant by it, just went around to the neighbor's house and asked her to take care of the carving knife. When she needed it, on a Sunday, she would knock on the neighbor's wall and the neighbor would pass it over the fence to her, and take it back when she'd finished. A carving knife was too good to throw away. These men got the women they deserved.

FIVE

AFTERMATHS

A fine, illuminating question:
what is independence?

—MILAN KUNDERA

18

NEVER AGAIN

S ometime in the mid-eighties, whilst the cold war was still on, I saw a documentary about Czechoslovakia in which a man in his thirties was talking to a camera from his flat in Prague, bravely in the circumstances. He said that every year, on the anniversary of the Soviet "liberation" of their country, everyone was told to put out little flags onto their balconies. He refused, in spite of the pleas of his friends. They said, for heaven's sake what does it matter, it's meaningless, and if you don't put the flag out your job prospects and those of your wife will be at risk, together with the future of your small children—and you're not helping the rest of us, either. Just go along with it, it's trivial. But he said: "This is the thin end of the wedge. They can't arrest me for not putting a flag out, but if I do what they say on this one small thing, then I have to do it on the next, perhaps bigger, thing and so on. And so by the time I end up saying no, whatever I'm doing is a hanging offense."

Totalitarian rule sets in by convincing you that you have no choice over small things like putting out flags, or choosing soap, or when and where you're allowed on the streets, let alone over big things like influencing governments. It does this by random, brutal

crackdowns on anyone stepping out of line, and by a pervasive network of surveillance—or just rumors of surveillance. It does it very
fast, once the foot's in the door. And the experience isn't easily forgotten by its victims. As an Arab saying has it, He who has been bit-
ten by a serpent fears the shadow of a rope.

During the war and after it, my father's two homelands, Czechoslovakia and Poland, were lost to him, first brutalized by the Nazi
regime, then swamped by Stalinist rule. A year after the war, Sydney Morrell described the general picture: "Deep down and hidden
were the people of Europe, but they had no voice. They were too
stunned by defeat to seek one and, when they recovered, the power
of the occupier was too strong." During the war, Czechoslovakia
had become a place of terror, blunted despair and opportunistic corruption, its plight screened from the rest of Europe. After the war,
especially after 1948 and the Communist takeover, it became a cut-
off state my father could no longer return to if he had wanted to. It
was Munich which had set this all in motion—"Munich," which
usurped even the name of Czechoslovakia's crisis and gave it a
German name. The effect of the betrayal on the morale of the
Czechoslovak people was devastating.

At first, however, from the summer of 1939, when Beneš set up his
regime in exile in England, there had still been resistance to the
Nazis. On the first anniversary of Munich, September 30, 1939,
four weeks after the West had declared war on Germany, the Czechs
boycotted Prague's public transport system in a show of passive
resistance, and distributed a leaflet urging a silent protest on their
anniversary of independence, October 28: "Since Hitler proclaims
our passivity abroad, mistaking it for peaceful and joyful acceptance of his protection, we need to show to the world that this criminal lies again. . . . Your duty is to protest silently but proudly
against the Teutonic criminals. . . . At 6 pm sharp all patriotic
Czechs will meet in the upper part of Wenceslas Square and at the

stroke of six will remain silent for two minutes." But in a mark of Hitler's personal fury, the demonstration was brutally broken up by police, who rounded up and arrested over a thousand students, and sent them off to concentration camps. At dawn on November 17, nine students, randomly selected, died without trial before a firing squad. All Czech institutions of higher learning were officially closed for three years (although in practice they would not reopen until after the war).

Thousands of Czechs escaped before the borders were closed in late 1940, but from then on skeptical compliance, opportunism and duplicity began to infect the spirit of those left behind under Nazi rule. The frontiers between resistance and collaboration were fluid and often the same people took part in both—as with Premier Alois Elias. The president led the way in submission: on the first anniversary of the "Protectorate," Hácha said to Hitler, "Today I feel an urge to call Sieg and Heil upon the glorious German weapons which also protect the Czech people."

The Nazi terror campaign launched against the Czechs in autumn 1939 included rumors of chemical and disease-spreading attacks. It aroused indignation abroad and made the Czechs more cautious about open displays of defiance. Many also knew that in England, Beneš was creating a Czechoslovak army and air force from exiled Czechs who had made their way to England from all over Europe. A year later, after the fall of France, this would enable Czech pilots to take part in the Battle of Britain in August 1940, which would make the Czechs, like the Poles, co-belligerents now, with a strong claim to restoration of their independence.

However, at home the screws were tightening. By September 1941, the Germans had got wind of Elias's double game as premier-cum-partisan, and changed their *Reichsproteckor* from von Neurath to the dreaded Chief of Security Police Reinhard Heydrich, one of the architects of the "final solution." A few days later, General Elias was arrested by the Gestapo. He made a false but abject recantation, and was executed eight months later. Heydrich now brought in martial law and a curfew, and set about coldly and systematically breaking the spirit of the Czechs. He made a distinction between two techniques of repression, "breaking" and "bending." He judged bending to be most suitable for Slavs, since they could not easily be broken thanks to their ability to bow before force, like a willow in the wind, and return to normal as soon as pressure ceased. Therefore, he planned to break them by a short spell of terror, to make bending more effective later, a policy used in all times by coercive interrogators and which he called *Peitsche und Zucker*—whip and sugar. "Breaking and bending" was a visible success. Soon the Czechs were back in a far more terrifying version of their old, pre–First Republic predicament: compliance masking inner reluctance. Worse still, it led them to behave like that all the time even if no threat was immediately present. They had, in effect, been brainwashed—and soul-washed.

By November 1941, Hácha was giving an example of someone who had been "broken" when he broadcast a submissive speech to the Czechs appealing to them to "fulfill their obligations to the Reich completely and sincerely in a manly and determined manner." In four months, Heydrich had done his breaking work: on January 19, 1942, he installed a new government, with Hácha still as president, lifted martial law and announced the release of the remaining students from concentration camps. In May that year he began to prepare to move on, perhaps to occupied France to repeat his "great success" in Czechoslovakia.

In London, however, Beneš and the Special Operations Executive (SOE) had been liaising as best they could with resistance within Czechoslovakia. The first SOE agent had been dropped into Czechoslovakia by parachute in April 1941. In the few months from the summer of 1939 until April 1940—before Heydrich came on the scene—some fifteen thousand people had been arrested on suspicion of resistance activities. Once Heydrich arrived, it became far more difficult. All the same, they hatched a plan for what would be the only assassination attempt the Allies ever made on the life of a leading Nazi.

On May 27, 1942, as Heydrich and his bodyguard left his country seat near Prague in his open-top Mercedes sports car for his office in Hradcany Castle, he was shot at by two Czech agents, Josef Gabčik and Jan Kubiš, who had been parachuted in through London. They then threw a bomb at the car, and escaped—one of them cycling away dripping blood, as Heydrich's bodyguard had shot at him. Heydrich himself turned out to be only injured, although he would later die of these injuries. Hitler ordered the immediate arrest of ten thousand "suspect" Czechs as revenge. Martial law was declared once more, and Germany's chief of regular police, Kurt Daluege, was brought in as successor to Heydrich. Everyone in the country then had to register within twenty-four hours on pain of death. All public gatherings, including sport and theater, were banned. German police made extensive searches throughout the "Protectorate": 1,148 people were arrested and 657 shot dead on the spot without trial. Addressing the nation three days after the bombing, Hácha warned that "whoever works against the Reich in the slightest way will be destroyed."

On June 4, Heydrich died in a Prague hospital. In the late afternoon his coffin was carried on a gun carriage through streets deserted by frightened inhabitants up to Prague Castle, where the Nazis staged a midnight funeral ceremony lit by torches. In Berlin, at a memorial service for Heydrich, Hitler told Hácha and his government that if any other such attempt were made, he would deport the whole Czech population. Then Hitler took more revenge, selecting at random the small village of Lidice outside Prague and ordering it razed to the ground. On June 9, the total male population of 192 was shot, together with 7 women; 195 women and 98 children were deported to Ravensbrück concentration camp, where 81 of the children were later gassed. Rumors were spread that every tenth Czech would be shot.

The long shadow of Heydrich was visiting the country even after his death, and the terrible weeks following his assassination came to be known as the "Heydrichiana." There were mass arbitrary arrests and executions and an atmosphere of shock, fear, uncertainty and brutality deliberately engendered in everyday life—what Daluege later hailed as "severe police measures, the frame of mind we have artificially produced, and the systematic fraying of the nerves, stimulating an increase of fear until rumours of an intended decimation of the entire nation were spread." As the respected Communist writer Julius Fuchik wrote from his condemned cell, "Death by bullet stalks the country like a plague and makes no distinction among its victims." The events made headlines in the world press, and there was outrage at this Nazi barbarity. In several countries around the world, starting with America, communities were renamed Lidice to show solidarity with the Czechs, and resistance to fascism.

The Nazis tried to track down Heydrich's assassins and on June 13 promised clemency to people who knew their whereabouts as long as they informed the police by 8:00 p.m. on June eighteenth. This was another petty chiseling in of terror, as the specific time and date became freighted with fear: what would the Nazis do if the deadline passed? Then, as a *coup de sadisme,* on the morning of the eighteenth the Nazis shortened the deadline by seven hours. Although fourteen people had known in advance about Gabčik and Kubiš's mission and thirty-five could have given information to the police, only one did: Karel Curda, who voluntarily surrendered. Gabčik and Kubiš and five other parachutist conspirators took refuge on the eighteenth in the Orthodox Church of St. Cyril and Methodius in Prague. On the tip-off from Curda, SS troops and police surrounded the church, and after several hours of violent battle the seven men all chose suicide within the church rather than surrender. The bishop of the church, three clergymen and all who assisted the parachutists—as well as all members of their families, in the Stalinist manner of "collective responsibility"—were executed, and the Orthodox Church as a whole was dissolved. Curda was paid off and lived in Germany under an assumed name until 1945. At the end of the war, he was extradited to Czechoslovakia, sentenced to death and executed for treason.

This was not the end of the retaliations: on June 24, Hitler ordered the deaths of all the inhabitants of Lezaky, a hamlet in eastern Bohemia which had operated a resistance radio communicating with the agents. Further, one thousand Jews were arbitrarily transported from Prague to extermination camps. Only one survived. And in October 1942, 252 people, including entire families, were massacred at Mauthausen concentration camp for alleged involvement in the plot against Heydrich.

Not surprisingly, the underground network set up by the parachutists disintegrated, and from now on the Czech underground was decimated. The terrible consequences of the assassination probably stemmed any further such attempts by the Allies, for in spite of the plan's boldness, it showed the disadvantages of individual bravery without backup and a longer game plan. The killing of one tyrant could not end the terror when another tyrant and a whole Nazi terror organization was still there to take horrific reprisals. "By his death," the historian Vojtěch Mastný writes sardonically, "Heydrich fulfilled his primary ambition—'pacification' of the Protectorate." Then, with the bitter, detached black irony to which the Czechs were now condemned as a national mood—and which, you sense, will have been Mastný's personal legacy from the role of his father as ambassador to Berlin at the time of Munich—he says of Beneš, "Despite the heavy toll, Beneš considered the sacrifices worthwhile because they had bolstered Czechoslovakia's position in case of a negotiated peace. Since the threat of such a peace, however, existed only in his imagination, this advantage was illusory."

With a further dusting of subdued irony, Mastný observes that "If determination was in such critically short supply among established European great powers—France and Britain—its shortage among Czechs—a small nation with inadequate political experi-

ence—need not cause much surprise. . . . The subsequent collaboration by some of the population damaged the nation's self-respect.
Democratic institutions alone, if not sustained by strong civic
spirit, are no guarantee against abject submission to force. More, in
societies where too many people have too much to lose, comfort
and affluence may become serious obstacles to resistance." Widen-
ing his scope, Mastný draws general conclusions:

> Yet we need not be negative. We know better than
> before that modern autocratic regimes, far from
> being omnipotent, suffer from serious weak-
> nesses. . . . The best protection is prevention. For
> any nation lucky enough to be enjoying freedom
> and independence, its self-respect, faith in its insti-
> tutions, and readiness to defend them, with the
> force of arms if necessary, are the best guarantee
> that its citizens would never have to resist any
> enemy under conditions of subjugation.

Under an agreement with the Western Allies, it was the Russian
Red Army that liberated Prague, on May 9, 1945. Beneš now came
back from exile in triumph to head a new independent government,
and on October 28, 1945, he gave a speech to the Provisional
Czechoslovak Assembly. It was the twenty-seventh anniversary of
his country's independence, which he had heard his old teacher
Masaryk proclaim from the foot of the statue of St. Wenceslas. His
own speech was now tinged with bitterness and *Schadenfreude:*

> In Prague on September 26th, 1938, we listened
> with deep emotion to a speech made in the Berlin
> Sports Palace by Adolf Hitler . . . a speech which
> was one of the most treacherous statements in his
> deceitful and inhuman life. Its climax was his fan-

tastic attack on Czechoslovakia and her President, addressed to us and the rest of Europe, in these words: "Here I stand and over there stands he. Things must be decided between us." True, this was a struggle of two irreconcilable worlds, of democratic Czechoslovakia and the Nazi Third Reich. But politically and personally the question was put correctly by Hitler. Seven bitter years have passed. There was our Munich defeat and the frightful disappointment inflicted by the Western democracies; there was Hitler's treacherous sneaking into Prague Castle; there was Ribbentrop's historically mendacious proclamation of the legal subordination of the Czech lands to the German Reich. There were unspeakable moral sufferings, bestial German persecution and years of moral humiliation. . . . Seven years of a frightful war, for us almost endless, of great German victories, of German inflated and uncivilized triumphs, accompanied by the most incredible German brutalities almost unequalled in history, which will remain for ever an indelible disgrace to the German nation. And in the end the crushing and merited military defeats of the German army, and the terrible fall of the political structure called Nazism and the Third Reich, which set out to rule the world for one thousand years and condemn our State and our people to a miserable existence under the scourge of the Master Race.

Today we, the Czechoslovak nation, are again standing with all our moral strength in our own free Prague, hallowed by great and glorious history, and we are looking across to shattered Berlin and Munich and to the ruins of the Third

Reich, our heads high, our conscience clear, in
the knowledge of a great historic victory and in the
knowledge that our great democratic national
truth has prevailed . . .

And Germany, with all her grandiose plans and
her historical falsehoods about our lands falling
legally under Germany, is lying in ruins, destroyed,
shattered, in chaos, with her people crushed and
morally shattered. It may take generations for her
to recover. At this moment it is we who call to our
nation and to the other nations: "Yes, there stood
Hitler and his Third Reich with all they stood for,
and here we stand."

Unfortunately for Beneš and Czechoslovakia, this would be a
brief reprieve, for the wound of Munich invited some settling of
scores. The adamant cry amongst the Czechs was "Never again
Munich!" and in 1945–46 the immediate form this policy of
revenge and self-protection took was for Beneš and his government
to expel the entire Sudeten German population—3 million—from
the Czech lands forever, sending them back to a Germany now too
morally and economically shattered to have much say in the matter.
The Western Allies sanctioned this vast, subsequently contentious
transfer of people—the greatest since the migration of nations—as
they too felt guilt, and a weary determination to stamp out all future
pretexts for warmongering by Germany.

Czech bitterness over Munich also translated into cynicism and
made it an easy target for Communist propaganda: indeed, Beneš
himself, on the rebound from the Nazism which had wrecked his
country and consigned many of his relatives to concentration
camps, had been partly won over by Stalin and communism once
Russia joined the Allies. He wanted—as he had always wanted—
Czechoslovakia to play the role of bridge between East and West in
postwar Europe, so he colluded in the high profile and votes the

Communists began to enjoy in Czechoslovakia from 1946 (and the practical presence of the Soviets on Czech soil as they were allowed, for example, to exploit Czechoslovakian uranium mines). Ironically, Munich had pushed Beneš into just the attitude Hitler had falsely accused him of before the war—sympathy for the Communists.

Masaryk's son Jan, in exile in the West during the war, had now returned to his post as foreign minister, and saw the score earlier than Beneš: "I went to Moscow," he wrote in 1947, "as Foreign Minister of an independent sovereign state. I returned as a lackey of the Soviet state." The following year, he "fell" to his death from a window in the Czernin Palace: "suicided." Shortly after a Communist coup that year brought the Soviet-dominated Communist Party into power, Beneš could no longer be under any illusions, and he resigned as president. A few months later, he died; as with Jan Masaryk, it was suspected at the time that he had been murdered or forced to commit suicide. From then on, Czechoslovakia was under Communist rule for over forty years. The brief period of liberalization in 1968, led by Alexander Dubček, was crushed by Russian-led Warsaw Pact armies, and Czechoslovakia then became the most tightly ruled nation in the Soviet bloc. But the thread of the past had not been lost: Dubček's "communism with a human face" could not have surfaced without the memory of Masaryk's legacy.

Whilst he was president, in April 2002, Václav Havel wrote an article evaluating the many subsequent criticisms of Beneš. In it, he stated:

> I am firmly convinced that the era of the dreadful
> dilemmas which Edvard Beneš had to face is now
> past. But I am also convinced that, should we ever
> have to face such dilemmas again, the personal and
> political story of Beneš could serve us all as a pro-

found lesson. For that story is one of the great dra-
mas of modern times. And every drama contains a
challenge. But how we understand that challenge,
and what we derive from it for ourselves, is a matter for our own conscience.

Before he was beheaded by the Gestapo in Berlin in September
1943 (two months before I was born), the Communist Czech writer
Julius Fuchik wrote a message to posterity:

> I ask only one thing of you: if you survive this
> epoch, do not forget. Do not forget either the good
> men or the evil ones. Gather up patiently the testi-
> mony of all those who have fallen for them and for
> you. Some fine day, today will be the past and peo-
> ple will speak of a great epoch and of the anony-
> mous heroes who have made history. I would want
> everyone to know that there are no anonymous
> heroes. They were all persons, with a name, a face,
> desires and hopes, and the anguish of the least
> among them was not less great than that of the first
> whose name will survive. I would like them all to
> be always close to you like persons whom you
> once knew, like members of your own family, like
> yourselves.

Trawling through Czechoslovakia's past had explained a lot about my father to me, but it was the fate of Poland which had affected his young adult life more actively. It was through my chance visit to Wanda and Lucjan, the neighbors of the Hungarian travel agent who helped me plan our Carpathian trip, that a vista opened up which would help fill in the rest of the puzzle.

"She is asleep," a man's voice had told me gruffly on the telephone when I rang asking for Wanda, just before setting off for Lviv in March 2001.

"I'm not asleep now," a voice retorted in the background.

"I'm sorry, did I wake her?"

"Yes, she's here," said the old man's voice, its curt non sequitur sounding just like my father. No softening pleasantries of the kind the English tend to cushion entrances and exits with, even telephonically. ("No, don't worry at all, she was just waking. She'll be glad to hear you. Would you mind waiting a moment? Good, good.")

Wanda grabbed the receiver and was all attention as I told her why I'd like to come and talk with them about prewar Lwow. Within a few moments she had told me the outlines of her story, in her still heavy Polish accent. She was a young married woman when war broke out, working as a general practitioner within a hospital. She was in a fortunate position, she said, because she came from a highly educated family and was part of the 10 percent of the Jewish population of Lwow allowed by the Poles to go to university—the same percentage as the Ukrainians were allowed. She said it as if it were normal for only 10 percent of a people to be allowed to study, and it reminds me of how contentious an issue the suspicion of underlying anti-Semitism in Poland is. Just that week I'd been reading in the newspapers about a book alleging that what had been thought to be a Nazi massacre of some eight hundred Jews in the village of Jedwabne in Poland during the war was in fact carried out by their Polish neighbors and "friends," people who had lived alongside them all their lives; more long-buried skeletons from the last century being unearthed.

"Lwow was very sophisticated and Polish-European at that time," Wanda says. "But then war broke out, and on November 6, 1939, three Russian soldiers came in middle of the night and took my husband away—'for interrogation,' they said. After one or two days I saw NKVD man who'd been with them in street, and I went up to him from behind and grabbed him and said angrily, 'Where have you taken my husband?' He looked straight ahead, not looking at me, and told me name of prison. I tried to take my husband food there three times, they wouldn't let me. I never saw him again. Then I was taken off to Kazakhstan, to a collective village, and that was not bad really, they treated us quite well. The Russians there were normal people, you know. One young man—he must have been about twenty-seven and I was twenty-nine—took me aside and said, 'If I ask you a question, will you promise never to tell I asked it?' And then he said, 'If the Poles win the war, will they murder me for what I'm doing now?' " She laughed as if that were the end of the story, but I asked how she had replied.

"Well, I said, 'If you didn't do anything wrong, nothing will punish you.' Then when Germans attacked Russia, we were released—an 'amnesty,' " she says derisively, "as if they had any right to call it that! So I joined Polish army in Uzbekistan— Anders's army, you know. We were evacuated through the Caspian Sea, and then went to Persia—well, Iran now—then to Baghdad and on to Palestine and Egypt. I became doctor for Polish ATS for invasion of Italy. I met my husband there—my second husband. He was with General Anders's army, too—the Polish Second Corps. After war, we wanted to be in Europe, and we came to England, where our diplomas were recognized."

"Goodness," I say, reeling from this whistle-stop tour of displacement. "Let's consider it normal," she says. "Our lives are normal."

I arranged to meet Wanda and her husband Lucjan a few days later. Meanwhile, I'd boned up on the Anders army. All I knew about it until then was that it was a branch of the Polish army, which originated for some reason in Russia, and which fought a battle at Monte Cassino. What I found—as with Munich—provided a context for my father's silence and gloom which would later help dispel them. As I filled in the picture of what happened to the Poles in the war, I was also filled with sadness and a mounting outrage in my chest that felt as if it had always been there, stifled, and had now found its source. Although most of this happened before I was born, this is the story I was born into, and one that for all sorts of reasons— sometimes necessary to national and international stability, sometimes hypocritical, sometimes cowardly—had to be suppressed. I felt like the boy in the science fiction story who always sensed that what he was being told, genially enough, wasn't the truth.

Wanda answered the door eagerly, tiny and bright-eyed, more like a seventy-year-old than an eighty-eight-year-old. In the hall we

passed a large framed engraving of Lwow in medieval times, its
hills rising like elephants' feet behind the town, an amiable lion settled into the right-hand corner symbolizing its origins: its founder,
the Kievan Rus prince Daniel of Galicia, built the town for his son
Leo—Lwow, city of the lion.

We sat in a front room whose shades of brown and maroon and
elegant, worn furniture had an Austro-Hungarian feel. Photograph
albums were spread out on an occasional table, and we later
repaired to the kitchen, where Wanda had prepared enough plates of
triangular ham sandwiches, cakes and biscuits to feed an army. At
one point Lucjan, ninety, but still tall and bearing traces of the
handsome man he is in the old albums, came shuffling in labori-
ously, too ill to smile, and sat with us for a while. He told of how
they went back to Lwow (as he still called it) in 1993 for a ceremony to honor the Jewish dead of the city, the first time they'd been
back since having to leave more than fifty years ago, and he looked
at me with stern sadness from behind his spectacles. "People asked
when we got back, 'Did you enjoy your holiday?' I said, it wasn't a
holiday, it was a pilgrimage." He told me this story twice before he
left, seeking out Wanda's hand with urgent tenderness to support
him into the room next door.

Wanda and I talked about their Hungarian neighbor, and of how
their friends still tend to be from central Europe. "The English are
children," she says, "ignorant children. When I was in school in
Lwow, I was taught about the amalgamation of the English coun-
ties. Here no one knows anything about central Europe. Even
Churchill knew nothing. By the end of the war England was negli-
gible, no longer an empire. And Churchill of course sold the Poles
out at Yalta. He was rude about the Poles—he thought them brave in
war but worse than cruel otherwise. Which is not true. He thought
they were greedy for land."

I had wanted to see Wanda to ask her about the Lwow she knew,
but once I found out about General Anders, and that she was part of
his army, it was that I most wanted to hear about. She told me how

she and her first husband had been sitting at home listening to the radio on August 23, 1939, when they heard the news which astonished and dismayed the world: that the arch enemies, Nazi Germany and Soviet Russia, had made a nonaggression pact. Her husband had looked at her and said: *"Finis Poloniae!"*

To anyone in the know, the German-Soviet Pact signalled that Poland's history would be devastatingly repeated; the country would be crushed again between its powerful neighbors, just as it had been in 1772, when it had been partitioned between Russia, Prussia and Austria, losing a third of its land. Until that time, Poland in its heyday—the Polish Commonwealth of the Kingdom of Poland and the Grand Duchy of Lithuania as it was—had enjoyed an early form of democracy, but one which had proved its downfall: fighting for its freedom against the Turks in the Battle of Vienna in 1683 had driven the feudal Turkish threat away from Europe for good but had also exhausted the Commonwealth's reserves; and the Polish parliament, whilst limiting the king's powers, also limited its own powers of action by allowing any one individual to veto a majority decision. Weakened by these and other factors, including a weak king, Poland was left prey to the land-hungry empires on either side, who moved in on the pretext of restoring order. In fact, Russia, Prussia and Austria had already made a secret pact in 1732 to partition Poland. Hitler knew his history when he approached Russia to make a similar secret pact in 1939. After 1772, and affected by the democratic, republican ideals of the new United States and of Revolutionary France, Poland tried to get itself in better shape in order to shake off the foreign influence. By 1791, it had the first codified constitution in Europe since the ancient Greeks', and the second in the modern world after that of the United States. It also had the first ministry of education in Europe, and planned partial emancipation of the serfs. All this served merely to provoke Russia and Prussia to invade more of the country, and in 1793,

Poland lost half its land in the second partition. The third partition came in 1795, when the whole of Poland was wiped off the map, parcelled out between Russia, Prussia and Austria. By 1797, even its name had been obliterated, and wouldn't be restored until 1918.

Many Poles captured during the fighting were sent by the Russians to Siberia—a dumping ground for "undesirables" since the seventeenth century—but thousands more escaped to Italy, where they joined Napoleon's army in fighting Austria, hoping to free their own homeland, a hope never realized. Both the exile to Siberia and the escape to Italy and France to fight on behalf of others, with no ultimate reward to themselves, would be replayed after 1939. Meanwhile, the Russians rubbed salt into the wound by calling their part of Poland "Vistulaland," reducing the strong romantic idea the Poles had of their nation from its Renaissance heyday onward to a geographical matter of lands around a river. "Vistulaland" even had something of cloud-cuckoo-land in it, playing on Poles' fears that their nation's existence was notional, not a reality.

Like all the other "succession" states of 1918, Poland regained its independence at a bad time, with the depression playing into the hands of its vast neighbors Russia and Germany as they fell increasingly under the power of the two most destructive dictators the world has known. Worse, these two powers harbored deep grievances against Poland. Both felt they had been cheated of their land in the re-created Poland (omitting to notice that they had taken those territories away from Poland previously), and both had been left out at Versailles. Both countries felt anger and humiliation at this remaking in the name of liberal democracy of the map of a part of the world they felt concerned them more than anyone else. The strength of their underlying resentment would fuel the Nazi-Soviet Pact, as two cunning tyrants, far better informed about the complex history of central Europe than the Western Allies, saw a way to steal a march on their rivals by checkmating them all in one surprise move. The Soviet Union felt that from 1934 onward it had tried to set up collective security with the West against Nazism, but Britain and France had shown nothing but bad faith and hypocrisy, intent on appeasing Hitler. So, according to Russia, it had to buy itself time (as my father had guessed). The Soviet Union had an additional grievance against Poland. The Red Army had invaded eastern Poland in the summer of 1920, wanting to get back the territories it had been forced to cede two years before, and also bent on a world revolutionary crusade of its own: to make Poland a highway through which Trotsky's Red Army would march into Germany to trigger a revolutionary uprising all over Europe. Poland seemed doomed against the might of the Red Army advancing on Warsaw, especially since the Soviets had already set up a puppet government-in-waiting for the country, under the most feared man in the USSR, its Polish-born head of secret police, Feliks Dzerzhinski. Yet Poland's army under Marshal Piłsudski managed against all the odds not only to turn the Red Army back from Warsaw but also to expel it from Poland, reduced to a rabble of fleeing refugees—which forced Russia to abandon its two-year-long push to Bolshevize Europe by force. It was a battle which Catholic Poles would know as the "Miracle of the Vistula," and which would rank in the Poles' memory as one of the keystones of their history, alongside that of the Battle of Grunwald (commemorated in the name of my father's *Bursa*) when they and the Lithuanians had driven back the Teutonic Knights to their west, and the epic Battle of Vienna, when they had halted the Turkish invasion to their east.

In all of these battles, Poland's role in defending the rest of Europe from Turks, Teutons or Bolsheviks arriving on its doorstep has, in its own view, gone unappreciated. The Soviets, of course, did not see the Battle of the Vistula as a miracle, but as a catastrophic humiliation. Lenin declared in September 1920 that it had inflicted a "gigantic, unheard-of defeat" on the cause of world revolution, and swore that, as for the Poles, "we will keep shifting from a defensive to an offensive strategy over and over again until we finish them off for good." In other words, from then on, a monumental revenge was in the offing. It took nineteen years almost to the day after Lenin's speech for the Soviets to gain that revenge, and it came when the Soviets marched into eastern Poland on September 17, 1939, in the wake of the Nazis' *Blitzkrieg.*

Meanwhile, just before the announcement of his pact with Stalin, Hitler had been preparing the ground for his own settling of scores. He told the League of Nations' high commissioner on August 11: "If the slightest incident happens I shall crush the Poles without warning in such a way that no trace of Poland can be found afterwards." At the same time one of his senior officers wrote uneasily in his diary that "It is the Führer's and Goering's intention to destroy and exterminate the Polish nation," adding darkly, "More than that cannot even be hinted at in writing."

So it was that Wanda's first husband knew at once what to expect when they heard of the pact between the two dictators. Poland's population of nearly 35 million (over double its pre-1918 population) was poised between Germany's 70 million and the Soviet Union's 170 million. Unless it had help from allies, the outcome was inevitable—even before anyone knew that the Nazis and Soviets had written in a secret protocol to their treaty providing for a joint attack on Poland and the Baltic States, and their division between Germany and Russia. Without the tacit assurance of the Soviet Union's compliance in this invasion, Hitler could not have risked a unilateral attack on Poland. This secret protocol and its implementation on September 17, 1939, when the Red Army marched into a Poland reeling from seventeen days of Nazi *Blitzkrieg,* changed the destinies of millions in central Europe, including my father.

"I tried everything to trace my husband after the soldiers had taken him off," Wanda says, "but I couldn't find out anything." Wanda's husband was a journalist, from an influential, non-Jewish Polish family. Her father was professor of classics and German at Lwow University, an "assimilated Jew," she says, like herself. As Jews and intellectuals, both were prime targets of the Nazis, and as "bourgeois" intellectuals, all three were prime targets of the Soviets in their program of terror and deportations to Siberia. As Solzhenitsyn wrote in *The Gulag Archipelago,* the Soviet police "took those who were too independent, too influential, too noteworthy; they took particularly many Poles from former Polish provinces. It was then that ill-fated Katyn was filled up; and then too that in the northern camps they stock-piled fodder for the future army of Sikorski and Anders."

Wanda managed to survive and work through the winter of 1939 living in a flat with her sister. "Then, on April 13, 1940, came knock on door at three in the morning and there were two Soviet soldiers there. 'Pack what you can and take it with you,' they said. My sister wasn't taken. I was put on train packed with other women, and children. It took us east for seventeen days and nights, and eventually it arrived in Semipalatinsk in Kazakhstan—on edge of western Siberia."

"Did they tell you why they were taking you?"

"No, no. But we knew. Everyone who had some relative in prison or in the army was sent to camps—this was doctrine of 'collective responsibility.' And they just put people in prison in first place, just like that, you know."

This train was in the second wave of mass rail deportations which the Soviets set up to travel to the outer reaches of their empire, following Russia's by-now-three-hundred-year-old pattern of packing off to the east all kinds of customers it perceived as awkward. The first batch of 110 trains had set off in mid-February, each train carrying some 2,000 people in subhuman conditions which led to frostbite, starvation and derangement. It was the second batch of 160 trains which had Wanda on board. She shrugs off my question about the ghastliness of conditions on the train, as if to say, of course, what do you expect, this was normal. I'm learning that her way of regaining control over her story, hijacked as it was by some appalling episodes of history, is to laugh it off and keep her strong sense of herself as someone who always had some room for maneuver and autonomy. At one point she says to me, "It's funny, no, all this?" and when I pull a face and object, she says, "Okay, tragicomic, let's say."

"We were allowed to do our business through a hole in the carriage floor, but always supervised by soldiers holding bayonets! When we arrived in Semipalatinsk, the local women stared at us in amazement as we got off the train, because we still had elegant coats on, fur coats even, with silk linings. They had been told we were Finns—because of Russian-Finnish War, which had just taken place. Stupid. As if Russian people wouldn't find out! The station at Semipalatinsk looked like a camp. We waited three days there for train to take us on to the *kolkhoz,* collective village."

Wanda and five other women, one of whom had two young daughters with her, were put in a clay peasant longhouse with a tin roof, one large communal room and a kitchen. They soon became friendly with the local Ukrainian, Kazakh and Russian peasants, who had come and given them cucumbers and vodka the day they arrived.

"The Russians were crazy for watches. It was a mania with them. They asked me to sell my watch, a Longines, but I wouldn't sell it. They first gave me the job of cutting potatoes, then I did some plowing." She pulls a wry, mischievous face. "I wrote back to my mother that I was 'working in my own profession.' " Wanda stayed in this collective village until November 1941, when she and four others were given rail tickets to travel the near two thousand kilometers from Semipalatinsk to Yangiyul in Soviet Uzbekistan, where General Anders was assembling his army.

She brings out a small, faded gray leather notebook she kept with her throughout the war, with dates and places noted in neat script—her anchorage found in places and dates, just as my father's was. I'm surprised she was allowed to keep this, and she shows me several pages where she'd cut off the top or bottom or both, judging it too dangerous to keep. I would have thought these excisions alone would be provocative to the authorities, which makes me realize how difficult it can be to decode the meaning of even the smallest, most tangible of things from the past. Wanda has marked the stages of her journey:

Znamenka 30.4.40
10.XI.41 Semipalatinsk

Then, after the "amnesty," when she joined Anders's army:

Krasnovodsk
Rasht
25.VIII.42 Hamadan
31.XI.42 Baghdad
5.I.43 Nazareth
18.IV.43 Kursk
23.IV.43 Ufa

General Anders, Wanda says, was "like Moses leading us out of the desert." Geographically, Anders's journey out of the Soviet Union, which British prime minister Harold Macmillan would later call "an epic," went in the opposite direction to my father's—east at first, to Joe's west. And militarily they were at opposite ends of the echelon: Anders would end up commanding the Polish army, and my father would be among the youngest foot soldiers in that army. But humanly they would share a common fate, the fate of most Polish servicemen who ended up in England during the war: vicarious despair.

.   .   .

Władysław Anders was born near Warsaw in 1892, into a country which had been subject to the Russian Empire for a hundred years, since the last partition. It was therefore in the tsar's army that he first served, until the Bolshevik Revolution of 1917 prompted many former Russian-dominated states to form their own independent armies. Anders joined the newly formed Polish army, which was embroiled in six border wars provoked by the Treaty of Versailles— the worst of them being the one with the Bolsheviks for Warsaw and eastern Poland.

By the time the Germans invaded Poland, Anders was a seasoned career officer commanding a Polish cavalry brigade in northern Poland—on the face of it the very type of officer the Poles have been caricatured for: highly skilled on horseback, dashing and patriotic, but no match for the new kind of mechanized *Blitzkrieg* Hitler launched on the world. Yet he would prove to be much more than that—an outstanding military strategist and the kind of general Norman F. Dixon in his book *On the Psychology of Military Incompetence* applauds for three qualities which redeem generals from their necessarily authoritarian and bellicose profession: flexibility, imagination and care for their men (and women, and children, in Anders's case).

In August 1939, Anders, like his compatriots, was well aware of Hitler's designs on Poland, plainly proclaimed. He'd witnessed the sequence of events: their neighbor Czechoslovakia dismembered and then invaded by Hitler, the Nazi-Soviet Pact and, in the days prior to the invasion, Nazi units massing on Poland's western and southern borders. Although, as Anders wrote in his memoirs (1949), "To me, as to most other soldiers, it was clear . . . that the military position of Poland in the coming war would be very difficult, if not hopeless," the Polish government announced a general mobilization on August 29. This was overruled—as Czechoslovakia had been at Munich—by Western governments still trying to maintain peace. In spite of the unpromising example of Munich, the Poles felt they had support in Neville Chamberlain's March 31 statement to the House of Commons that "if any action clearly threatened Polish independence and . . . the Polish government accordingly considered it vital to resist with their national forces, His Majesty's Government would feel themselves bound at once to lend the Polish Government all support in their power." Two days after the Nazi-Soviet Pact, on August 25, 1939, this Anglo-Polish Agreement was signed and strengthened to guarantee joint Anglo-French military intervention if Poland were attacked. However, Britain was already equivocal in its attitude toward Poland, saying one thing and doing another. The day after Chamberlain's statement, on April 1, 1939, *The Times*—now the unofficial mouthpiece of the government—wrote an editorial preparing the way for pulling the rug out from under the guarantee it had given to Poland, just as it had done with Czechoslovakia the previous year.

This equivocation had not, however, yet percolated through to the Poles. So once the Nazi planes began raining bombs on Poland on September 1, 1939, in the world's first *Blitzkrieg,* and their 3,200 tanks (against the Poles' 313) were penetrating the country from the north, west and south in a carefully planned pincer movement, the Polish army, including Anders and his brigade, fought fiercely to play for time, certain—especially when Britain and France declared war on Germany on September 3—that the Allies would be coming to their aid. A long fortnight followed, when the planes in the skies were still only those of the Luftwaffe, and no help or even information came. The Polish infantry and cavalry, poorly equipped and undermanned, could only fight a rearguard action, with great courage, and no strategy. In the face of the waves of German attack from the west, the only way to go was east, which Anders and other units did as slowly as possible, fighting all the way.

A British editor and teacher working in Poland at the time, Denis Hills, remembers those two weeks:

> As the days passed village squares filled up with
> peasants in smocks and moccasins who had been

mobilised but had no movement orders or transport. It was rumoured that the British fleet had
sailed into the Baltic and that the RAF was flying
to Poland's help. The weather stayed cloudless, the
countryside ominously quiet. Day after day the
peasants looked up at the blue sky and saw no
vapour trails. Then refugees began to arrive by car
from Warsaw—lawyers, artists and writers, people
who had the resources and initiative to save themselves, and they brought the first signs of panic.

In his memoirs, Anders echoes the sentiments: "High overhead,
squadron after squadron of aircraft could be seen flying in file, like
cranes, to Warsaw. Railway lines were cut, and crowds of refugees
were trying to escape to the eastern provinces. Military communications became almost impossible. The shadow of disaster had
already begun to loom." Long columns of civilians were out on
the roads fleeing the invaders, and the whole country was over-
hung with German planes, flying low to attack them with machine
guns. As commanders fell, Anders took over more and more
brigades, gathered from the remnants of various cavalry regiments.
On their way east, they passed through burning villages with
bodies strewn on the ground, including those of civilians and children: "the nature of the new war," wrote Anders, "was already
clear." After two weeks of fighting, "few of us had more than the
briefest snatches of sleep. . . . Now an utter weariness seized hold
of us. We could barely keep our eyes open. Our poor horses
were in a similar plight." He recalls his brigade's frame of mind by
September 17:

> What was happening in the west, we wondered,
> and when would the French and British start their
> offensive? We could not understand why our allies
> were so slow in coming to our assistance. While

we were talking some of us fixed up the wireless
and began combing the ether for news. And the
news, when we heard it, stunned us. Soviet troops
had crossed the Polish frontier and were advancing
to the west! All eyes turned to me. We had no order
from anywhere, no directions whatever. What were
we to do?

The terms of Britain and France's guarantee of military intervention were that "limited offensive operations" would start three
days after Polish mobilization, and a "full offensive" within fifteen
days. On the sixteenth day of the war, they were pledged to send
into action between thirty-five and thirty-eight divisions. In the
event, no offensive was even planned, let alone carried out. At the
Nuremberg Trials, the German general Alfred Jodl said that "if we
did not collapse in 1939, that was due only to the fact that during
the Polish campaign" the seventy-six British and French divisions,
which faced by then thirty-two German divisions, "were completely inactive." Half a century later, the British historian Norman
Davies wrote:

Colourful stories about sabre-swinging cavalry-
men charging the steel hulls of Panzer tanks hardly
do justice to the record. The Poles inflicted over
50,000 casualties on the Wehrmacht, and were still
fighting hard when the entry of the Russians on the
17th September sealed their fate. Their perfor-
mance was certainly more creditable than that of
the British and French forces when they in their
turn faced the German Blitzkrieg eight months
later. Meanwhile, in September, the Western Allies
had not fired a shot in Poland's defence. The last
Polish unit in the field capitulated at Kock on the
6th October.

On the ground, hundreds of thousands of Polish soldiers, going east to escape the Nazis, were faced now with what to many was an even worse fate: the Red Army invading from the east—the same Red Army my father and Zbyszek had also been escaping as they scurried back to Lwow. Memories of the Red Army's previous invasion in 1920 were still vivid to many of the soldiers, including Anders. The invasion was particularly bitter since Poland had non-aggression treaties with both Germany and the USSR; often the paraphernalia of democracy can, it seems, be dismantled at a stroke when the greater power wills it.

Describing this moment, Anders's personal and national history seep into his writing: "Russia had violated the Polish-Soviet agreement at a most critical moment and had flung herself like a hyena against the defenceless rear of the fighting and bleeding Polish army." He decided to move south toward Lwow and then on to Hungary, the only remaining escape route, only to hear that Lwow had now fallen to the Germans.

> From the east the Soviet forces were thrusting ever deeper into Polish territory. To escape to the south, we must hurry. Speed, speed was our cry. But so tired were the men and horses that they could hardly move. Soldiers slept in the saddle. . . . We could not order a halt as the men, once dismounted, fell so soundly asleep that they could not be roused.

Poland was rapidly partitioned again, just as the secret protocol had provided. The far west of the country was incorporated into the German "Reich," the center became a new administrative district which the Germans called the "General Government," and the east of the country, beyond the rivers Bug and San, came under Soviet rule. The General Government, with its headquarters in Krakow, immediately brought in a campaign of terror. Every sign of Polish life was suppressed and all universities, colleges, schools, theaters, publications, museums and bookshops were closed down. In the biggest purge of university intellectuals by the Nazis, 30 percent of the teaching staff at Krakow's famous university were seized and shot without trial within the next few months. On September 27, Albert Forster, Nazi officer in charge of the Danzig area, said, "I was appointed by the Führer . . . with the clear instruction to Germanise the land again . . . to eradicate within the next few years any manifestations of the Polish nationality, of no matter what kind . . . whoever belongs to the Polish nation must leave this country." Nazis were given free rein to treat Poles with a vicious cruelty that was even more brutal for the Polish Jews.

East of the rivers, including Lwow, the Soviets took over and immediately brought in curfews, shortages, martial law, and a reign of terror similar to that of the Nazis: what Joe had experienced. The difference was one of presentation. The Red Army claimed to be invading Poland to offer "protection" to western Ukraine and western Byelorussia according to the "wishes" of the local people, whereas Hitler operated openly by decrees. Thus the rigged National Assembly in Lwow on October 27 resolved "unanimously" to request the Soviet Union to take the occupied Polish territories within their boundaries; thus on November 1 western Ukraine was "incorporated" into the USSR, as was Byelorussia the next day. Three days before, the Russian foreign minister Vyacheslav Molotov had said, "After one quick blow, first from the Germans, and next from the Red Army, nothing remained of the misshapen monster created by the Treaty of Versailles." Although Nazi behavior was more sadistically barbaric and lawless than the Soviets', the effects of terror on the local populations were similar, and there was a high degree of cooperation between the Gestapo and the NKVD—to the absurd extent of the NKVD's denouncing German Communists to the Gestapo. This is when the Soviets began arbitrarily to deport Poles from the regions they occupied to labor camps in Arctic Russia, Siberia and Kazakhstan—a deportation my father most likely narrowly escaped when he bribed his way out of the prison courtyard. An estimated 2 million would be sent east during 1939 to 1940, and at least half of them would die within a year. This was part of a deliberate Soviet policy to annihilate the Poles through starvation rather than—it was said—"wasting a bullet" on them, and to clear eastern Poland of Poles, in order to repopulate it with Russians.

Once the Soviets moved in, Anders and his men turned south, hoping to get to Hungary via Romania, but they soon ran out of ammunition, fuel and food, and their horses were starving. By September 27, Anders decided they must split into small groups to try to reach Hungary, in view of the vast number of Soviet troops concentrated in the area; but as the group passed through Sambor, they found themselves surrounded and had to fight their way out in hand-to-hand combat. Anders, badly wounded, suffered two hemorrhages, and begged his companions to leave him and escape. They refused, even when he passed out for most of the night. The next day they managed to get him to the next village, where someone informed on them and they were arrested and separated. Anders was taken off to a prison cell in Lwow. A Soviet officer told him: "We are now good friends of the Germans, together we will fight international capitalism. Poland was the tool of England, and she had to perish for that. There will never again be a Poland."

Like many other Poles, Anders refused to join the Red Army, and was interned in appalling conditions. When he arrived in his vermin-infested cell in Lwow, he was so badly wounded he was barely able to move, even on crutches. To make matters worse, it was the most severe of winters, with temperatures 30 degrees below freezing. There were no washing facilities, and he had frostbitten hands, a suppurating face, hands and legs, all of which went untreated. With the robust self-respect that never seemed to desert him and that he would confer on his army in due course, he demanded a visit from a doctor, the return of his clothing, glass to be put in his windows, and a daily bread ration—none of which came. "In spite of the great resilience of my constitution, I became extremely thin and I was so weak that I no longer felt any pain from my wounds and frost-bite." There would also be "ruthless searching of the natural cavities of my body. They did not even neglect to hunt through the long beard which had grown during my imprisonment and which was stiff from pus that had run into it from my frost-bitten face and frozen nose. I was kicked and beaten on these occasions."

Like other prisoners, he was regularly dragged out of his cell for interrogations. "Brutal and basic torture became the norm for those regarded as enemies of the state," a recent historian has written. "Sleep deprivation, night interrogation, beatings and the everlasting threat of reprisals against relatives and colleagues remaining in occupied Poland were the accepted method of extracting 'confessions' of anti-Soviet intrigue." There were fourteen official categories of "enemies of the state," including "Volunteers of all other armies other than the Bolsheviks, citizens of foreign states, persons who have travelled abroad, aristocrats, landowners, wealthy merchants, bankers, industrialists, hotel and restaurant proprietors, the staff of the Red Cross" and—with an arcane paranoia about anything with a whiff of internationalism—"persons who are esperantists or philatelists." However, even these manically wide-ranging categories barely got invoked as the Red Army, backed by the NKVD, swooped down randomly on any target.

Suddenly, on February 29, 1940, Anders was taken out of his cell and put on a train for several days without being told why. He found that he'd been transferred to the notorious Lubyanka Prison in Moscow, headquarters of the Soviet secret police. This vast building had a history of arrest and execution going back centuries, its vaulted dungeons originally designed to torture the estranged wife of Peter the Great. Its use had lapsed until 1917, when it became a prison again. Once again, Muscovites hurried by with their eyes averted, just as passing forebears had crossed themselves to ward off evil. It had been expanded to accommodate the NKVD, and had a new head, forty-one-year-old Lavrenti Beria, whose out-ward respectability masked a vicious sadism. Lubyanka was termed facetiously a "luxury prison," since only people who were of special interest to the NKVD were sent there. Indeed for Anders, conditions improved considerably; they could hardly have got worse. He had his first wash for many months and was given a glass of tea "with two lumps of sugar, as well as watery, but hot soup, and two spoonfuls of pearl barley. At that time, after many months of starvation, it seemed a royal banquet." However, everyone was forbidden to speak except in a whisper, so that the prison was "strange and eerie . . . the general impression was one of sinister silence."

The interrogations, however, continued at full volume. They pumped him for information on everything from who had run the Lwow underground organization to who had called on him in hospital and what they had talked about. One time he would be shouted at and hit, another he would be offered cigarettes. He was "disturbed by the officials' unusual outspokenness to me about what one would have thought to have been secrets of high policy. It seemed that the Soviet authorities were so over-confident that they did not take into account at all that I might some day be released." "Don't think," they told him there, "we're genuine friends of Germany: we hate only the English more. But, as soon as the Germans are weakened after the defeat of France and Great Britain, we will push forward and occupy the whole of Europe." He was also shown their file on him, with photographs taken of him at the Olympic Games in Amsterdam and at an international horse show in Nice, none of which he'd known about. "We have such a file," they told him, "for every military and political personage in the whole world. The Soviet Union has long arms."

When Anders's cellmate told him that he had no idea why he'd been arrested, he "rocked with laughter," writes Anders, "when I expressed my amazement. He said at least nine-tenths of Russian prisoners do not know why they have been arrested, since an anonymous denunciation is sufficient to send them to prison." Much later, the Polish writer Jozef Mackiewicz would describe this atmosphere of fear, which the Soviets immediately transplanted into the Polish territories they invaded: "People had become very dangerous. All one needed to do was to go to the authorities and make a deposition. The accused was finished."

As a general—and perhaps too as someone who turned up at international horse shows—Anders would have been deemed a class enemy, a "bourgeois." But he took a keen interest in his enemy, as he did in everything, and read thoroughly the Bolshevik literature they were allowed in prison. His conclusion was that Stalin's tactic was derived from Lenin's, which "authorises any ruse, cunning, unlawful method, evasion, concealment of truth, attempts to provoke disputes and divisions among partners and adversaries; and recommends a continual offensive by all means, open and secret. It is well known that communism discards all 'bourgeois' principles of ethics and morality." Marxism's justification for such dissembling means in pursuit of an end it saw as historically inevitable was that it regarded conventional ethics and morality as merely a smokescreen for bourgeois ideology. Other dictators in the twentieth and twenty-first centuries would take Stalin as their model, Hitler leading the way.

Once again Anders was taken out from his cell to an unknown destination, this time in a Black Maria. He was terrified that he would be taken off to the "torture prison" of Lerfortovo, but in fact he was taken to Butyrki Prison in Moscow, where he was kept in solitary confinement for months (just as the poet Mayakovsky had been, thirty-two years before). Day and night a powerful light was directed at his eyes, which became so filmed over with pus that he feared he would lose his sight. In September 1940, he was hauled out of seven months of total isolation and sent back to the Lubyanka, where he was put in a cell with seven others. It was here that he heard for the first time "the stunning news that France had surrendered, that the Germans had occupied Denmark, Norway, Holland and Belgium; Paris had been taken! The fall of Great

Britain was imminent. Italy had entered the war on the German side. The shock was overwhelming. Had the Polish sacrifice, which had given the Allies a breathing-space, been in vain?"

Although he had been deprived of information about the outside world, he was an eyewitness to the Stalinist purges within Russia through his fellow prisoners. He became an involuntary archaeologist, able to date accurately the layer of the purge a prisoner had been captured in. At first, it puzzled him to find that three out of four prisoners were themselves members of the Communist Party. They were most reluctant to give the reasons for their arrest. Only when they were particularly distressed after a night interrogation and had returned to the cell bleeding and tortured would they "complain and swear for fifteen or twenty minutes." Nearly all the prisoners, Anders wrote, were of Jewish extraction, many arrested for alleged sympathy with Trotskyism. Soviet prisons showed that far from a few individuals being arrested for "hindering the progress of Bolshevism"—as official claims went—hundreds of thousands were being liquidated after "workers' trials." One opposition after another was eliminated by Stalin and his party, who then openly adopted the program of their adversaries. By these kinds of tactics, most of the population had been coerced into conformity by 1938.

"And if one realises," Anders writes, "that Bolshevik legislation, unique in the world, admits the principle of so-called collective responsibility, and that with the convicted all their relations, friends and acquaintances—however distant the connection—are put into prisons and prison camps, it is easy to guess how many millions filled the Soviet gaols at that period, and how many recruits were enlisted for forced labour for the purposes of the Five-Year Plan." Or, as a recent study puts it, using records that have come to light since the dissolution of the Soviet Union and that corroborate Anders's observations half a century before, "Rule by terror was the essence of Stalinism. No previous tyrant since ancient times had dared discipline his subjects in such ruthless fashion. . . . Victims were chosen in arbitrary fashion. Most of them had no association with any opposition tendency and a number were loyal Stalinists of unimpeachably proletarian credentials." By the time Anders was interned, Stalin had already murdered millions of his own people, including most of his army officers in 1937. (Such figures are notoriously hard to check, but just under 900,000 Russians were actually executed, and at least 10 million—some sources say over double that figure—perished in the gulags.)

The Soviet officials Anders had dealings with "never disguised their detestation of the British, and reviled them at every opportunity." The Germans, he says, they dreaded, but at the same time regarded "with a peculiar respect." Perhaps, he surmises, this was because for years before the 1914 war many Germans had held key posts in the Russian Empire. Perhaps, too, there was a perverse respect for the fact that in the previous war, the Germans had always defeated the Russians, even when outnumbered, and obviously despised them. Furthermore, it was the Germans who had sent Lenin and other Bolshevik leaders to Russia in 1917; and thousands of German technicians had stayed in Russia after the Revolution and helped to build up the Soviet heavy industries. Certainly—as Anders was not yet in a position to know—part of Hitler's success in the early months of the war was thanks to the Soviet shipping of raw materials such as oil, timber, metals and agricultural produce through to the Germans. In turn, Germany supplied machinery and arms to the ailing Soviet economy.

Knowing the two countries, Anders guessed this mutual assistance would not bear up for long, and when he heard the distant sounds of air raids and antiaircraft guns, he knew that Russia and Germany were at war, although it was days before it was admitted. The news that its ally had launched an attack on it, and that 3 million Nazi soldiers were marching toward Leningrad and Moscow, gave the Soviet Union a shock similar to the one it had given the world with its pact of August 1939. (This in spite of the fact that in the previous six months Stalin had been given over a hundred intelligence warnings about such an attack—one even from the German ambassador—but had angrily dismissed them as disinformation.)

Almost at once, Anders's treatment changed. He was allowed to shave regularly, his food improved, and he was suddenly treated with respect and "the soul of courtesy." On August 4, at the civilized hour of 4:00 p.m., instead of the early hours of the morning, he was taken to meet Beria and his assistant Merkulov, who offered him a cigarette or some tea. "I asked whether I was a prisoner or a free man—the answer was: 'You are free.' I then asked for tea and a cigarette." How false were the Germans, they told him, who had so unexpectedly attacked the Soviet Union. Now the Poles and Russians must live in harmony and bury the hatchet, with the sole aim of defeating the Germans. They told him that the Soviet Union had just signed a treaty with Great Britain, together with a Polish-Soviet Agreement, under which not only would there be an amnesty for all Poles, but a Polish army would be formed. He, Anders, had been appointed commander of this army by the Polish authorities, with the consent of the Soviet government. They were, Anders says, "extremely friendly." Did he have any difficulties or requirements? He took immediate advantage of the question to ask for the release of a prisoner known to him who was under a death sentence, and a measure of their extreme friendliness was that it was accorded at once.

Anders had been in prison for twenty months in all, seven of those in solitary confinement. His "anti-Soviet" stance was no blind prejudice, but informed and well earned. It would be criticized later in England by politicians leaning fashionably to the left to counter England's own sociological schisms—often influenced ideologically by the Spanish Civil War—but who had no experience of what was really happening in Communist Russia. George Orwell knew this, writing as war broke out in 1939 that "the overwhelming majority of English people have no experience of violence or illegality. If you have grown up in that sort of atmosphere it is not at all easy to imagine what a despotic regime is like. . . . To people of that kind such things as purges, secret police, summary executions, imprisonment without trial etc., etc., are too remote to be terrifying. They can swallow totalitarianism *because* they have no experience of anything except liberalism." Many idealistic intellectuals in Britain, blithely ignorant of the practice of terror, were hoodwinked in this way. Anders, however, had grown up in Russia, knew it intimately in both its tsarist and its Bolshevik phases, spoke Russian fluently, and had almost been liquidated by the Russians.

After the war, the Soviet Union's huge losses—18 million people estimated killed in the fighting, by far the highest number of any nation—earned it respect and sympathy, and its propaganda thereafter, that the Soviet Union alone had fought fascism and stopped the Nazis in the Second World War (the propaganda I had witnessed in Berlin in 1958), entrenched the country's view of itself as uniquely suffering and heroic. Undoubtedly the victory at Stalingrad was the turning point of the war, and the Russian people's courage and suffering is not in question. But, Anders writes, the Soviets' victory also "used the blood of the human reserves of those nationalities considered to be the most opposed to the totalitarian and centralist policy of the Soviet Union. They were bled white . . . Leningrad was defended by Ukrainians, and few of these defenders remained alive." This kind of statement, no less than the truth, would contribute to Anders's being considered "political" in postwar England, in the kind of coded put-down which in England could be an economical, bloodless version of the sadism of Beria.

Although "still too weak to drink vodka" at the end of August, so that others had to stand in for him at banquets, Anders put his energy into tracing and regrouping all Polish prisoners of war in Soviet labor camps—in the process discovering to his dismay how many there were, some 2 million. He realized at once, as did his colleague General Sikorski—who had also escaped Poland and had since become prime minister of the Polish government-in-exile in London—that thousands of officers had gone missing, completely unaccounted for. Anders also realized that he was not just creating an army but an opportunity to evacuate as many Poles as possible from intolerable conditions.

"I succeeded in obtaining from the Soviet authorities permission to . . . create a Women's Auxiliary Service. I knew that besides the men, thousands of our women and girls were in prisons, and huge numbers of them were in concentration camps. They were certainly willing, and also entitled, to give all their strength to the national service. I also knew that in the circumstances we had to face it was the only way to save their lives." Wanda was one of these women, and I understand now why she was so furious that Stalin should get away with calling the release of these illegally taken Polish prisoners an "amnesty," as if it were a gesture of magnanimity.

Yet although Anders could form an army—financed by Soviet and British lend-lease credits—and was on good terms with the respected Soviet marshal Zhukov (whom my father had quietly bearded in Lwow), he was subordinate in operational matters to the Soviet high command, and wasn't given proper supplies. When General Sikorski visited Anders's forces near Moscow in the terrible winter of 1941, with temperatures plummeting to 56 degrees of frost, he was appalled at how starved, underequipped and unfit for combat they were—even though, thanks to Anders, their morale was high. Something clearly had to be done, especially since Stalin wanted to split up the Polish army and send divisions of it to the front at Stalingrad, as it was technically under Soviet command and half financed by them.

Anders and Sikorski went to meet Stalin at the Kremlin. Anders, evidently as strong a presence in face-to-face negotiations with Stalin as he was within his army, managed to block the attempt to coopt his army. He did this by refusing to let his men fight until they were restored to health, and could fight together as an army, not as units. Knowing Stalin's tactic of fielding "subject" nations at the front line, he did not want to volunteer his men and women, so recently escaped from the horror of prisons and camps, for convenient cannon fodder. Anders and Sikorski also managed to persuade Stalin that Anders should evacuate some 100,000 of his Poles from northern Russia to warmer climes in the south, near Yangiyul in Uzbekistan. Stalin agreed partly because he thought they would perish en route—as indeed many of them did—and partly because he wanted any Polish army as far away as possible from Poland, which he was intending to take back under Russian rule. Anders and Sikorski also pressed Stalin on the matter of the thousands of Polish officers who seemed to have simply disappeared in the spring of 1940, and about whose fate they had the direst forebodings. What had happened to them? Anders asked Stalin directly. Stalin answered with a shrug and the fanciful suggestion that "they had probably escaped to Manchuria."

Field Marshal Lord Alanbrooke, now in command of the British forces, was in Moscow at the same time with Churchill, and he describes in his diary a meeting with Anders. (No doubt for reasons of security, this is one of the entries he wrote retrospectively.)

> Anders' visit was of course of some interest. . . . When he came into my hotel sitting room he beckoned to me to come and sit at a small table with him. He then pulled out his cigarette case and started tapping the table and speaking in a low voice. He said: "As long as I keep tapping this table and talk like this we cannot be overheard by all the microphones in this room!" I must confess that till then I had not realized that my sitting room was full of microphones. I learned to realize that all rooms in Moscow had ears! Anders then proceeded to tell me that hunt as he might he could not discover a large consignment of Polish prisoners which comprised most of the men of distinction in most walks of life. He had followed one clue half way across Siberia and then it fizzled out. He said

he was certain that they were either being liquidated in one of the Siberian Convict Camps or that
they had been murdered.

In fact, as Mikhail Gorbachev finally admitted when he was
president in 1990, Stalin had had some fifteen thousand officers
murdered—most of them teachers, doctors, artists and other civilians who had volunteered to defend their country against Hitler.
Their hands were tied behind them and they were shot in the back
of the head and buried in mass graves at Katyn, Starobelsk and
Ostashkov. The Nazis uncovered the mass grave at Katyn Forest in
April 1943 and their propaganda minister broadcast the fact that the
Soviets had committed this atrocity; unfortunately, this accurate
news came from such a suspect source that it could be quickly dis-
counted by those with an interest in doing so. For most of the rest of
the century, East and West would collude in the lie that it was the
Nazis who had killed the officers.

Once established in Yangiyul in January 1942, Anders's army
lost some seventy people a day to typhus and dysentery, but grew
strong culturally, with theaters, classes, swimming, football and
musicals set up to create a mini-Poland, particularly for the thousands of children amongst them. In April, Anders flew to London to
see Sikorski and Churchill, and in July to Moscow to see Stalin, to
try to persuade them to let him take his army further on to Persia.
No doubt his main imperative was to get his army as near as he
could to Poland, by however circuitous a route, in order to defend
his country—preferably alongside the Allies—but he also needed
to get it out of the Soviet sphere of influence. His experience told
him that whatever the Allies might think, if the Soviets "liberated"
Poland from the Nazis, they had no interest in establishing a free
Poland. Anders succeeded finally in gaining permission to evacuate
his people, like the Pied Piper—or, as Wanda said, like Moses leading his people out of the desert—into Persia, where the Allies
needed a protective force for their oil fields.

20 | TOURISTS

Wanda has brought out a video of a Polish-made documentary about Anders and his army and we sit transfixed together watching it. She hunches forward on the edge of her chair, her right eye more hooded and slightly downwind of her left, like Picasso's portrait of Gertrude Stein. For the first time, I watch Anders moving and understand why he could command such respect and loyalty. He is lean, taller than most of those around him, and in individual encounters his dark eyes, made more striking by his shaven head, like Yul Brynner's, sparkle with attention. His responsibilities, past suffering and military training (including two years in military school in Paris before the war) give him gravity and economy of movement, particularly when he delivers a bracing speech to the young boys he wants to lead back to help rebuild Poland after the war. "He moves like a Buddhist monk," I say, "relaxed and alert." Wanda laughs. "Oh no! Far from that, not a monk at all—he was very appetizing. To the ladies, you know." Her eyes light up. "Yangiyul. That's where I joined the Anders army! Look—can you stop the video for a moment?"

She gets out a Polish book on the women's units within the Polish army from 1918 onward (published in London in 1995) and

General Anders in 1944

leafs through it to show me diffidently a picture of herself in a group of women and men laughing and full of verve. She tells me why: they had just been issued British army uniforms, but the hats hadn't arrived, so they'd been given Australian army issue instead, dashingly curled up at one side like cowboy hats. Hence the mirth—something I could never have guessed from looking at the picture without her. Her young face gazes out at me from the photograph, pretty, relaxed and rather modern, and I can see why she found some of the inanities that the war threw up funny, and why she survived so well. She had a natural zest—and still has, at eighty-eight. "You looked lovely," I say. "I looked like a mushroom." She laughs. I want to include the picture in this book, but she refuses, just as she demurs in letting me use Lucjan's and her real names. "I wouldn't want people to think I was pushing myself forward, many people went through far worse things, we are just small people. And, you know, Jews are always accused of being pushy, I don't want that."

In spite of the spirit and energy and the well-turned-out look of the Anders army in both book and video, endemic diseases and cold nights that caused undernourished people to freeze to death in their tents were a frequent concern. Anders sent an urgent telegram to this effect to Sikorski, which was what on the face of it led Stalin to give permission for them to make a swift evacuation to Persia via the Caspian Sea. Welfare organizations like the Red Cross and the Polish-American Relief Organization helped in hospitals and hostels along the way in Isfahan, Teheran, and—"what was the name of the port that's now Rasht?" Wanda asks me peremptorily. I've no idea, and don't even know where Rasht is. "You are an islander," she says, and when she sees my face fall, adds, "you don't want to be, but you are."

I suddenly feel the dismay of a small child not being included in the game. Before, I'd sent her my biography of Isabelle Eberhardt and she'd read it all of a piece, through the night. This had pleased me, especially when she'd said, "You are a European." Now I felt this privilege had been withdrawn, and my disappointment quickly turned to denial and dismissiveness. These émigrés, I thought, they're so bound up in their own experiences in the past, and so arrogant. I was conveniently calling on the English part of me, having suddenly been rejected as a European. This dismissiveness, of course, is what the English and others have often experienced individually with émigrés, and why they often haven't hung around to get a fuller story. More panoramically, this is part of what the Soviet Union experienced when its former ally Germany turned on it: hurt pride. And this is what the Germans and Russians had experienced at Versailles: hurt pride and ostracization. What a task it is even for one individual not to overreact when criticized. To try to salve my pride, I reflect that Wanda and her husband have no children, and that children can make you a little more careful about bursting people's bubbles. They have no children, Wanda has already told me, because after the war they made a conscious decision not to bring children into a world that could produce such horrors. This decision seems to go against her seeing the events as funny, or even tragicomic, and, although ambivalence is the most human response in complex situations, I also know that in the end actions speak louder than words.

Now Anders and his army are seen embarking at Krasnovodsk in summer 1942 to sail across the Caspian Sea in two desperately overloaded ships to Pahlevi (now Rasht), in Persia (now Iran). "There was exhaustion, starvation, sickness," says the commentator in the video, who balances his clipped Scottish tones with the occasional wild swoop on a word, "but the troops *adored* and respected Anders." Civilians were installed in and around Teheran, and whole small Polish towns were built. "They had the best of contacts with the Arabs, because they had never been *tainted* as a colonial power," the commentator says approvingly. We watch an orphaned bear they adopted as mascot as he pals around with them, drinking beer, showering and clowning. He will end up in the Edinburgh Zoo at the end of the war, always perking up at the sound of a Polish voice.

However—and this the video doesn't tell us—by now Anders's army was becoming something of an embarrassment to the British government and even to the Polish government-in-exile, who did not know what to do with it without offending the Soviets. In April 1942, just before Anders had begun his evacuations to Iran, he had flown to London to speak with Sikorski and the British high command. Field Marshal Alanbrooke wrote in his diary:

> There are two opposed camps in the Poles now, Sikorski and those in England wish to transfer a large contingent home to form force here, the others wish to form Polish forces in the Middle East. Personally I am in favour of the latter. Any forces in the Middle East will be a Godsend to us.

Understandably, Anders was wanting to build up his men, still weak and undertrained, into a cohesive fighting force before pitching them into battle in Europe, as well as to supervise the care of the hundreds of undernourished children in his band (whom we watch smiling eagerly out at the camera, unaware of their concave chests and bone-arms). Understandably, too, for his part Sikorski wanted to field reinforcements where he was, in England, to contribute to the Allies and strengthen his homeless government's position; he also wanted Polish forces as near to Poland as practicable, ready for after the war. The difference between the two men was that Sikorski didn't have Anders's intimate experience of the Soviet regime. As for the Soviet Union, not only was it suffering terrible losses and deprivations in what was now a yearlong war with Germany but in August 1942—a few months after Anders and his army arrived in Persia—the Nazis launched what would be a ferocious seven-month battle for Stalingrad. Hence, perhaps, Stalin's bitter epithet for Anders's army: "Sikorski's tourists." (That August, Alanbrooke met Stalin for the first time and wrote in his diary: "He is an outstanding man, there is no doubt about that, but not an attractive one. He has got an unpleasantly cold, crafty, dead face, and whenever I look at him I can imagine him sending off people to their doom without ever turning a hair.")

Anders and his army moved on across the deserts to Iraq, where they met up in May 1942 with another Polish brigade, the Carpathian Rifles, which had been formed in Syria in 1940, and had a long series of battles behind them, including Tobruk. It was then that the joint army was officially given the name of the Polish Second Corps. It was also then that Anders met up with a singer from Lwow, Renata Bogdanska. "Anders took everything by *storm*," the commentary tells us, as a Chopin piano sonata plays to a crescendo in the background. "This front-line love affair concluded after the war with the general's second marriage. He was subjected to social *condemnation*. He was no longer invited to society *events*. The royal court then did not *tolerate* divorcees."

We watch the new Second Corps moving on to Palestine, where they train as a fit and cohesive fighting force for the first time. Here some three thousand Jewish soldiers desert from the army, most of them to join Irgun and Haganah. One of these soldiers was Mena-hem Begin, future prime minister of Israel. "The British protest violently," says the commentator, as these soldiers will then engage in terrorism against the British military authorities. Although deser-tion was punishable by death in Polish military law, Anders refused to take action against them, saying, "They are at home and they want to fight for their own country." This would not have stood Anders in good stead with the British authorities.

Something else had happened, too, two months before, which had changed the political balance radically for Anders and the Poles—something the video again doesn't mention. In February 1943, Hitler's army had been decisively beaten at Stalingrad by the Russians, in an outcome that turned the tide of the war, giving Stalin and the Soviets immense moral authority within the Allies. It also meant that the Allies felt themselves in no position to object to what Stalin might do within his own "sphere of influence." Stalin took immediate advantage of this to send a note to the Polish gov-ernment in London to say that all Poles remaining in the Soviet Union would be considered Soviet subjects. This was a red alert to Anders and Sikorski. And it was shortly after this, in April 1943, that the Nazi propaganda minister announced that German troops had found mass graves in the forest of Katyn, near Smolensk, which they claimed were those of some 4,500 (they thought at the time) Polish officers massacred by the Russians in 1940.

General Sikorski immediately asked the Red Cross to investi-gate the report. Stalin responded with a blanket denial and by abruptly breaking off diplomatic relations with the Polish govern-ment, as if he were the injured party. This rupture was in his long-term interests to provoke anyway, as he had already set up his own Communist-led government to install in Poland after the war, and was in the process of recalling a Polish officer, Zygmunt Berling, who had deserted from Anders's army, to form a rival, Communist Polish army within Russia. Sikorski vehemently objected to

Stalin's behavior over Katyn, but was overruled. This was partly because the Allies needed the might of Russia on their side at a point when they were planning to invade France, partly because President Roosevelt needed to persuade Russia to enter the war against Japan with him, and to back the emerging United Nations, and partly because Poland was a small player in a much larger game; but it was also more nebulously personal.

To Churchill, the Poles under Sikorski were beginning to be irksome in his wooing of Stalin. His biographer Martin Gilbert writes that "to Churchill, Poland was always 'slightly beyond the pale,' not one of the countries to which he was emotionally drawn." Another biographer puts it down to Churchill's very personal take on Poland's reincarnation after Versailles: "But then [Churchill] was deeply suspicious of the new Poland that emerged through the Treaty of Riga, with its extended frontiers taking in Lwow and Wilno, and so he felt that this was some sort of distortion . . . he felt that the whole Polish concern with their eastern frontier was an obsession born of something unnatural in 1921." (As opposed to the cold-blooded massacre of fifteen thousand men, which he did not condemn as "unnatural.") Stalin cleverly played on this, and got additional revenge for the humiliation of the Battle of the Vistula, by telling Churchill that in 1919 England's own foreign secretary, Lord Curzon, had proposed the very frontier that the Russians were insisting on: it was called the "Curzon line," so it must be all right. Poland, he told Churchill, was land-grabbing and warlike, and had taken this territory from Russia in 1921 (the fact that Russia had previously taken it from Poland in 1772 was ignored again). Churchill, whose understandable first priority was now for the Allies to defeat Germany with the crucial help of the Russians, could not afford to acknowledge any grievance against them, however egregious. The upshot was that "the British government believed that the Katyn massacre was highly embarrassing and should be ignored as much as possible." Foreign Minister Anthony Eden's private secretary sent a memo on April 21 saying, "The

Poles have fairly upset the apple-cart. They will need very firm treatment if they are not to upset the peace settlement and wreck Anglo-Soviet unity." Five days later, Churchill was of the same mind: "There is no use prowling around the three-year-old graves of Smolensk."

A month after that, Sikorski visited Anders and his army in Iraq. Anders writes, "From the first talks I had with him I saw that some one had turned him against us in the Middle East. It transpired that he had been warned in London against visiting us, because there was believed to be a plot against his life and because the army was reported to be undisciplined and too prone to meddle in politics."

It was in these circumstances that ten weeks later, on July 4, 1943, Sikorski was killed in an air crash over Gibraltar, along with six crew and ten other passengers, including his daughter. Only the pilot, a Czech, survived. Rumors were rife at the time that Stalin had engineered this crash, or even that he'd done so with Churchill's complicity. It was investigated by the Foreign Office at the time and by a secret inquiry in 1969 at the behest of Prime Minister Harold Wilson. The first inquiry concluded that there was no sabotage; the second, that sabotage could not be ruled out. As we shall see later, recently declassified evidence now endorses this second judgment. Certainly, it was, on the face of it, a fortunate piece of timing for Stalin, and even for Churchill. With Sikorski gone, the Polish government-in-exile had only weak leaders to hand; Stalin was let off the hook over Katyn; and Churchill didn't have to contend with a strong opponent who might "upset the apple-cart" with Stalin. When Anders heard the news, he wrote: "It was a profound shock to the whole army. To me it brought great grief, for we had respected each other." He says nothing of theories of sabotage, limiting himself to noting that "there is every reason to believe that if it had not been for his death the Polish cause would have been much better defended later."

. . .

Three days after Sikorski's death, Winston Churchill paid the general an orotund tribute in the House of Commons, which was fulsome in its praise of the Polish war effort and apparently supportive of Poland's future independence. He called Sikorski's death "one of the heaviest strokes we have sustained," and termed him "the embodiment of that spirit which has borne the Polish nation through centuries of sorrow and is unquenchable by agony." He lauded Sikorski's gathering together of a Polish army of over eighty thousand men in France, which "fought with the utmost resolution in the disastrous battles of 1940. Part fought its way out in good order into Switzerland, and is today interned there" (the option my father's unit had refused), and "Part marched resolutely to the sea, and reached this island" (including Joe). However, the speech contained key phrases which must have rung warning bells for Anders and his men (phrases I've italicized):

> [Sikorski] personally directed that movement of resistance which has maintained a ceaseless warfare against German oppression in spite of sufferings as terrible as any nation has ever endured. (Hear, hear.) This resistance will grow in power until, at the approach of *liberating armies,* it will exterminate the *German ravagers* of the homeland. . . . He was a man of remarkable preeminence, both as a statesman and a soldier. *His agreement with Marshal Stalin of July 30th, 1941, was an outstanding example of his political wisdom.* Until the moment of his death he lived in the conviction of the common struggle and in the faith that a better Europe will arise in which a great and independent Poland will play an honourable part. (Cheers.) We British here and throughout the Commonwealth and Empire, *who declared war on Germany because of Hitler's invasion of Poland and in*

fulfilment of our guarantee, feel deeply for our Polish allies in their new loss.

We express our sympathy to them, we express our confidence in their immortal qualities, and we proclaim our resolve that General Sikorski's work as Prime Minister and Commander-in-Chief shall not have been done in vain. (Cheers.)

The phrase about declaring war on Germany "in fulfilment of Britain's guarantee," whilst technically true, no doubt had a hollow ring to men who had fought for a month under the assault of the *Blitzkrieg,* with no help on the horizon. Otherwise, the "ravagers" of Poland are labelled as only German (although the Soviets had invaded half of Poland too); the "liberating armies," Anders knew, would be the far-from-liberating Red Army, and the pointed reference to Sikorski's "political wisdom" in making an agreement with Stalin showed that he'd been made to toe the line of European realpolitik. The appointment of the inexperienced Stanisław Mikolajczyk, Sikorski's deputy, to take over as Polish prime minister increased Anders's concern.

By the time of the Teheran Conference four months later, from November 28 to December 1, 1943, Churchill's subtext was becoming clear, although as yet behind closed doors. It was now that he, Stalin and Roosevelt secretly agreed—without allowing the Poles any representation—that Russia should keep all the eastern Polish territory it had illegally taken through the Nazi-Soviet Pact, when its Red Army marched into Poland. The strains of this period on all the key players cannot, of course, be minimized. Roosevelt was already very ill at this time—as well as clinically depressed—and he was preoccupied with the forthcoming elections in his country. Churchill, too, was physically exhausted by the stresses of a long war; at this stage he had little room for maneuver now that Russia and America had effectively taken over the running of the war, and his priority was to bring about the early defeat of Germany, whatever the cost, for which he needed Russia on board. There were also pressing concerns that Russia might make a separate peace with Germany if ruffled, and that the new "secret weapons" Germany was known to be producing—which would turn out to be the V1s and V2s—would soon be launched against England. In addition, Stalin had one key negotiating advantage over Churchill and Roosevelt that wouldn't emerge until decades later: the "Cambridge Five" agents were sending through highly classified intelligence which gave Stalin superior knowledge of the cards in the other men's hands. It paved the way for this most important political gain of his, agreement to the Soviet Union's keeping its 1941 gains in Poland.

For whatever the mitigating circumstances, the fact still stands that a vast nation which had illegally invaded a sovereign nation with one sixtieth of its landmass, and which had arbitrarily imprisoned and murdered millions of its people, was being handed the spoils of its crime on a plate. Not only that, but the sacrificial victim was being forced to smile and keep quiet as it went to the altar, or it might "upset the apple-cart." Wanda—who became a captain in Anders's Polish army—tells me matter-of-factly that there was a special meeting for officers in Palestine at which they were told to "keep their mouths shut about what had happened in Russia because it might endanger their relatives and friends at home, and those left behind in Russia"—"collective responsibility" again. The Poles were being muzzled, and it would not be for the last time.

When, in January 1944, the Red Army arrived in Poland, it was clear proof of what the signs had been pointing to over the past months: that Poland was going to be sacrificed to Stalin, without its consent, by her own Allies. The men who were fighting in the Polish armies would no longer have a free homeland to go back to. For most of the men of the Anders army particularly, who had experienced Soviet camps, to go back to a Soviet-ruled Poland would be a fate worse than death.

On top of all this, Poland's army was now fielded into a battle
that was already morally tainted, that many thought a lost cause and
a suicide mission, and that had been unsuccessfully waged three
times in the previous months by the Allies: the battle for Monte
Cassino.

Wanda and I follow Anders's "wandering army" on the video as it
sets out from Palestine via Egypt to North Africa, where, Anders
wrote, "I met American units for the first time in my life. I was
struck both by the physical fitness of the men and by the high quality of their kit and equipment." It was here that the Polish Second
Corps joined up with the Allies under the overall command of the
British Eighth Army—fresh from its victories under General Mont-
gomery at El Alamein and in Sicily—and of the American Fifth
Army, in order to invade Nazi-occupied Italy. Now the Polish Second Corps landed in southern Italy—the "soft underbelly of
Europe," as Churchill called it—and began to move north alongside
Allied troops from Algeria, Brazil, Britain, France, India, New
Zealand and the United States to try to take Rome. In May 1944
time was at a premium because the Allied invasion of Nazi-
occupied France was planned for the following month, and they
needed to defeat the German units in Italy so that they couldn't
come to the assistance of their colleagues in France.

The trouble was that the road to Rome was blocked by what
seemed an impregnable fortress: the vast monastery of Monte
Cassino, which had been taken over as a stronghold by the Nazis.
This was the fortress and run of hills that the Allies had tried, and
failed, to take in devastating battles in September 1943, and again
in January and February 1944. For five months Monte Cassino had
been the closest parallel to the stalemate in the trenches of the First
World War.

By May 11, when they were due to go into battle, there was
great ambivalence in the Polish camp. On one hand, morale was

high: in fighting with the Allies for Italy, they were fighting for their country, just as at the Battle of Britain in 1940 Polish airmen had already distinguished themselves, providing an initial 13 percent of the pilots—and by the end 20 percent—including the Polish 303 Kosciuszko Squadron, named after the Polish national hero, which shot down more enemy airplanes than any other squadron. Harold Macmillan visited Second Corps for the first time in Italy and was struck by "first, the remarkably high standard of drill, discipline, appearance and 'tenue' of the Polish troops. I had not seen anything to equal it during the campaign, except perhaps (I write as a one-time Guardsman!) in the Brigade of Guards. The second impression was more subtle and more difficult to define. It was an extraordinary sense of romance—not gaiety, exactly, but chivalry, poetry, adventure. It was more than a military formation. It was a crusade. . . . General Anders himself was the natural leader, as well as the formal military leader, of this knightly army. Behind his firm military bearing was—and is—the ardour of a boy." At this stage Macmillan knew nothing of what Anders had gone through to get to this point, and when he later found out, he wrote: "What is almost incredible to me is that, after such experiences he should have retained such physical and intellectual vigour. . . . He spared no pains; he shirked no problem; he evaded no difficulty. He gave all he had. . . ."

However, if morale was high, Anders and his army were full of foreboding because of the disquieting sequence of political events. Anders wrote:

> We entered the battle zone feeling very depressed at the political situation. As the Germans withdrew westwards from Poland, their terrorism increased, while the Russians as they advanced towards Vilno and Lwow made it clear through their press and radio that they considered the territories that they had obtained by their alliance with Germany in

1939 to be their own. . . . There was a feeling too
that the Teheran meeting in December 1943
between Churchill, Roosevelt and Stalin, had
resulted in an understanding being reached at
someone else's expense.

Anders had in mind particularly Churchill's recent speech of February 22 making public some of the secret agreements made at
Teheran. "We never agreed," Churchill said, "to the Polish occupation of Vilno in 1920 and Russia's present demands to secure its
frontiers are nothing but common sense and justice." The news
came as a bombshell to the Polish troops. If they had known about
it, a Foreign Office minute of March 27, a month later, would have
been even more devastating: "Despite Polish arguments to the contrary, there is nothing inconsistent with British interest in the existence of a Poland under strong Soviet influence."

In spite of the previous reverses over Monte Cassino, the Allies
were now beginning to sense victory. The Germans had been
repulsed in Russia, Mussolini had been deposed the previous July,
Rommel had been driven out of North Africa, the Allies had landed
in Sicily, the invasion of France was imminent. General Alexander's order of the day to his soldiers before battle as commander in
chief of the Allied Armies in Italy rang with Churchillian cadences:

> The Allied armed forces are now assembling for
> the final battles on sea, on land, and in the air to
> crush the enemy once and for all. From the East
> and the West, from the North and the South, blows
> are about to fall which will result in the final
> destruction of the Nazis and bring freedom once
> again to Europe, and hasten peace for us all. To us
> in Italy has been given the honour of striking the
> first blow. We are going to destroy the German
> Armies in Italy.

This bracing speech was bolstered by a clandestine reason why Alexander and the Allies could feel confident of victory in this and future battles: the fact that they could decipher the Germans' Enigma code. They knew how much under strength the German forces at Monte Cassino now were, and much else besides. And one of the chief reasons they had cracked it—which took most the rest of the century to emerge—was that a Polish mathematician, Marian Rejewski, had deciphered Enigma in 1933 and the Poles had then taken it upon themselves to hand over all their knowledge to the British and French in a historic meeting near Warsaw in July 1939. The first word of the role Enigma and its code-breaking counterpart Ultra played in the war only emerged in 1974. Since then it has been acknowledged that "At minimum, Ultra saved lives by shortening the war by two years, at most it saved civilization."

It is important to what is to come to note Rejewski's story up to this point. The Poles had been very active in the field of decipherment ever since the Polish-Russian War of 1919–20, when they had managed to break the Russian cipher. Indeed, this cracking of the code had played a large part, unknown for years, in the "Miracle of the Vistula"—not, after all, the supernatural miracle it had been billed, but a matter of brainwork behind the scenes. Piłsudski's early alarm about Hitler's intentions led him to appoint Rejewski to the Polish General Staff Cryptological Service in 1932. Enigma was the most complex code to date: the number of possible encoding positions was 5,000 billion trillion trillion trillion trillion, or 5 to the power of 86 zeros. By January 1933, in a few intensely creative weeks, working alone and in complete secrecy, Rejewski had broken this initial code—although because of the top-secret nature of the work he was engaged in, and because of the British attitude to the Poles after the Soviets had switched sides, he wouldn't be given recognition until a few years before his death. After the German invasion of Poland, Rejewski fled to Romania, and the first Allied mission he visited was the British, where the staff of the embassy were too busy to listen to him. "If anyone at the embassy had shown some interest in his case," an expert wrote more recently, "he might have become one of the glories of Bletchley." Rejewski then fled to France and worked with French and other Polish cryptologists from 1940 to 1942, when the head of French code-breaking did recognize the importance of what Rejewski was doing, calling it "this incredible adventure, unequalled in any country in the world." Rejewski escaped occupied France for Britain in 1943. By the time Anders and his army were squaring up to their first major battle at Monte Cassino, he was serving in the Polish army in London as a cryptologist (although, as the intelligence historian Christopher Andrew points out, "the fact must be stressed, without any link with Bletchley [Park]; the British authorities left him, as well as all other Polish cryptologists, in complete ignorance of what they were doing").

Monte Cassino is a high medieval hill town crested by one of the largest and most imposing abbeys in Europe, founded by the patriarch of monks, St. Benedict. It has been a holy site from ancient times, first as a temple to Apollo—god of light, poetry, music, healing and prophecy—and then as a fount of the flow of gentle, diligent civilization for all Western Europe through the saint and his followers, the Benedictines. Paradoxically, however, because of its height and strategic position southwest of Rome, Monte Cassino has also been the key to military control of Rome for most of the Christian era, and subject to periodic sackings.

For these reasons, after the Italian armistice of September 3, 1943, the Nazis had taken over the 1,700-foot hill and its surrounding foothills in an attempt to stem the Allied advance. They at once flooded the surrounding countryside and mined the area with what Martha Gellhorn, who—after the Spanish Civil War, and after Munich, was now with the Allied armies as a war correspondent—called "their ever-lasting mines: the crude little wooden boxes, the small rusty tin cans, the flat metal pancakes which are the simplest and deadliest weapons in Italy." Given the numinous nature of the monastery, full of rare manuscripts and works of art, the Allies knew they were faced with a dismaying decision: in order to make the vital breakthrough in this phase of the war, they would have to attack the monastery. They first bombed it in September 1943, to no avail—except that it led the enlightened Colonel Schlegel of the Hermann Göring Panzer Division, one of the crack Nazi units defending the hill, to evacuate the treasures and works of art from the monastery and hand them to the Italian government.

The Allies' next attack took place on January 17, 1944, but after heavy casualties on both sides, they had to retreat. By this time the looming vastness of the abbey hanging in the clouds up on the hill, and thought to be full of Nazis, was inducing in the Allies down below what one of the combatants described as "mass psychosis." As one U.S. corporal put it, "The abbey was this big black building that was killing us." Its strategic position was indeed vital to the course of the war, and stalemate had set in over the winter; but what the Allies did next came as much out of the darker reaches of the psyche as out of military strategy. It's as if, once the dogs of war are let loose, the most sacred places seem to draw the most destructive fire that human beings can muster; as if they are a reproach to the powers of devastation and have to be brought to heel.

On February 15, after distributing leaflets warning all the civilian population to leave because they would be bombed from the air, the Allies launched the most intensive bombardment on the abbey that any single building would be subject to during the whole course of the war. U.S. bombers alone dropped 5 tons of explosive for every German in the area. It was the first time bombers from England had attacked an Italian target. The monastery was pulverized; there was shock around the world. One of Italy's leading archaeologists declared: "To remain silent in the face of such horrible manifestations of the fury of war . . . would be tantamount to being culpable of indifference, or worse, of cowardly acquiescence, not only in the eyes of our contemporaries, but also in the eyes of future generations." The obliteration of the abbey added a moral backlash to what was already one of the most brutal and protracted conflicts of the war; and still, after all that, what remained of the abbey and the hills had not been taken. There was a renewed attack on March 15 at which, amongst others, the Gurkhas showed notable bravery, but it was called off on the twenty-third after a loss of a further three thousand men.

It was in this general climate that Anders and his Second Corps were brought in to fight their first battle after their travels—after their "long nightmare which defies concise description," as the historian Adam Zamoyski puts it—a climate of partial loss of moral footing, attrition, and urgency. At the same time, they were hugely spurred on by their alarm at what was happening to their homeland. Anders told them, "When you fight for Monte Cassino, you fight for Poland. Let lions live in your hearts." The fifty-thousand-strong Polish Corps went into battle on May 11 at 11:00 p.m. Wanda and I watch the black-and-white footage of the soldiers waiting in the dark and preternatural stillness before it starts, then lit up by flashes and explosions; then, after days of harrowing fighting, being taken back down the hill, wounded, on stretchers. "Surgery went on around the clock." A soldier raises the Polish flag over Monte Cassino on the eighteenth, and raises the British flag alongside it— "playing fair," as the Scottish commentator puts it. A bugler plays the sequence of notes which a lone bugler famously sounds every hour from the tower of Mariacki Church in Krakow.

After the Poles had gone on to fight other critical battles in Italy, including Anzio and Ancona, Field Marshal Lord Alexander of Tunis wrote in 1949 that Anders and his troops were

> one of the outstanding formations of the British
> 8th Army . . . the Poles played a part which gained
> the admiration of their comrades and the respect
> of their enemies. They fought many a victorious
> battle alongside their Allies, but their greatest was

at Monte Cassino. Only the finest troops could
have taken that well-prepared and long-defended
fortress. When the Polish standard floated proudly
from the ruins of the monastery, it signalled the
march to Rome.

Wanda and I watch King George VI presenting Anders with the
Order of the Bath for this battle. The Polish government in London
created 48,498 special commemorative military crosses for them.
Yet, although he took pride in the victory on behalf of his men and
country, Anders's account of it in his memoirs shows he felt its hollow side:

> The battle field presented a dreary sight. There
> were enormous heaps of unused ammunition and
> here and there heaps of landmines. Corpses of Pol-
> ish and German soldiers, sometimes entangled in a
> deathly embrace, lay everywhere, and the air was
> full of the stench of rotting bodies. There were
> overturned tanks with broken caterpillars and oth-
> ers standing as if ready for an attack, with their
> guns still pointing towards the Monastery. The
> slopes of the hills, particularly where the fire had
> been less intense, were covered with poppies in
> incredible numbers, their red flowers weirdly
> appropriate to the scene. All that was left of the oak
> grove of the so-called Valley of Death were splin-
> tered tree stumps.

There was a high cost to Second Corps: 281 officers killed,
wounded or missing, and 3,503 from the ranks. In all, with the bale-
fully suggestive zeros of approximate figures, the Allies lost 40,000
men during the four battles for Monte Cassino spanning five
months of 1944, and the Germans 25,000 men. Anders wrote of the

battle what could be an epitaph for so much of the war: "It was a collection of small epics, many of which can never be told, for their heroes took to their graves the secret of their exploits."

Meanwhile in Poland news of this victory reached the Home Army, led from London by Sikorski's successor Mikolajczyk, which was maintaining a strong network of resistance against the Nazis. By this time the Allied armies had occupied Belgium, Luxembourg and nearly all of France, whilst—more pertinently and alarmingly for the Poles—they saw the Soviet "liberators" now occupying Estonia, Latvia, Lithuania, Romania, and moving in toward Yugoslavia, Hungary and Czechoslovakia. By July, the Soviet Red Army was closing in on Warsaw, together with the Soviet-dominated Polish Berling army. Spurred on by Anders's feat, and knowing that if they didn't move against the occupying Nazis now, the Red Army would do it for them and then claim the prize of Poland, on August 1, 1944, the Home Army in Warsaw rose against the Nazis. It was an uprising long in the pipeline; the Home Army ran to some 350,000 members and had, extraordinarily, managed to produce an underground newspaper every day throughout the war.

As often with the Poles, it was an extraordinary feat of bravery, and a strategic failure. Twelve thousand Polish Home Army troops were mustered, secretly and minimally equipped with weapons, against twenty thousand Wehrmacht, SS and police troops with tanks, artillery and planes. The Poles held out for four days, until, arsenals and foodstocks depleted, they requested Allied airdrops through their government-in-exile in London. These came, but since the Soviets—although technically now allies—refused to allow the planes to land on their soil, the Polish, British and South African pilots had to make perilous flights from a base near Brindisi in Italy, flying 1,700 miles there and back over enemy-occupied territory. This proved to be a suicidal task, as far more were shot down than got through. The Soviets themselves had planes which were only one hour's flying time from Warsaw. Although Stalin claimed that he couldn't help the Poles out in Warsaw because his armies were not in a position to beat the German forces, in fact the Russians deliberately lagged behind at this point in reaching Warsaw in order to let the Germans raze Warsaw and extinguish the Home Army for them.

Churchill and Roosevelt tried to intercede with Stalin, but the Soviet leader was intransigent. The fact was that the Nazis and Soviets had had the same policy with respect to the Poles from the start: mass deportations and exterminations of the Poles who were under their rule from the moment they invaded, a depolonization of the occupied areas and extermination of the Polish intelligentsia. They now shared a common aim: to destroy Warsaw. The difference between the Nazi and Soviet policies was that the Soviet was just that much more cunning; they would let the Nazis do the fighting for them. The war log of the German Ninth Army for this period notes that "For days after the German operations aimed at destroying the Soviet Third Armored Corps had ended in this region, the Moscow broadcasting station continued to report strong German attacks east of Praga and dressed up this news with detailed descriptions of battles that were completely fictitious."

The civilian population of Warsaw now joined in the fight and for six weeks held out against an increasingly vengeful and brutal counterattack by the Nazis, who sent in execution squads which slaughtered their way through the town, setting fire to Home Army hospitals full of wounded, and driving unarmed Polish civilians before them to screen them from fire. Neal Ascherson, who calls the Warsaw Rising "one of the supreme events of Polish history," says that "It brought to an awful climax the romantic tradition of armed uprising which stretched back to 1794. It convinced most of the generation who took part in it that in modern conditions that tradition no longer had a place: after another such rising, there would be no Poland left." But he adds that it was also "a time of freedom . . . which left a hot residue of pride to keep the nation warm through the bleak years that followed." They would need it. Hitler ordered that Warsaw be annihilated so that no settlement would ever arise there again. When his army had finished, 93 percent of Warsaw's buildings were destroyed.

And then the Red Army and Berling did move, crossing the Vistula to Warsaw on September 16. The final surrender of the Home Army in Warsaw came on October 2, 1944. In all of the war, Warsaw would be the only Allied capital city to be involved in combative warfare.

Even before the final fall of Warsaw, Churchill was publicly siding with Russia over the border issue. In a speech to the House of Commons on September 28, he said: "Territorial changes in the frontiers of Poland there will have to be. Russia has a right to our support in this matter. . . . I have fervent hope that Mr. Mikolajczyk, the worthy successor of General Sikorski, a man firmly desirous of friendly understanding and settlement with Russia . . . wants a united Polish government." As Churchill implies, Mikolajczyk was more biddable than his predecessor, a fact testified by the fact that the new commander in chief of the Polish Army, General Kazimierz Sosnkowski, who would not preside over this sacrifice of all that his men were fighting for, was relieved of his position. In his farewell to the Polish soldiers his bitterness is bridled by dignity: "I understand very well that if in 1939 our nation was the first to oppose the Germans, if the fjords of Norway, the sands of Africa, the mountains of Italy and the fields of France, the plains of Belgium and Holland witnessed our fighting, if Warsaw still fights amongst the ruins and a sea of flame, it was not to see Poland at the end of the war being presented with a demand to resign the rights of sovereignty she possessed when five years ago she took her stand against aggression beside the allied nations."

As soon as he heard of the defeat, Anders sent a telegram to his president:

In my great anxiety and concern to maintain the
morale and unity of the Army Corps, I have to
report that the soldiers reject every thought of a
possible organisation of a Polish government
under Russian occupation, with the participation
of traitors and Soviet agents. All have vividly in
mind the similar events which have taken place in
Estonia, Lithuania and Latvia, and they also
observe with great attention present events in
Rumania, Bulgaria and Yugoslavia.

It was no wonder that, as Martha Gellhorn observed from her van-
tage point alongside the Allies in Italy, "All the Poles talk about
Russia all the time. . . . They follow the Russian advance across
Poland with agonized interest." She saw their anguished dilemma:

It is a long road home to Poland, to the Great
Carpathian mountains, and every mile of the road
has been bought most bravely. But now they do not
know what they are going home to. They fight an
enemy in front of them and fight him superbly. And
with their whole hearts they fear an ally, who is
already in their homeland. For they do not believe
that Russia will relinquish their country after the
war; they fear that they are to be sacrificed in this
peace, as Czechoslovakia was in 1938. It must be
remembered that almost every one of these men,
irrespective of rank, class or economic condition,
has spent time in either a German or a Russian
prison during this war. It must be remembered that
for five years they have had no news from their
families, many of whom are still prisoners in Russia or Germany. It must be remembered that these
Poles have only twenty-one years of national free-

dom behind them, and a long aching memory of
foreign rule.

Then she notes, "But I am not a Pole; I belong to a large free country and I speak with the optimism of those who are forever safe."
Remembering individual soldiers she has spoken with, often still
very young, she writes, "it seemed to me that no American had the
right to talk to the Poles, since we had never even brushed such suffering ourselves."

For the record, among the major combatants, approximate estimated figures for the total of those who died during World War II
are: 18 million Russians, 6 million Poles (3 million of them of Jewish background), 1,505,000 Yugoslavs, 563,000 French, 466,000
from Britain and the Commonwealth (357,000 British within
that), 413,000 Greeks, 298,000 Americans, and 225,000 Czechs.
Amongst the Axis powers, the Germans lost 4,200,000, the Japanese 1,972,000, the Romanians 500,000, the Hungarians 490,000,
and the Italians 395,000. In all, the Allies lost some 28 million individuals to the war and the Axis countries around 45.5 million: a
total of over 73 million dead.

Poland lost 22 percent of its population in the war, a higher percentage of its population than any other prewar state. About 89.9
percent of Polish war losses, Jews and Gentiles, were "victims of
prisons, death camps, raids, executions, annihilation of ghettos,
epidemics, starvation, excessive work and ill treatment."

20 | POLES APART

Politically, things continued on the same ominous tack. Whilst occasional lip service was paid by Roosevelt or Churchill to a "strong, free and independent Polish State," it became increasingly clear that the Teheran Conference of November–December 1943 had sewn up Poland's fate. Even the new prime minister, Mikolajczyk, resigned the following year, on November 24, 1944, in protest against the Allies' lack of support for the Warsaw uprising and over the question of Poland's eastern frontier. This meant that the unity of command and purpose in the Polish government was further weakened, giving the British free rein to bypass the Poles, and allowing Stalin to exploit their internal differences at Yalta. As for Anders himself, when he attempted to object and intervene, he was accused of "meddling in political matters."

By the time of the Yalta Conference of Churchill, Roosevelt and Stalin, which took place at Yalta in the Crimea on February 4–11, 1945, Poland was definitively sacrificed to the "liberating armies" of the Soviet Union. When Churchill returned to Britain from Yalta, he said: "Poor Neville believed he could trust Hitler. He was wrong. But I don't think I'm wrong about Stalin." For his part, Roosevelt had been predisposed toward backing Stalin ever since his aide,

Harry Hopkins, had engaged in two long meetings with the Soviet leader in July 1941, shortly after Germany had invaded Russia, and at a point when most people, including Stalin, thought the Nazis would *Blitzkrieg* Russia out of existence within weeks in the same way they'd done with Poland. Hopkins and Stalin came to an understanding which had changed the face of Roosevelt's policy toward Russia. Before, he'd been wary; after Hopkins's visit, Roosevelt courted Stalin. In February 1940, Roosevelt had said, "The Soviet Union, as everybody who has the courage to face the facts knows, is run by a dictatorship as absolute as any other dictatorship in the world"; by March 1942, three months after America had declared war on Japan and Germany after Pearl Harbor, Roosevelt was saying to Churchill: "I know you will not mind my being brutally frank when I tell you I think I can personally handle Stalin better than your Foreign Office or my State Department. Stalin hates the guts of all your top people. He thinks he likes me better, and I hope he will continue to do so." By the time of Yalta, the truth was also that Stalin already had all the trump cards anyway: the Russians had beaten Hitler, the Red Army was occupying the whole of Poland, and they had over one hundred divisions at the gates of Berlin. As for the Allies' forces, they were dispersed all over the world.

"Bah!" Wanda says. "Roosevelt was an idiot by that time—feeble-minded. And his adviser was Hopkins—you know who I mean—he was a kind of Soviet agent." The Polish government denounced the Yalta Agreement, describing it as "the Fifth Partition of Poland, now accomplished by her Allies." Anders wrote in his memoirs:

> There followed a few days in which we Poles were numbed and bewildered. Then there was a violent reaction in the army as the men realised the great injustice that had been done to them. Each had trusted that at the end of his struggles, toil and suf-

fering he would be able to return to his own country, his family, his cottage, his trade or his piece of
land: now he knew that the reward for his efforts
and his comrades' sacrifices was to be either further wandering in alien lands, or a return to a country under foreign rule. Only a sense of discipline
and confidence in their officers prevented the men
taking precipitate and uncontrolled action.

In these circumstances, Anders applied to the Allied authorities
on February 13 to withdraw his troops from battle sectors, saying,
"I cannot in conscience demand at present any sacrifice of the soldiers' blood." His men had nothing left to fight for. And when Field
Marshal Alexander refused his request, replying that there were no
spare troops to relieve the Poles, Anders—his military duty over-
coming his feelings in a way that can only be imagined—gave his
assurance that in these circumstances he and his troops would carry
on. At the very same time, with the duplicity that had characterized
the British government's dealings with the Poles, the Foreign
Office prepared itself to abandon the London Poles as "a lost cause
and an obstacle to good relations with Moscow."

However, one of the American generals reasoned with Anders
that Roosevelt must have considered the existence of 4 million
Poles in the United States, even if only for political reasons, and
therefore, "if with Churchill he signed this catastrophic agreement,
he must have obtained guarantees of which we know nothing con-
cerning conditions which will be established in Poland in future."

Anders secured a personal meeting with Churchill over the matter, who simply told him "irascibly":

> It is your own fault. For a long time I advised you
> to settle frontier matters with the Soviet Union and
> to surrender the territories east of the Curzon Line.

> Had you listened to me the whole matter would
> now have been different. We have never guaran-
> teed your eastern frontiers. We have enough troops
> today, and we do not need your help. You can take
> away your divisions. We shall do without them.

Indeed, although Anders was now made commander in chief of the
Polish forces, all further conferences with Field Marshal Alanbrooke, Churchill and others were cancelled. "I was made to feel
the cold reserve of the British," he wrote, adding: "Such was the
position of the Commander-in-Chief of the Polish forces in the
sixth year of the war, on the eve of victory. . . . I had no time to
grow embittered. Events followed one another, and I had to keep
pace with them and adapt myself to circumstances."

Events, alas, were marked by more perfidy from Albion. On the
one hand, Churchill pledged that Poland would have free elections
under Stalin; on the other, in the House of Commons an amendment
expressing regret at the decision to surrender to a third power the
territory belonging to an Allied country, in violation of Article II of
the Atlantic Charter, was rejected by 396 votes to 25. Again, on one
hand, King George VI wrote an appreciative letter to Władysław
Raczkiewicz, the president of Poland, on May 8, 1945, saying:

> It will ever be to Poland's honour that she resisted,
> alone, the overwhelming forces of the German
> aggressor . . . the gallant Polish soldiers, sailors
> and airmen have fought beside our forces in many
> parts of the world and everywhere have won their
> high regard. In particular, we in this country
> remember with gratitude the part played by Polish
> airmen in the Battle of Britain which all the world
> recognises as a decisive moment in the war. It is
> my earnest hope that Poland may, in the tasks of
> peace and international cooperation which now

confront the allied nations, achieve the reward of all her courage and sacrifice.

Yet on the other hand, when on March 5 invitations to the San Francisco Conference drawing up the United Nations Charter were sent out to forty-four nations, Poland was not amongst them. And, most shocking of all, leaders of the Polish wartime resistance who went on a negotiating mission to Moscow simply "disappeared," until sixteen of them turned up on a "show" trial for the outrageously trumped-up crime of "collaborating with the Germans." None of the Allies raised a finger to help them, or a voice in protest.

By summer 1945, matters were out in the open: on June 18, the Soviets set up their own puppet government, the Provisional Government of National Unity, in Warsaw, which the British recognized on July 6, simultaneously officially de-recognizing both the Polish government-in-exile and the Polish forces. When Anders vigorously protested, he was called "politically controversial." (I ask Wanda how the British government can have done such a thing. "Britain was like a chopped-off pair of hands after the war," she replies. "It had lost its empire. Russia was the only power left in Europe.") These betrayals of Poland were condoned by a silent world, and indeed, as Hope points out, were encouraged by "Some leftist sections of the British press, sympathetic to the Soviet media, who began to brand Anders and his Poles and the Polish government as 'fascists' and warmongers. Max Beaverbrook's 'rightist' Express group also took an early pro-Soviet stance, with its newspaper playing a key role in belittling the Poles."

Lord Beaverbrook's paradoxical flirtation with the left dated from a visit he had made to Russia in 1929. This had led to his intervening in British political life against the Poles' interests; for example, the *Daily Express,* almost alone among British newspapers, had condemned Chamberlain's March 1939 guarantee to Poland against German aggression, and in 1943, behind the scenes, Beaverbrook had drafted for Churchill the first, dismissive message repudiating Polish complaints about the massacre at Katyn (although Churchill didn't in the end use this draft). In October that year the Soviet Union awarded Beaverbrook the Order of Suvorov for his pains, which entitled him, amongst other things, to such privileges as twenty rubles a month, exemption from income tax or call-up and free travel all over the USSR once a year in which he was to be given priority and specifically "free use of soft plush seats." To top this egalitarian bonanza, his descendants were entitled to inherit all these privileges too. No doubt these esteemed bonuses weighed somewhere in the balance when he said in 1944, "the friendship of Russia is far more important to us than the future of Anglo-Polish relations."

Meanwhile, Anders described the lot of all Polish servicemen in 1945 as "Despair, coupled with humiliation and anger," and Adam Zamoyski notes that "their isolation had become total." Seeing this, and knowing that all Polish soldiers who returned to Poland—as they were actively being encouraged to do under the new Labour government of Attlee in England—would be suffering reprisals and punishment, Anders sent a memo to the British government stating that it seemed the Polish population was the most neglected in Europe, and worse treated than the Germans. Furthermore, they had been deprived of legal protection because of the withdrawal of recognition from the London government and the unsympathetic attitude of the Warsaw government. This memo, he said, "simply disappeared as a stone thrown into water."

Writing half a century later of the West's silence over the trials of the Polish wartime leaders in Moscow, Norman Davies says that "Of all the moral surrenders demanded by the Grand Alliance of the Western democracies with the Soviet Union, none was more obscene than this." It was not as if the Moscow Trials were censored from the West: the proceedings were openly published in England for all the world to read, yet the world watched in silence. "The fate of the Polish Government and its loyal adherents," Davies writes, "was painful in the extreme."

. . .

To add insult to injury, and extraordinarily, the Poles were now invited to neither the V-E Day or the later V-J Day victory celebrations—a startling measure of Britain's guilt and denial. Anders found himself watching from his hotel in the Strand the great rejoicing as hundreds of thousands celebrated the end of the long war in 1945, a rejoicing in which he could not take part. With stoic understatement, he wrote, "I must simply state that we were robbed of those great days at the end of the war."

The following year, on June 8, 1946, a Victory Parade was held in London in which the Polish soldiers and sailors again were not invited to take part. A token twenty-five airmen from amongst those who fought in the Battle of Britain were invited, and they declined, since their army and navy were excluded. Polish soldiers, Anders said sadly, felt more embarrassment than anger at the treatment, because they knew that the other ordinary soldiers from all countries would miss them. Many voices were raised in their defense, including that of MP Robert Boothby, who told the House of Commons: "we never lifted a finger to help the Poles." Churchill's voice was now amongst them, even though he had been one of those in some measure responsible for putting Poland in this position. He was no longer prime minister but in opposition, and the nature of the Soviet regime in Poland was dolefully clear to him. "Poland is denied all free expression of her national will," he said, deploring how the Soviet-dominated government

> do not dare to have a free election. The fate of Poland seems to be unending tragedy, and we, who went to war, all ill-prepared, on her behalf, watch with sorrow the strange outcome of our endeavours. I deeply regret that none of the Polish troops, and I must say this, who fought with us on a score of battlefields, who poured out their blood in the

common cause, are to be allowed to march in the
victory parade. They will be in our thoughts on that
day. We shall never forget their bravery.

The day before the Victory Parade, Macmillan wrote Anders a
personal note saying, "tomorrow we are to celebrate our victory . . .
I tell you this frankly; that with all the legitimate joy and pride in
every British heart will be mingled much sorrow and even shame."

For a later generation, Norman Davies sums up the score:

> In the Battle of Britain in 1940, Polish pilots
> accounted for some 15% of enemy losses, thus
> contributing significantly to the salvation of Great
> Britain. Yet no reciprocal gesture was ever made
> by the British, either in 1939–40 or in 1944–5, for
> the salvation of Poland. At Lenino on the Ukrain-
> ian Front in October 1943, at Monte Cassino in
> Italy in May 1944 and at Arnhem in September
> '44, Polish units showed immense courage and
> suffered heavy casualties in the course of opera-
> tions of doubtful value. . . . The considerable Pol-
> ish effort in the war against Hitler was not matched
> by any corresponding benefits relating to Poland's
> future destiny.

At the Nuremberg Trials of 1945 to 1947, the Katyn massacres
were swept under the carpet, and no British government has ever
acknowledged that the Soviets and not the Nazis were responsible
for the atrocity. Although Poland lost the one-hundred-fifty-mile
strip of her eastern marches, it was compensated by being given
a similar amount of land to the west, to include Danzig (now
Gdansk), Stettin (Szczecin), and Breslau (Wroclaw). This seemed a
fair deal to the Allies, except that the effect, as Stalin intended, was
to bring the Soviet Union, having Sovietized Poland, closer to

Berlin and the West. What Stalin's Machiavellian policy also did—
like King James in settling Scottish Protestants in Ulster to be "a
thorn in the side of Popery"—was to provoke German sensibilities,
which would then license the Red Army to defend Poland's western
flank.

As for the West, after the war it was faced with a new "Polish
problem": thousands of Polish soldiers with no country to return to.
In Britain, the new Labour government under Attlee set up a Polish
Resettlement Corps with the aim of demobilizing the Polish forces
as quickly as possible and persuading as many of them as it could to
return to Poland. In a final ceremony for Second Corps in Italy on
June 15, the unit's commanders read out a statement:

> ... According to the decision of our allies with
> whom we fought side by side all the time for the
> common cause of freedom, the Independent Polish
> Forces are to be demobilized. . . . Today the world
> understands that Poland is ruled by servile agents
> of Moscow. . . . We are deeply convinced that we
> were always loyal to our allies at times most per-
> ilous for them. In spite of this, however, there were
> no Polish soldiers parading on V-day.

For the British, it was hard to understand the reluctance of Polish soldiers to be demobilized, and this caused them to feel some
annoyance, particularly since the soldiers appeared to be being kept
at British expense. Once again, as in the thirties, it was difficult for
Western countries like America and Britain to understand the
nature of the Stalinist regime, the use of any means to twist the facts
of what had happened, and the vicious reprisals against a fallen foe
at any level. So, Norman Davies writes,

> The remnants of the Home Army were not simply
> suppressed, they were put on trial as "bandits,"

"smugglers," or "Fascist collaborators." Returning
Polish soldiers and airmen, who had fought for the
allied cause at Monte Cassino or in the Battle of
Britain were arrested as "imperialist agents." The
Polish Government in London was not merely
ignored; it was officially declared to have been
"illegally" convened by the "Fascist" constitution
of 1935.

He adds that "The Poles who chose to stay in the West were treated
as outcasts and pariahs." This meant they were getting stereophoni-
cally denied and repudiated, on one side by their former homeland,
and on the other by their new homeland—which they hadn't chosen
to come to.

Harold Macmillan, after reading Anders's memoirs, noted that
other readers, like him, "will realize what must have been the effect
upon the Polish army of the successive political blows which fell
upon them. The General," he said, "has not exaggerated their
effects; he has minimised them, for that was the role which he
steadfastly and consistently followed." So it is poignant to read
Anders's cry in his epilogue: "Why was this done, why was the
most faithful of the allies sacrificed, an ally who could not be
accused of any breach of promise, of any denial of his obligations,
or of any neglect in making the supreme effort? It was done to
appease Russia. It was done because Russia demanded that Poland
be sacrificed as the price of her further cooperation with the west."
And he spells out the dangers of the Soviet regime as he had intimately known it:

A Soviet citizen . . . is completely deprived of any
contact with the outer world, and all he can learn of
it must come from official Soviet sources . . . his
idea of the outer world is one of pure fantasy. And
it must be stated that not the least of the great evils

that the Nazis did in the world was that of giving
the Soviet nations an entirely false impression of
Europe and her culture ... the regime itself [is] a
dictatorial police pyramid which makes every
Soviet citizen not only an object of pressure and
exploitation, but also himself an atom in a colossal
machine of persecution and exploitation.

What this meant for the Poles in Soviet Poland after the war was
that all contact with the Polish émigrés—often their relatives and
friends—became a treasonable offense. For the Poles who stayed in
England, like my father (who, although born Czechoslovak, had
come in with the Polish army), contact with anyone inside Poland
was fraught with probable danger for both sides, all the worse for
being unspecified. Whilst Poles who had fought with the Soviets
were welcomed home as heroes, those who had died alongside the
Western Allies were blotted out of the record. History was rewrit-
ten, from school textbooks upward, to show how the war had been
won by the Soviet Union alone, and all mention of the names of
Sikorski and Anders was forbidden. "The effect of this massive
deprivation on Polish consciousness," Davies points out, "was one
of prolonged trauma. Not only were Poles condemned to bear the
deaths of their 'lost generation' in silence, and to overcome their
separation from the 'lost provinces'; they were even expected to
sever their ties with their friends and relations abroad." The worst
irony was that when finally the official documents of the wartime
episodes crucial to the Poles were published, in the 1950s and
1960s, the Poles in exile were vindicated: but by that time the cold
war had set in and Poland was beyond reprieve.
    Davies, writing in 1986, before the collapse of the Soviet
Union, noted that all was, however, not lost:

The Polish peasantry survived the War largely
intact, and, in the unprecedented birth-rates of the

postwar years provided the biological reserves from which Poland's depleted substance could be replenished. The Polish Emigration abroad preserved a fuller record of the Second World War than officially exists in Poland. Its memoirs, recollections, and publications ... are serving even now to enrich the consciousness of a younger generation eager for knowledge. .... In face of these survivals, the military and political triumph of the Soviet camp may yet prove to have been a superficial and temporary episode in Poland's 1,000-year history. The wounds were deep, but total destruction was defied.

After the war, most of the Polish soldiers settled throughout Western Europe, often in the places where they had landed. Altogether only 17.9 percent of Polish forces in Britain opted to return to Poland, and by October 1949 there were nearly 162,000 Poles resident in Britain. British trade unions were resolutely opposed to the Poles' employment, fomenting a climate of suspicion and distrust against them, and threatening a series of strikes. They were egged on by Beaverbrook's newspapers, which accused them of "taking away jobs from the British worker" and of being "anti-Soviet warmongering fascists."

All Polish ex-servicemen now became aware of dramatic changes in public attitudes, not least the men of Second Corps (whose contact with the British had been the least of all Polish forces). Overnight, the valiant Poles became "black marketeers and 'womanizers.' " The slogan "Poles go Home" appeared everywhere, and there were press and parliamentary sources suggesting that the Poles were being maintained in idleness in the Resettlement Corps. It was perhaps no wonder that over a thousand Polish air veterans emigrated to Canada after the war.

My father would be one of those handled by the Polish Resettlement Corps, one of the 82.1 percent who opted to stay in Britain rather than return to a Soviet-dominated Poland. The mathematician and decoder Marian Rejewski, whose work had arguably contributed to "at least shortening the war by two years, and at most, saving civilization," took the other route, opting to return to his family in Poland in 1946. There he held second-rate positions, "his former life in the west making him a rather suspect person." However, after 1974, when the existence of Enigma and Ultra—and his key part in the decoding—were revealed, he began to gain some recognition, and in the last five years of his life, until his death in 1979, some popular acclaim.

It was when Poland's fate as a vassal of the Soviet Union became clear, in 1949, that Macmillan summed up his reactions to reading Anders's memoirs of his long march and its aftermath:

> It is an epic. Like the march of the Greeks under Xenophon, it will long remain a classic of military prowess and courage. Alas, though the Greeks at last saw the sea, which meant for them the final stage in the journey, this Polish force, starting from the prison camps of Eastern Europe, traversed Asia, Africa and Western Europe, only to find, at the end of so much heroism, disillusion and despair.
>
> No Englishman or American can read this record without a sense not only of sympathy, but of something like shame. . . . Perhaps on our side, we may recall some of the immense anxieties under which our statesmen suffered, and the burdens which they bore. In our treatment of Russia during World War Two there was, no doubt, much wishful thinking. There was also much uncertainty and many dangers. . . . Yet I do not believe we have seen the end of Polish freedom.

He was right. By 1988, Premier Wojciech Jaruzelski's Communist-led government in Poland was faced with £39 billion (about $59 billion) of debts, and major strikes, led by Solidarity leader Lech Wałesa. Ironically—with fitting historical revenge—Wałesa began what would become the unravelling of the Soviet Union from the port of Gdansk, one of the prizes of Sovietized Poland. In a climate made possible by Mikhail Gorbachev's arrival as president of the USSR, Jaruzelski acknowledged electoral defeat in August of that year and brought in a measure of power-sharing. By August the next year, Poland had the first non-Communist government in Eastern Europe since the Second World War.

On September 3, 1992, the standard of the Polish air force was brought back to Poland aboard the presidential plane, escorted by four hundred former pilots, including sixteen commanders of Polish squadrons based in Britain during the war. In a moving ceremony, it was handed over to the cadets of the Polish air force training school at Deblin, which had trained so many of the airmen.

All this, I know from my reading, will be the aftermath of the Poles' story. For the moment, Wanda and I watch Anders toward the end of his life, now married to Renata, with a daughter and living modestly but happily in Brondesbury Park in northwest London, in a house very similar to Wanda's own. His fate was to be fêted as an individual by those who knew the score—we see him being greeted by President Kennedy—but never to get the collective recognition for his country and men he'd striven for, and never to go back to a free homeland. We hear of Anders's death in a London hospital on May 12, 1970, the anniversary of the first day of the Battle of Monte Cassino. At his request, his remains are taken to Monte Cassino on a special RAF airplane and buried amid the graves of his men, which the surviving soldiers paid for themselves at the time out of their pay. "He did not live to see his dignity reinstated," says the video commentator, "nor *respect* expressed for a great military commander. There were two wreaths from German war veterans. There were *no* flowers from Warsaw. The legend though undermines this, survives and remains intact. It says, 'Let those who are responsible bow their heads in expiation.' Let them say, 'Excuse us, General.' At least that." Two wreaths from German war veterans. So many individuals behaved thoughtfully, and honorably.

We've spent the whole afternoon, while Lucjan sleeps, talking and watching the film. I'm concerned that this is taxing Wanda, and taking precious time. But she is fizzing with intelligence and interest. She shows me what she's reading: John Barron's book on the KGB, Mary McAuley's *Politics and the Soviet Union,* the memoirs of General Berling's widow, *To Be Near the Truth*—"trying to clear his name," she says—and for light relief Nancy Mitford's *Love in a Cold Climate.* Also there is a book by Roland Perry called *The Fifth Man,* which later on will help me fill in a missing dimension crucial to the Poles and to my father's story, that of secret intelligence.

I ask what happened to her parents and first husband—whom she continually tried to trace in her travels with Anders's army. She brings out files, and letters, all stashed away carefully in transparent folders. Her last letter from her husband, its folds a gaping cross from being handled, was written from a hospital in Russia in September 1941. She knew he must have perished there. There were no records given by the Russians from these camps, these gulags. A typewritten letter from a friend tells her in 1946 the news she probably already knew, in substance, that her parents had been taken to concentration camps and had "perished" there, too. All her family—her brother, her cousins, aunts and uncles—had been lost in the concentration camps.

I ask her what was the worst time of all for her. "Ah," she says, almost perking up. "No one has ever asked me that before." She looks around for a moment, then says: "I was going to say, being taken off in train. But no, we still had hope. They said, your husband will be free, don't worry. And we didn't know, we didn't know

Germans would kill the Jews—were killing Jews. No, second worst was worst—when you realized what happened, and you lost hope."

As we move to the door, she says, "You know, being deported to Siberia was good thing, for me as a Jew! If I hadn't been deported by Russians, I would have been taken off to concentration camp. I was lucky." She smiles challengingly at me. In a gesture which by its specificity and forgiveness magics away the horrors of the time she lived through, she gave her father's books, she tells me—his fine translations of Martial, of Catullus, of Ovid—to the Department of History of Classical Philology at the University of Munich. This, I think, is why she is free and young in spirit.

SIX

STATES OF MIND

The very thing that parents try to
hide is what will preoccupy a child
the most, especially if a major
parental trauma is involved.

—ALICE MILLER

22 | REPTILIAN BRAIN

On the face of it, making the audiotapes had been cathartic in our lives. My father had become lighter-hearted, jokier, and had visibly shed at least a dozen years, and most of his frowns. He was demob happy. He would write letters now, very good letters, his handwriting opening up like his feelings since he had unburdened himself of his complex, unsolicited past. For his seventieth birthday in 1990, I gave him a watch with a cartoon of Einstein and the legend "Relative Time" in the middle. Around the edges were the numbers "1-ish," "2-ish," and so on. I liked the pun (especially coming from a relative), and the spirit behind it, and knew he would, too. He liked jokes, and liked the dry, wary Australian sense of humor, which accorded so well with his own.

Somehow, though, I hadn't been able to write the book. The exigencies of earning a living, together with something unresolved about the story—which expressed itself in not being able to find a form for it—meant that it got put on the back burner. And then an incident occurred which suggested the story wasn't quite over yet. It was 1993, and I was visiting Australia again, this time to take a trip with my parents up to the Great Barrier Reef. We were taking

Joe in the garden at Wallsend, 1993

three weeks to drive up from Newcastle to Cairns and back—a distance of some 6,500 kilometers. Joe was now seventy-three, and he thought it was time for us all to make "the trip of a lifetime" while we could.

We went in July, their winter, to avoid the heat of the Queensland summer. We drove through the lush, rolling hills behind Byron Bay and Brisbane, bathed in golden sunshine and almost English except for their sudden peaked, red, rocky hills. Then came the monotous kilometers of sugarcane country, with their bulbous cane toads creeping around inside. We passed through endless creeks, their names spelling out bluntly the tale of men's first encounters with them, just as Cape Tribulation, Mount Warning, Lake Disappointment and Lake Deception do. Plentiful Creek, Emigrants' Creek, Deep Creek, Little Pig Creek, Graveyard Creek, Kangaroo Creek, Duck Creek, Deadman's Gully, Magpie Gully, Spider Creek, Devil Devil Creek, even Creek Creek. I said I'd heard that to double a word in the Aboriginal language was a way of saying "very." My father laughed, and said he had a better idea, which is that they were deaf, and needed everything said twice.

He said this with fellow feeling, because deafness by this time was beginning to be an issue. He'd been going slightly deaf for a while, which he put down to the noise of the Stuka and other bombings in the war, and the Morse code machines. It looked as if his corporal's sardonic prediction of going deaf by the age of thirty was belatedly coming true. What we all failed to notice for a long time, since my mother had an eccentrically extrovert conversational style, was that she was going profoundly deaf as well. She felt that this, too, must have been a result of the war—of the Blitz—since deafness wasn't otherwise in the family. Just as communication had opened up between us, this new subtle impediment was brought in to hamper the kind of spontaneous, redundant remarks that are the stuff of life. Few things in ordinary conversation are interesting enough to bear loud, slow repetition, and so the ones that weren't began to be edited out, just as the distance across the globe and the early morning or late evening calls had imposed their own constraints. New kinds of no-go areas were threatening, and we would have to beware that what was said didn't become that much more two-dimensional than ordinary language, another kind of Morse code. Around the house notices had begun to appear: FAX SWITCHED ON? KEYS? WINDOWS LOCKED? I half expected: SSHHH. WALLS HAVE EARS. My father had fashioned a device for the telephone that made it ring far more loudly and shrilly than usual, and added a flashing red light, so that to ordinary ears a telephone call now felt like being hunted down by the police.

On the way up to Cairns we went to the usual tourist sites, visiting rainforests and crocodile farms. At one, we saw a man feeding a crocodile in a large pool. The crocodile, with its zigzag grinning jaw, ambled into one end of the murky pool, whiplashing its scaly tail behind, before disappearing under the brown water. The man took a dead chicken round to the other side of the now-still pool and held it out on the end of a stick. There was a long silence; then at the man's feet the waters erupted like a volcano and a prehistoric jaw rocketed out vertically to snatch it in one gulp. It was awesome, archetypal—and strangely familiar emotionally.

We waited for good weather to go out to the Great Barrier Reef, but none came, so we went out on a chilly, overcast day, the wind ruffling the choppy sea against its grain. I was seasick overboard and as I hung there in my puking misery, I heard myself say between bouts to a kind young New Zealand doctor who offered assistance: "the irony is . . . I present a radio program . . . called *The Art of Travel*," which I did at the time. Once we were anchored, a new, leaner me donned a wet suit, snorkel, flippers and goggles, and slipped into the deep water, which was thronging with flickering, gaudy fish.

Under the waterline, there was a sudden beatific silence and a whole new universe, tethered only by my snorkel breaths. Shoals of silver fish with yellow tails like frisky kisses darted around me, tiny ultramarine fish skittered in and out between them, bigger flat fish kitted out in black-and-white zigzags with vermilion tails came up to my goggles and peered at me with the sweet confidence of Eden, and a huge, ugly brown groper fish looking like a Cyclops grumped at me curiously. In the background, down below on the raked reefs, a supple yoga class of iridescent turquoise, black, brown and maroon sea anemones softly waved and breathed, sea slugs shimmied and clams with brilliant colored insides trilled their frilly mouths. This is what the earth must have been like for some of its first inhabitants: pulsing with life, packed with sensuous information and exuberance, at ease in its realm, its *Reich*.

It was on the way back home from Cairns that the incident occurred. We'd stopped off for a swim at a deserted bay fringed with pines. Joe stayed in the car, parked on sandy scrubland above the bay, reading a newspaper. As we came back from the sea, we noticed another vehicle parked there, too, a beat-up Volkswagen van with a couple of men and a girl outside it, looking at the van and scratching their heads. I asked if anything was wrong, and one of the men said, with slightly veiled eyes, "Oh, we've broken down, we need some . . . oil, I think. Could you give us a lift?" I was just saying sure when Joe, who had wound down the car window about three inches, and was on red alert, called out: "There are shops down other end of bay, it's not far." In spite of this, the man went off to get his backpack and made for our car, by which time my mother and I were getting in. The man was on the shifty side, but I only felt threatened to the extent of getting in the back, so that if there was trouble, we'd be behind him. But when my father, who was getting increasingly agitated, saw the man coming toward him with a backpack, he went berserk, suddenly shouting: "No backpack! No backpack!" his arms and eyes akimbo. He ordered us to shut and lock all the doors.

The man's jaw dropped and he looked on in astonishment as Joe drove off and left him standing. Later that evening, Joe rationalized that there had been tales of two murders on nearby Ellis Beach the previous year—and indeed later that year two backpackers would be murdered on a beach not far away—so logically he was justified in taking firm steps to protect us all from potential threat. And yet . . . His reaction was excessive and, with the distance of years and geography, I suddenly saw that behavior I'd accepted as simply part of his character was a jarring overreaction.

That it took me another three years to put words to all this might seem strange. I can only say that the literature on the subject was just beginning to come into the public arena, and that for all I know I had a share of denial. And it's perhaps not surprising that secrets long buried take time to surface. The term was of course "shell shock," or post-traumatic stress disorder (PTSD), as it's now called. I first encountered a description of this syndrome in Daniel Goleman's book of popular psychology, *Emotional Intelligence,* and was struck by his phrase that it was a kind of "learned fearfulness." The phrase immediately seemed to describe my father's no-go territory, the hinterlands whose contours I'd taken on subliminally. Of course. Fear underlay his silence, and his occasional outbursts, and

at the root of the fear was his experience of terror: the literal "Great
Terror" in Soviet Lwow, terror sliding across the frozen San to the
sound of a rifle shot, terror under fire in France. If all this had had
the physical effect of permanently affecting his eyes, what must it
have done to his mind? Goleman's implicit answer was mind-
opening to me: according to new neuroscientific research, trauma
could physically alter the limbic circuitry of the brain. "Changes in
these circuits," he wrote, "are thought to underlie PTSD symptoms,
which include anxiety, fear, hyper-vigilance, being easily upset and
aroused, readiness for fight or flight, and the indelible encoding of
intense emotional memories."

Each of these symptoms was Joe's, I recognized with rising
excitement, including the unusually well-etched memories he had
of his year of displacement and war. And Goleman also identified
other chemicals which are brought into play in circumstances of
terror and fear, and which simultaneously kick in to do quite the
opposite, to blunt the feeling of pain: "This appears to explain a set
of negative psychological symptoms long noted in PTSD: anhedo-
nia (the inability to feel pleasure) and a general emotional numb-
ness, a sense of being cut off from life or from concern about
others' feelings. Those close to such people may experience this
indifference as a lack of empathy." And I had, I had—as my mother
had, too, and still did. Reading this, it suddenly seemed to me that
I'd been living alongside a syndrome rather than a father as I grew
up, even though, like the science fiction story I'd read, on the surface everything appeared to be normal, even banal. I was seized
with a melodramatic picture of my father having something alien
clamped onto him, like something from a horror movie. I always
knew that the man underneath was unusually intelligent and sensitive, but he was often glimpsed through a glass darkly. I'd sensed—
taken for granted even—that my father's hair-trigger jumpiness had
something to do with the war, but I'd never consciously understood
what this meant: that the losses and dislocations the war had visited
on him might have left a part of him damaged—an identifiable part

of the neural network, if the new neuroscientific findings were right. And then there was its counterpart: the psychic numbing. Put together, these two things meant that his emotional responses would always have been to some degree out of kilter; not only did the world never feel safe, always on the brink of an emergency, but how he related to those close to him was atrophied in some near-mechanical way.

The nature of PTSD is that it washes over you in a rage that is often dumb—words fail you, you are just prey to this immobilizing beast. This muteness is something that anyone who has had a normal, nontraumatized background would find difficult to understand. New research suggested that this was because a specific part of the left hemisphere of the brain called Broca's area, which governs speech, is turned off like a tap when someone reexperiences trauma. This in turn is because the essence of PTSD is that the traumas have been registered in the old, "reptilian" part of the brain—the fast-track fight-or-flight part, the amygdala—without being referred either to the more evolved neocortex, which usually encodes experiences for us and puts them into context, or to Broca's area, which gives words to them. So, when something taps into an old trauma, it's felt simply as an overpowering, inarticulate physical state:

> This probably means that during activation of a traumatic memory, the brain is "having" its experience. He or she may be physiologically prevented from translating this experience into communicable language. When PTSD victims are having their traumatic recall, they may suffer from speechless terror in which they may be literally "out of touch" with their feelings.

This sabotaging experience can mean that for the rest of their lives, people suffering from PTSD may be prone to depression, irritability and aggression, and find it almost impossible to make personal relationships. In her book on shell shock, Wendy Holden says that "they can be helped to live with their trauma, but there is no cure—a salutary thought for those responsible for the defence of the nation." This sentence could be usefully given to anyone responsible for deciding to go to war, for we do not yet build into the estimated cost of war a future cost: its knock-on toll to those who survive it, and those who come after and who try to get out from under its shadow.

During and after the Second World War in Britain there was less PTSD than for the First, perhaps partly because the cause of defeating such a noxious regime as Hitler's was clear-cut and worthy. However, the chaotic Normandy Campaign of June 1940, which Joe was caught up in, and the retreat from Dunkirk induced wholesale shell shock, as did the Burma Campaign and the Japanese prisoner-of-war camps later.

What hasn't been noticed is that at the end of the war the Polish soldiers would have been potentially far more susceptible to the effects of trauma than, for example, their Dunkirk counterparts. Not only had most of them come through traumatic journeys to get to the front—as Anders and his men, and my father, had done—but at the end of it their homelands were no longer safe to go back to. Even more crushing, their suffering in the war was abruptly nullified: they were cut out of the Victory Parade, their story was largely airbrushed out of the victors' account of the war, and they were faced with graffiti of "Poles Go Home." Anecdotally, many people in England remember that surviving Poles were often treated as funny refugee foreigners. One cameo of how they were viewed by local village children comes in Lorna Sage's autobiography, *Bad Blood:*

> you could lose yourself until you slowed to a dazed
> standstill and seemed a very passable village

idiot. . . . Quite a few people were doing this at the
time around Hanmer, including solitary patients in
blue hospital uniforms from a wartime camp at
Penley a few miles away, mostly Polish and suffering from TB. Juvenile Hanmer lore had it that they
were Germans and when a gang of us got together
we'd bravely jeer at them for losing the war. They
took no notice, just wandered on, staring sadly into
space.

The Polish culture of valor and patriotism, and the way the country
had had to get used to the shocks of war and occupation, no doubt
gave Poles an added degree of toughness; but I notice that Joe's
friends Ted and Stan both died prematurely of alcoholism, and neither reached anything like his full potential.

Czechoslovak soldiers were subject to similar potentially trau-
matizing stresses, but to a lesser degree. The image of both Poles
and Czechs in British minds, if they have one, is of the dashing and
decidedly uncrushed pilots who took part in the Battle of Britain;
but this doesn't take account of what happened to them later. The
Czechoslovak soldiers in the West had no homeland to return to
either, but they benefited from residual English guilt about Munich
in their reception. Nor were they perceived as a threat to employment in England in the way the Poles were—only 4,938 Czech
troops and their families were evacuated from France, for example,
as compared to some 90,000 Poles from all over Europe. Also their
exiled government under Beneš was pro-Stalin, so toed the Allied
line after 1941. Stalin, too, was pro-Czech, so Churchill, who had
always stood up for Czechoslovakia even before Munich, didn't
have to drop it like a hot brick to please Stalin. (I note that the
Czech Club in London still has a prominent picture of Churchill on
its walls, and the Polish Hearth Club does not.)

What helped the Poles and Czechs who opted to stay in Britain
above all was group solidarity, which is why the still-flourishing

Polish Hearth Club was set up in London after the war, dedicated to preserving the history of the Polish campaigns in its Sikorski Museum, and to fostering its own people in a network of educational, social and religious activities. Unfortunately for him, my father slipped through this net, although his friends Ted, Stan and Władek provided valuable solidarity. Time, money and class factors prevented him from joining the Polish Hearth Club, but also paradoxically the social withdrawal induced by whatever degree of "shell shock" he had prevented him from taking steps to ameliorate it. Something else inhibited him too, which I had yet to learn about.

Before reading about PTSD, it would have seemed to me obvious that war induces a stress that can seriously damage people's lives, that it comes automatically with a health warning. As Martha Gellhorn says:

> War is the crime against peace. War is the silver bombers, with the young men in them, who never wanted to kill anyone, flying in the morning sun over Germany and not coming back. War is the sinking ship and the sailors drowning in a flaming sea on the way to Murmansk. . . . War is the casualty lists and bombed ruins and refugees, frightened and homeless and tired to death, on all the roads. War is everything you remember from those long ugly years. And its heritage is what we have now, this maimed and tormented world which we must somehow restore.

This rang bells for me when, after visiting my parents in 2000, I went to see a Yugoslav doctor who works at a National Health Service clinic set up in London in 1986 to treat post-traumatic stress. Dr. Kristina Dionisio is tall and shapely, and gestures a lot with expressive hands. She looks exhausted. The clinic she works for deals with thousands of refugees who come from fraught conditions abroad—particularly, when I go to see her, from Kosovo. The clinic was overloaded with work, with a huge waiting list. There are fourteen thousand refugees in Greater London alone, she says. When they arrive, they think they're losing their minds, and this can be reinforced by the series of choppings and changings from place to place that is the best the system can do for them. There is fear and lack of trust and language is always a problem. She says all this is something English people cannot really understand. It's June 2000, and a terrible train crash at Paddington has just taken place. She says, in order to appreciate what it feels like to be the people she sees, you would have to imagine being in a train crash, escaping from that, then being shot at as you cross the road, then getting home to find your home burnt down, then running away and finding yourself in an unknown country where you don't speak the language.

Yet by this time I'm also aware that the treatment of trauma has been driven by clinical fashion, and that today a reaction has set in against the very existence of PTSD. As the historian Ben Shephard puts it, by the end of the twentieth century, "Even as the trauma bandwagon rumbled on in the wider society, some of its builders were trying to get off it." First of all, it had become politically implicated in compensation litigation, particularly in the United States, giving victims all too much financial reason to score high on the checklist, or abnegate responsibility for their lives; second, the standardization of the syndrome for precisely these purposes had made it a clumsy, artificial construct, unable to do justice to the range of symptoms. In addition, none of the therapies that had been successively in fashion from World War I onward—ECT, "deep sleep," insulin-induced coma, rehabilitation centers, peer group therapies, debriefing—seemed to have had a substantial effect on the patients. There was also another view about PTSD, suggested in one of the old-fashioned words for it, "malingering," which was that it didn't exist, or rather that it was a fig leaf for weakness or cowardice. This view was the main reason, it seemed to me, why men might resist having any part in it, for fear of appearing a wimp or invalid in some way. I guessed that my father's reaction to the suggestion that he suffered from any kind of "syndrome" would be to shrug it off with bafflement and irritation.

So, before I went to see my parents in the first month of the new millennium, after a long gap, I spoke with two eminent professors in London who take the view that PTSD doesn't exist. Simon Wessley of the Maudsley Hospital in Hampstead—whose father perhaps not coincidentally happened to be Czech and fought in the war—took the sanguine view that PTSD was invented after Vietnam by a group of U.S. military psychiatrists opposed to the war, and that it was a "neat way of making perpetrators into victims." He thought it was a symptom of a litigious society, which had become addicted to "victimology" and sanctioned people's making money out of things that happened to them which were just part of the ups and downs of life. He laughingly deplored what he called the emphasis on the "ambulance-chasing glamour of war trauma as opposed to, for example, the depression of mothers coping with life in Camberwell." Worse, he deplored people who "make their living out of being a second-generation survivor": which was suddenly getting a bit too close to home.

I also spoke with an old friend, the distinguished expert on pain, Patrick Wall, who was himself terminally ill. He said with an elegant smile that there was no clinical evidence for PTSD, and that the war had simply broken down some people's identities. They themselves rather than the war were to blame for this, and were flawed personalities. He shocked me by saying of Primo Levi that "he didn't do too well in Auschwitz." In awe as I was of Patrick's lifetime of expertise, I still felt that this was a view only someone firmly rooted in his own country might take, especially if that country was England. After hearing the outlines of my father's story, his wife, Mary, said, "Your father led a charmed life, didn't he?" "*Charmed?*" I repeated, amazed, as until then I'd thought my father had had singularly bad luck, pitched into the eye of each breaking storm. But as soon as she'd said it, I felt it was true, and it made me feel much better for my father, and I knew it would make him feel better, too. Lucky Joe.

When I returned to Australia in January 2000, I found that an episode in my parents' lives had presented Joe synchronistically with the concept and diagnosis of PTSD. In the years since my last visit, my mother had become completely deaf. As she was otherwise fit and lively, she had decided to have the new cochlear implant operation the Australians pioneered, which had restored some hearing to her. In an effort to improve the quality of life for her, Joe had devised a couple more attachments for the telephone— one to enable her to hear it ring and the other to help her hear a voice on the telephone. My mother's audiologist was interested in these inventions and invited my parents to an open day for the cochlear implant scheme in Sydney. She suggested that Joe should bring the devices with him so that he could help others by making a few more if desired.

The gathering took place in the courtyard of what turned out to be a former juvenile detention center. Having set up his stall, as it were, my father suddenly freaked out, cutting off all communication with anyone trying to speak with him and insisting that my mother and he leave at once to take the two-hour train back to Newcastle. There was no explanation to anyone, least of all my mother. This was the kind of incident I remembered from childhood—the abrupt shutdowns and withdrawals—and which I'd taken for granted as being part of him. But this time a perceptive stranger, the audiologist, was witness to it. Her own father, a German, had fought in the war and she had recently come to realize that he had been suffering from PTSD. She tactfully put it to my father that he might be carrying this burden too, and might like to look at some helpful literature on it.

So, when I spoke with Joe, I found him already prepared intellectually for the idea. On the other hand, as we sat looking at the digest of scientific papers the audiologist had sent, and at my boiled-down bullet points, I could tell that none of it was really getting through to him:

- persistence of a "startle" response or irritability
- flashbacks
- continual state of free-floating anxiety or hypervigilance
- proclivity to explosive behavior
- fixation on the trauma
- an overall constriction of life
- disturbed dream life, including vivid nightmares
- avoidance/denial: attempts to blot out the experience—"I just don't want to talk about it"
- psychic numbing
- withdrawal/isolation: shuns friends, neighbors, family—"leave me alone." Gets annoyed at being bothered with petty concerns of everyday life. "The hurt feelings this engenders in those rebuffed may lead to a vicious circle of avoidance."

The vocabulary was often abstract even if English was your primary language, and the list of symptoms a little dismaying if it was all being applied to you. I was concerned not to bring artificial distress into Joe's life: he had survived and adapted to his experiences with resourcefulness and success, and had a well-earned, agreeable life. In a few months, he would be eighty. I was no expert on anything medical, and was temperamentally inclined to stay with the poets' intuitions on such things. I didn't want the bullet points to be literal ones, reactivating old wounds.

So we went through the points fairly lightly and I asked him if he thought each one applied. On the questions of "explosive behavior" and "startle" response, he listened attentively and agreed this might apply to him, and I noticed they did soon begin to prove helpful concepts to him in tempering his overreactions in everyday life. And he himself made the connection with Eureka-like excitement that the courtyard in Sydney had reminded him subconsciously of the courtyard in Lwow, and that he was suddenly back there, in a position of terror, needing at all costs to get out. I recalled how one of the symptoms of PTSD was "becoming panicky in rooms or crowds where [you] are unable to negotiate a clear route of escape."

I asked him then about the "psychic numbing" bit, suggesting that from my point of view I thought he had been far more silent and uncommunicative than the average person, particularly over feelings. He said no, he didn't talk much, and he had a rational explanation for it: it started at Bravington's, where no one talked because everyone was having to concentrate on fine instrumentation, and then it carried on at BCURA, where the same thing applied. There was not only no necessity for talk, but any noise would have been dangerous, because concentration was essential. What about the lunch hour? I asked. He said he played chess at lunchtime, and there was no need for speech. QED for each of our readings: his that it was entirely rational; mine that he was rationalizing a resistance to communication that was present anyway. Still, sure though I was that these elements in him were hangovers from his war experiences, I was aware how reductive this kind of labelling could be. Having to define oneself not as a living, individual human being but as a syndrome or case history is unwelcome to anybody of spirit.

At this point I felt it was time to put an end to the journey into the past with my father. It must have been taxing as well as liberating for him, although he has never said so. While the jettisoning of a burden had been cathartic, dwelling too much on it would tip into morbidity. The aim of therapy for PTSD is apparently "not to be

haunted by the past, but to be in the here and now." It was time for
us to do that: to go off for walks and swims, to play games, to talk
of the events and people around us, to find the world out there.
My father took me aside gently one day and said: "I've got one request. Would you mind very much calling us Dad and Mum from
now on?"

For Dad's eightieth birthday we found him an old Omega watch,
roughly from the period when he'd lost his. And if that young Russian guard is out there somewhere, an old man now, I hope you're
enjoying the Omega watch, too. My father is enjoying the freedom
you gave him.

23 | SPOOKS

Because I believed that my father was home and dry when he reached England, I hadn't thought too much about what he'd been doing during the four final years of the war. I'd taken "radio communication" at face value, linking it with pictures of him with his headphones on alongside boxes bristling with plugs, bigger versions of the one he'd made me as a child. Then, when I was back in Australia in 2000, he mentioned in passing that during this time he'd been a spy—a radio spy. He'd given clues before, but it took the word "spy" for me to wake up to what was at stake. When I began to question him more, I found that once he reached England, far from being home and dry, he had faced pressures as great as the dislocations of exile and war. It was the cold war just as much as the "hot" war that dictated his silence, and it had needed the cold war to thaw for the silence to be lifted. Looking back, I realized I hadn't been wrong at the beginning when I'd felt I would have to ask the right questions in order to measure up to him.

When my father was summoned down from Scotland to Stanmore in London on December 1, 1941, he was posted to what was offi-

Joe in radio communications, 1942

cially known as the Administrative Unit (Radio Section) of the Polish Ministry of Defense, which was the headquarters of the Polish
commander in chief. For three weeks he worked in radio communications, receiving and sending ciphered messages in Morse code
between the headquarters and the Home Army in Poland, as well as
to and from resistance elsewhere in enemy-occupied parts of
Europe like France, Norway, Sweden and Hungary. He and his colleagues, who included Władek, Stan and Ted, had no idea what
these messages contained; they simply passed them on for decoding to others. Their work was at the lowest level of communication
duties, my father says, except that Stan was later promoted to being
a decoder (which he didn't like, because it meant he now had the
privilege of paying for his uniform).

In the first year of the war, Polish military intelligence was
working in close cooperation with the British, and with the British
Special Operations Executive (SOE), set up in July 1940 to "coor-

dinate all action, by way of subversion and sabotage, against the enemy overseas." Clandestine warfare courses were being run from English country estates, their owners often moving out of the main house, or moving out altogether, to facilitate operations. Well over two thousand men and women from the Polish armed forces volunteered to be sent into occupied Poland for underground operations, and it was the coded messages of those selected, amongst others, which were being received by Polish radio communications.

After the first three weeks, my father was transferred briefly to a large house called Dower House, within walking distance of his previous location at Ridgeway Street in Stanmore. This was no longer a two-way radio communications center, but only a listening post—eavesdropping, as he said. He was there for just three nights, as part of a group of eight, but he deduced that he was listening in to German submarine communications in the Atlantic. The British army major in charge transcribed their information and passed it on to the Admiralty, or to Bletchley Park. Two men in the group were dealing with decoding, one of whom had been part of a group deciphering Egyptian hieroglyphics before the war.

My father was perhaps being tested there, because after those three nights in early January 1942, he was sent to a special unit dedicated to listening in to coded communications from Russia, from both military and political sources. No doubt his aptitude for abstract mathematics, as well as his ability to keep quiet, had been noted and played a part in this posting. The men were not supposed to know what they were listening to or where it came from, but, he says, you could soon recognize a station by its manner of transmitting. "It's like handwriting, there would be different tone to each station, different style. Nowadays it would be called surfing; you'd surf the wavelengths until you found signature you were looking for. After about two months, the other men—more experienced than I was—would say kind of, 'Oh, that must be Boris,' so I started to guess what we were dealing with. On other hand, we were at lowest level of spying game, and overall feeling was, the less you know,

the better off you are. Overall picture was of umbrella of secrecy."
So what he was allowed to know—and what he cared to know—
was limited, even though from now on he would be doing this job
most nights for three years until the end of the war. It was when he
had just been assigned these duties that he met my mother, which is
why he had been so cagey with her about his work and even his
name.

In spring 1943, just after the Nazis' revelations about Katyn,
and after Stalin had theatrically broken off relations with the Poles,
my father's unit was enlarged and moved out to a country house at
Boxmoor, set in extensive grounds not far away, with orchards, sta-
bles and a tennis court (an estate given by Queen Elizabeth I to her
favorite, the Earl of Leicester, who then donated it for the use of the
local people). Even so, accommodations were overcrowded, and
two Nissen huts were built for this unit of some sixteen men to
sleep in. Władek, as a sergeant and professional soldier, had been
sent off to nearby Chipperfield Lodge, where he would work in military radio communications, in touch with the Anders army
amongst other branches of the Polish armed forces. My father's
group, Unit 2, had a more undercover task in collecting intelligence
on the Russians. Not only was the unit's existence secret from the
Russians, but after the revelations of the Katyn massacre in spring
1943, its communications were not automatically passed on to the
British either—the Polish high command having become more
wary of the intentions of the British government. It would become
even more so after Sikorski's death three months later.

So there were two parts within the Radio Unit of the Polish
chief of staff: Unit 6—Władek's—and my father's, Unit 2. Unit 6
dealt with two-way communications with the military, and Unit 2
dealt with one-way listening: intelligence. The difference is
reflected in the way the communications of Unit 6 were sent to Polish headquarters in the Rubens Hotel in Victoria, central London,
by teleprinter, whilst those of Unit 2 were decoded at Boxmoor, and
sent through to the hotel by courier. Also, Unit 2 was financed sep-

arately from all other Polish radio communications centers. Unit 2 was in a league of its own, its intelligence-gathering independent of both regular military activity and often its host country.

The fact that the Poles had no direct contact with the Russians after Katyn put them in an anomalous position: they were the enemy of their ally's ally. Because of their well-founded fears about Russia's intentions toward Poland, and because of their suspicions and concern about what had happened to their missing fifteen thousand officers, and what might happen to the hundreds of thousands of other Poles locked within Russia, they had an overriding need to monitor Russian activities independently. Some of this intelligence was passed on to the British, and Polish intelligence in general was the backbone of Allied intelligence during the war, something which has not yet been acknowledged (although there are books in the pipeline that will reveal its extent). It may have suited the British to get much of their intelligence on the Russians from the Poles so that they were not seen to be eavesdropping too much on their ally. But at the end of the war, in 1945—when they de-recognized the Polish government-in-exile—the British authorities curtailed all transmission by the Poles to Poland. Since then, one Polish historian has told me, the British have been silent over admitting the great role Polish intelligence played in the war out of guilt at how the Poles were treated thereafter—and guilt at their own intelligence lapses.

My father, detailed to this job whether he wanted it or not, felt that this "eavesdropping" work, low-grade as it was, put him potentially on a KGB black list the moment the cold war kicked in—and this threat hung over him, as only he (and Ted, Stan and Władek) knew, right up until the dissolution of the Soviet Union. After the war, he was a spy left out in the cold, as Churchill and then Attlee began to court Russia and dropped their Polish allies. In spite of his low level in the hierarchy, my father knew enough from his time in Lwow to understand that the threat was real—a threat not only to him but also, thanks to "collective responsibility," to my mother and me, as well as to his family in Poland. But he also knew that even if he had wanted to talk about it, no one in England would have taken him seriously. His fear was augmented by the fact that he'd escaped from the Russians in the first place in Lwow, and so already felt wanted by them. From then on, he felt he couldn't trust people, as he didn't know what their allegiances might be. Once, a Russian approached him in the street in Stanmore asking him questions about who he was, and he acted dumb and saw him off, but this terrified him and preyed on his mind. And although (as I've recently found out from the War Office) he had two standard British medals from the war, the War Medal and the Defence Medal, it took him eight years to get British citizenship, during which time those two CID men turned up on our doorstep unannounced to interview him. No wonder we never had a telephone.

In March 1946, Winston Churchill, now replaced as prime minister by the Labour leader Clement Attlee thanks to an electorate weary of war rhetoric, gave a famous speech in the United States ushering in the new era of the "cold war":

> I have a strong admiration and regard for the valiant Russian people and for my wartime comrade, Marshal Stalin. There is deep sympathy and goodwill in Britain—and I doubt not here also—toward the peoples of all the Russias and a resolve to persevere through many differences and rebuffs in establishing lasting friendships. It is my duty, however, to place before you certain facts about the present position in Europe.

> From Stettin in the Baltic to Trieste in the Adriatic an iron curtain has descended across the Continent. Behind that line lie all the capitals of the ancient

states of Central and Eastern Europe. Warsaw, Berlin, Prague, Vienna, Budapest, Belgrade, Bucharest and Sofia; all these famous cities and the populations around them lie in what I must call the Soviet sphere, and all are subject, in one form or another, not only to Soviet influence but to a very high and in some cases increasing measure of control from Moscow.

He went on to issue a warning: "In a great number of countries, far from the Russian frontiers and throughout the world, Communist fifth columns are established and work in complete unity and absolute obedience to the directions they receive from the Communist center."

What Churchill knew, as my father knew, was that we were now in an unsafe world, a different kind of unsafe world. It was the world I grew up into, the postwar world, and it was proposed as the safest world we had yet had: "You've never had it so good" was Prime Minister Harold Macmillan's slogan when he came to power in 1957. At school in southeast London, we looked up into the sky during the elections and saw two airplanes boldly writing BACK MAC in vapor trails across the blue, a flamboyant gesture of a piece with Macmillan's sporting a white Russian fur hat when he went to meet Khrushchev at the Kremlin—the first flickers of style to animate a gray and conformist postwar Britain.

For my father, the cold war meant he always felt he was a potential candidate for the knock on the door in the middle of the night. Hence the hammer under the pillow. If he had said any of this at the time, it would have seemed histrionic to the English—just as Polish intelligence reports about the horrors of the treatment of Jews in concentration camps were dismissed, we now know, by the British Foreign Office as "exaggerated" and consigned to the wastepaper basket. Yet, with hindsight, there was genuine reason for fear, as my father suspected. Recently, I asked him how he thought Australia had helped in liberating him from the anxieties of his past, and he wrote a picturesque answer: "After demobilisation I wanted to remain invisible in society, to meld with the crowd, so that comparing to a nest of ants I would not be recognisable. I feared for you and your mother and for my family on Continent if I could be traced. At the time we arrived in Australia, I found myself in a nest of so many insects, instead of ants only, that I felt safer for being just another unmatched insect." He also said he was happy from the start to come to Australia because he had been *invited* to come, whereas in England he was always aware of having come uninvited.

His underlying fears in England were exacerbated by the turn of events after the war; it was not, after all, peace that followed the end of the Second World War in Europe, as we were led to believe, but half a century of volatile armed truce, with the cold war between the Soviet Union and the West being fought actively by proxy elsewhere—in Korea, in Vietnam, and also covertly on our doorsteps. By 1971, just before British prime minister Edward Heath named 105 Russians in Britain as Soviet agents and had them dispatched back to the Soviet Union, there were some 400 Soviet agents or spies in the country, run by 25 Russian intelligence officers—numbers that had been steadily swelling during the sixties. Finding out why they were in Britain makes me realize why it had become particularly appealing for my father to leave for the other side of the world in November 1971, at the height of the cold war, and after the Heath government's action in expelling the spies had brought a new low in Anglo-Soviet relations.

It had started in the late 1920s, when the NKVD had already formulated a plan for infiltrating Britain's intelligence establishment. Communism was an attractive proposition to many people in Britain after the horrors of World War 1, in which ordinary foot soldiers could be seen to have suffered inordinately to further the interests of the ruling classes and the establishment, which the war had served in many ways. The dismay at the betrayal of working people's interests, further fuelled by the Great Depression, would translate in the twenties and thirties into hunger marches, general strikes and miners' strikes. As early as 1920—a year after the creation of the first Communist International—this disillusion had helped fuel the formation of the British Communist Party. The Bolsheviks in the Soviet Union, propelled by their own 1917 revolution, wanted to change the world order, and Britain was a prime target. As the Communist Party of Britain was still putting it in 1991: "capitalist Britain had the oldest and most cunning ruling class, and was at the centre of world imperialism." In these circumstances, the NKVD in Moscow began to target these cunning ruling classes with its own cunning—a cunning honed into sophisticated techniques of psychological infiltration during the Bolsheviks' long underground struggle against imperial Russia. The NKVD wanted to infiltrate British Intelligence, but didn't want to use eager and hotheaded working-class Communist Party members for the purpose. They wanted to undermine the establishment from within. And they were after top secret information, which an ordinary party member would be least likely to have access to. So they patiently targeted bright, idealistic young men who were born into the establishment, and on their way to positions of influence and power within it, but who had Marxist leanings.

Four of these young men, who would have a great influence on the unfolding of the war and of the climate of the cold war in Britain afterward, were Anthony Blunt, Guy Burgess, Donald Maclean, Kim Philby and John Cairncross, all recruited from the elite Cambridge University society known as the Apostles. Since the society was a self-selecting coterie of people already inclined to conspiracy and arrogance, infiltrating the Apostles was an economical and, as it turned out, highly effective way for the KGB to get to the heart of future English powerbrokers. During the war, Blunt, Burgess and Maclean worked for M(ilitary) I(ntelligence) 5, the British version of the FBI, a counterintelligence service responsible for internal security in the country. Philby worked for its other arm, MI6, which gathers information about "the actions and intentions of persons outside the British Islands" for defense and foreign policy purposes (equivalent to the CIA). Thus, throughout the war, there was a phenomenal hemorrhage of classified information from MI5 and MI6 to the Soviets. In 1941 alone, the London residency of the NKVD forwarded to Moscow 7,867 classified political and diplomatic documents, 715 on military matters, 127 on economic affairs and 51 on British intelligence. The following year Donald Maclean's documents forwarded to Moscow filled up more than forty-five volumes in the Soviet secret service archives. From summer 1942 to summer 1943, the fifth agent, John Cairncross, was even working at Bletchley Park, transmitting decrypts back to his bosses in Moscow.

In retrospect, from spring 1943 onward—when my father began his work at Unit 2, and when the Katyn revelations led to Soviet-Polish relations being broken off—this secret flow of classified information from London became particularly treacherous for the Poles. As far as we know, this was unknown to the British government and intelligence services at the time, although the Poles were evidently taking general precautionary measures against the new British-Soviet entente by splitting off Unit 2 from connections with British intelligence. Still, any information they did share with the British intelligence services about their activities in trying to plan an independent Poland after the war, as Sikorski was trying to do, was—as we know in retrospect—likely to be channelled to Stalin through the Cambridge Five, ensconced in key positions in MI5 and MI6. Some of the classified information to the Soviets concerned the politically sensitive subject of the Poles.

To find what that information might have been, I went to the Public Record Office in Kew, outside London, to look at the declassified secret service files on Sikorski. Leafing through the memos and letters written in the large, jumpy typeface of old typewriters, I found that a large proportion of the documents on him at this period were deleted in the sixties—which, ambiguously, could be a cover-up or mere pruning for shelf space. Yet even from this partial view, it was clear that Sikorski was already perceived as a problem a year before his death—not only by the British secret services but also by his own Polish colleagues. He was criticized in a "MOST SECRET AND CONFIDENTIAL" memo "From a Most Reliable Source" in May 1942 for his tendency to "stray about the world, making himself important," and in March that year he had already been the subject of what looked like a sabotage attempt, when an aircraft he was about to board for America caught fire. There was another incident in November 1942, when Sikorski was again about to take off for America, and both engines of his plane failed within seconds of takeoff. Undaunted, by February 1943 he was still straying about the world—again to the United States—where a secret memo reported that "Sikorski's aim was to unite all the scattered forces into a single force to defend Poland against the Russians after Germany's collapse." It was also noted that Sikorski's private talk "revealed a deeply hostile attitude towards Russia," although he was being "publicly conciliatory"—and this was two months before the Katyn revelations.

Meanwhile, the double agent Donald Maclean, the most effective of the five spies, now had the post of administrative liaison at the Foreign Office with Allied troops in Britain—which meant at this time mostly the Poles and French. So, as it happens, Maclean was the first man to convey the news of the Nazis' discovery at Katyn to Sikorski, and to note his reactions. He reported back to Moscow that Sikorski wanted to put great pressure on Stalin over Katyn and embarrass him as much as possible with the Allies. Stalin was furious. He and Sikorski had locked horns personally ever since the Polish-Soviet War of 1919–20, as Sikorski had commanded one of the armies at the Battle of the Vistula which turned back the Red Army so humiliatingly. The unresolved matter of the joint border added to festering historical animosities between the two countries, and now there was the matter of the hundreds of thousands of Polish prisoners Stalin had taken.

Just after the Nazis' revelations, Churchill admitted privately to Sikorski on April 15, 1943, over lunch at 10 Downing Street that "The German revelations are probably true. The Bolsheviks can be very cruel." In fact, from a long, detailed report sent to him two days before by the British ambassador to the Polish government— and which Churchill had forwarded to Roosevelt—Churchill knew very well that the allegations were true. However, he did not want to upset the delicate relations with the only remaining power that could help the Allies win the war against Hitler, and so he strove to calm matters between Stalin and the Poles. He told Sikorski some days later that his intended riposte to Stalin would be a "declaration of mortal war," and that conciliation was "the only line of safety for the Poles and indeed for us." It was now that he said, "There was no use prowling morbidly round the three-year-old graves of Katyn." However, later, on August 13, 1943, the same ambassador, Sir Owen O'Malley, put the moral position lucidly in a letter to President Roosevelt:

> We have been obliged to appear to distort the normal and healthy operation of our intellectual and moral judgements; we have been obliged . . . to restrain the Poles from putting their case clearly before the public, to discourage any attempt by the public and the press to probe the ugly story to the bottom. In general we have been obliged to defect attention from possibilities which in the ordinary affairs of life would cry to high heaven for elucidation . . . we have in fact perforce used the good name of England like the murderers used the little conifers to cover a massacre; and, in view of the immense importance of an appearance of Allied

unity and of the heroic resistance of Russia to Germany, few will think that any other course would have been wise or right.

On the night of April 27, Churchill redrafted the communiqué in Sikorski's name, telling Roosevelt: "We have persuaded them to shift the argument from the dead to the living and from the past to the future." And the inspired bargain that he dreamed up was that in exchange for keeping quiet over Katyn, the Poles should be given back all the remaining Polish soldiers and prisoners in Russia, who would join the nascent Anders army in Persia. It was a prisoners-for-no-questions deal. "We think the request is reasonable," Churchill commented, asking Stalin to consider it "in the spirit of magnanimity." For its part, Britain would ensure "proper discipline" in the Polish press in Britain—that is, it would be muzzled. Churchill also added that he'd urged the Poles not to make "charges of an insulting character" against the Soviet government, and that "I am glad to tell you that they have accepted our view and that they want to work loyally with you."

Now, thanks to Maclean's reporting back to Moscow from his position close to the Poles, Stalin knew this was not true, and that the Poles had been silenced against their will. Toward the end of April 1943, Maclean was asked to let Moscow know Sikorski's (top-secret) travel itinerary, and he told the Russians that the leader planned to meet with Polish forces (led by Anders) in Teheran, then fly on to Cairo and Gibraltar and meet other exiles there in July. Sikorski had had previous warnings of sabotage, and when he set off for Cairo, three separate members of his government received anonymous calls falsely reporting that Sikorski's plane had crashed on takeoff with no survivors. This crash did not materialize, and Sikorski flew on to Gibraltar as planned. However, there was a hitch when a request came through for Sikorski to delay his takeoff from Gibraltar as the Soviet ambassador to Britain, Ivan Maisky, needed to make a refuelling stop there en route to Moscow. Now that

Polish-Russian relations were so poor, it would be a diplomatic incident if Maisky and Sikorski were to find themselves in close proximity. Maisky himself later said that it would not have been difficult to smuggle a sabotage agent onto Sikorski's plane, in what became a last-minute frenzy to load and check it—but Maisky's supposition in his 1965 memoirs was that the Germans had done it. Three years later, John le Carré resurrected the CIA's long-held suspicion that Stalin was behind the crash, for the agent in charge of security operations in Gibraltar at the time—head of the SIS's Iberian Section—happened to be none other than Kim Philby. And back in London, the man responsible for the security of the missions of Allied governments in London, including the governments-in-exile, was Anthony Blunt.

It was in this circumstantially suspicious context that on July 4, 1943, Sikorski's plane took off from Gibraltar, observed by the British governor, by saluting Poles and various officials—who included the British actor, then a major, Anthony Quayle. Within their appalled sight, the plane took off, only to stall and then go into a slow nosedive into the sea. All but the Czech pilot were killed. Many Poles ran distraught to the end of the runway, whilst others, close to Quayle, began to sob and cry out, "This is the end of Poland, this is the end of Poland!" And once again, for a long time, it would be so. Other passengers included Sikorski's daughter, members of the Polish military from a major general to a lieutenant, and two British MPs, one of whom, Victor Cazalet, had been British party liaison officer to Poland since 1940, and was now special adviser to Sikorski.

There have been recent allegations that Cazalet carried onto the plane documents proving that Russian soldiers had murdered the Polish officers at Katyn. Also on the plane—unknown to Sikorski—was the head of the British Intelligence Service in the Middle East. Whatever the origin of the jammed controls which precipitated the crash, the Polish leadership in exile had been decimated. As an

American historian has said, "If Philby had a hand in arranging Sikorski's death, it would have been by far his greatest wartime coup. For not only was Sikorski greatly admired by Churchill and Roosevelt, but even Stalin, whom Sikorski did not fear, treated him with respect. He was also the only one who could hold together the faction-ridden Poles. His death was as disastrous as it would have been had England lost Churchill in 1940 or had the United States lost Roosevelt in 1942. Once he was eliminated, Poland's fate was sealed."

When he heard the news of Sikorski's death, Churchill is said to have wept. The remaining Polish leadership demanded an immediate investigation, sure that either the KGB or the Nazis were implicated. There was much general speculation at the time about who had been responsible—the Germans, the KGB, Churchill, or other Poles competing for power with Sikorski—and to quash this and satisfy the Polish leadership, Churchill ordered a Foreign Office inquiry. Maclean volunteered the man for this investigation, his friend Victor Rothschild (alleged by some to have been the "fifth man" in the ring of spies, and the subject of one of the books I had seen on Wanda's table). Rothschild flew out, examined the remains of the aircraft, and concluded that there was no way of proving whether there had been sabotage or who might have been responsible. His report was not only deemed to have dealt with the matter for good but was also kept secret. This suited the Russians; but the Poles were left with the feeling of having been muzzled once again, and that there had been a cover-up.

I wrote to ask my father what he and his Polish colleagues had thought about Sikorski's death at the time and he replied anecdotally:

> From the time of entering into what I call the spy cell, we had no military training, and when the body of General Sikorski arrived by train in Lon-

don (I think it was Victoria station), all we could
supply was four soldiers who were skilled enough
to do present arms and so forth. The point though
is that Churchill was there, and as the coffin was
being taken out and carried, he lit a cigar. This
apparently did not go down very well.

The blows of Katyn, Sikorski's death, Yalta and the snub over
the Victory Day celebrations caused increasingly heavy hearts and
polarized loyalties in Poles stranded in England after the war, leaving them with a burden of honorable silence and unvoiceable mistrust. Yet the complexity of the imperatives facing the Allies,
together with the political wrangling amongst the Poles' own leaders, did not allow the Poles a clear-cut sense of blame. Moreover,
they could not object because they were at the mercy of the country
which was sheltering them, their host, which had offered them suc-
cor and pay and much else—often, as with my father, people with
wives and families. In all kinds of individual ways, particularly
within the armed forces, the British had shown the utmost tact,
respect and affection for their Polish colleagues. To whinge about
your hosts is bad form in any right-minded culture, and for the most
part, my guess is that like my father they were too fastidious to
complain. Most must have understood England's position, as they,
too, had come from a part of the world where sometimes the lesser
evil had to be accepted for the greater good. But the descent of an
iron curtain "from Stettin to Trieste," cutting them off from their
families in "Red Poland," exacerbated their silence, as nobody
wanted to upset the precarious balance of peace and provoke the
grizzly Soviet bear, especially under a nuclear umbrella.

The position of the ring of spies also altered as the cold war set
in, as they were now plain traitors, passing secrets to an enemy
country. Burgess and Maclean stayed at the Foreign Office, delivering a flow of information on Western policy to Moscow throughout

the forties, from top-secret nuclear plans to progress on the formation of NATO and the Marshall Plan. The two men began to be suspected, but defected secretly in 1951 before they could be caught,
only to surface publicly in Moscow in 1956. Philby was head of the
Soviet Section of MI6 in 1951, and immediately came under suspicion. But although he was relieved of his intelligence duties that
year, it wasn't until 1955 that he was dismissed altogether—and it
was a full eight years before he fled to the Soviet Union, in 1963.
The following year, Anthony Blunt, who had meanwhile become
Keeper of the Queen's Pictures and been knighted, "confessed" in
exchange for immunity from prosecution.

My father, reading in the *Daily Mirror* the revelations of double-
dealing and defections—and of the apparently curious leniency of
the British intelligence services toward Philby and Blunt—would
have felt a particular alarm at the long and seemingly ubiquitous
arm of the KGB. For although spy satellites began to operate in the
sixties, making much of this individual intelligence redundant,
other spy scandals—virtual spymania—quietly detonated throughout the decade and into the seventies: George Blake; the Americans
Peter and Helen Kroeger; "Gordon Lonsdale," alias KGB colonel
Konon Trofimovich Molody; John Vassall; and then the Profumo
affair. Even John Stonehouse, the MP who faked his death by
drowning and later surfaced in Australia, was thought to be a Czech
intelligence agent. (Later, after my father had left for Australia,
there would be the murder of the Bulgarian dissident Georgi
Markov, killed in the street by an umbrella tip charged with the
lethal poison ricin; and even as late as 1985 the KGB double agent
Oleg Gordievsky would be spirited back to Moscow, drugged and
interrogated, then smuggled back out by MI6.)

For my father, reading about these episodes would have been a
different experience from that of the rest of us in England, often

unaware of what was at stake, and finding it all an amusing piece of Grand Guignol. For anyone with antennae alert to the dangers of the KGB, and with a past that could be called to account, the whole era of the cold war meant an endemic state of vigilance. And his apprehension was no fantasy: a recent exhibition in the Czech Republic about Czech and Slovak exile in the twentieth century mentions that "To many it will be news that during the communist regime, some who escaped were hunted down, kidnapped, brought back to the then-Czechoslovakia, and executed."

Recently my father told me: "I've never felt secure. I only began to feel secure when the Berlin Wall came down. Until then I was trying to be a nobody—I felt safer that way. I felt safer not being known than being protected. Basically I was afraid to be seen. There was just—fear." In these conditions, not mentioning anything about his past at all was, he felt, the only way to protect himself and those close to him. As Alfred Duff Cooper put it to those under his command during the war: "there is only one way to keep a secret. There are not two ways. That way is not to whisper it to a living soul—neither to the wife of your bosom nor to the man you trust most upon earth."

Just before I flew to Australia last time, I went to the London archives of the Polish Underground Army, sequestered in a sprawling Edwardian house of dusty, scholarly elegance where everything, even the typewriters, seems to have been preserved in its 1945 state. I wanted to find out if they had any information on Unit 2. The rooms were buzzing with Polish talk and bustling with energetic scholars, many elderly. The librarian gave me information on the unit from a Polish book published in 1973 called *Thank You Our Compatriots*. There I found my father's name on a list of all those who had worked in radio communications, together with those of Władysław Kordys, Tadeusz Danecki and Stanisław Badzioch. I could hear the shock in his silence when I told him on the telephone. We then found that Unit 2 was referred to in that book, which was devoted solely to Polish radio communications during the war, but only once—and only to dismiss it. What it said was: "The headquarters of the Battalion of Radio Communications of the Chief of Staff was located at Dower House in Stanmore. The battalion consisted of two companies: the radio-telegraphic company and the company that was gathering intelligence. With the latter we shall not be dealing."

When I got to Australia, my father showed me a passage from Simon Singh's book *The Code Book: The Science of Secrecy from Ancient Egypt to Quantum Cryptography,* which I'd given him on a previous visit. It concerned Marian Rejewski and the existence of Ultra and Enigma, all first revealed in *The Ultra Secret* (1974), by former MI6 colonel Fred Winterbotham. Singh wrote:

> Those who had contributed so much to the war effort could now receive the recognition they deserved. Possibly the most remarkable consequence of Winterbotham's revelations was that Rejewski realised the staggering consequences of his pre-war breakthroughs against Enigma. After the invasion of Poland, Rejewski had escaped to France, and when France was overrun he fled to Britain. It would seem natural that he should have become part of the British Enigma effort, but instead he was relegated to tackling menial ciphers at a minor intelligence unit in Boxmoor, near Hemel Hempstead. It is not clear why such a brilliant mind was excluded from Bletchley Park, but as a result he was completely unaware of the activities of the Government Code and Cypher School. Until the publication of Winterbotham's book,

> Rejewski had no idea that his ideas had provided
> the foundation for the routine decipherment of
> Enigma throughout the war.

Dad looked at me—his eyes now steadier, his nystagmus, so it seemed to me, having all but disappeared over the past year—and said, "He will have been working days at Boxmoor decoding what we collected in night." For three years this would have been the case—and he hadn't known. We read the allegedly complete list of people working in Polish radio communications in *Thank You Our Compatriots* and found no mention of a Marian Rejewski. This book was published in 1973, a year before the first revelations came out about Ultra, and when set against Singh's paragraph saying Rejewski was at Boxmoor, it's an interesting discrepancy. It means that Rejewski was there, but unacknowledged (possibly operating under a pseudonym). This in turn suggests a possible reason why such a brilliant mind should have been relegated to "tackling menial ciphers at a minor intelligence unit in Boxmoor": for the Poles, nothing, not even winning the war, could compare with the importance of monitoring Russia's intentions toward their homeland.

Clearly, there are boxes-within-boxes of not knowing, like Russian dolls. As far as we were concerned, I hadn't known my father's story, and he hadn't known what he was caught up in. This is probably the way the world is organized: you solve one mystery, only to hit upon another. Since we're undeniably placed on a small planet within an infinite mystery, there's no reason to think that our individual lives wouldn't replicate the bigger pattern.

The more my father and I look into the complexities of what was going on secretly at the end of the war merely between the Poles, Russians, Germans and British, the more we feel that this is where we bow out of the story. The details of the intricate web are for others, more versed in these matters, to pursue. In the end, secrecy is second-rate, but many people don't have the luxury of realizing that. As Richard Gid Powers says in his introduction to Daniel Patrick Moynihan's *Secrecy:*

> What secrecy grants in the short run—public support for government policies—in the long run it takes away, as official secrecy gives rise to fantasies that corrode belief in the possibilities of democratic government. All because of secrets locked away foolishly and in the end, it would seem needlessly. Secrecy is a losing proposition. It is, as Senator Moynihan has told us, for losers.

On the other hand, secrecy at Bletchley Park contributed to winning the war. And one cannot fail to notice that the two current leaders of major world powers, President Putin and President Bush, are respectively a former head of intelligence services, and the son of a former head of intelligence services.

24 | KRAKOW

We sit in the tiny Prowincja café in Krakow on ul. Bracka, around the corner from the main square, breakfasting on cheese, tea with lemon and freshly baked white bread with honey. Roger and I have taken a tram in from our room in the Kazimierz district on the outskirts of the city—the former Jewish quarter, its buildings still so intact and unreconstructed since the Second World War that it was used for Steven Spielberg's film *Schindler's List*. Graceful old mid-nineteenth-century buildings molder there, as elsewhere in the city, shrouded in pollution and grime—ripe, it seems to me as a Londoner, for gentrification. Western consumerism has a foothold here already: on the way in, we pass signs for Tesco Supermarkets, Jackpot & Cottonfield, Morgan, and an advertisement for "aristocratic" Earl Grey tea.

Although my father never came to Krakow, Roger and I decide to end our journey here, knowing it's an interesting city and not wanting to miss it. We arrived yesterday evening, to snowflakes falling soft and straight down, a curtain-raiser to the magic of the city. Krakow is built around a castle on a hill with a river running alongside it: that fairy-tale triangulation. The river is the Vistula, the castle is Wawel Castle, the hill is Wawel Hill, home in legend to a dragon slain by Prince Krak, founder of Krakow. The city has the biggest medieval square in Europe, the Rynok Glowny—which, like all good medieval squares, is not square at all but improvised to please the eye and fit the lie of the land. At one corner are the twin towers of the Mariacki Church, asymmetrical and ornate, like king and queen chess pieces. From the top of the taller and more delicate of the two Gothic towers, pricked with floodlights at night, a lone horn blower sounds his horn every hour at each corner of the tower, stopping short suddenly mid-note: in memory of the moment when the original medieval bugler, sounding the alarm at the sight of approaching Tatar armies, was silenced abruptly by an arrow piercing his throat. These were the notes echoed in May 1944 by that lone bugler on the hill, when the Poles took Monte Cassino. The city center has few parking restrictions, indeed not too many cars. Yet there are Internet cafés, gently funky restaurants and bars with delicious food. Our favorite is Gospoda C. K. Dezerter, which includes on its menu "Mulled mine" and "A broad of cheese variety: regular cheese, moldy cheese."

As we sit in the Prowincja café, with its antique lace curtains and bare-brick vaults, a young man in full leather gear comes in and takes off his fur-lined, ear-flapped aviator's cap to reveal a completely bald head. We hear a brass band outside and see a motley group of decoratively dressed soldiers marching past toward the square. Tagging along to see what's happening, we find the huge square thronging with people in the light drizzle. It's difficult to make out what's going on. The brass band shuffles onto a podium in the square, its members grinning in their four-cornered hats and Ruritanian uniforms of royal blue, gold, pink and black, whilst two broadcasters from Radio Krakow take to the microphone in front of them. Dignitaries come up and give speeches to rippling applause, whilst in another part of the square soldiers lay wreaths on a monument, swinging their khaki capes as they turn smartly on their heels, the white plumes on their hats dampened by the moist air. Toward the edge of the square farthest from the Mariacki Church, a metal hoist rises high above the scene with a couple of figures up on its platform. We keep hearing the name "Horowitz." Eventually I ask one of the broadcasters what's going on and she says that the Krakow-born photographer Ryszard Horowitz is up on the hoist taking a photograph of the square packed with well-wishers to send to Pope John Paul II, former archbishop of the city and also born near Krakow, for his eighty-first birthday in May. The date—March 24, 2001—has been chosen because it's the anniversary of the uprising against the Russians led from the square over two hundred years ago by the Polish national hero Tadeusz Kościuszko, also from Krakow—hence the wreath-laying. The chance combination of these three names in this square—Kościuszko, the Pope and Ryszard Horowitz—takes me back to questions over the core of the Nazi horror and Poland's part in it which I left hanging in the air. It also takes me back to silence.

Kościuszko, born in 1746, was one of the first to embrace the ideals of democracy and equality in the post-Enlightenment air, but grew to manhood just as his country lost its independence for the first time in 1772. Since he couldn't fight for his ideals in truncated Poland, he volunteered for the American War of Independence, where he became fêted for his military prowess, and was made an American citizen. He returned to defend his country against Russian armies in 1792, but to no avail, as the king decided that to avoid future inevitable defeat, he would capitulate to the Russians. A stream of outraged reformist intellectuals and officers left Poland, including Kościuszko, only to see the Prussian army invade the country from the other side, and effect the second partition in 1793. Meanwhile, Kościuszko was given honorary French citizenship by the new Revolutionary government in Paris, something that would give Poland's enemies the excuse to brand him and Poland in general Jacobin once the Revolution had turned sour. With tsarist armies massing again on its eastern borders, in 1794, Kościuszko came back to the Rynok Glowny in Krakow, and it was now, on March 24, that he swore to wage war for his country's independence.

In French Revolutionary fashion, armed only with scythes and pikes, the Poles fought off a well-equipped Russian army—a success that had an inspirational effect on the country. He hadn't, however, counted on the prior secret agreement between the Prussians and Russians, and on the day of battle he found his 14,000 men confronted by the combined forces of 25,000 Russians and Prussians. After exemplary bravery, Kościuszko was wounded on the battlefield and taken prisoner to St. Petersburg. As he fell on the field, he cried out, "*Finis Poloniae!*"

It was the end of Poland for over one hundred and twenty years, but Kościuszko became a hero not only to patriotic Poles and to the new American republic, but also to the Romantic movement in Europe; Keats wrote him an ode of praise. Released from prison on condition that he never return to Poland, he went back to America, where he became a lifelong friend of Thomas Jefferson. Although he never returned to his eradicated homeland, his body was taken back to Krakow and lies in the vaults of Wawel Castle alongside those of the kings of Poland.

In the nineteenth century, the country's erstwhile freedoms sat badly with the Russian tradition of absolutism, and there were more uprisings. After 1848, Polish exiles fought "for your freedom and ours" in almost every nation in Europe, a foretaste of things to come. Later in the century, Poland's plight attracted the sympathy of the new Socialist movements in Europe: so much so that Marx and Engels said the liberation of Poland should be "the single most important immediate objective of the workers' movement." Thus Poland managed to get tarred simultaneously with the brush of revolutionary Marxism and landowning feudalism.

Meanwhile, the great waves of Polish emigration began, largely to the United States and to Paris. The first was in 1830, when some ten thousand Poles left for Paris, including Chopin and the Poles'

great poet Adam Mickiewicz—a mass transfusion from one country
to another exceeded only by that of the Jews from Austria and Germany a hundred years later. Another distinguished exile was Joseph
Conrad, born Józef Korzeniowski to Polish parents in Russian-
occupied Ukraine in 1857. His father, arrested and imprisoned by
the Russians for "revolutionary patriotism," had died when Conrad
was eleven and was buried in Krakow. Conrad left the city for a sea-
faring life, but later decided to come back to show Krakow to his
English family. He chose a bad time: August 1914. War suddenly
broke out around them, and they found themselves overnight in
enemy territory. On the night of general mobilization, as Poles were
again being corralled into battle to fight for a nation not their own—
this time for Austria-Hungary, which had helped swallow their
land—Conrad sat devastated in his hotel room with Polish friends.
He wrote:

> I saw in those faces the awful desolation of men
> whose country, torn in three, found itself engaged
> in the contest with no will of its own, and not even
> the power to assert itself at the cost of life. All the
> past was gone, and there was no future, whatever
> happened; no road which did not seem to lead to
> moral annihilation.

It was a gloomy if realistic prediction, but Conrad lived to see it
proved wrong, as Poland regained full independence in 1918, with
the composer and pianist Paderewski its moving force and first
prime minister. That things should go so wrong so soon afterward,
and remain so for half a century after the war had ended, was the
most bitter irony of many in Poland's history. Yet Hitler's ghost has
suffered worse ironies: thanks to him, Germany ended up with less
territory—less *Lebensraum*—than it had before he came to power,
more international opprobrium and more international impotence;
and 3 million Sudeten Germans, far from being given more "living

space" and rights, were entirely expelled from their ancestral land. Above all, he had paved the way for exactly what he was trying to avoid: the complete takeover of Eastern Europe, and half of his own nation, by Communist powers.

I think of how the Prussian Bismarck saw Poland as a "seasonal state," one that was there sometimes and not at others, like snow, or roses. He had a political interest in seeing it that way, because this diminished its territorial solidity, making it ripe for trampling on. Yet I wonder what it must do to your psyche, to belong to a place which is there sometimes and not at others. Apart from anything else, it must make part of you go underground, waiting for the right season to come. Part of my father went underground for a long time, like both his fatherlands. His season has come again, like those of the Czech Republic, Slovakia and Poland, though for all of them it is a late-flowering season.

There's been a slight break in the rain, but it's just beginning to drizzle down again. Up on the hoist, the baseball-capped figure of Ryszard Horowitz says something in Polish through a loudspeaker and everyone laughs and waves their umbrellas in the air. He clicks his camera. Then the hoist comes down slowly, like an elephant's trunk, and Horowitz, in sunglasses in spite of the weather, is surrounded by autograph seekers and fans. Around the edges people begin to disperse, but many, like us, are held captive by the atmosphere emanating from this odd mix: Kościuszko, Ryszard Horowitz, the Pope. A huge, benign crowd in a medieval square. A small figure high up on a hoist, looking down.

I wonder what the occasion meant to the photographer up there, and when we get back to England, I contact Horowitz in New York. He generously takes the time to tell me:

> The city decided to combine my photo session with Kościuszko's anniversary. Local media de-

voted tremendous amount of effort to promote our
event to attract as many people as possible. Everything from thousands of posters, newspaper articles, TV coverage, etc. On the day of the shoot, as
you remember, it was raining. I had a window of
opportunity, long enough to take five exposures,
before people, close to 20 thousands put up their
umbrellas and were ready to disperse. I brought
my own view camera and film, and only after the
shoot I found out that there was no lab in Krakow
able to process 8×10 film . . . and we needed it the
following day for the media. Only after many
attempts we managed to convince one private
photo lab owner to process my film. In the course
of it, he destroyed two sheets of my exposed film,
so out of the three remaining one exposure was
slightly blurred because of wind and crowd movement, the second was perfect and the third one
exposed lots of umbrellas people began to open up
to protect themselves against dashing rain. In other
words, we were all very, very lucky. I don't have to
tell you the outcome of this entire affair had I not
been able to produce an image. . . . From professional point of view this must have been the most
hair rising [sic] experience in my 30 year career
and fortunately it all had dawned upon me only a
couple of days later when I was already on a plane
back to New York. Think of the potential 20 thousand Polish enemies, one disappointed Pope in
addition to Kościuszko's ghost all following poor
me to the end of the world.

I ask him how he felt looking down on that crowd and he writes
that he'd lived in the square in a top apartment right in front of the

town hall tower—"I was a very successful art student surrounded by some of the most incredible people of the era. Krakow of the mid-fifties was a magical place in spite of the communism." He'd shot a documentary there and knew that in order to get the view he wanted, he would have to get higher than any surrounding building, so he managed to persuade the Krakow fire department to lend him the rig. "Talking to and controlling such a crowd made me feel like a rock star."

I've also found out that Ryszard Horowitz was one of the youngest people to survive a Nazi concentration camp—sent in when he was three, almost preverbal, and not emerging again until the camps were liberated. His story goes into the heart of the war's darkness, giving a glimpse of what happened to Polish Jews who didn't escape Nazi Poland, as Wanda had been "lucky" enough to do, and as my father, a non-Jewish Czechoslovak with "a charmed life," had managed to do.

Horowitz was born in Krakow in May 1939 (another bad year to arrive there), and spent his infant years with his family in the Krakow ghetto of Podgorze—one of nineteen large ghettos which the Nazis created in Polish cities and towns from March 1941, calling back into existence the idea of Jewish ghettos abolished the century before. The demented Nazi bureaucracy managed to formally designate Ryszard a prisoner at the age of twenty-two months, arrest him in March 1941 and log the reason for his arrest in po-faced Kafka-speak: being Jewish. Having herded Jewish people into concentrated areas, Hitler then took his pathological obsession one stage further after the Wannsee Conference in early 1942, and began to set up extermination camps to liquidate mass numbers of them—the "final solution" to a "Jewish question" of his own making. As word got around of this, Ryszard's parents sent their son, not yet four, and his eight-year-old cousin off to a country village to be sheltered by relatives. A few weeks later, on March 13–14, 1943, the Nazis, at the height of their power, went to the ghetto and took anyone not able-bodied—some two thousand old,

sick, and very young—and shot them, ferrying their bodies by
truckloads to a mass grave in Plaszow in the Krakow suburbs, near
a forced-labor camp they'd established the previous summer. Rationalizing this with a word, as with *Führer* and *Lebensraum,* they
called it an *Aktion.* Most of the rest of the inhabitants were taken to
the labor camp of Belzec, and some eight thousand others to the
labor camp at Plaszow, run by the sadistic SS commandant Amon
Goeth—the camp and commandant featured in Thomas Keneally's
book *Schindler's List* and in the subsequent film. It was to this
camp, ten kilometers outside Krakow, that Ryszard's parents and
relatives were taken.

In 1943, Plaszow was a relatively small and insignificant labor
camp. From inside the camp, Ryszard's family heard that the village they had sent their son to was about to be "liquidated," like the
Podgorze ghetto. His father, Dolek, had by then been given a job in
the camp in charge of supplies, and managed to get Ryszard and
his cousin smuggled into Plaszow—a rare case of people actually
wanting to get in. Ryszard's mother, Regina, found a way of taking
the four-year-old boy into her bunk at nights and then getting
him away to the men's section of the camp before the morning roll
call. Ryszard's uncles, the Rosner brothers, used their violin and
accordion-playing skills to become musicians to Amon Goeth—
as Spielberg's film shows. Then Dolek managed to get Regina,
Ryszard and his daughter Niusia onto Otto Schindler's list of people allowed to work at his armaments and enamel factory in
Krakow—a harsh, Dickensian fate for a four-year-old, but infi-
nitely better than what was in store in Plaszow. However, by late
spring 1944 the factory was closed down in the face of the advancing Russians, and Ryszard and his family were sent back to Plaszow. Within days of their return, the Nazis ordered "unproductive"
adults and children to be sent off from Plaszow to the now fully
operational Auschwitz, where they would be gassed. Fourteen hundred adults and 286 children were sent to their deaths, but Ryszard

was one of ten children to escape, sheltered in the barracks of the Jewish police.

Ryszard stayed on at Plaszow until October 15, 1944, when Schindler managed to set up another so-called armaments factory, in Brünnlitz, Czechoslovakia—now the Nazi "protectorate" of Bohemia-Moravia. Schindler himself, born twelve years before my father, had originated in the "Sudetenland" of Czechoslovakia, and had been one of the Sudeten Germans—mostly Social Democrats—who were appalled at the Hitler-Henlein attitude toward the Czechs and their manically escalating demands. Now, Schindler arranged for eight hundred more men and five boys from Plaszow to be sent to his Czech factory in cattle trucks—among them Ryszard and his father, cousin and uncle. Even then they were not safe, because one day soon afterward when Schindler was away, the new camp commander of the Brünnlitz garrison came and rounded up all the children in the factory, with their fathers, and dispatched them to Auschwitz. Sometime in January 1945, the men were separated from the boys; Ryszard's father was sent off to Mauthausen camp, and Ryszard, still only five, was left alone in Auschwitz. He has said that he cannot remember the bizarre life that went on there, as he couldn't understand it (it didn't, after all, make sense); what he remembers vividly is the barbed-wire fence. When I ask him how he survived the next few days, he answers:

> I wonder as much as you do . . . to some extent I owe my life to Roman Gunz who looked after me after my father was snatched to Mauthausen camp. Roman was a close family friend from before the war who in Auschwitz was put in charge of German warehouses. They contained military gear as well as some food. When things got rough he would hide me there and for a while he placed me in a hospital full of contagiously ill inmates that

> was unlikely to be visited by the Nazis. Years later
> I met with Roman and his family who like me
> immigrated to New York. Unfortunately I was
> immature enough at that time to inquire about our
> Auschwitz experience. He has passed away soon
> after.

The last remark reminds me of the inhibitions I'd felt about approaching my father's no-go areas, and of how effectively my father, and Roman Gunz, and thousands like them, have barricaded their experiences from the light of day—and for good enough reason. You feel with some justice that you are too ignorant and inexperienced to frame the right question, let alone be worthy of understanding the answer. Yet Horowitz's "unfortunately" and "immature enough" show how he, like me, had accepted the burden of being at fault in inquiring. It has a ring of one of the most deplorable of the Nazi legacies: that, thanks to some human quirk of feeling guilt at being treated badly, the oppressors left their *victims* carrying the burden of silence and shame, instead of the other way around.

On January 27, 1945, the Russians, so long bruited as on their way, like something in a ghost story, finally arrived at Auschwitz. Hearing of their impending arrival, the Nazis had been attempting to destroy all evidence of the camps, including burning hastily buried bodies. Now they lined up a group of the children in the camp to be shot, Ryszard amongst them. Then, he writes in an essay.

> an officer arrived on a motorcycle. I remember him
> getting off the motorbike and saying that the Rus-
> sians were coming, were really close, and that all
> the German soldiers must leave at once. When the
> Russians arrived they had a film crew with them
> and they lined all of us kids up again and marched

us between the barbed wire fence towards the camera. They also placed us next to the gallows, I suppose because it was a vivid background, and filmed us there. Then they took me to an orphanage in Krakow.

Ryszard's parents had survived the camps and the war, but had no idea that their son had done so, too. So from the orphanage he was taken in by a woman who had taken her nephew under her wing. This nephew, six years older than Ryszard, and born Raimund Liebling, had been in the Podgorze ghetto with the Horowitzes, but had been smuggled out the day before the ghetto was destroyed, and spent the rest of the war hidden as a Gentile. There had been a saving grace for the boy: he'd taken a precocious interest in photography, and now had a willing acolyte in six-year-old Ryszard. Across the city, photography was intervening in another way in his life, as Ryszard's mother watched a free Russian showing of film of the Red Army liberating Auschwitz, and fleetingly spotted her son amongst the released boys. Searches through the Jewish Relief Organization revealed Ryszard's whereabouts, and they were reunited after seven months. The entire Horowitz family had survived the camps—the only family of the whole Jewish community in Krakow to do so.

Not surprisingly, when he got home, the boy was grave, withdrawn and suspicious of strangers. He was reluctant to wash, gobbled down his food as quickly as possible, hid uneaten portions of bread under the sofa or his pillow and would bang his spoon and fork on the table in an obsessive rhythm, mimicking a camp ritual of protest and hunger. I can't imagine such a camp ritual in the face of Nazis, who shot people for less, and ask Ryszard why they allowed it. He says, "Sometimes some pretty weird and highly improbable things took place and were condoned by the Germans. Your guess is as good as mine."

His parents tried to put the past behind them and lead a "normal" life, not talking with their children about what had happened. As Ryszard's paternal grandparents were still alive, his parents stayed on in Krakow, although most of the rest of the family had left the country as soon as they could after the war. Because of this, Ryszard says, he had a stable, happy home life. One small, suggestive cameo shows the legacy of dislocations the Nazis' unhinged actions bequeathed to the next generation: "As a result I had an experience—really rare for European Jews of my generation—of being put to bed as a child by my grandfather."

There is a picture of Ryszard a year after he'd left the camps: now looking groomed and cared for in a sailor suit, but earnest and wary. Behind Ryszard, with a gnomish face and ears sticking out, looking younger rather than six years older, is Raimund Liebling, the boy photographer who would change his name to Roman Polanski—and, in the postwar future, live out personal horrors of his own. The two men, now in their sixties, Ryszard in New York and Roman in Paris, are still friends. For both of them, art was the great liberator. For Polanski, only recently has he been able to contemplate incorporating his Auschwitz experience into a film, *The Pianist,* which has earned him the industry's highest awards, as well as some oblique absolution for past misdeeds.

For his part, Horowitz studied photography in New York under Richard Avedon and Alexey Brodovitch, pioneering the new possibilities of digital prestidigitation, conjuring up images of pin-sharp clarity where sky, birds, models, skyscrapers, sunbursts or sea metaphormose into one another, opening up masterly new possibilities of how things might look if unmoored from gravity and reintroduced to each other. Although there is an aspect like the camps sometimes, in that there's no logical coherence yet everything is presented as if it's orderly and real (like the formal arrest of a twenty-two-month-old infant), the pictures simultaneously transcend this surreal effect. Fragmentation and shatterings there are, often, but they burst with wit and color. Horowitz is starting to return to Poland regularly to teach at a new art academy in Warsaw,

Ryszard Horowitz (foreground) and Roman Polanski as boys, 1947

seeding back the creative riches he drew on in Krakow into a Poland that's reborn—once again. "All the Poles seem to be highly charged," a New York friend of his says.

My guess would be that this high charge—which I recognize in my father, in Stanley, Władek and Ted, and in myself, at one remove—derives from the Poles' periodic lack of a homeland. It would tend to make you more taut and alert than the average settler. Perhaps the tendency in Jews toward a similar highly strung note comes from their—more long-standing—lack of a homeland, albeit offset by the centripetal force of their culture and religion. This

does not, however, account for the close association between Poles
and Jews, which long predates Poland's troubles as a nation: it was
in 1346 that Kazimierz the Great first encouraged the Jews to settle
in Poland, protecting them from persecution at a time when they
were suffering pogroms all over Europe. This meant that by 1790,
just before the partitions, Jews already constituted 10 percent of
Poland—by far the largest Jewish settlement in the world, which is
how it would remain until the outbreak of the Second World War.

But Poland's traditional tolerance of Jews became corrupted by
influxes of Jews escaping Russian pogroms in the East, causing
overcrowding and poverty in these regions, and also by an increasingly desperate Polish nationalism. It was easy to suspect Jews,
inclined to internationalism, of not being sufficiently committed to
the Polish cause. By the twentieth century, another factor added to
growing tensions: Jews were beginning to play a role in the emerging Socialist movements. The first mass Socialist party in Russia
was the General Jewish Workers' League of Lithuania, Poland and
Russia, set up in 1897, and a direct ancestor of the Mensheviks and
Bolsheviks. This meant that the Poles were potentially wary of a
growing connection between "their" Jews and the new, Bolshevik
version of their traditional enemies, the Russians. Underneath all
this lay the still latent anti-Semitism of a profoundly Catholic
country.

Since the war, the Catholic Church has, bit by bit, tried to accept
its responsibility for its own historical part in anti-Semitism, and
for its silence in the face of the trucks and wagons shuttling across
Europe under the ignominious rule of the Nazis. I ask Ryszard
Horowitz how he, as a Jew who had been through the concentration
camps, felt about sending the Pope a card. "I like the guy," he says.

I think how there are good silences and bad silences, just as there
are good secrets and bad secrets. It was an honorable and impres-

sive silence kept for nearly a quarter of a century by the men and women at Bletchley Park about the role of Enigma. As for secrets, a healthy rule of thumb for life in ordinary times seems to be that you should never have secrets apart from good ones. The difficulty comes in extraordinary times, when out of the blue conflict and violence put inordinate stresses on unsupported individuals. Keeping quiet is the instinctive way to cope: the "freeze" part of the dinosaur mechanisms of freeze, fight or flee.

It occurs to me that my father did all three: froze, fled and fought—and then froze again, when the cold war came. Part of him was put into cold storage throughout the cold war, and it took the warmth of Australia to bring him fully back to life. It may well be that his unusual youthfulness for an eighty-two-year-old is partly due to that accidental cryogenics—he was "frozen" as a young man and has a lot of catching up to do. A flash recognition of this came three years ago, when my children, now grown up, were with my parents again in Australia, too, which made him positively frisky. When I mentioned how well they all got on, he laughed and said immediately, "But I'm their age!" Yet it has by no means all been positive. His chrysalis of silence undoubtedly slowed his progress—and mine, too, by osmosis—and led to more years than one would have wished spent lost in a taciturn limbo. Jung said, "The keeping of secrets acts like a psychic poison, alienating their possessor from the community." This could have felled my father from inside, had he not made the break for Australia with my mother—fleeing unpropitious circumstances for the second time— or had the Soviet Union not collapsed, or had I not finally got around to asking him some questions.

Yet he did not, of course, merely respond to the three "dinosaur" imperatives, but, as I now see, was quietly ingenious and inventive at every turn in making the best of bad circumstances—just as Ryszard Horowitz's family were, as Wanda was, as so many millions throughout the two world wars have been. They survived, and

Ryszard Horowitz's photograph of Krakow Square, March 2001

we all survived because of them. And my father had another saving grace: a great interest in the physics of the outside world, in the stars and in the universe. If art saved Ryszard, then science nourished my father's life force. Art and science, worthy lodestars. And they beat you, Hitler, you with your signally bad taste in mental furniture. Science beat you with the decoding of Enigma, with radar, with the atomic bomb. Art would beat you because you were, of course, a bad artist. And intellect in general beats you in the end, though after far too long, because you had contempt for it, and drove some of the best minds of the century—who were, as they had often had been, German—out of your valuable country, to enrich the democratic world you so despised.

.   .   .

Ryszard Horowitz's photograph of the square in Krakow has its own Web site, and also a zoom facility, enabling you to come in closer and closer to the crowd. The closer in you get, the more the perspective is slightly skewed, so that the faces begin to look like the Gothic faces carved in the huge limewood polyptych in the Mariacki Church behind them, which depicts scenes from the life of Christ and his family. The closer in you go, too, the grainier the picture, like something from Antonioni's *Blow-Up*. At every click I expect to see some cutpurse sidling away with swag whilst the faces all look up more or less smiling into the camera. I expect to see us, too, but perhaps that was the moment we'd gone off briefly to get new film ourselves. The faces seem identifiably Polish: tough and canny, men and women alike. The one word you wouldn't use of most of them is naive. I'm surprised to see so many old people there, happy to have their pictures taken, many smiling at the camera, a few still etched into scowls and looking wary. Infants are held up to the camera by their parents.

25 | STATE OF THE MIND

Meanwhile my father, taking over to Australia with him in 1971 surely the largest collection of used nails, screws, bolts, bits of piping, wire and oddments ever carried on a liner by a single individual, has constructed a future out of it all, having started at the age of twenty-one with nothing but a horse blanket and a past which threatened to ambush him. Perhaps I've made a similar bricolage with words, being my father's daughter. If my father had died young, I might never have known most of this, since there is barely a trace of him in any record, and no one is around who knew his story. And if he had died young, he would have remained an enigmatic figure: a handsome young man in a sepia photograph who became a troubled young man in uniform, someone who must have had a bad war.

As for me, what the Czechs and Poles have given me is vastly increased *Lebensraum:* living space of the mind and heart, the best sort. I expand my world by identifying with the Czechs' combination of idealism, irony and rooting for the vernacular. And with some fancy footwork I also manage to identify with the panache and romanticism of the Poles, and even—cruising for a fall—with their bravery. If I conveniently occlude their downsides like drunk-enness (Polish) or ambivalence (Czech) or dull-wittedness (Slovak, which is the nationality my father would be now), that seems all right to me, too, since although I've been in all three states now and then, I don't aspire to stay there long.

There's a very particular gift the Poles and Czechs have unwit-tingly given me, too: release. Release from my own oddball, shack-ling fantasy of continuity and stability and family life—from *Life with the Lyons* to the country estate. I've derived this expectation of what ought to be—solid settler life—from my English background, although I've always felt at one remove from it, as if I were mouthing the words eagerly to a hymn sheet I didn't have. But many people feel that way, I would guess, of any nationality, including the English. It's probably called alienation, and I don't want to glorify it. What the Czechs and Poles seem to propose is another realm, another *Reich,* the realm of no-solid-ground-under-your-feet, the liberating realm of people who have periodically not had a state to be in, but who keep their values, their vocabulary and their wit.

And in my imagination, seeing what appalling devastation has been wreaked over the last century by the bullish nation-state, and continues to be so, I conjure up a notion of cybernations, released from the gravity of power play, pooling the good things. Not pos-turing. In this light, I see the Czechs' wry, radical, human self-questioning as an asset with which they might lead the way—as Masaryk did, ahead of his time, with his United States of Europe—instead of apeing the self-important solidity and armies of more established nation-states, which have caused so much grief. For when it comes down to it, the Czechoslovaks had an army, a very good army indeed, and it got them nowhere. A good defensive army and good morale were useless in maintaining life and self-respect when coveted and targeted by others, and when their friends let them down. Perhaps it's possible to outgrow armies, and put the money and effort elsewhere. The tongue-in-cheek uniforms of the Hradcany Castle guards might set the tone, as could Václav Havel's farewell speech on preparing to leave office as president:

> I've discovered an astonishing thing: although it might be expected that this wealth of experience would have given me more and more self-assurance, confidence, and polish, the exact opposite is true. In that time, I have become a good deal less sure of myself, a good deal more humble. You may not believe this, but every day I suffer more and more from stage fright. . . . And while other presidents, younger than me in terms of their time in office, delight in every opportunity to meet each other, or with other important people, to appear on television or deliver a speech, all of this simply makes me more fearful.

I can't imagine a president of any other country delivering such a speech. It seems to echo Masaryk's words: "we are gifted, no doubt about that, but we are somewhat unstable, not circumspect enough, and shall I say, politically green." The acknowledgment of political greenness, or fearfulness, is new territory in itself in a world led by slogans—"mental furniture"—of "good" and "evil" and by "spin." It's relaxing, like any truth. Perhaps this awareness—psychological awareness, historical awareness—could be substituted for the twin sentinels of defense and aggression.

It was odd not to have known what and who my father was fighting for, as my schoolfriends knew with their fathers. Now I do know what he was fighting for, and what other Poles and Czechs were fighting for, and what lay behind what they were fighting for. And I know something else: my father, too, was in the forces. He was in the forces that swirl around all the time, sometimes and in some places more violently than others—the forces of life and death. And he's free of secrets now, and free of fear, and it's a gain in *Lebens-raum* and *Liebensraum* for all of us. What lies underground now is merely his geographical past: his birthplace of Hnonje in Slovakia swallowed up by an artificial lake from a dam, just like the bend in the river where he crossed the San.

So what about the parachute, I ask him, where did that come from—you didn't do any parachuting in the end, did you? No, not in war, he says. "But in third year at Lwow we did military training, which included parachute training—one afternoon a week for some thirty weeks." "But our parachute surely didn't come from there?" "Oh no, I bought it after war," he says. "They were selling them off."

And why, I ask him, was he so ferocious about forbidding people to smoke? "Oh, I was smoking so much in war—about fifty cigarettes a day, I would put one in mouth and find I already had one in there! Cigarettes were easier to get than food. They were our food. But then when I was at Boxmoor, I suddenly found I couldn't catch country bus I'd been able to run for at 440 yards distance before, so I said to Ted, 'If you order me to stop smoking, I will give up.' He agreed and said, 'I order you to stop smoking.' So I did, but I was unapproachable for months afterward. And at Warwick Road, I had twenty Players on mantelpiece to show myself I could resist temptation."

And finally, his flickering eyes: I discover, in quizzing my father's optician, that nystagmus is something you are born with, not something you could ever get from shocks. This is itself a profound shock to me, after all my pattern-making. Now that I specifically ask, he says he can remember being told as a child by a doctor to keep his eyes still, so he must have had it then. And it turns out that the improvement in his condition is thanks to the expertise of

Joe in Wallsend, 2003

his optician, and nothing to do with our journey into the past together. This reminds me not to cling to insights, and stories; they serve us so far, and no further.

There's been another companion on our journey, though, that won't go away, which rumbles around like thunder and boomerangs back just when we think it has gone. What about that companion, Dad, war, that stalker who threw your life and mine off balance, what can anyone like you and me do about its bullying presence? It's February 2003, terrorism is rife and the second Gulf war is looming. My father pulls his jokey face, and I can tell he's just remembered a good one. "Well, as far as I'm concerned, if they're after me, first they've got to find Australia, then they've got to find Newcastle, then they've got to find Wallsend, then they've got to find this house, and by that time I won't be there, I'll be down at pub and be drinking Jack Daniel's." No, seriously, Dad (he never goes to pubs . . .). "Seriously, only thing that will stop war," my father says, "is when human beings are endangered species. And there are lot of meteors lining up out there at moment."

I lie on the rough brown horse blanket in the garden at Wallsend, New South Wales, Australia, in the February heat, unfashionably soaking up the sun. If I open an eye, I see the letters "CM" outlined in yellow on its border, and then "*AEV 1936.*" A relic from another country, the past.

NOTES

3: **DREAM STATE**

43   "In his book *Czechoslovakia's Case for Independence*": Dr. Edouard Beneš, *Czechoslovakia's Case for Independence* (London: George Allen & Unwin, 1917), p. 3.

44   "We were a small nation": *President Masaryk Tells His Story*, recounted by Karel Čapek (London: George Allen & Unwin, 1936), p. 225.

4: **SLUMP**

49   "It is our desire": Karel Kramář speech, November 14, 1918, in Radomír Luža, *The Transfer of the Sudeten Germans: A Study of Czech-German Relations, 1933–1962* (London: Routledge & Kegan Paul, 1964), p. 32.

50*ff*   All unspecified biographical material about Adolf Hitler has been taken from the following sources: Alan Bullock, *Hitler: A Study in Tyranny* (London: Penguin, 1990); William Carr, *Hitler: A Study in Personality and Politics* (London: Edward Arnold, 1978); Joachim Fest, *Hitler,* translated from the German by Richard and Clara Winston (London: Weidenfeld & Nicolson, 1987); Adolf Hitler, *Mein Kampf,* introduction by D. Cameron Warr, translated by Ralph Manheim (London: Pimlico, 1992); Peter Hoffmann, *Hitler's Personal Security,* translated from the German (London: Macmillan, 1979); Walter C. Langer, *The Mind of Adolf Hitler* (London: Secker & Warburg, 1973); H. R. Trevor-Roper, ed., *Hitler's Table Talk 1941–44* (London: Weidenfeld & Nicolson, 1953).

52   "In modern war"; "In truth, the German superman": Tomáš Garrigue Masaryk, *The Making of a State: Memories and Observations 1914–1918* (Prague: 1925, London: George Allen & Unwin, 1927), pp. 317, 319.

6: **LWOW-USTIANOWA, 1939**

84   "We shall introduce here": E. Zimmerman and H. A. Jacobsen, *Germans Against Hitler, July 20, 1944* 5th ed., trans. Allan and Lieselotte Yahraes (Bonn: Press & Information Office of the Federal Government, 1969), p. 195.

7: LVIV-USTIANOWA, 2001

91   "For me, like the more": U.S. Secretary of State Madeleine K. Albright,
     Remarks at the Tomáš Masaryk Statue unveiling ceremony, Prague
     Castle, March 7, 2000. As released by the Archive Site for the U.S. State
     Department.

8: BALIGROD, 1939 AND 2001

135   "an episode so dreadful": Neal Ascherson, introduction, in Waldemar Lotnik
      with Julian Preece, *Nine Lives: Ethnic Conflict in the Polish-Ukrainian
      Borderlands* (London: Serif, 1999), p. 7.
137   "We reacted to their attacks": Lotnik, *Nine Lives,* p. 46.
142   "We do not conceal": Ibid., p. 221.

9: A "FARAWAY COUNTRY"

145*ff*   All quotations from Sydney Morrell in this and subsequent chapters are
          taken from his memoir of the Munich period, *I Saw the Crucifixion* (London:
          Peter Davies, n.d. [1939]).
150   "Although there was much in the Nazi system": Christopher Andrew and
      Vasili Mitrokhin, *The Mitrokhin Archive: The KGB in Europe and the West*
      (London: Allen Lane, The Penguin Press, 1999), p. 85.
153   "camouflage our movement": Luža, *Transfer of the Sudeten Germans,* p. 78.
153   "Is the Prime Minister aware": *Parliamentary Debates,* Commons, 5th
      series, vol. 335, (May 4, 1938) p. 858.
154   "The Czechs must": J. W. Brügel, *Czechoslovakia Before Munich: The
      German Minority Problem and British Appeasement Policy* (Cambridge:
      Cambridge University Press, 1973), p. 163.
154   "The war in the east": Luža, *Transfer of the Sudeten Germans,* p. 156.
155   The countdown ran: Hugh Skillen, *Spies of the Airwaves: A History of
      Y Sections During the Second World War* (Pinner, England: H. Skillen,
      1989), p. 31.
155   "Both Hitler and Goering": Brügel, *Czechoslovakia,* p. 164.

10: MOBILIZATION

162   "presented one of the most valuable": Luža, *Transfer of the Sudeten Ger-
      mans,* p. 137.
162   "the general instruction": Ibid., p. 132.
162   "With Henlein and Hitler": Luža, *Transfer of the Sudeten Germans,* p. 129.
163   the "official German view": Ibid., p. 134 n.

164 "a Birmingham Unitarian": Compton Mackenzie, *Dr. Beneš* (London: George G. Harrap & Co. Ltd, 1946), p. 230.

167 "Where are we going?": *Documents of British Foreign Policy 1919–1939*, ed. E. L. Woodward and Rohan Butler (London: HMSO, 1949), 3rd series, vol. 2, (cited hereafter as *DBFP*) p. 74.

168 "Insomnia is spoiling": Ibid., p. 116.

168 "I was a little consoled": H. R. Trevor-Roper, ed., *Hitler's Table Talk 1941–1944* (London: Weidenfeld & Nicolson, 1953), p. 488.

170 "if Hitler carries the day": *DBFP*, p. 684.

170 "I take it that Von Kleist": Ibid., p. 686.

171 "I do wish": Ibid., p. 257.

171 "Henlein threw off his mask": Luža, *Transfer of the Sudeten Germans*, p. 133n.

173 "I have never heard": William L. Shirer, *Twentieth Century Journey: A Memoir of a Life and the Times*, vol. II: *The Nightmare Years 1930–1940* (Boston: Little, Brown, 1984), p. 336.

173 "Unfortunately I did not get: *DBFP*, pp. 253–54.

174 "We know how intolerable": Brügel, *Czechoslovakia*, p. 251.

11: "SMALL FRY"

179 "So I said 'Hold on' ": *DBFP*, p. 339.

181 "it was impossible": Brügel, *Czechoslovakia*, p. 259.

183 "In the circumstances": *DBFP*, p. 407.

183 "It's a sorry business": Ibid., p. 655.

183 "President Beneš was greatly": Ibid., p. 416.

184 "1. Czech Government": Ibid., p. 424.

185 "Dr Krofta who was": Ibid., p. 426.

186 "The French Minister": Brügel, *Czechoslovakia*, p. 280.

189 "The partition of Czechoslovakia": Mackenzie, *Dr. Beneš*, p. 220.

190 "Do I understand": *DBFP*, p. 463.

191 "Every few steps": Shirer, *The Nightmare Years 1930–40*, p. 345.

192 "He, Mr Chamberlain": *DBFP*, p. 499.

194 "Every possible opportunity": Patricia Meehan, *The Unnecessary War: Whitehall and the German Resistance to Hitler* (London: Sinclair-Stevenson, 1992), p. 4.

195 "After reading your letter": *Parliamentary Debates*, 5th series, vol. 339 (September 26, 1938), p. 21.

195 "would not conceal from me": *DBFP*, p. 626.

196 "The President [Beneš] telephoned": Ibid., p. 604.

197 "replied to the appeal": Mackenzie, *Dr. Beneš*, p. 232.

197 "The Munich Conference": William Strang, *Home and Abroad* (London: André Deutsch, 1956), p. 144.

198 "roughly that accorded": Mackenzie, *Dr. Beneš*, p. 232.

198 "This led to a tirade": *DBFP*, p. 631.

199 "To the professional": Strang, *Home and Abroad*, p. 146.

200 *"Prime Minister:* He was": *DBFP*, p. 635.

12: "A NICE QUIET SLEEP"

203 "The President and the Government": Luža, *The Transfer of the Sudeten Germans*, pp. 150–51.

203 "We have had to choose": *Documents on German Foreign Policy, 1918–1945* (Washington, D.C.: Departments of State and Public Institutions, 1949–), from the Archives of the German Foreign Ministry, Series C (1933–37), *The Third Reich: First Phase*, IV, pp. 4–5.

204 "It was clear": Strang, *Home and Abroad*, p. 148.

205 "My good friends": Neville Chamberlain, *In Search of Peace: Speeches 1937–1938* (London: Hutchinson, n.d. [1940]), p. 303.

205 "Before giving a verdict": *Parliamentary Debates*, 5th series, vol. 351 (October 3, 1938), p. 45.

206 "President Beneš, despite": Luža, *Transfer of the Sudeten Germans*, p. 154.

207 "It was not Hitler": Josef Korbel, *Twentieth-Century Czechoslovakia: The Meanings of Its History* (New York: Columbia University Press, 1977), p. 134.

207 "If the world is not": *Keesing's Contemporary Archives* (London: 1931–86), October 1, 1938.

207 "the Nazis had achieved": Sheila Grant Duff, *A German Protectorate: The Czechs Under Nazi Rule* (London: Macmillan, 1942), p. 12.

207 "the memory of the bitter": Brügel, *Czechoslovakia*, p. 299.

208 "practically put the causes": Luža, *Transfer of the Sudeten Germans*, p. 151.

208 "The moral of that moment": Martha Gellhorn, *A Stricken Field* (London: Virago, 1986), p. 306.

208 "My poor friend": Strang, *Home and Abroad*, p. 153.

208 "We have sustained": Ibid., p. 149.

209 "The peace of Munich": *Keesing's*, October 1, 1938.

209 "I was caught up": *Parliamentary Debates*, 5th series, vol. 339 (October 3, 1938), pp. 30–40.

212 "By the failure": Meehan, *Unnecessary War*, p. 9.

213 "That is a really dreadful": Ibid., p. 386.

213 "Munich was Hitler's": Mackenzie, *Dr. Beneš*, p. 322.

13: LEARNING TO KEEP QUIET FAST

216 "The crowds moved slowly": Gellhorn, *Stricken Field*, pp. 12–13, 25.

217 "The 'democratic vistas' ": George Orwell, *Inside the Whale and Other Essays* (London: Penguin Classics, 2001), p. 18.

218 "Our soldiers having": Vojtěch Mastný, *The Czechs Under Nazi Rule: The*

Failure of National Resistance 1939–42 (New York & London: Columbia University Press, 1971), p. 17.

218 "Physically, I was": Mackenzie, *Dr. Beneš*, p. 248.

219 "the international outlook was": Ibid., p. 246.

220 "determination to take the Czech": Mastný, *Czechs Under Nazi Rule*, p. 18.

222 "otherwise German aircraft": Luža, *Transfer of the Sudeten Germans*, p. 178 n.

223 "When twenty years ago": Mastný, *Czechs Under Nazi Rule*, p. 55.

224 "being definitely released": Mackenzie, *Dr. Beneš*, p. 247.

224 "A tortoise coming": Ibid.

225 "I must end with": Ibid., p. 250.

226 "Do not believe that": Luža, *Transfer of the Sudeten Germans*, p. 183.

15: **BLITZKRIEG**

246 "My estimate is that": Martin Gilbert, *A History of the Twentieth Century,* vol. II: *1933–1951* (London: HarperCollins, 1998), pp. 309–10.

246 "there was no hurry": Ibid., p. 270.

247 "This is one of the most awe-striking": Ibid., p. 308.

248 "hard lot to announce": Winston Churchill, Speech to the House of Commons, June 4, 1940. *Parliamentary Debates,* 5th series, vol. 361, p. 787.

16: **CHAMPAGNE**

259 "Any man who suffers": General Stanisłas Maczek, *Avec mes blindés* (Paris: Presses de la Cité, 1967), pp. 121–22.

259 "Effectively General Maczek": Andrzej Suchcitz, "General Stanisław Maczek" in J. L. Englert and K. Barbarski, *General Maczek and the Soldiers of the First Armoured Brigade* (London: Polish Institute and Sikorski Museum, with the Polish Cultural Foundation, 1992), p. 10.

264 "impatient we all were": Maczek, *Avec mes blindés,* p. 124.

275 "Unlike the Polish Government": Andrzej Suchcitz, *Poland's Contribution to the Allied Victory in the Second World War* (London: Polish Ex-Combatants' Association in Great Britain, 1995), p. 11.

276 "On behalf of the Government": Leon Koczy, *The Scottish-Polish Society: Activities in the Second World War* (Edinburgh: Scottish-Polish Society, 1980), introduction.

17: **"SUNLIT UPLANDS"**

281 "What General Weygand": Churchill to the House of Commons, June 18, 1940. *Parliamentary Debates,* vol. 362, p. 59.

284 "more jittery": Jane Waller and Michael Vaughan-Rees, *Blitz: The Civilian War 1940–45* (London: Optima, 1990), p. 298.

18: **NEVER AGAIN**

292 "Deep down and hidden": Sydney Morrell, *Spheres of Influence* (New York: Duell, Sloan and Pearce, 1946), p. 5.

293 "Today I feel an urge": Mastný, *Czechs Under Nazi Rule*, p. 156.

295 "whoever works against": Ibid., p. 214.

296 "severe police measures": Ibid., p. 218.

296 "Death by bullet": Julius Fuchik, *Notes from the Gallows* (New York: New Century, 1948), p. 74.

297 "By his death": Mastný, *Czechs Under Nazi Rule*, p. 221.

297 "If determination was": Ibid., p. 223.

298 "In Prague on September 26th, 1938": Mackenzie, *Dr. Beneš*, p. 339.

301 "I am firmly convinced": President Václav Havel, article published in several European newspapers, including *Le Monde* and the *Süddeutsche Zeitung*, on April 19, 2002.

302 "I ask only one thing of you": Luža, *Transfer of the Sudeten Germans*, p. xxi.

19: **"FINIS POLONIAE!"**

303*ff* All quotations by General Władisław Anders in the following chapters are taken from his memoir *An Army in Exile: The Story of the Second Polish Corps* (London: Macmillan, 1949).

309 "we will keep shifting": George Weigel, *Witness to Hope: The Biography of Pope John Paul II* (London: HarperCollins, 2001), p. 18.

310 "If the slightest incident": Gilbert, *Twentieth Century*, vol. II, p. 251.

311 "took those who were too independent": Alexander Solzhenitsyn, *The Gulag Archipelago 1918–1956: An Experiment in Literary Investigation* (London: Collins & Harvill Press, 1974), vol. I, p. 77.

315 "As the days passed": Denis Hills, *Return to Poland* (London: The Bodley Head, 1988), p. xiii.

317 "if we did not collapse": Martin Gilbert and Richard Gott, *The Appeasers* (London: Weidenfeld & Nicolson, 1963), p. 330.

317 "Colourful stories about": Norman Davies, *Heart of Europe: A Short History of Poland* (Oxford: Oxford University Press, 1986), p. 65.

319 "I was appointed by": Jozef Garlinski, *Poland in the Second World War* (London: Macmillan, 1985), p. 27.

319 "After one quick blow": Ibid., p. 31.

321 "Brutal and basic torture": Michael Hope, *Polish Deportees in the Soviet Union: Origins of Postwar Settlement in Great Britain* (London: Veritas, 1998), p. 15.

321 "enemies of the state": Norman Davies, *God's Playground: A History of Poland*, vol. II: *1795 to the Present* (Oxford: Oxford University Press, 1961), pp. 447–48.

324 "Rule by terror": Lionel Kochan and John Keep, *The Making of Modern Russia* (London: Penguin, 1997), pp. 396–97.

325 This in spite of the fact: Andrew and Mitrokhin, *Mitrokhin Archive*, p. 122.

326 "the overwhelming majority of English": Orwell, *Inside the Whale*, p. 26.

329 "Anders' visit was of course": Field Marshal Lord Alanbrooke, *War Diaries 1939–1945*, ed. Alex Danchev and Daniel Todman (London: Weidenfeld & Nicolson, 2001), pp. 301–302.

20: TOURISTS

334 "There are two opposed camps": Alanbrooke, *War Diaries*, p. 252.

335 "He is an outstanding man": Ibid., p. 301.

337 " 'slightly beyond the pale' ": quoted in Hope, *Polish Deportees*, p. 29.

337 "But then [Churchill] was": H. Pelling, *Winston Churchill*, quoted Ibid.

337 "the British government", "The Poles have fairly upset", "There is no use prowling": Ibid., p. 44.

339 "[Sikorski] personally directed": Churchill to the House of Commons, July 7, 1943, *Parliamentary Debates*, 5th series, vol. 390, pp. 1946–47.

341 Stalin had one key negotiating advantage: Andrew and Mitrokhin, *Mitrokhin Archive*, p. 148.

343 "What is almost incredible": Harold Macmillan, introduction to Anders, *An Army in Exile*, p. xv.

344 "Despite Polish arguments": Hope, *Polish Deportees*, p. 50.

344 "The Allied armed forces": Anders, *An Army in Exile*, p. 173.

345 "At minimum, Ultra saved": *Secrets of the War: I—The Ultra Enigma* (U.S.A.: I.M.A., 1998), documentary film.

345 "If anyone at the embassy": Christopher Andrew and David Dilks, eds., *The Missing Dimension: Governments and Intelligence in the Twentieth Century* (London: Macmillan, 1984), p. 132.

346 "this incredible adventure": *Station X: The Codebreakers of Bletchley Park* (London: Channel 4, 1998), p. 9.

346 "the fact must be stressed": Andrew and Dilks, eds., *Missing Dimension*, p. 39.

346 "their ever-lasting mines": Martha Gellhorn, *The Face of War* (London: Virago, 1986), p. 125.

347 "The abbey was this big," "To remain silent in the face": Grand Island Films project: http://www.mindspring.com/~gif212.

348 "one of the outstanding formations": Field Marshal Lord Alexander of Tunis, foreword to Anders, *An Army in Exile*, p. v.

351 "For days after the German": Stefan Korbonski, *The Polish Underground State: A Guide to the Underground, 1939–1945*, trans. Marta Erdman, East European Monograph Series, no. 39 (Boulder: Eastern European Quarterly, 1978), p. 189.

351 "It brought to an awful climax": Neal Ascherson, *The Struggles for Poland* (London: Michael Joseph, 1989), p. 133.

353 "It is a long road": Gellhorn, *The Face of War*, p. 118.

354 "victims of prisons": Richard C. Lukas, *The Forgotten Holocaust: The Poles Under German Occupation 1939–1944* (New York: Hippocrene, 1997), p. 39.

21: **POLES APART**

355 "Poor Neville believed": Melvyn P. Leffler, *The Specter of Communism: The United States and the Origins of the Cold War, 1917–1953* (New York: Hill and Wang, 1994), p. 44.

356 "The Soviet Union, as everybody": Wilfried Loth, *The Division of the World, 1941–1955* (London: Routledge, 1988), p. 29.

356 "I know you will not mind": *Churchill and Roosevelt: The Complete Correspondence.* vol. I, *Alliance Emerging: October 1933–November 1942:* ed. Warren F. Kimball (Princeton: Princeton University Press, 1984) p. 421.

358 "It will ever be to Poland's": cited Anders, *An Army in Exile*, p. 270.

359 "Some leftist sections": Hope, *Polish Deportees*, p. 51. Martin Gilbert in *The Appeasers* also notes that the *Daily Express* was "hostile to the Poles, and to Anglo-Polish commitments."

360 "the friendship of Russia": A. J. P. Taylor, *Beaverbrook* (London: Hamish Hamilton, 1972), p. 559.

360 "their isolation had become": cited in Hope, *Polish Deportees*, p. 52.

360 "Of all the moral surrenders": Norman Davies, *Heart of Europe*, p. 96.

361 "do not dare": cited in Anders, *An Army in Exile*, p. 300.

362 "tomorrow we are to celebrate": Ibid.

362 "In the Battle of Britain": Davies, *Heart of Europe*, p. 96.

363 "According to the decision": Anders, *An Army in Exile*, p. 299.

363 "The remnants of the Home Army": Davies, *Heart of Europe*, p. 106.

364 "The General has not exaggerated": Harold Macmillan, introduction to Anders, *An Army in Exile*, p. xv.

365 "The effect of this massive": Davies, *Heart of Europe*, p. 107.

365 "The Polish peasantry survived": Ibid., p. 108.

367 "his former life in the west": Andrew, *Missing Dimension*, p. 39.

367 "It is an epic": Macmillan, introduction to Anders, *An Army in Exile*, p. xvi.

22: **REPTILIAN BRAIN**

378 "Changes in these circuits": Daniel Goleman, *Emotional Intelligence* (London: Bloomsbury, 1996), p. 205.

379 "This probably means that": Bessel A. van der Kolk, Alexander C. McFarlane and Lars Weisaeth, eds., *Traumatic Stress: The Effects of Overwhelming Experience on Mind, Body and Society* (New York and London: Guildford Press, 1996), p. 232.

380 "they can be helped to live": Wendy Holden, *Shell Shock* (London: Channel 4 Books, 2001), p. 151.

380 "you could lose yourself": Lorna Sage, *Bad Blood* (London: Fourth Estate, 2000), p. 105.

381 only 4,938 Czech troops: "Some Polish Contributions in the Second World War," The Bletchley Park Reports, no. 15 (July 1999), p. 17.

382 "War is the crime against peace.": Gellhorn, *Face of War*, p. 198.

383 "Even as the trauma": Ben Shephard, *War of Nerves* (London: Jonathan Cape, 2000), p. 391.

386 persistence of a "startle" response: derived from Laurence Miller, *Shocks to the System* (New York and London: W. W. Norton & Co., 1998), pp. 11–12, and the American Psychiatric Association's *Diagnostic and Statistical Manual of Mental Disorders (DSM-III)*, 1980.

23: SPOOKS

394 "I have a strong admiration": Winston Churchill, speech at Westminster College in Fulton, Missouri, March 5, 1946. In *Churchill Speaks: Winston S. Churchill in Peace and War, 1897–1963*, ed. Robert Rhodes James (London: Windward, 1981), pp. 877–84.

395 "exaggerated" and consigned: Dr. Jan Ciechanowski, "The Polish Underground and the Intelligence Connection" (lecture presented at Bletchley Park, January 10, 2002).

398 a phenomenal hemorrhage of classified: Andrew and Mitrohkhin, *Mitrokhin Archive*, pp. 119, 149, 156.

399 "stray about the world, making": Public Records Office, Kew Gardens, KV/516. P.F. 60518 (44a).

399 "Sikorski's aim was to": Ibid. (66).

400 "The German revelations": *The Diaries of Sir Alexander Cadogan 1938–1945*, ed. David Dilks (New York: G. P. Putnam's Sons, 1972), p. 520.

400 In fact, from a long, detailed report: *Churchill and Roosevelt: The Complete Correspondence.* vol. II, *Alliance Forged: November 1942–February 1944:* ed. Warren F. Kimball (London: Collins, 1984), p. 389.

400 "There was no use prowling": Churchill's telegram to Sikorski, marked "Most Secret and Personal," April 26, 1943, quoted in Hope, *Polish Deportees*, p. 44.

400 "We have been obliged": *Churchill and Roosevelt*, vol. II, p. 398.

402 "none other than Kim Philby": Verne W. Newton, *The Cambridge Spies* (New York: Madison Books, 1991), p. 57. His source is an undated CIA publication, *Intelligence in Recent Public Literature*, released under the Freedom of Information Act, November 14, 1980.

402 There have been recent allegations: BBC Radio 4 program "One Night in Gibraltar," January 2001.

403 "If Philby had a hand": Newton, *Cambridge Spies*, pp. 57–58.

403 alleged by some to have been: notably by Roland Perry in *The Fifth Man* (London: Sidgwick & Jackson, 1995). Rothschild's most recent biographer, Niall Ferguson, however, writes in *The World's Banker* (London: Weidenfeld & Nicolson, 1998), p. 997: "Years later there would be speculation about Victor's relationship with the Cambridge spies, culminating in the false allegation that he was the 'fifth man.' "

406 "To many it will be news": *British Czech and Slovak Review* (February–March 2003).

406 "there is only one way": Alfred Duff Cooper, *Old Men Forget: The Autobiography of Alfred Duff Cooper (Viscount Norwich)* (London: Rupert Hart-Davis, 1953), p. 203.

407 "Those who had contributed so much": Simon Singh, *The Code Book: The Science of Secrecy from Ancient Egypt to Quantum Cryptography* (London: Fourth Estate, 1999), p. 188.

409 "What secrecy grants": introduction to Daniel Patrick Moynihan, *Secrecy: The American Experience* (New Haven & London: Yale University Press, 1998).

24: KRAKOW

414 "I saw in those faces": Joseph Conrad, *Notes on Life and Letters* (London: Dent, 1921), p. 229.

420 "an officer arrived": Jon Blair, *Ryszard Horowitz* (Krakow and New York: Wydawnictwa Artystyczne: Filmowe Warszawa & M. M. Art Books, Inc., 1994), p. 12.

425 "The keeping of secrets": Carl Jung, *Modern Man in Search of Soul,* quoted in Sissela Bok, *Secrets: On the Ethics of Concealment and Revelation* (Oxford: Oxford University Press, 1986), p. 8.

25: STATE OF THE MIND

430 "I've discovered an astonishing thing": President Václav Havel, "A Farewell to Politics," *New York Review of Books,* vol. 49, no. 16, October 24, 2002.

433 CM *AEV 1936:* My guess has been that this stands for something like *Corps Militaire, Armée Equestrienne de Versailles.* I've tried to get it deciphered properly with the kind help of French army archivists, but in the end General J. J. Senant, head of the *Service Historique de l'Armée de Terre,* informs me that they have regretfully drawn a blank. Thank you, all the same, *mon Général.*

PERMISSIONS ACKNOWLEDGMENTS

Grateful acknowledgment is made to the following for their permission to quote from previously published material: Mrs. Renata Anders for excerpts from General Anders's memoirs *An Army in Exile: The Story of the Second Polish Corps* (London: Macmillan, 1949); Granta for excerpts from Martha Gellhorn's *A Stricken Field* (London: Virago, 1986) and *The Face of War* (London: Virago, 1986); Oxford University Press for excerpts from Norman Davies, *God's Playground: A History of Poland*, volume II (Oxford: Oxford University Press, 1983), and *Heart of Europe: A Short History of Poland* (Oxford: Oxford University Press, 1984). Every effort has been made to trace the heirs of Sydney Morrell, without avail; the author would be delighted if they would contact her.

The author would also like to thank Ryszard Horowitz for his generous permission to use his photographs of Krakow and of himself when young, both copyright © Ryszard Horowitz, 2003.

A NOTE ABOUT THE AUTHOR

Born in London, **ANNETTE KOBAK** studied modern languages at Cambridge University and creative writing at the University of East Anglia. She has written an acclaimed biography of the traveler Isabelle Eberhardt and translated her novel *Vagabond* from the French. She presented the series *The Art of Travel* on BBC Radio 4 and reviews travel books and fiction for the *New York Times Book Review* and *The Times Literary Supplement*. She is currently the editor of the magazine *The Cut*.

A NOTE ON THE TYPE

The text of this book was set in a typeface called Times Roman, first designed by Stanley Morison (1889–1967) for *The Times* (London) and introduced by that newspaper in 1932. Among typographers and designers of the twentieth century, Stanley Morison was a strong forming influence—as a typographical adviser to the Monotype Corporation, as a director of two distinguished publishing houses, and as a writer of sensibility, erudition, and keen practical sense.

Composed by North Market Street Graphics,
Lancaster, Pennsylvania
Printed and bound by R. R. Donnelley & Sons,
Harrisonburg, Virginia
Maps by David Cain
Designed by Anthea Lingeman